CARL LOTUS BECKER

The History of Political Parties in the Province of New York 1760–1776

With a Foreword by
ARTHUR M. SCHLESINGER

The University of Wisconsin Press
Madison · 1960

Published by
THE UNIVERSITY OF WISCONSIN PRESS
430 Sterling Court, Madison 6, Wisconsin

SECOND PRINTING
First printing, 1909, as No. 286 of the
Bulletin of the University of Wisconsin
History Series, Vol. 2, No. 1

Printed in the United States of America

FOREWORD

It is seldom that a doctoral dissertation becomes a minor classic of historical literature, but *The History of Political Parties in the Province of New York, 1760–1776* by Carl Becker, written over fifty years ago, is still a seminal work for students of the American Revolution. Becker, who was thirty-six in 1909 when he published the study, had spent his early boyhood on a farm in Blackhawk County, Iowa, then taken his A.B. and Ph.D. degrees at the University of Wisconsin with an intervening graduate year at Columbia, and taught European history successively at Pennsylvania State College, Dartmouth and, from 1902, at the University of Kansas. He was to leave Kansas in 1916 and, after a year at the University of Minnesota, assume the chair of modern history at Cornell, there to continue until his retirement in 1941. He died in Ithaca on April 10, 1945, at the age of seventy-one.

Becker was fortunate in the variety and quality of the history professors under whom he studied in his apprentice years: Frederick J. Turner, Charles H. Haskins and Victor Coffin at the University of Wisconsin (the first two afterward of Harvard), and Herbert L. Osgood, John W. Burgess and James Harvey Robinson at Columbia. Of his initial course with Turner he wrote many years later, "Until then, I had never been interested in history; since then, I have never ceased to be so." To the example of these inspiring teachers, he tells us in his Preface, he owed his greatest debt in the preparation of his dissertation, though it is to be noted that only one of the group was a specialist in the field in which his subject lay. They, for their part, could hardly have found a student more appreciative of the doors they opened up to him, more discriminating in seeking what would contribute most to his own intellectual development, and more addicted to turning over in his mind what he heard and read.

Although Professor Turner had suggested that he write a history of American nominating conventions, the subject in Becker's hand became something very different, touching only slightly the intended theme and then but for a limited period and in a single colonial area. Instead he provided the first genuinely searching analysis for a given province of the clash of economic and social interests which over a short sixteen years led the people to the unforeseen goal of Independence in company with the sister colonies. Even the title of the study falls short of describing the contents, for Becker was more deeply concerned with the background forces at work than with the political machinery—committees, parties, public meetings, conventions and the like—through which the forces functioned, though these, too, he examined with painstaking care. The key to the whole matter, he said in words which historians have never ceased to echo, was the struggle over the question of "home rule," on the one hand, and over "who should rule at home," on the other.

Though the treatise is heavily documented, Becker was master of his material instead of letting it master him. He wrote with clarity combined with the insights of a musing mind, thus foreshadowing the literary artist he was to become. He, however, gives little evidence of his later preoccupation with eighteenth-century intellectual history. There is only the barest allusion to colonial political theory, no consideration of the Enlightenment as a possible influence on patriot thinking, and only scanty reference to the bitter contest between the Presbyterians and the Anglicans which at times convulsed New York politics. The work is primarily a politico-economic account, and from that point of view later researches have been able to alter the picture only in matters of detail. The chief oversight perhaps was his failure to take into account the long postwar depression following the Peace of 1763, which underlay much of the American dissatisfaction with the new parliamentary legislation.

For some years after his dissertation appeared Becker continued to write in the colonial field, but a significant change of emphasis occurred from the material factors at play to things of the mind and the spirit. In 1915 he published *Beginnings of the American People*, a general sketch from the discovery of the New World to the close of the Revolutionary War, with greater consideration now given to the intellectual and psychological forces involved. In 1918 came *The Eve of the Revolution*, traversing the same period as his dissertation but from the standpoint of "the quality of the thought and feeling of those days" and covering all the colonies. Then, in 1922, followed *The Declaration of Independence*, accurately described by its subtitle as *A Study in the History of Political Ideas*, and finally, in 1926, *The Spirit of '76*, an essay in a collaborative volume, which personalized the reactions of an imaginary New York merchant to the successive stages of the quarrel with Britain. Except for the last, which represented a return to the subject matter of his doctoral thesis though from a very different angle, all these writings revealed his increasing absorption in the ideological aspects of the colonial revolt and in the European sources from which the patriot spokesmen drew inspiration. The outcome of this new orientation was his best-known volume *The Heavenly City of the Eighteenth-Century Philosophers* (1932), in which he shifted his ground wholly to the far side of the Atlantic. Becker's philosophical bent also led him in these later years to write essays, afterward collected in book form, on the grave issues confronting America and mankind in his own day.

The reprinting of the present treatise, the first and perhaps the least remembered of his publications, is a boon to students of American history. In his Preface he terms it a "modest essay," but it is much more than that. In research method as well as in content, objectivity and interpretation it is a model of what a work of historical scholarship should always strive to be.

Arthur M. Schlesinger.

Cambridge, Massachusctts, October 27, 1959.

PREFACE

Under the inspiration of one of Professor Turner's illuminating suggestions, I began, while a graduate student at the University of Wisconsin several years ago, to collect material for a history of the nominating convention in the United States. That great work remains still unpublished, having fined itself down to the modest essay which is now presented. Even so small a venture would have been still further delayed, or rendered impossible altogether, but for the ready assistance that has been accorded at every turn. In this connection, it is a pleasure to mention the officers and assistants of the libraries where most of the material was collected: The Library of the Wisconsin Historical Society; the Library of the New York Historical Society; the Library of Columbia University; the Lenox Library; the New York State Library at Albany. I owe much to the suggestions and criticisms of Professor Wilbur C. Abbott, formerly my colleague, now of Yale University, and of Professor Frank H. Hodder, my present colleague in the University of Kansas. But I owe most to the example of certain inspiring teachers: Frederick J. Turner, Charles H. Haskins, Victor Coffin, Herbert L. Osgood, John W. Burgess, James H. Robinson.

The editor of the *Political Science Quarterly* has kindly permitted me to use an article printed in that journal for March, 1903. With few changes, it appears as chapter V of this essay. The editor of the *American Historical Review* has very generously accorded me a similar privilege with respect to articles which were printed in that journal for January and October, 1901, and October, 1903.

CARL BECKER.

Lawrence, Kansas, February 3, 1909.

CONTENTS

THE HISTORY OF POLITICAL PARTIES IN THE PROVINCE OF NEW YORK, 1760-1776

CHAPTER I

PROVINCIAL PARTIES AND PARTY POLITICS. 1700-1769

The American Revolution was the result of two general movements; the contest for home-rule and independence, and the democratization of American politics and society. Of these movements, the latter was fundamental; it began before the contest for home-rule, and was not completed until after the achievement of independence. The history of revolutionary parties, if properly understood, must be regarded, therefore, from the broader, as well as from the narrower, point of view. And if we are so to regard it, a brief consideration of the general character of provincial politics is indispensable.

Previous to 1765, the central fact in the political history of New York was the contest between the governors and the assembly. The contest was doubtless inevitable, for the governor and the assembly represented different interests and opposing principles; the governor, including under this term all officials receiving their appointments directly from the king, represented the English government,[1] while the assembly, which had been virtually forced upon the proprietor, represented the colony.[2] Theoretically, doubtless, the interests of the colony were iden-

---

[1] Poor, *Charters*, 1: 786. *Magazine of American History*, 8: 315, 598.

[2] *New York Col. Doc.*, 3: 317, 331. *Col. Laws of New York*, 1: 109. For the establishment of representative machinery, see *Col. Laws of New York*, 1: 121, 122. *New York Col. Doc.*, 13: 575. *Mem. Hist. of New York*, 1: 408. *Doc. Hist. of New York*, 1: 748; 3: 700. Rutgers, *Orange County*, 32, 45. Smith, *Dutchess County*, 48. *Council Journal*, 1931.

tical with those of the English government; but in fact the assembly looked at the empire from the local point of view, while the English government looked at the colony from the broader imperial standpoint. To those who were shaping an imperial policy, New York occupied a position of peculiar importance. But the assembly was little interested in imperial policy; it was greatly interested in local needs. Protection for the moment, rather than security for the future, was its motto. Trading upon the necessities of the empire, it therefore used its position to exact tremendous concessions in the practice of local self-government.

But the governor and the assembly not only represented different constituencies; they also represented opposing principles. After 1688, it is true, colonial administration was gradually transferred from the king in council to Parliament acting through various administrative boards. It was a change, however, which involved possibilities for the future rather than present achievement, for the governors received their instructions from a ministry that was usually the master rather than the servant of Parliament. The forming administrative bureaucracy which directed colonial affairs was in fact dominated by ideals of government that drew their inspiration from the monarchical traditions of the past. The colonial assembly, on the other hand, while it did not rest upon manhood suffrage, did rest upon a suffrage that was uniform, and if in theory it represented the popular will imperfectly, in fact it guarded the general interests with even an over-scrupulous care.

Three questions stand out prominently as central issues in this long quarrel. The assembly early asserted, and rather successfully maintained, its claims to supremacy as a legislature. It appropriated to itself the title "General Assembly,"[3] refused to allow the council to amend money bills,[4] controlled all appropriations,[5] and attempted, though with indifferent success, to secure frequent elections.[6] The assembly tried, throughout

---

[3] *Col. Laws of New York*, 1: ch. 1.
[4] *Assembly Journals*, 184, 188.
[5] *Ibid.*, 1: 706.
[6] *Col. Laws of New York*, 2: ch. 650. *New York Col. Doc.*, 6: 136.

the colonial period, to control the judiciary. Until the end of Burnet's administration, the issue was the power of the executive to establish and control superior courts;[7] after Burnet's time, the issue shifted to the tenure and salary of judges, and the right of appeal to the king in council. Technically, the governors won every point, but, through an organized bar, the assembly was able in the end to control the judiciary effectively.[8] It was in the field of administration, however, that the assembly won its most signal success. It insisted successfully on an elective treasurer.[9] Appropriations were limited, save in rare instances, to one year;[10] and, beginning with Van Dam's administration,[11] money bills were made more and more specific, both as to the purposes for which and the agents by which the appropriations were to be expended.[12] Even salaries in the army were granted in some cases by individual appropriation.[13] The constant and excessive use of specific appropriations went far towards reducing the administrative function of the governor to a mere form; Hunter, Clark, and Clinton all admitted that, unless the king took the colony in hand, it would be necessary to turn the whole business of government over to the assembly.[14]

This all but continuous contest between governor and assembly was fundamental in determining the character of provincial parties. It was a dispute that centered in divergent interpretations of the colonial governmental system; and in the presence of this vital question, questions of policy were forced into the background. Strictly speaking, therefore, there were no political parties; there were rather two centers of influence,

---

[7] *Doc. Hist. of New York*, **1**: 147, 148. *New York Col. Doc.*, **5**: 295, 298, 359, 844, 848, 884. *Assembly Journals*, November 24, 1711; November 25, 1727; July 30, August 10, 1728.

[8] Colden, *Letter-Book*, **1**: 149, 150, 208, 231. *New York Col. Doc.*, **7**: 469, 470, 471, 479, 483, 500, 705, 706, 709, 762, 763, 773, 803, 814, 815.

[9] *Col. Laws of New York*, **1**: ch. 159.

[10] *Assembly Journals*, **1**: 352, 354, 706. *Col. Laws of New York*, **1**: ch. 280.

[11] *Col. Laws of New York*, **1**: ch. 105.

[12] *Assembly Journals*, **1**: 352, 354, 704, 744, 792, 797, 800; **2**: 61, 68, 86, 173, 181, 203, 243, 246, 247, 259. *New York Col. Docs.*, **6**: 412, 456. *Col. Laws of New York*, **1**: ch. 290; **3**: chs. 675, 676, 741, 742, 743, 745, 764, 783, 793, 832, 847, 970.

[13] *Col. Laws of New York*, **3**: ch. 847.

[14] *New York Col. Docs.*, **5**: 356; **6**: 150, 160, 598.

and the only division that was permanent was that between the men who at any time were attached to the governor's interest and the men who made use of the assembly to thwart that interest. Now, there was no constant factor operating to hold any group of men to the governor's interest. Not being thoroughly identified with the colony, only while he was in a position to grant special favors or insure the continuance of those already granted, could the governor hold individuals or factions, and the so-called popular party was likewise not a permanent group, but a residuum, as it were, composed at any time of those who were without the sphere of executive influence.

If political conditions determined the nature of party alignment, party methods were equally determined by social and economic conditions. From this point of view, there may be distinguished three distinct classes, of which the most important was that small coterie of closely related families of wealth, commonly known as the aristocracy.[15] The early governors were instructed to attach to themselves, by grants of land and special privilege, men of ability through whose influence they might hope to control the colony.[16] And it was in no small degree the liberal land grants by the early governors that served in fact to establish the peculiar social conditions that characterized New York in the eighteenth century. By the close of Cornbury's administration, in any case, a very large part of the most valuable land in the province was in the hands of a few families.[17]

In Richmond County, on Staten Island, there were few large estates in the English period, and the county was one of the least influential, politically, in the entire province.[18] On Long Island, the estates of Remsen, Rapalje, Nicoll, and Smith embraced some two hundred square miles of the most valuable land in Kings, Queens, and Suffolk counties.[19] Livingston and Van

---

[15] Kip, *Olden Time*, 14, 15. De Lancey, *Origin and History of Manors*, in Scharf, *Westchester County*, 1: 130. Colden, *Letter-Book*, 1: 362, 363, 459, 468; 2: 68, 167, 168, 223, 224, 398, 399.

[16] *New York Col. Doc.*, 3: 331, 369, 685, 819; 4: 285.

[17] *Doc. Hist. of New York*, 1: 749.

[18] Clute, *Staten Island*, 16–19, 20, 44, 48, 58, 71.

[19] Stile, *Brooklyn*, 1: 49, 55, 70, 78. Bayles, *Suffolk*, 197–199, 226, 228, 229. *New York Col. Doc.*, 4: 1137. Valentine, *Hist. of New York*, 239. *Magazine of Am. Hist.*, 13: 1; 18: 361.

Cortlandt, whose property was chiefly in Albany and West-chester counties, also had small possessions in Kings County.[20] On Manhattan Island the most valuable estates were those of Stuyvesant, Bayard, Heathcoate, De Lancey, and De Peyster.[21] The counties of Ulster and Orange, west of the Hudson, were exploited by land companies early in the century, but few of the large grants were permanent.[22]   The county of Westchester contained six manors, which together covered more than half of the entire county. Morrisania, Fordham, and Pelham, in the south, were comparatively small, but Scarsdale, belonging to Caleb Heathcoate, Cortlandt Manor, and Philipsburgh covered approximately four hundred square miles of the choicest land in the province.[23]   In Dutchess County, the Philipse family had a second estate, larger than the manor,[24] which made that family second only to the Van Rensselaers in landed possessions. Beekman and Schuyler had possessions in Dutchess County,[25] which also contained the Great or Lower Nine Partners patent.[26] In Albany County lay the Livingston Manor[27] and the princely estate of Van Rensselaer,[28] together covering nearly a million acres on both sides of the Hudson. The Schuyler property was mainly in Albany County,[29] and the estate of Sir William John-son, patented at a later date, was within the original bounds of Albany County.[30] Closely associated with the land-owning fam-

---

[20] Stile, *Brooklyn,* **1:** 60, 72.

[21] Valentine, *Manual,* (1857), 498; (1861), 536; (1864), 563-623, 665. Valentine, *History of New York,* 228, 233, 236, 242, 243, 379. *Council Journal,* 115. *Doc. Hist. of New York,* **4:** 1035 ff. Scharf, *Westchester County,* **1:** 169. *Mem. Hist. of New York,* **2:** 224, 225, 257.

[22] Rutgers, *Orange County,* 22, 23, 26, 27, 28, 131, 353.

[23] Scharf, *Westchester County,* **1:** 91, 156, 157, 159, 160. *New York Col. Doc.,* **2:** 619; **3:** 303; **6:** 29, 56. *Mem. Hist. of New York,* **2:** 216, 217. Valentine, *Hist. of New York,* 239, 243, 244. Smith, *Hist. of New York,* 179. Valentine, *Manual,* (1864), 665. Schuyler, *Colonial New York,* **1:** 187.

[24] Smith, *Dutchess County,* 43, 44.

[25] *Ibid.*

[26] *Ibid.,* 43.

[27] Schuyler, *Colonial New York,* **1:** 286. *Doc. Hist. of New York,* **3:** 608-841.

[28] *New York Col. Doc.,* **1:** 383; **7:** 911; **8:** 383; **9:** 1039. Schuyler, *Colonial New York,* **1:** 208 ff.

[29] Schuyler, *Colonial New York,* **1:** 99 ff. Tuckerman, *Philip Schuyler,* 20. Campbell. *Annals of Tryon County,* App. 46 ff.

[30] Stone, *Life of Sir William Johnson,* is the best life of Johnson. *Cf.* also, *New York Col. Doc.,* **7:** 532. Campbell, *Annals of Tryon County,* 29.

ilies were the wealthy merchant families of New York, such as Van Dam, Cruger, Walton, Floyd, Rutgers, Ludlow, and Alsop.[31]

The manorial estates were the homes of a numerous tenantry. Land was sub-let by tenures that served to establish relations of a quasi-feudal nature between the proprietor of the estate and its inhabitants. Freeholds were ordinarily granted for life, though sometimes in fee. Leaseholds were more common than freeholds, though there was apparently no sharp distinction between the two sorts of grant. The manorial privileges included the right to hold courts—leet and baron, (a privilege rarely used), sometimes the right of avowdson, and in three cases the right of representation in the assembly.[32] The tenant system was also common on the non-manorial estates,[33] and while the non-manorial proprietors were without some of the distinctive privileges of lords of manors, their wealth and the relations they sustained to their tenantry, gave them an influence that was frequently determinative in the county in which they lived.

From the landed and commercial aristocracy, must be distinguished the mass of the freemen and freehold electors. Freemen were those who had purchased the privilege of engaging in certain occupations within the corporations of Albany and New York,—wholesalers, retailers, and independent handcraftsmen. The fee for ''freedomes'' was 5£ in New York; in Albany, 3£, 12 sh. for merchants, and 36 sh. for artisans.[34] The number of freemen was small; so late as 1790 there were only forty-five in Albany and ninety-three in New York,[35] an insignificant proportion of the total electorate of either county. The electoral freeholders were those who possessed, free of incumbrance, an estate in fee, for life, or by courtesy, of the value of 40£.[36] In 1790 the

[31] Valentine, *Manual* (1865), 713; (1869), 845. *Mem. Hist. of New York,* 4: 522, 523, 524, 525. *New York Col. Doc.,* 6: 153. Valentine, *Hist. of New York,* 234, 240.

[32] Scharf, *Westchester County,* 31 ff. Dawson, *Westchester County,* 1-4.

[33] In 1753 there were "Upwards of 120 families" on the estate of Sir William Johnson. *New York Col. Doc.,* 7: 532.

[34] *New York Hist. Soc. Coll.* (1885), 48, 239, 240. *The Charter of the City of Albany,* 11, 12.

[35] *New York Hist. Soc. Coll.* (1885), 53-238. A census of the Electors and Inhabitants in the State of New York, 1790; *Broadsides,* 1.

[36] *Col. Laws of New York,* 1: chs. 1, 74. *Cf.* Dawson, *Westchester County,* 4, note 4.

proportion of electors to the total population was approximately 12 per cent., which, applied to the colonial period, would give a voting population of 2,168 in 1698, and 20,256 in 1771.[37] These numbers are in fact too large,[38] and, for the present purpose, they must be still further reduced by deducting the freemen and the freeholders who were members of the aristocracy. In the early period the enfranchised freeholders were mainly outside the manors, but later the manorial freeholders increased steadily; in 1775, Colden informed Dartmouth, the freeholders within the manors of Livingston and Rensselaerwick were sufficient to control the elections of Albany County.[39]

The third class was made up by the unfranchised: freeholders whose estates were valued at less than 40£, or were encumbered, leasehold tenants, and those who labored for others—clerks, journeymen, day laborers, and "the shiftless, characterless class which encumbered the city of New York during the colonial period." This class was sometimes courteously designated as the "inhabitants," sometimes as the "mechanics," to distinguish it from the freeholders and the merchant freemen.[40] It is perhaps safe to say that over half of the male population above the age of twenty-one years was without political privilege of any sort. In the early period, this class was hardly a factor in the political problem; in the revolutionary period the very absence of privilege became a matter of tremendous significance.

As a result of the political and social conditions that have been here described, the aristocracy was able in large measure to control provincial politics. Organization prevailed, not so much within the so-called parties,—the court party, and the popular party; their personnel was too unstable for that,—as within the aristocracy as a social class. The leaders within this class stood, as it were, between the governor and the assembly, using either

[37] A Census of the Electors . . . 1790; *Broadsides,* **1.** *Greenleaf's New York Journal,* January 27, 1791.
[38] *Doc. Hist. of New York,* **1:** 689–697.
[39] *New York Col. Doc.,* **8:** 565. "The freeholders in the Manor of Livingston . . . are as numerous as those either of Kings County or Richmond. Their militia are upwards of 650 men." The Case of the Manor of Livingston ` *Broadsides,* **1.** *Cf.* Dawson, *Westchester County,* **4,** note 3.
[40] Dawson, *Westchester County,* **4,** note 3.

as occasion demanded. When the governor was the real center of influence, with lands to grant or sinecures to offer, ambitious men with favors to ask turned to him and supported him. But with titles secure and position achieved, their dependence on the governor decreased; and in the later period the leaders of the aristocracy in increasing numbers identified themselves with the assembly. Some families, such as the Philipse, it is true, remained loyal to the governors. On the other hand, Robert Livingston, after spending the best years of his life worming a great estate out of the government, entered the assembly and almost at once found himself at odds with the governor, his descendants becoming the most distinguished leaders of the popular party.[41] Even De Lancey, who is best known as the leader of the court party, having secured a life-appointment to the chief-justiceship of the province, became the chief political enemy of Clinton during the remainder of his administration.[42]

For political purposes, the organization of the aristocracy rested upon the surviving feudal principle of the personal relation: personal loyalty, rather than faith in a proposition, was the key to political integrity. The principal means by which this personal bond was established, aside from the economic relation of tenant to proprietor, was the marriage relation. An effective political influence was established, not by securing control of a "machine" within a party, but by inter-relating one's family with the aristocracy as advantageously as possible. Without wealth and powerful family connections, an "interest" could hardly be established, save in some rare circumstance where exceptional ability was united with a unique situation, as in the case of Sir William Johnson.[43] A man of ability and wealth, on the other hand, who extended his family connections judiciously, readily became a power in his community, if not in the province at large.

The principal families of wealth, commercial and landed, have already been named; they were precisely the families most prominent in political affairs previous to 1765. How closely they

[41] Schuyler, *Colonial New York*, 1: 242-273.
[42] Keys, *Cadwallader Colden*, 133, 142. *New York Col. Doc.*, 6: 417, 578.
[43] *Cf. Am. Hist. Review*, 6: 265 ff.

were related by marriage, it may be worth while to mention in some detail. The children of the first American Schuyler married with the families of Van Cortlandt, Van Rensselaer, Livingston, and Verplanck. The second generation of Schuylers married with the Van Cortlandts, Van Rensselaers, Livingstons, Bayards and De Peysters.[44] The Van Rensselaers married principally with the families of Van Cortlandt, Schuyler, Nicoll, and Livingston.[45] The Livingstons were connected with the families of Van Dam, Schuyler, Van Rensselaer, Beekman, Smith, and Ten Broeck.[46] The Philipse family married with the Van Cortlandt, Morris, and Robinson families.[47] The first generation of Van Cortlandts was connected with the Schuylers, Philipses, and Van Rensselaers; later generations with the families of De Peyster, Van Schaach, Bayard, De Lancey, Beekman, Van Rensselaer, and Schuyler.[48] The Floyds and Nicolls of Long Island were closely inter-related with the Van Rensselaers.[49] Among the relatives mentioned as present at the funeral of Abram De Peyster in 1767, are the names of Van Cortlandt, Beekman, Bancker, Rutger, Livingston, De Lancey, Van Horne, Philipse, Schuyler, Stuyvesant, Jay, and Roosevelt.[50] Caleb Heathcoate, of Scarsdale and New York, was closely related to William Smith, James De Lancey, and Stephen Van Cortlandt.[51] Colden, William Walton, Judge Thomas Jones, and the families of Beekman, Watts, Van Rensselaer, Verplanck, and Cruger, were related to De Lancey, as, less directly, were also the families of Morris, Ludlow, Rutger, and Wilkins.[52]

It has been well said that "these families . . . directed the infant colony. They formed a coterie of their own, and gen-

---

[44] Schuyler, *Colonial New York*, 1: 185. *New York Marriages*, 341, 342.
[45] Schuyler, *Colonial New York*, 1: 208. *New York Marriages*, 425.
[46] Schuyler, *Colonial New York*, 1: 286. *New York Marriages*, 235.
[47] Schuyler, *Colonial New York*, 1: 187. *New York Marriages*, 1, 300. *New York Col. Doc.*, 6: 56, note. Scharf, *Westchester County*, 1: 169.
[48] Valentine, *Hist. of New York*, 243, 244. Schuyler, *Colonial New York*, 1: 187 ff.
[49] Bayles, *Suffolk County*, 229. Valentine, *Hist. of New York*, 239.
[50] Valentine, *Manual* (1861), 556; (1851), 556. *New York Marriages*, 108.
[51] Valentine, *Manual*, (1864), 665. *Doc. Hist. of New York*, 4: 1035.
[52] *New York Marriages*, 20, 94, 445. *Doc. Hist. of New York*, 4: 1035. Smith, *Hist. of New York*, 2: 142, 143. *Mem. Hist. of New York*, 2: 224, 225; 4: 522, 523. Scharf, *Westchester County*, 169.

eration after generation married among themselves.''[53]   Aside from the close inter-relation by marriage, the conditions which made it easy for them to control nominations and elections are not far to seek. The voting population was small, ranging from about 2,000 in 1698 to 23,000 in 1790.[54] A large proportion of the electorate resided within the manors and on the large estates, especially in the later period. It was said that in 1770 the free-holders in the manors of Livingston and Rensselaerwick were sufficient to control the elections of Albany County;[55] and in fact the Albany elections were largely determined by the Van Rensselaers, Schuylers and Livingstons, for it was taken as a matter of course that tenant voters would follow their land-lords.[56] In Westchester County an even larger proportion of the electors were within the six manors,[57] and elections were power-fully influenced, if not determined, by Philipse, Cortlandt, and Morris. In other counties the economic and social relations of landlord and tenant were hardly so pronounced a feature of the situation, but the prestige of landed wealth and social position was everywhere sufficient to confer an excessive influence upon a few men.[58]

The wide-spread indifference to political matters served also to strengthen the great land owners. Until the middle of the century, and until a much later date in the rural districts, the democratic ideal was without significance. The aristocratic flavor which everywhere permeated society prevented the common man from taking the initiative, and even from expressing independence of judgment on political questions. To look up to one's superiors and follow their lead was quite the proper thing;

---

[53] Kip, *Olden Time*, 14.

[54] A Census of the Electors . . . 1790; *Broadsides*, 1. *Greenleaf's Journal*, January 27, 1791. *Doc. Hist. of New York*, 1: 689–697.

[55] *New York Col. Doc.*, 8: 565. Hugh Wallace to William Johnson, February 4, 1771; Johnson MSS., 20: 87.

[56] Kip, *Olden Time*, 16–18.

[57] In 1769 about five-sixths of the population of the county was within the six manors, and at least one-third within the two largest, Courtlandt and Philips-burgh. Scharf, *Westchester County*, 1: 91, 92.

[58] In 1769, R. R. Livingston failed of election from Dutchess county "Owing to all the tenants of Beekman and R. G. Livingston voting against him." P. R. Livingston to Philip Schuyler, February, 1769; Lossing, *Life of Schuyler*, 1: 238.

for the leaders it was largely a matter of making their position known.[59] In the country this indifference had a physical as well as a moral basis. The counties were large, traveling difficult, and the infrequent elections, which often were not of striking importance, were called whenever the governor saw fit, and sometimes at such short notice that the voting population such as it was could not be got to the polls.[60] Finally, no secret ballot or Australian system safeguarded the independence of the voters. The elections were held at the county town, under the supervision of the sheriff. The candidates, who were usually present, were publicly announced, and a vote was taken by "show of hands." If this "view" did not clearly indicate the result, a poll was resorted to: each voter, under oath, registered his name and the location of his freehold; by his vote he declared to the world in whose "interest" he stood.[61]

While these conditions prevailed, machinery for the nomination of candidates was unnecessary. Candidates were, in the phrase of the time, "sett up" by private personal agreement among those leaders whose "interests" were likely to carry the election.[62] If candidates sometimes apparently set themselves up, it was doubtless only after having received the assurance of support from respectable interests. A common man who ventured to follow his own inclination, rather than the cue of a leader, was certainly doomed to failure, besides laying himself open to censure. In 1733, when Lewis Morris was set up for Westchester County, there appeared an opposition candidate by the name of Foster. When the polls were closed and Morris was declared elected, Foster wished him much joy, and very humbly said "he hoped the late judge would not think the worse of him for setting up against him, to which the judge re-

---

[59] Dawson, *Westchester County*, 1 ff.   Clute, *Staten Island*, 82.   Kip, *Olden Time*, 17, 18, 26.

[60] "As to the present election it was appointed so suddenly by the sheriff that it was impossible to collect the votes of this extensive county, particularly as the roads are so bad and the rivers impassable."   William Johnson to Dr. Auchmuty, January 25, 1769; Johnson MSS., **17: 51**.

[61] *Col. Laws of New York*, **1: 406**.   Scharf, *Westchester County*, **1: 110**. *New York Journal*, November 5, 1733.   Bolton, *Westchester County*, **1: 136**.

[62] This point has been discussed in some detail in *Am. Hist. Review*, **6: 260** ff.

plied, he believed he was put up against his inclinations, but that he was highly blameable.''[63] The question was not, what are the candidate's principles, but, whom is Colonel Philipse for?

Generally speaking, these conditions prevailed throughout the colonial period, and at every election aristocratic methods of political management were in striking evidence. Yet one can perceive from an early date, particularly in connection with the city elections, the beginnings of new methods, essentially democratic, which were destined ultimately to transform politics altogether. These beginnings accompanied the rise of democratic ideals which tended to lessen the influence of the upper classes, and to give weight to the common man. These new ideals, so characteristic of the latter half of the eighteenth century, may doubtless be assigned to general causes; but in New York two more particular influences were at work. In the first place, the colony was a part of the English frontier, and the conditions inseparable from a frontier community were levelling here as elsewhere. The absence of a law of entail served in some cases to break up the great estates.[64] In any case, a certain democratic flavor always characterized the aristocracy inasmuch as it was based on wealth and not on birth. Inevitably the equality of opportunity that put so high a premium upon ability and industry in economic life, could not but aid in breaking down distinctions which artificial conditions had established in social and political life.

The political situation contributed to the same end. It has been said that the constant struggle between governor and assembly was the result of the rising democratic spirit. At best this is but a half truth. Technically the assembly did not represent the people; it represented a privileged class whose interests were in reality threatened by the spread of democratic notions. The assembly represented the people only in the sense that it protected the whole colony against executive encroachments. This identity of interest concealed for a time the latent hostility be-

---

[63] *New York Journal,* November 5, 1733.
[64] Schuyler, *Colonial New York,* 1: 187.   *New York Col. Doc.,* 6: 29.

tween privileged and unprivileged within the colony. Legally the governor's authority was unassailable. In resisting that authority, therefore, the assembly was forced to seek its justification in arguments from natural right and general welfare. A local and an aristocratic assembly could not consistently oppose monarchical and external authority by pleading the natural rights of a class or the general welfare of the few. The practical result of the assembly's long contest with the governors was thus to foster the theory of political equality; to give life to the notion that governments derived, or ought to derive, their authority from the consent of the governed. At a later time, when these notions began to yield their proper fruit in the demands of the unfranchised for political recognition, the land owners began to draw back. For the present their attitude served only to encourage the very spirit which threatened their peculiar privileges.

Whatever the cause may have been, the result of the rise of the new ideas was gradually to transform political organization. As men learned that they might have opinions of their own in such matters, some broadly generalized theory of political right, or governmental policy, or social change, rather than some powerful personality or traditional leader, was sure to claim their allegiance. The great families, the traditional leaders, found it necessary, therefore, particularly in the city, to modify their methods of political management. They found it increasingly necessary to win over their "interest" to every measure and to every ticket by force of reason, or what passed for reason. This modification, the beginning of which we are now to trace, took two directions, corresponding to the two chief characteristics of the old method: private and informal nominations of candidates by the leaders gave way to nominations by public meetings of the rank and file; the personal relation, as a means of holding the voters in line, was replaced by appeals to the voters' intelligence or interest, in the form of public letters or resolutions setting forth the principles for which the candidate stood.[65]

---

[65] Similar tendencies have been observed in English politics in the late eighteenth century. *Cf.* Lecky, *England in the Eighteenth Century*, 3: 373. Stephens, *English Thought in the Eighteenth Century*, 1: ch. 8, sec. 2.

The first step[66] towards the public mass meeting for purposes of nomination, appears to have been the formal announcement of the candidate in the public prints. As early as February, 1739, the voters of the city of New York were informed that ''whereas a great number of the freeholders and freemen of the said city have agreed and resolved to choose the following persons to represent them: towit. . . . Your vote and interest are desired at the ensuing election, on Tuesday, the 13th March next.''[67] With little variation similar announcements were made at each succeeding election during the colonial period.[68] Although these announcements seem to imply a meeting of the freeholders and freemen, they were at first doubtless the result of consultations among the leaders only. They are significant, however, precisely because they show that the leaders were now finding it desirable to create the illusion of a popular nomination; it was coming about that great numbers constituted as good a political asset as great names.

Inevitably, however, the hypothetical meeting back of the public announcement became a reality, the secret consultation of the leaders broadened out until it became a meeting of the faction or the party. The exact stages in this transformation cannot be reproduced,[69] but by 1769 the public mass-meeting for nominating purposes was an established fact. The election of that year was a conflict between the Livingston and the De Lancey factions, the former being supported by the lawyers and the Dis-

---

[66] Popular meetings for naming delegates were sometimes held in the Dutch period. They do not represent the growth of settled methods of political action, however. *Cf. New York Col. Doc.*. 1: 390, 554, 555 ; 2: 159, 374, 375, 394, 579, 680, 701, 702 ; 14: 109, 112, 218, 219. *Records of New Amsterdam*, 6: 395, 396. *East Hampton Records*, 1: 241 ; 2: 101, 103, 134, 135. Ricker, *New Town*, 27, 31, 52, 63, 83, 103, 104, 107. Stiles, *Brooklyn*, 1: 108. Schoonmacher. *Kingston*, 44, 45.

[67] *New York Gazette*, February 20–27, March 13–20, 1739. Valentine, *Manual*, (1865), 744. *New York Col. Doc.*, 5: 982.

[68] *New York Weekly Post Boy*, October 17, 1743 ; June 24, 1745 ; December 21, 1747. Valentine, *Manual*, (1865), 751, 779, 821, 823. *New York Gazette*, January 18, February 15, 1748 ; July 30, 1750 ; January 20, 1752 ; January 1, December 18, 1758. *New York Mercury*, December 23, 1758 ; February 15, 22, 1768. Watts to Monckton, January 23, 1768 ; Chalmers' MSS., 3. *Mass. Hist. Soc. Coll.*, 10: 599.

[69] Sedgwick, *Life of Livingston*, 65. Jones, *History of New York*, 1: 5, 6. *New York Gazette*, February 3, 17, 1752.

senters, the latter by the church and the mercantile interest. The old members of the assembly from the city were James De Lancey, James Jauncey, and Jacob Walton, of the De Lancey faction, and Philip Livingston, of the Livingston or popular party. Livingston had tried to arrange a compromise by which each party should select two of the four candidates. To this proposal De Lancey was unwilling to accede, but he was ready to accept Livingston as a candidate with himself, Jauncey and Walton. Wednesday, January 4, public meetings of both factions were assembled, each of which sent a messenger to Livingston inviting him to stand. He replied that he "could not join with either party." Upon receiving this answer, the De Lancey meeting, which was assembled at the *Exchange*, proceeded to nominate De Lancey, Walton, and Jauncey, and in the next number of the *Mercury* a card appeared, signed by these three, thanking the freeholders for "The generous approbation you have shown of our past conduct by nominating your late members," and informing them that, Mr. Livingston having declined serving, "Mr. John Cruger . . . has been prevailed upon to join us at the earnest solicitation of a great number of the inhabitants." Meanwhile, on January 5, a second meeting of the popular party was assembled. John Morin Scott was chosen chairman and it was unanimously agreed to support Philip and Peter V. B. Livingston, John Morin Scott, and Theodore Van Wyck. The usual card, announcing the ticket and soliciting the vote and "interest" of the electors, appeared in the next number of the *Mercury*.[70]

The rise of the formal public meeting for nominations represents one phase of the transformation of the old method of political control. The second phase centers in the effort to formulate in published documents the principles or the policies for which the nominated candidate stands. In the measure that the personal relation could no longer be relied upon for holding the party in line or for insuring the loyalty of the candidate to the interests of the voters, it was natural that common opinions

---

[70] *New York Mercury*, January 9, 1769. Sedgwick, *Life of Livingston*, 146, 147. John Wetherhead to William Johnson, January 9, 1769; Johnson MSS., 25: 125. Lossing, *Life of Schuyler*, 1: 236. *Cf.* Johnson MSS., 17: 34, 40.

on the part of the electors should be sought for attaining the first, and a tacit or explicit pledge by the candidate for the second.

Of letters and broadsides addressed primarily to the voter, with the object of defining the issues for him, there are many examples, beginning with 1748.[71] But the most striking instances are connected with the elections of 1768 and 1769. In the former election, the candidacy of John Morin Scott was bitterly opposed by the merchants, and a series of broadsides was issued[72] which clearly indicate the new methods for effecting party alignments. "The sincere friends of Trade and Prosperity of the City of New York," so runs one of these sneets, "present their good wishes to the respectable tradesmen and other electors; and hope they will join Heart and Hand to hinder a lawyer being chosen to represent this commercial city." Rather more pointed was the following: "Jack Bowline and Tom Hatchway send their service (damn compliments) to the freeholders and freemen, and beg they would in order to try how the land lies, take an observation, and they will find: 1st, that the good people are supported by trade and the merchants; 2nd, that the lawyers are supported by the people."[73] The two other issues of these elections—the religious quarrel, and the supplying of the British troops—elicited rather more serious discussions, in which both sides were set forth with much clearness.[74] In both elections the voters were as fully informed of the position of the opposing candidate as modern voters are through the party platforms.

From addresses directed primarily to the voter, may readily be distinguished others directed primarily to the candidates; and as the object of the former was to bind the voter to the candidate,

---

[71] A Word in Season, September 26, 1736; Broadsides, 1. Mechanic to the Worthy Inhabitants of New York; Ibid. A Plain Answer . . . August 21, 1750; Ibid. New York Gazette, January 18, 25, 1748; February 24, 1752. New York Mercury, February 17. November 17. 1755. Jones. Hist. of New York, 1: 6. Sedgwick, Life of Livingston, 104. Valentine, Manual (1866), 703.

[72] Mostly published by Holt. The excellent collection in the Lenox Library has been summarized in Bulletin of the New York Public Library, 3: No. 1, pp. 23–33.

[73] Lenox Broadsides, 23, 24. Leake, Life of John Lamb, 41.

[74] Lenox Broadsides, 24–26.

the object of the latter was to bind the candidate to the voter. Expressions of satisfaction for past services appear as early as 1734,[75] and it was a simple transition to indicate what conduct would prove satisfactory in the future. The early documents were generally expressions of individual opinion, but when the public mass-meeting came into use for nomination, the formulation of precise instructions by the whole constituency, or what passed for the whole constituency, became a common practice. During the stamp act troubles an effort was made to instruct the city representatives,[76] and in 1769 and 1770, instructions were formulated at public meetings with respect to three particular measures which were then occupying the assembly.[77] Such proceedings were already regarded as altogether proper, and the representatives themselves, on one occasion, replied that they were always ready to give careful attention to ''constitutional instructions from a majority of their constituents.''[78]

From this discussion of provincial politics it should be quite clear that the two main tendencies which produced the revolution were already well defined when Grenville began his experiments in colonial administration. The so-called contest for home rule was primarily a continuation of the long contest between governor and assembly. The governor's quarrel was taken up, as it were, by the ministry and Parliament; while the assembly was supported more unanimously than ever, so far as the main point was concerned, by the colony. But the assembly could not deal so effectively with parliamentary measures as it had dealt with the measures of the governor. The governor was dependent on the assembly for legislation, but a law of Parliament could be resisted effectively only by the refusal of the whole colony to recognize it. It thus happened that the assembly was early replaced by extra-legal committees and congresses as the chief institutional means for maintaining colonial rights.

---

[75] New York Journal, October 7, 1734.

[76] New York Gazette, November 28, 1765. New York Mercury, December 2, 1765.

[77] Broadsides, 1. New York Mercury, April 17, June 5, December 18, 25, 1769; January 8, 1770. Lenox Broadsides, 27. Doc. Hist. of New York, 3: 528, 534, 535.

[78] New York Mercury, January 22, 1770.

Now the establishment of this extra-legal machinery was the open door through which the common freeholder and the un-franchised mechanic and artisan pushed their way into the polit-ical arena. But their presence there, their violent and irrespon-sible methods of procedure, were altogether unwelcome to the land-owning and merchant aristocracy. The stamp act riots at once revealed the latent opposition of motives and interests be-tween the privileged and the unprivileged,—an opposition which the war itself only half suppressed, and which was destined to reappear in the rivalry of Federalist and Republican. From 1765 to 1776, therefore, two questions, about equally prom-inent, determined party history. The first was whether essential colonial rights should be maintained; the second was by whom and by what methods they should be maintained. The first was the question of home rule; the second was the question, if we may so put it, of who should rule at home.

CHAPTER II

THE STAMP-ACT. RADICALS AND CONSERVATIVES

After the conclusion of the French wars, the way was open for a more careful attention to colonial affairs; the extension of colonial territory made such a step necessary, while the settlement of European affairs by the Peace of Paris made it possible. The enforcement of the trade acts first engaged the attention of the government. Aside from the violation of the molasses act of 1733, which was virtually countenanced by the authorities, illegal trade had been a subject of very little complaint since about 1720, but during the Seven Years' War there developed an extensive contraband trade with Holland, and with the French, either directly by means of flags of truce, or through the neutral islands, particularly St. Eustatia.[1] Even before the war was over an effort had been made to meet these conditions, writs of assistance being issued to facilitate the work of the customs officials, and when Grenville became prime minister in 1763 there was a general overhauling of the customs service—among other things the establishment of naval officers at the principal ports to encourage "fair trade by the prevention of smuggling."[2] The merchants of New York were mainly well satisfied with these measures, it may be supposed, since they

---

[1] As early as 1752 Clinton complained of the extensive trade with Holland in tea and gunpowder. *New York Col. Doc.*, 6: 765. *Cf.* Hardy to the Lords of Trade, July 10, June 14, 1757; *ibid.*, 7: 271, 226. Colden to the Lords of Trade, December 7, 1763; *ibid.*, 584. *Annual Register*, 1765, p. 20. For the importance of St. Eustatia in Revolution, *cf.*, *Am. Hist. Rev.*, 8: 683.

[2] *Annual Register*, 1765, pp. 18, 22, Colville to Governor Hopkins, October 22, 1763; Arnold, *Rhode Island*, 2: 246. As early as 1757 De Lancey had suggested "a small nimble sailing vessel to cruise from Sandy Hook and off of Block Island and down the sound." *New York Col. Doc.*, 7: 273. *Cf.* Holland to Grenville, October 14, 1764; *Grenville Papers*, 2: 247.

had already complained of the lax inspection that prevailed in New England ports and to the southward.[3] Probably, therefore, the measures of Grenville for suppressing illicit commerce would have been successful had they not been part of a more general scheme of colonial control.

For Grenville proposed to establish part of the British army in the colonies and to raise a revenue from them for supporting it. The first measure for raising a revenue was the sugar act of 1764, which was a revision of the earlier act of 1733. The act of 1733 laid a duty of $9d$ per gallon on rum, $6d$ per gallon on syrups and molasses, and 5 $sh.$ per cwt. on sugar (except sugar from the dominions of Spain and Portugal) imported from American plantations not British into the British colonies.[4] These duties were not intended to raise a revenue, but to regulate commerce simply. As the law had never been enforced, it had served neither purpose. But the sugar act of 1764, as the preamble asserted, was expected to accomplish both ends. Certain new duties were laid on indigo, coffee, wine, and silks; the duty on molasses was reduced to $3d;$ the importation of rum was prohibited. Very stringent measures were taken for the enforcement of the new law, among other things the extension of the admiralty jurisdiction to cases arising under it. The revenue was to be paid into the Exchequer to be devoted to the defense of the colonies. Both duties and forfeitures arising under this law, as well as under the law of 1674, were required to be paid in silver, a provision which, often unnoticed, had practical consequences of the highest importance.[5]

While several laws were passed at the same time for encouraging colonial trade in other directions,[6] New England complained loudly that the sugar act would destroy the commerce of the colonies.[7] The assertion was certainly an exaggeration, to

---

[3] Colden to the Lords of Trade, December 7, 1763; *New York Col. Doc.*, **7:** 584, 585.

[4] 6 *George III.*, ch. 13.

[5] 4 *George III.*, ch. 15. For revenue laws prior to 1764, *Cf. Pol. Sc. Qu.* **22:** 20 ff.

[6] *Annual Register*, 1765, p. 22.

[7] Tyler, *American Revolution*, **1:** 55. Weeden, *Econ. Hist. New Eng.*, **2:** 753.

say the least, for in fact colonial commerce fell off but little during the following years.[8] But the policy of Grenville at least required a considerable readjustment of trade relations—an adjustment no less necessary for New York than for New England. The prohibition of the importation of rum, for instance, and the heavy duty on sugar, eliminated two of the principal commodities which the New York merchants received in exchange for their flour, while the 3d duty on molasses was claimed to be still prohibitive—a claim largely justified by the subsequent reduction of the duty to one penny.[9] Nevertheless, but little complaint was heard in New York, or at least whatever complaint existed was soon merged in the far more general opposition to the second measure of Grenville—the stamp act. That the government was contemplating the passage of a stamp act, had been known for some time. The colonial agents protested, but when Grenville assembled them for consultation they could suggest no other practicable scheme, and in February, 1765, the measure became a law.[10]

The stamp act required that stamped paper be used for practically all legal documents and customs papers, for appointments to all offices carrying a salary of 20£, save military and judicial offices, for all grants of privilege and franchises made by the colonial government, for licenses to retail liquors, for all pamphlets, advertisements, hand bills, newspapers, almanacs, and calendars, for packages containing playing cards and dice. The paper was to be printed by the government, and sold by officers appointed for that purpose. As in the sugar act, no money save silver could be accepted; and further to safeguard this clause in both acts, a law had already been passed in 1764 providing for the abolition of bills of credit as legal tender in the colonies.[11] It was estimated that the tax would net the government 60,000£. yearly—a tax which, divided among a population of over a mil-

---

[8] Almon, *Remembrancer*, 1: 117. Anderson, *Annals of Commerce*, 4: 42, 43, 59, 82, 104, 115, 126, 134, 142, 154, 162, 170.

[9] *Annual Register*, 1765, p. 22. 6 *George III.*, ch. 52.

[10] 5 *George III.*, ch. 12. Rumors of the stamp tax were current as early as 1763. *Cf.* Lott to Monckton, October 13, 1763; Chalmers' MSS., 4. For the authorship of the stamp-act, see *Grenville Papers*, 2: 373, note; 374, note.

[11] 4 *George III.*, ch. 34.

lion, was thought to be not excessive,[12] nor unreasonable, indeed, inasmuch as it was to be devoted to the defense of the colonies themselves.

The violent opposition which presently developed was nevertheless directed towards the stamp act primarily, although it must not be forgotten that the stamp act came as a sequel to the sugar act and the currency act of the preceding year. The wordy orators, of the popular party particularly, denounced the new tax as unconstitutional, and historians have too frequently, following their lead, neglected other phases of the question. The more important ground of opposition to Grenville's policy was economic rather than political. The new tax was not excessive, but in two respects it was with some justice regarded as a serious burden; it would frequently be inconvenient to secure a proper supply of the required paper, especially in the interior of the colony, and more especially it would prove a serious drain on the supply of silver which had never been more than barely sufficient to pay the English balances,[13] and was less so than ever now that the sugar act dues were to come out of it, and paper money shortly to be abolished. This difficulty was pointed out at the time, but it did not in fact become a serious problem for some years—not until the paper currency was actually retired in November, 1768. The further treatment of the sugar act and the currency act will therefore be reserved for a later chapter, in their proper connection with the mutiny act. The present chapter will deal only with the stamp act.

The election of 1761 had placed the assembly in the control of the popular party, of which the Livingstons, William Smith, and John Morin Scott were the leaders. Naturally, therefore, the opposition to the commercial and financial policy of Grenville was at first directed by the assembly, as opposition to the governors had always been. October 18, 1764, after the sugar act and the currency act had been passed, and the stamp act was all but assured, the committee consisting of the representatives from New York County, which had been appointed to correspond

[12] *Parl. Hist.*, **16:** 183.
[13] *Cf. New York Col. Doc.*, **5:** 685, 738 ; **6:** 116, 179.

with the colony's agent in England, was authorized to be "also a committee during the recess of the house, to correspond with several Assemblies, or committees of Assemblies, on the continent, on the subject-matter of the act, commonly called the Stamp-Act, of the act restraining paper bills of credit in the colonies, from being legal tender, and of the several other acts of Parliament lately passed, with relation to the trade of the northern colonies: and also on the subject of the impending dangers, which threaten the colonies, of being taxed by laws to be passed in Great Britain."[14] After the passage of the stamp act in the following winter, the assembly still directed the opposition; it approved of the suggestion of Massachusetts for a continental congress,[15] and left the appointment of delegates to the committee of correspondence.[16] When the congress finally assembled in New York, October 7, 1765, the committee itself, consisting of John Cruger, Philip Livingston, R. R. Livingston, William Bayard and Leonard Lispenard was admitted as the New York delegation.[17] The resolutions drawn up by congress asserted in moderate and conciliatory language: (1) That the stamp act was unconstitutional inasmuch as the colonies could be legally taxed only by their own representatives; (2) That the payment of the various duties laid by the new laws was, "from the scarcity of specie . . . absolutely impracticable," and would "render them unable to purchase the manufactures of Great Britain,"[18] resolutions which, although the New York delegates felt they were not authorized to sign them, were afterwards confirmed by the assembly.

With the adjournment of the congress, October 25, 1765,[19] the work of the assembly, as a leader of the opposition, was for the time being finished; it had used the means open to it; there was nothing to be done but wait for the reply of the home gov-

[14] *Ass. Journals*, 780. Niles, *Princ. of the Rev.*, 159. Dawson, *Westchester County*, 60, 61.
[15] Colden to Conway, September 23, 1765; Colden, *Letter-Book*, **2**: 35.
[16] *New York Mercury*, October 14, 1765. Niles, *Princ. of the Rev.* 158.
[17] *New York Mercury*, October 14, 1765.
[18] Niles, *Princ. of the Rev.*, 163.
[19] New York letter, November 8, 1765; Adolphus. *England*, **1**: 598. *Cf.* fragment, dated October 26, 1765; Chalmers' MSS., **3**.

ernment. But long before any reply could reach the colony, even assuming that it would be a favorable one, the stamp act would be in operation. The only alternative to submission was to find some other method of resistance, more immediately effective than mere official protest. The issue had in fact so shifted that the assembly alone could no longer meet it successfully: a governor it could quite effectively thwart, because a governor was dependent upon it for legislation; but it had no similar hold on Parliament. Direct Parliamentary legislation like the stamp act could be successfully resisted only by the refusal of the whole colony to give effect to it. The way was thus opened for the establishment of extra-legal organizations to direct popular activity, and for the entrance of the unfranchised classes into the political arena as the main stay of such organizations.[20] It was the entrance of this class into the contest, and the measures which it or its leaders proposed to carry out in that contest, that created the first broad distinction between radicals and conservatives.

The distinction was not, however, at once apparent. All classes alike were opposed to the distribution of the stamps; and conservative land owners and merchants saw little harm in popular demonstrations if they could be kept within control and directed to proper ends.[21] Even before the Stamp-Act Congress, there had been some stirring broadsides, and during July and August popular excitement had steadily increased.[22] The first

[20] Deane to Root, May 20, 1785 ; *Deane Papers,* 4: 349, 350.

[21] "The very men who have now fallen into such a pleasant dream of loyalty and obedience, in the time of the Stamp-Act were most of them 'patriots of distinguished note,' " etc. 4 *Am. Arch.,* 3: 1735.

[22] "The new tax gives the highest disgust . . . the duties are thought to be beyond all reasonable bounds." (The Sugar Act is doubtless meant.) Smith to Monckton, May 30, 1765 ; Chalmers' MSS., 4. August 31, James McEvers resigned as stamp distributor. Colden, *Letter-Book,* 2: 27. "You will think the parties are mad, Holt particularly, who has been cautioned over and over again and could have been prosecuted, but people's minds are so inflamed about the Stamp-Act, it would only be exposing government to attempt it." Watts to Monckton, September 24, 1765 ; Chalmers' MSS., 3. *Cf.* Colden, *Letter-Book,* 2: 44. The question of appeals from colonial courts to the king in council contributed also to the popular excitement. *Ibid.,* 89. *Hist. MSS. Com.,* Rep. xi., Pt. 5, pp. 331, 332. Smith to Monckton, November 8, 1765 ; Chalmers' MSS., 4.

step[23] towards active resistance to the stamp act appears, nevertheless, to have been taken October 17, five days before the stamps were expected. On that day there appeared a notice in the *Gazette* calling a meeting of the "friends of liberty and the English constitution," in order to form "an association of all who are not already slaves, in opposition to all attempts to make them such."[24] The notice (which was not signed, nor was any date apparently set for the meeting) was one which at the moment expressed the quite general sentiment. The expected arrival of the stamped paper and more especially the action of the lieutenant-governor in preparing the fort to receive it,[25] had aroused a feeling of resentment that was as indiscriminating as it was intense.[26] All classes for the moment were at one; merchants, we are told, "will send for no more British manufactures, shop keepers will buy none, gentlemen will wear none."[27] When Captain Davis' ship presently arrived, Tuesday, October 22, the situation was critical. By the direction of Colden, the frigate had been stationed just outside the Narrows, and the ship bearing the stamps was brought to anchor under the guns of the fort. The council was shortly summoned, three only out of seven attending. After much argument Colden was advised to hire a sloop to remove the goods from the ship so that the stamps could be got at. No sloop, however, could be hired, and the king's ship, Garland, had to be used for that purpose, seven packages of stamped paper being in this fashion presently deposited in the fort.[28] To the landing of the stamps no resistance was made, but on the night of the 23rd some notices were posted about the city, signed *Vox Populi*, "bidding the persons who first used stamped paper to take care of Home, Person, and

---

[23] Colden asserts that a secret correspondence had been carried on throughout the colonies, the object of which was to prevent by force the distribution of the stamps. Colden to Conway, September 23, 1765; Colden, *Letter-Book*, **2:** 33. I have come across no evidence in support of this.

[24] *New York Gazette*, October 17, 1765.

[25] Colden, *Letter-Book*, **2:** 44.

[26] R. R. Livingston to General Monckton, November 8, 1765; Chalmers' MSS., **4.** Printed in *Mass. Hist. Soc. Coll.*, Ser. IV., **10:** 559. A long and detailed account of the stamp act riots of November 1st to 5th. The letter is unsigned, but is in the hand of Livingston.

[27] Livingston to Monckton, November 8, 1765; Chalmers' MSS., **4.**

[28] Colden, *Letter-Book*, **2:** 47, 54, 55.

effects,"[29] and as the 1st of November approached—the day set
for the distribution of the stamps—still more formidable threats
continued to be thrown out in the same manner.

If there were individual men of property who were already
beginning to look with distrust upon the growing indignation
of the mob, no step was yet taken to check it. The merchants,.
as a class at least, were prepared to encourage the rising opposition. October 31, a meeting of merchants and others was held
at George Burn's tavern, where the first non-importation association was formed. It was resolved neither to import any more
English goods, nor to sell any on commission after January 1,
1766, until the stamp act was repealed. About two hundred
merchants, it was said, subscribed to these resolutions, which
were strengthened by a separate agreement of the retailers not
to "buy any goods, wares, or merchandise of any person or persons whatsoever," shipped after the new year.[30] It is also
stated,[31] though no authority has been found for it, that a committee of five was appointed to correspond with the merchants
in other colonies. Although the meeting separated peaceably,
some boys and sailors, who had been attracted to the tavern by
the rumor that "there was a design to execute some foolish
ceremony of burying liberty," paraded the streets in a
"Mobish" manner, whistling, breaking a "few glass win-
dows,"[32] and threatening "particulars that they would the next

---

[29] Livingston to Monckton, November 8, 1765; Chalmers' MSS. 4. Colden,
Letter-Book, 2: 47. *New York Col. Doc.*, 7: 770.

[30] *New York Gazette*, November 7, 1765. Dawson, *The Park and its Vicinity*,
9, 10. *Montressor Journals*, 336. *Mag. of Am. Hist.*, 1: 369, 370. The agreement appears to have been kept pretty well—partly because, there being no
stamps to be had, vessels could not legally sail any way. Imports from England
to New York in 1764 were approximately 515,416£; in 1765, 382,349£; in
1766, 330,829 £. The falling off in Pennsylvania, Maryland, and Virginia
was about the same; in New England it was very slight; in the Carolinas
imports increased slightly in 1765; in Georgia there was an increase from 18,
338£ in 1764 to 67,268£ in 1765. Almon, *Remembrancer*, 1: 117. Dawson,
Sons of Liberty, 87, note 2. The New York agreement was entered into by
forty-eight merchants at Albany. *New York Mercury*, January 27, 1766.

[31] Leake, *Life of Lamb*, 14, 15. Dawson, *Westchester County*, 84. Neither
Livingston nor the *Gazette* mentions the appointment of a committee. *Cf.
Mem. Hist. of New York*, 2: 367, note.

[32] Livingston to Monckton, November 8, 1765; Chalmers' MSS., 4.

night pull down their houses.''[33] The next night a much more
formidable mob did in fact parade the streets, proceeding, in
spite of the effort of the mayor and council to disperse it,[34] to
the fort, where the lieutenant-governor, who had during the day
added to h's unpopularity by ordering the marines to the fort,[35]
was hanged in effigy. Stones and bricks were thrown aga:nst
the barred doors, and with every accompaniment of insult the
soldiers were called upon to fire. Receiving no reply, the gal-
lows, effigy, and the chariot of the governor, were transported
to the Bowling Green and there burned in a fire kindled with
boards from the fort inclosure. After sacking the house of
Major James, who had threatened to cram the stamps down the
people's throats, the mob ended its debauch by rifling some
baudy houses.[36]

This sort of thing brought men of property to a realization
of the consequences of stirring up the mob. A little rioting
was well enough, so long as it was directed to the one end of
bringing the English government to terms. But when the destruction of property began to be relished for its own sake by
those who had no property, and the cry of liberty came loudest
from those who were without political privilege, it was time to
call a halt. These men might not cease their shouting when
purely British restrictions were removed. The ruling classes
were in fact beginning to see that ''liberty and no taxation''

---

[33] "31st Oct., 1765. Several people in mourning for the near issue of the
stamps and the interment of their liberty. Descended even to the Baggammon
boxes at the Merchant's Coffee-House being covered with black, and the dice
in crape. This night a mob in three squads went through the streets crying
"Liberty," at the same time breaking the lamps and threatening particulars," etc.
Montressor Journals, 336.

[34] "On the night of the first of November, there passed through the streets
a mob, the most formidable imaginable. The mayor and aldermen had met
at the city hall in order to prevent anything of the sort, and at its com-
mencement endeavored to prevent it with their constables and threw down the
effigy they were carrying, but the persons attending ordered it to be taken up
again in the most magisterial manner, and told the mayor, etc., they would
not hurt them, provided they stood out of their way." Livingston to Monckton,
November 8, 1765 ; Chalmers' MSS., 4.

[35] Colden, *Letter-Book,* 2: 52.

[36] The lieutenant governor's loss was estimated at 195£ 3 sh. Colden, *Letter-
Book,* 54. Livingston to Monckton, November 8, 1765 ; Chalmers' MSS., 4.
Montressor Journals, 337.

was an argument that might be used against themselves as well
as against the home government. The doctrine of self-government, which for so many years they had used to justify resistance to the colonial governors, was a two-edged sword that cut
into the foundations of class privilege within the colony as well
as into the foundations of royal authority without. Dimly at
first, but with growing clearness, the privileged classes were beginning to perceive the most difficult problem which the Revolution was to present to them: the problem of maintaining their
privileges against royal encroachment from above without losing
them by popular encroachments from below. It was this dilemma
that gave life and character to the conservative faction.

The beginning of the conservative reaction may be said to
date from November 2, 1765, the day following the burning of
the governor's effigy. In the morning of that day it was publicly reported that the people, far from being satisfied with the
violence of the preceding night, were determined to attack the
fort and destroy the stamps.[37]   Whereupon R. R. Livingston,
who up to this time had been convinced that ''nothing could be
done by going out,'' went to Mayor Cruger and offered his services in suppressing the project.   Meanwhile, Colden, who had
lost all hope of distributing the stamps, agreed to place them on
board the man of war.   Pleased with these concessions, Livingston, Duane, and other influential men, assisted by the captains
of some vessels (sailors were prominent in the mob element) determined to make a serious effort to keep the peace.   They
''went into every part of the town, spoke to many persons . . .
and every now and then had hints of the intended design.''
After a time seven or eight men were seen to assemble opposite
the Fields with torches in their hands, being soon surrounded
by a ''strange sett'' from all quarters.   With the greatest difficulty Livingston and his associates succeeded in disbanding a
part of the crowd; and when a declaration finally came from

---

[37] Letters were sent to Colden threatening his life.   Colden, *Letter-Book*,
2: 80.   *New York Col. Doc.,* **7:** 774.

the governor to the effect that he "would not meddle with the stamps at all," the rest also dispersed.[38]

The project of taking the stamps was, nevertheless, not abandoned. The next day, Sunday, November 3, a notice was posted at the Coffee House, signed *Sons of Neptune*, urging the people to disregard the advice of the "peaceable orators" of Saturday night, and fixing the time for assaulting the fort on Tuesday, November 5. The conservative leaders were now thoroughly alarmed. They called a meeting of the citizens at the Coffee House on Monday morning, where many attended, but few had courage to speak out, being afraid of the "secret party" whose strength none could know. Livingston, nevertheless, made a speech picturing the horrors of "mob government," and setting forth the necessity of suppressing the design of the mob, which threatened to plunge the city into civil war. The governor now made another concession. He invited Livingston, Cruger and some others to the fort and to them declared that he would not suffer the stamps to be delivered.[39] A broadside was accordingly issued stating that "The governor acquainted Judge Livingston, the mayor, Mr. Beverly Robinson, and Mr. John Stevens this morning, being Monday the 4th of November, that he would not issue nor suffer to be issued any of the stamps now in Fort George." This statement was signed by the four names mentioned, and there was added the rather ambiguous assertion that "the freeman, the freeholders, and inhabitants of the city . . . are determined to keep the peace of the city, at all events, except they should have other cause of complaint."[40] Still the "people" were not satisfied, and a counter broadside was issued calling the citizens to meet in the Fields on Tuesday, November 5, at 5 o'clock, and to come armed.[41] Tuesday morning the common council met, and in a written document, which was conveyed to the governor at 4 o'clock by the mayor and aldermen in person,

[38] Livingston to Monckton, November 8, 1765; Chalmers' MSS., 4. Colden's declaration was published as a broadside. *Broadsides,* 1. *Cf. Mass. Hist. Soc. Coll.* Ser. IV., 10: 581. Colden, *Letter-Book,* 2: 80. Mercantile Library MSS., 42, 43.

[39] Livingston to Monckton, November 8, 1765; Chalmers' MSS., 4.

[40] *Broadsides,* 1. Chalmers' MSS., 4. Quoted in Lamb, *New York,* 1: 729.

[41] *Broadsides,* 1.

proposed that the stamps be surrendered to them. The mob was already assembled to know the result, and Colden, after asking the advice of the council and of General Gage, gave up the stamps in return for a receipt signed by the mayor.[42]

With the stamps safely lodged in the city hall, the mob dispersed. But four days later Watts wrote to Monckton[43] that the situation was still critical, "of which the stamp act is the foundation," and he suggested that a repeal of the law would "calm the storm very soon." It was not a repeal, however, but a second shipment of stamped paper, that Sir Henry Moore brought towards the middle of November when he came out to take charge of the colony.[44] The new governor made no effort to distribute the stamps, and his conciliatory measures pleased the people immensely.[45] But the radical alarmists were not satisfied until the second shipment of stamps was lodged with the first in the city hall—a result which was achieved, once more through the intervention of the corporation, on Saturday, November 16.[46]

The November riots marked the first stage in the separation of radicals and conservatives. The rioting was carried on mainly

---

[42] Livingston to Monckton, November 8, 1765; Chalmers' MSS., 4. Colden, Letter-Book, 2: 57. Mem. Hist. of New York, 2: 363. Seven packages were receipted for. Three, left in the ship of Capt. Davis, were probably for Connecticut. For the attitude of the government towards this proceeding cf. Parl. Hist., 16: 118.

[43] November 9, 1765; Chalmers' MSS., 3. Cf., however, New York Col. Doc., 7: 773.

[44] November 13, 1765, on the Minerva. Colden, Letter-Book, 2: 66. New York Mercury, November 18, 1765. There were seven boxes of stamps for New York, and two for Connecticut.

[45] "He takes every method to ingratiate himself with the people." Colden to Conway, December 18, 1765; Letter-Book, 2: 66. "Sir Harry seems to be an easy, sensible, well-bred man, and experienced in business, every body likes the change extremely, indeed nobody could come amiss so they were but rid of the old man." The first question put to the council was "whether it would be possible to issue the stamps, answered, unanimously, no." All consented to restoring the fort to its former state "the old man at his elbow among the rest." Watts to Monckton, November 22, 1765; Chalmers, MSS., 3. Cf. Cal. Home Office Pap., 1766–1769, No. 41. The new governor was favored with congratulations by a deputation from the Sons of Liberty who also erected a "pyramid" in the Fields in his honor. New York Gazette, November 21, 1765. Moore thought Colden had exaggerated the danger from the people. Moore to Hillsborough, May 9, 1768; New York Col. Doc., 8: 67.

[46] New York Gazette, November 21, 1765. New York Mercury, November 18, 1765.

by the unfranchised mechanics and artisans, sailors, and the rough element of the city generally, under the lead of men like John Lamb, Isaac Sears, and John Morin Scott. There is even at this time some indication of a secret organization of these elements; Livingston speaks of the "secret party" whose strength was unknown; one of the broadsides was signed *Sons of Neptune*, another *Vox Populi*, still another *Free Sons of New York*. There is no evidence, however, at this time of any specific organization calling itself the *Sons of Liberty*. That term, which was used widely, after Barre's speech in Parliament,[47] to designate those who opposed British measures, had no technical significance in New York until a later date. What is clear is that during the November riots the more radical elements in the population were drawing together, as the more conservative men of property and political privilege began to protest against the use of mob violence as a means of resistance.

For the moment, the disposal of the stamped paper had put an end to mob violence. But another issue, involving violence of a certain sort perhaps, very shortly arose, which contributed to the further differentiation of the two factions. Carefully guarding the stamps in the town house effectively prevented the use of them; but it did not repeal the law; those business transactions for which the law required stamped paper must therefore cease altogether or be carried on as before without stamps. The first alternative constituted a legitimate and peaceable method of resistance; the second involved a kind of violence inasmuch as it necessitated a violation of law.

From the first, it appears that the law was ignored in some respects. The newspapers were published as usual, and handbills were a conspicuous feature of the contest from first to last. Holt, at least, publicly announced his intention of violating the law absolutely,[48] and doubtless the same course was pursued with respect to many of the business transactions that figured in the stamp act list. But inevitably general business activity was

---

[47] *Parl. Hist.*, 16: 38. *Cf.* Walpole, *Mem. of George III.*, 2: 56. Lecky, *Eng. in the Eighteenth Cent.*, 4: 74. note. Frothingham, *Republic*, 175, note 3.

[48] *New York Gazette*, November 7, 1765. The notice was run in each issue until December 26.

largely curtailed. Apart from the non-importation agreement
of the merchants,[49] the requirement of stamped paper for all
clearances and bills of lading, probably operated to stop much
of the foreign trade:[50] many merchants of wealth preferred the
legal method of resistance, and they largely controlled the foreign trade; besides, it was doubtful what reception would be
given in foreign ports to cargoes without properly attested bills
of lading,[51] and the frigate in the harbor made it difficult for
vessels to sail without legal clearances.[52] The stoppage of foreign trade soon affected retail business, in spite of the encourage-
ment given to domestic manufactures.[53] The merchants with
large capital, and the wealthy classes generally, could afford to
wait; in some respects the situation doubtless created for them
a temporary monopoly by which they might even profit.[54] But
the retailer without reserve capital was soon sold out; the artisan
and mechanic, and the day laborer found themselves out of
employment. Before the end of November, the former classes
began to suffer, and the situation offered an opportunity for a
renewal of political agitation by the radical leaders.

To the radical leaders, indeed, the stoppage of business was
in itself a kind of tacit recognition of the legitimacy of the

---

[49] There were at least two instances in which the association was forced upon
those who inadvertently or deliberately broke it. Late in April the *Sons of
Liberty* waited upon Capt. Hathorn of the ship Prince George. They were
informed that the cargo was shipped in ignorance of the association, and it
was readily turned over to them. The cargo was branded with the New York
arms and held for re-shipment at the first opportunity. *New York Mercury,*
April 28, 1766. For another instance, see *Mem. Hist. of New York,* **2:** 379.

[50] It is stated, nevertheless, November 8, that the merchants "ventured out
their vessels with unstamped cockets; nor have the officers of the customs the
hardiness to refuse them any of the necessary documents." New York Letter;
Adolphus, *England,* **1:** 597.

[51] "At present nothing is done in a commercial way, the stamps cannot
possibly be distributed, and if vessels should be permitted by this and other
governments to go without them, it is uncertain what treatment they would
receive abroad." Watts to Monckton, November 22, 1765; Chalmers' MSS., **3.**

[52] "In this port alone the men of war stop the shipping, unless a few that
steal out by night." Watts to Monckton, December 30, 1765; Chalmers' MSS.,
3. "No vessel will be allowed to go out of the harbor." Moore to Conway,
December 21, 1765; *New York Col. Doc.,* **7:** 802.

[53] *Annual Register,* 1765, pp. 55, 56.

[54] Colden wrote that if the non-importation agreement were enforced, "People
in America will pay an extravagant price for old moth-eaten goods and such
as the merchants could not otherwise sell." Colden to Lords of Trade, December
6, 1765; *Letter-Book,* **2:** 78.

stamp act. They believed, too, that this pretended form of resistance was little more than a device of the government to reduce the colony, through pinching poverty, to the necessity of complying with the law. And that, indeed, was after all the crux of the matter: in the long run the only alternative to the resumption of business without stamps was the resumption of business with stamps.[55] The radical leaders, therefore, addressed themselves to the task of putting "business in motion again in the usual channels without stamps."[56]

For this purpose they had recourse to the customary device of a mass meeting. Hitherto, so far as the radicals were concerned, the latter end of the mass meeting had usually been the riot. But in the present instance their plan appears not to have involved mob-violence; instead they hit upon the design of an appeal to the city's representatives, to whom they assumed the right of issuing instructions. Accordingly, "after some previous meetings of the gentlemen who have all along made the principal opposition to the Stamp-Act," a notice was posted in all parts of the town, November 25, requesting "freeholders, freemen and inhabitants of the city and county" to meet at Burn's tavern "in order to agree upon some instructions to be given to their representatives in general assembly."[57] That those instructions would request the representatives to use their influence to secure a resumption of trade without stamps was well known; that the

---

[55] *Cf.* Watts to Monckton, November 22, 1765; Chalmers' MSS., 3. In the absence of the "appearance of any remedy [for the decay of trade] or any proposal to that end, they [the radicals] thought it high time to better themselves . . . Since the discontinuance of business itself is a sort of admittance of the legality of the Stamp-Act, and has a tendency to enforce it; and since there is just reason to apprehend that the secret enemies of liberty have actually a design to introduce it by the necessity to which the people will be reduced by the cessation of business . . . whereas if the Stamp-Act, as being unconstitutional, was entirely disregarded, and business went on as usual, it is plain it would never take place here." *New York Gazette,* November 28, 1765. *Cf.* Watts to Monckton, December 30, 1765; Chalmers' MSS., 3. Governor Moore predicted that the ruin of commerce would force the people to give up the contest. *New York Col. Doc.,* 7: 802.

[56] *New York Gazette,* November 28, 1765.

[57] *Montressor Journals,* 340. *New York Gazette,* November 28, 1765; *New York Mercury,* December 2, 1765. There was a rumor that Philadelphia was on the point of accepting the stamps. *Cf.* Joseph Allicocke to——, November 21, 1765; Lamb MSS., (1765-1766).

unfranchised "inhabitants" were to be used to swell the radical
ranks and carry the instructions was equally obvious. For both
reasons the leading men of property and of political influence
were opposed to the meeting; they were opposed to all illegal
methods of resisting the stamp act, whether in the form of
rioting or of carrying on business in violation of law; they believed naturally that all matters of the kind should be settled
by the legal voters only, and not by the unfranchised. The entrance of the unfranchised into the political arena was as dis-
tasteful to them as the early November riots had been, for their
political supremacy was threatened by the one as their property
rights had been endangered by the other.

The meeting could not well be prevented however, though the
notices, it is said, were pulled down by those "hostile to the design."[58] By political management, it might nevertheless be diverted from its original purpose. Accordingly, on the day appointed for the meeting, the conservatives attended in large
numbers,[59] and by an ingenious device, the precise nature of
which is not clear,[60] appointed a committee of their own, laid
aside the resolutions prepared by the radical leaders, and adopted
others in their stead.[61] November 27, the committee, including
William Livingston, William Smith, James De Lancey, and John
Morin Scott, waited upon the representatives with these resolutions.[62] The instructions[63] began by urging that it could not be

[58] New York Mercury, December 2, 1765.

[59] It was said that the meeting consisted of about 1,200 people. New York
Gazette, November 28, 1765.

[60] "One or more of the company supposed to be previously instructed, proposed
some particular gentlemen present to be appointed as a committee for the county.
These gentlemen without the general consent of the people agreed to the proposal on condition they might be joined by several other gentlemen present who
were named." The exceptional character of these men prevented any objection
being made. They then took the lead, although they were not the prime movers,
and diverted the meeting from its real design. New York Mercury, December
2, 1765.

[61] The resolutions originally prepared were published in the Mercury, December 2, 1765.

[62] The Committee consisted of: Henry Cruger, John Van der Spiegel, David
Van Horn, James Jauncey, Walter Ruthford, John Alsop, William Livingston,
William Smith, Jr., William Hicks, J. M. Scott, James De Lancey, John Thurman,
Jr. The only member who ever became a thoroughgoing radical was J. M. Scott,
who at this time was not openly associated with the radicals. New York
Gazette, November 28, 1765.

[63] New York Gazette, November 28, 1765. New York Mercury, December 2,
1765.

unreasonable, for constituents "in this constitutional way," to formulate their wishes; they conceived that no tax should be laid save by gift of the people; that jury trial, without appeal, should be preserved; that internal taxes were unconstitutional. These principles the representatives were urged to maintain to the utmost of their ability. In return, the committee was assured that the assembly had already taken these matters into serious consideration.[64]

The radical resolutions, which had meanwhile been published in the newspapers, were in sharpest contrast to all this. They expressed the highest regard for constitutional government, and for the British Parliament, but enumerated various "encroachments" which had been made in years past upon their liberties, mentioning particularly the stamp act as being subversive of everything valuable in the British constitution. For that reason, the representatives were urged to prevent its execution by means of "legislative sanction to the transacting business as usual without stamps,"—a sanction which was to be secured by withholding the salary of every officer who refused to discharge the duties of his office precisely as though no stamp act had ever been passed.[65] At the same time a curious diatribe, purporting to come from the Sons of Liberty, was conveyed to the assembly through the clerk, of which, however, the radical leaders denied all knowledge, offering in fact to aid in detecting the author.[66]

---

[64] New York Gazette, November 28, 1765. For the assembly resolutions cf. ibid., December 26, 1765.

[65] New York Gazette, November 28, 1765. New York Mercury, December 2, 1765.

[66] The paper was delivered to the clerk in a sealed envelope, November 26. It was as follows: "Gentlemen of the House of Representatives you are to consider what is to be done first drawing of as much money from the Lieutenant Governor's sellery as will Repare the fort and on spike the guns on the Battery & the nex a Repeal of the gunning act & then there will be a good Militia but not before and also as you are a setting you may consider of the Building act as it is to take place next yeare wich it Cannot for there is no supply of some sort of the materials Reqhired this law is not ground on Reasons but there is a great many Reasons to the contrary so gentlemen we Desire you will do what Lays in your power for the good of the public but if you take this ill be not so conceited as to say or think that other people know nothing about government you have made these laws & say they are Right but they are Rong & take away Liberty, Oppressions of your make gentlemen make us SONS OF LIBERTY think you are not for the public Liberty, this is the general opinion

The assembly, as we have seen, had opposed the stamp act, and it had approved the resolutions of the Stamp-Act Congress. But it was strongly conservative: it was opposed to all violence; it was especially opposed to having political matters referred to the unfranchised for decision. Unquestionably, therefore, it was well pleased with the result of the meeting of November 26, and in December it accordingly embodied the instructions of that meeting in a series of resolutions that were moderate enough to satisfy even the most conservative.[67] The failure of their plans, and the conservative resolutions of the assembly did not discourage the radicals, however; they continued their efforts to secure a resumption of business without stamps,— with what success it is difficult to say. From one source we learn, for instance, that the lawyers met December 20, and resolved to exercise their notarial powers as before;[68] from another, that only two or three voted for this resolution.[69] Many merchants, doubtless, were willing enough to venture cargoes, if they could secure clearances that would be accepted in foreign ports; December 3, Watts writes that the "Men of war stop the shipping, unless a few that steal out by night." He nevertheless predicted that there would be trouble soon unless the colony was "put upon a footing with our neighbors;"[70] and in March it was reported to the secretary of state that "several vessels"

---

of the people for this part of your conduct By order signed one and all, FREE-DOM." *Doc. Hist. of New York*, **3:** 495. The assembly voted the letter scandalous and offered a reward of £50 for the detection of the author. Dawson, *The Park and its Vicinity*, 15, note. *New York Mercury*, December 16, 1765.

[67] "The last resolves of the Assembly concerning the present circumstances are very well. Why have they not been so moderate long ago? The effect would have been favorable and their conduct honorable. We set the house afire and then endeavor to put it out." Hasenclever to Johnson, December 23, 1765; Johnson MSS., **11:** 279. For the resolutions referred to, see *New York Gazette*, December 26, 1765.

[68] Friday last the gentlemen of the law met "and resolved to carry on business as usual without paying any regard to- the Stamp-Act." *New York Mercury*, December 23, 1765.

[69] *Freeman*, writing in 1770, states that the lawyers were waited on by a committee of twelve which desired them to go on without stamps, but that there "were only three or four of the profession who voted for going on." *New York Journal*, April 19, 1770. No courts were held, but in January some lawyers prepared a memorial to Governor Moore requesting that the common pleas be held as usual. The Governor refused. *New York Col. Doc.*, **7:** 805, 810.

[70] Watts to Monckton, December 30, 1765; Chalmers' MSS., **3.**

had been "cleared out by the customs-house officials at New York with unstamped paper."[71] Probably the necessities of the case proved stronger than patriotic resolutions, and we may conclude that, on the whole, there was an increase in the amount of business done in violation of law.

However much it may have been, it was far from satisfying the radicals; and they soon came to the conclusion that the execution of the act could be prevented only by the destruction of the stamps in the city hall.[72] December 23, the *Sons of Liberty*, a name now coming into common use to designate the radicals,[73] held a meeting (the inciting cause of which appears to have been the arrival, a few days before, of a stamped letter-pass from Quebec,) to determine what was best to be done. According to Montressor,[74] they debated whether to burn the stamps or send them back to England, while Hasenclever, writing to Johnson, says that the latter was decided upon.[75] In any case, an attack upon the city hall was expected, and the mayor and council, we are told, assembled the "better sort of citizens,"

---

[71] Lords Admiralty to Conway, March 30, 1766; *Cal. Home Office Pap., 1766–1769*, No. 102. *Cf.*, Moore to Lords of Trade, January 14, 1767; *New York Col. Doc.*, **7**: 891; and *Freeman* in *New York Journal*, April 19, 1770. Whatever business required the Governor's sanction was impossible; no letter passes, for instance, were granted to traders to the interior, nor grants for the New Hampshire lands. *New York Col. Doc.*, **7**: 807, 818.

[72] It appears that the radicals had never been satisfied with the disposition of the stamps on November 5. November 21, Allicocke wrote that the stamps had been "decently interred" in the City Hall, where they would remain unless taken out to be "sent back." Joseph Allicocke to —— November 21, 1765; Lamb MSS., (1765–1766.) The stamps "are continually under a city guard in the City Hall, and what will finally become of them we cannot tell. The populace threaten another insurrection, are to meet this afternoon (it is said) upon the common to consult upon compulsory methods, which puts the officers of civil justice almost at their wits 'end." Smith to George Whitefield, December 6, 1765; *Hist. MSS. Com.*, Rep. XI., Pt. 5, pp. 331, 332.

[73] "Sth [December, 1765.] The *Sons of Liberty*, as they term themselves," etc. *Montressor Journals*, 343.

[74] "23 [December, 1765.] Assembled a mob for householders' votes—yea or nay to burn the stamps or send them to England back. Undetermined." *Montressor Journals*, 343.

[75] "The Sons of Liberty, so they stile themselves, pretend to take by arbitrary force the stamps out of the town house and send them to England." Hasenclever to Johnson, December 23, 1765; Johnson MSS,. **11**: 279.

at eleven o'clock, to prevent the execution of the design.[76] In fact, however, no attack was made, and the stamps remained in the city hall. The radicals devoted themselves for the present to securing very formal resignations and humble apologies from those who had been appointed as stamp distributors.[77] The appearance of a stamped letter-pass raised a tumult,[78] and early in January ten packages of stamps, which arrived in the brig *Polly* from London, were forcibly taken and burned in the ship-yards at midnight.[79]

The time now seemed ripe for the formal organization of the radicals under the style of the *Sons of Liberty*. The lead-

---

[76] "Our political affairs are in great confusion. Today will be decided if the moble will command the town, or will be subjected to the better sort of citizens. The latter are called by the mayor and corporation to meet at the City Hall to resolve upon the point." Hasenclever to Johnson, December 23, 1765; Johnson MSS., **11:** 279.

[77] The first stamp distributor appointed for New York was James McEvers. *New York Mercury*, July 7, 1765. He resigned August 30. Colden, *Letter-Book*, **2:** 27. *New York Col. Doc.*, **7:** 761. David Colden applied for the office in a letter to the Commissioners of the stamp office, October 26, 1765. Colden, *Letter-Book*, **2:** 51. Apparently, however, Peter De Lancey was appointed, for, upon his arrival late in November, he publicly resigned, after being waited upon by a committee, November 27. *New York Gazette*, December 2, 1765. December 2, James McEvers was put through the same ordeal. *Ibid.*, December 9, 1765. *New York Mercury*, December 9, 1765. But the fear of stamp distributors extended to those of other colonies. Z. Hood, the Maryland collector, fled from Maryland and came to New York in September, afterwards going to Long Island. A company of patriots from New York waited upon him at Flushing, and offered him the alternative of resigning or leaving the province. He signed a formal resignation November 28, 1765. The following day the company returned to New York in "several divisions", carrying flags and banners bearing the inscription "Liberty, Property, and No Stamps." *New York Mercury*, December 9, 1765. For this action the patriots received the thanks of the Maryland *Sons of Liberty*. *New York Gazette*, December 26, 1765. *Cf.* Colden to Conway, September 23, 1765; *New York Col. Doc.*, **7:** 760.

[78] December 19, 1765, Capt. Blow arrived from Quebec, bringing a stamped letter-pass from Governor Murray. It was posted in the Coffee House, and Friday evening a mob paraded with effigies of Grenville, Murray, and Lord Colville. *New York Mercury*, December 23, 1765. In February information was received from Philadelphia of the receipt of a stamped letter-pass from Louis Pintard. Friday, February 14, the *Sons of Liberty* waited upon Pintard, who made a humble apology. The people. we are told, were hardly restrained from destroying his "person and effects." *New York Gazette*, February 17, 1766. *New York Mercury*, February 17, 1766.

[79] *New York Mercury*, January 13, 1766. *New York Gazette*, January 13, 1766. "11th January, 1766. Advertisements placarded throughout of the general approbation from the Sons of Liberty of those sons that burnt the stamps the other night." *Montressor Journals*, 345. *Cf. Cal. Home Office Pap.*, 1766–1769, No. 84.

ers of the party were well known; secret meetings had been held from time to time to determine their policy; towards the end of November, the term *Sons of Liberty* was already used to designate them.[80] Whether any formal organization bearing that title existed before 1766 is not known;[81] but on January 7, the very day the brig *Polly* sailed into the harbor with the detested stamps on board, they at least threw off the mask of secrecy that had hitherto somewhat veiled their actions, and publicly declared their organization and their principles. The meeting was held at the house of Mr. Howard, where a "great number of gentlemen, Sons of Liberty, assembled . . . in consequence of an invitation from some of the members of their society." "After setting forth and declaring their rights and liberties, their firm adherence to the English constitution . . . and showing the unconstitutional nature of the Stamp Act . . . the following resolutions were agreed to by a great majority. Resolved: That we will go to the last extremity and venture our lives and fortunes effectively to prevent the said Stamp-Act from ever taking place in this city and province. Resolved: That any person who shall deliver out or receive any instrument of writing upon stamped paper . . . agreeable to the said act, shall incur the highest resentment of this society, and be branded with ever-

---

[80] I do not find the term *Sons of Liberty* used to designate the ultra-radicals before the November riots. The placards of early November were signed *Sons of Neptune, Vox Populi, Free Sons of New York*, etc. November 9, Colden wrote to Conway, describing the methods of the radicals, but makes no mention of the term. November 21, the *Mercury* speaks of the *Sons of Liberty* sending a deputation to Sir Henry Moore. The same day Allicocke mentions "us Liberty boys." Lamb MSS., (1765-1766). November 26, an anonymous letter to the assembly already quoted uses the term. *Doc. Hist. of New York,* **3:** 495. December 8, Montressor speaks of "The Sons of Liberty as they term themselves." *Journals,* 343. December 23, Hasenclever mentions "The Sons of Liberty, so they stile themselves" Johnson MSS., **11:** 279. From January 1766, the term was commonly used to designate the radicals.

[81] If there was a formal organization of the radicals before January, 1766, there are but slight traces of it. The papers of John Lamb, who was the secretary of the society, consist of letters only. The earliest letter is from Jos. Allicocke, dated November 21, 1765. The letter indicates that there was at that time some sort of a secret society. With the letter there were enclosed several sealed packets, the disposal of which was carefully indicated. The next letter in the collection is dated January 15, 1766. The bulk of the correspondence for this period is in February and March. The letters are enclosed in a packet marked (1765-1766).

lasting infamy. Resolved: That the persons who carry on business as formerly on unstamped paper . . . shall be protected to the utmost power of this society . . . Resolved: That we will to the utmost of our power maintain the peace and good order of this city so far as it can be done consistently with the preservation of our rights and privileges.'' It was agreed to meet regularly for the future, once a fortnight unless more frequent meetings became necessary.[82]

If the radicals expected that this open avowal of their position would add to their strength, they were fated to disappointment. They appear to have been troubled by internal dissensions;[83] and if there was no absolute decline in numbers, certainly there was no gain. The extreme radicalism of their position,[84] as well as their partiality for parades, dinners, the burning of effigies, and such proceedings,[85] alienated the ''better sort'' as completely as ever; on the other hand, now that the real strength of the society became better known, as secrecy disappeared, there was less hesitation in opposing it than there had been at first. But above all, the danger which the *Sons of Liberty* saw in such a lurid light, was not equally apparent to others. The stamps had long rested quietly in the city hall, the last shipment having been even more effectively disposed of. No serious effort had been made to force them upon the colony; the council invariably advised

---

[82] *New York Gazette,* January 9. 1766. *New York Mercury,* January 13, 1766.

[83] "19 [January, 1766.] The Sons of Liberty assembled at night in the Fields and bespoke a large supper, but upon some disagreement (which is generally the case) they broke up and dispersed as soon as it came on the table, leaving only half a dozen." *Montressor Journals,* 347. Montressor was strongly prejudiced against the radicals.

[84] *Cf. New York Gazette,* January 2, 9, 16, 23, 30, 1766. *New York Mercury,* January 27, 1766. "26 [February, 1766.] The Sons of Liberty arrived at that pass as to have the utmost indifference regarding their manner of expressing themselves." *Montressor Journals,* 350. "27 [February, 1766]. The New York inadvertant Sons of Liberty make no scruple of publ'cly declaring that they are for shaking off the yoke of dependency of their mother country." *Ibid.,* 351. The Providence committee wrote. February 17, 1766, that they were prepared to take up arms in resistance to the stamp act if necessary. Lamb MSS.. (1765-1766).

[85] "6 [February, 1766]. This night several children were dispersed by the watchman . . . for parading the streets with 3 effigies and candles, being about 300 boys." *Montressor Journals,* 349. *Cf. ibid.,* 345, 350, 351, 353, 355, 357.

against any such attempt,[86] and the governor's policy was to limit as much as possible the transaction of business without stamps, and then wait until the economic pressure should bring the people to accept the stamps voluntarily.[87] Unquestionably, there was a strong probability that such a policy would succeed in the long run; but the danger necessarily appeared greater to the *Sons of Liberty,* whose followers were recruited from the poorer classes, than to the conservative and well-to-do. To the conservatives, it must have appeared that the *Sons of Liberty* were urging them to provide against a danger which was largely illusory, by methods which they were not in favor of using if it had been real. It is not surprising, therefore, to learn that the *Sons of Liberty* were "much concerned that the gentlemen of fortune don't publicly join them,"[88] a complaint that was echoed from Philadelphia, where, it was admitted by the committee, the society was weak on account of "dissentions in Provincial politics."[89]

But nothing disheartened the radicals: both fanatic and demagogue were incited to renewed activity by indifference or active opposition. If they were weak in numbers, they might find strength in a further unity of purpose and of organization; failing to receive general approval at home, the society sought for support in other colonies.[90] February 4, it was unanimously resolved, in pursuance of this policy, to appoint a committee to correspond with those outside of New York who were in sym-

---

[86] *Cf. Mem. Hist. of New York,* 2: 375.

[87] His conduct as well as his correspondence bears th's out. *Cf. New York Col. Doc.,* 7: 802, 810. Late in January Watts commended the governor for acting coolly and letting the stamps alone. Watts to Monckton, January 6, 20, 1766; Chalmers' MSS., 3.

[88] "4th [February, 1766]. Meeting of the Libertines who seem to decline, being much concerned that the gentlemen of fortune in the town don't publicly join them. They formed a committee of correspondence with the Liberty boys in the neighboring provinces." *Montressor Journals,* 348.

[89] Letter from Sons of Liberty at Philadelphia to New York, February 15, 1766: Lamb MSS.. (1765-1766).

[90] The correspondence of th's date indicates that there had been hitherto no inter-colonial union of the radicals. The prospect of union gave much pleasure in Connecticut and Philadelphia; union was necessary, according to Major Durckees of Norwich, in order to resist "our most inveterate enemies." Durckees to Sears, February 10, 1766; Lamb MSS., (1765-1766). *Cf.* Letter from Philadelphia, February 15, 1766: from Providence, February 17, 1766; from Upper Freehold, April 28, 1766; *ibid.*

pathy with the purposes of the association,[91] and at the next meeting, the original resolutions of January 7 were republished with an additional clause giving expression to the new project.[92] The committee, of which John Lamb was the secretary, began a correspondence with the counties of New York, and with all of the colonies to the north and as far south as South Carolina.[93] During February and March the work of uniting the radicals throughout the continent was carried on. From the correspondence of Lamb, and from the New York newspapers, it may be ascertained that the ramifications of the society extended at least to Albany,[94] Huntington,[95] Oyster Bay,[96] and Fishkill[97] in New

[91] "At a meeting of The Sons of Liberty last Tuesday evening at the house of Mr. Howard . . . a committee was appointed . . . in order to correspond with the Sons of Liberty in the neighboring colonies." *New York Gazette,* February 6, 1766.

[92] This meeting was held February 15. The added resolution declared that the safety of the colonies depended upon the union of all against the "enemies of his Majesty and the Colonies." *New York Mercury,* February 17, 1766. *New York Gazette,* February 11, 1766.

[93] Sons of Liberty in New York to Connecticut, February 20, 1766; Lamb MSS., (1765–1766). This letter is in the hand of John Lamb. It acknowledges the receipt of a letter from Connecticut, and states that letters had been written to all provinces as far south as South Carolina.

[94] There is only one letter from Albany before the repeal. It is dated January 15, signed "Albany," and addressed to "Messrs. J. Allicocke and I. Sears." There is another letter of May 24 which expresses the general joy at the repeal. Lamb MSS., (1765–1766). For the organization of the Albany Sons of Liberty, see *New York Mercury,* January 27, 1766.

[95] Huntington letter is dated February 24. It accompanied a series of resolutions, identical with those adopted by the society at New York. A committee was also appointed to correspond with the "Sons of Liberty in New York and elsewhere." The letter is signed: John Hobart, Gilbert Potter, Thomas Brush, Cornelius Conklin, Nath. Williams. Lamb MSS., (1765–1766). *New York Gazette,* February 27, 1766. *New York Mercury,* March 3, 1766.

[96] Meeting held at Oyster Bay, February 22, and resolutions adopted identical in substance with those of New York. The committee consisted of Benjamin Townsend, Rowland Chambers, Geo. Townsend, Geo. Weeks, Barach Sneething, Michael Weeks, and J. Sel [ies]. Sons of Liberty at Oyster Bay to Sons of Liberty at New York, February 22, 1766; Lamb MSS., (1765–1766). *New York Gazette,* February 27, 1766. *New York Mercury,* March 3, 1766. Onderdonck *Doc. and Let. of Queens County,* 13.

[97] The *Sons of Liberty* organized in Fishhill, Dutchess County, although the Lamb papers contain no letter from them. A meeting was held April 26. Three resolutions were adopted: Though faithful subjects of King George. they claimed that the stamp act was unconstitutional, and declared themselves "ready at the shortest notice to assist our brothers with both lives and fortunes . . . to defend our liberties, and deliver our posterity from political slavery. AMEN. GOD SAVE THE KING." Signed, Sons of Liberty. *New York Gazette,* May 15, 1766.

York, and to various towns in the provinces of New Hampshire,[98] Massachusetts,[99] Rhode Island,[100] Connecticut,[101] New Jersey,[102] Pennsylvania,[103] Delaware,[104] and Maryland.[105] Letters

[98] In response to the New York letter, a meeting was held at Portsmouth, Saturday, February 10, 1766. *New York Gazette,* February 27, 1766.

[99] The correspondence with Boston was carried on largely by way of Connecticut and Rhode Island. *Cf.* Letters from Providence, February 17, 1766; Lamb MSS., (1765-1766). One letter in the collection is from Boston directly. It is undated, and is in reply to a suggestion for a "union . . . for our common interests." It appears that the Boston radicals had already formed a sort of club. "Spent the evening with the Sons of Liberty at their own apartment in Hanover Square, near the tree of liberty. It is a counting room." Adams, *Diary,* January 15, 1766; *Works of John Adams,* 2:'178. This is the first mention of the *Sons of Liberty* I have found in the diary. The names and occupations of those present are given, mostly artizans or small tradesmen. There were, we are told, pipes, punch, wine, biscuits, cheese and such conversation as is heard at all clubs. February 5, Adams received a letter from the society stating that "the colonies (we mean New York and Connecticut) have entered into certain reciprocal and mutual agreements, concessions and associations, a copy of which we received by express the last Sunday, with their desire to accomplish the like association with us." The letter goes on to say that the object of the association is to counteract the inveterate enemies of American liberty, etc. *Ibid.,* 183.

[100] The letter from Providence expresses delight at the prospect of union. The *Sons of Liberty* there are firm against the stamp act, and will take up arms if necessary; at two hours' notice they will bring three thousand men under the "tree of liberty." Letter from Providence, February 17, 1766; Lamb MSS., (1765-1766).

[101] The Norwich *Sons of Liberty* were pleased with the idea of union, which they said was necessary on account of "inveterate enemies." Major Durckees to Isaac Sears, February 10, 1766; Lamb MSS., (1765-1766). March 6, resolutions were passed at Fairfield. *New York Mercury,* April 7, 1766. A meeting at Hartford, March 25, appointed a committee for the Colony. *New York Gazette,* April 7, 1766.

[102] The Upper Freehold, Monmouth County, did not reply to the New York letter till April 28, when a committee of five wrote that the *Sons of Liberty* had organized according to the suggestions of the New York society. Only a small number attended the meeting, the great majority of the inhabitants being absent for reasons "best known to themselves." Committee in Upper Freehold to New York, April 28, 1766; Lamb MSS., (1765-1766). *New York Mercury,* May 12, 1766. February 25, there was a meeting at New Brunswick, but whether in response to the New York letter does not appear. *New York Mercury,* March 3, 1766. In Woodbridge a committee was appointed, and resolutions were passed in response to the New York letter. *Ibid.,* March 10, 1766. April 1, the *Sons of Liberty* in Sussex County organized in the same way *Ibid.,* May 12. 1766.

[103] February 15, the *Sons of Liberty* in Philadelphia had not yet appointed a committee, but they promised to do so. They admitted that they were weak because of "dissentions in provincial politics." Sons of Liberty, Philadelphia, to New York, February 15. 1766 : Lamb MSS., (1765-1766). The same day William Bradford wrote that some stamps, passing through the city to the

were sent to South Carolina, but to what extent there were organized societies of the *Sons of Liberty* in Virginia and the Carolinas, I have not been able to determine. To add to the strength of the association, a congress of the *Sons of Liberty* was proposed;[106] but the repeal of the stamp act made the realization of this scheme unnecessary.

After the repeal, indeed, the *Sons of Liberty*, as a formal organization, was dissolved, although the leaders had declared that they would maintain their organization, and work for the repeal of all duties, and the abolition of the post-office and the admiralty courts.[107] As no records were kept, or at least none preserved,[108] it is impossible to say whether there was a formal dissolution or not. At any rate the meetings ceased, and we are told that the members divested themselves of homespun clothes, being supposed to remain only with homespun hearts.[109] The last official correspondence of the Society preserved in the Lamb papers,[110] bears date May 24, and in July, Montressor tells us that the meetings had ceased, and that the name of a *Son of Liberty* was no longer "to be ever heard of."[111] Nicholas Ray, writing from London, proposed to form a club of ten or twenty members, to be called the Liberty club, to meet monthly, and

---

South were burned at the Coffee House "with loud acclamations." Bradford to Lamb, Sears, Robinson, Wiley, and Mott, February 15, 1766; *ibid.*

[104] Organization of Essex County, with resolutions, March 15, 1766. *New York Gazette,* April 7, 1766.

[105] *Sons of Liberty* at Baltimore promised to "cooperate." Sons of Liberty at Baltimore to New York, March 8, 1766; Lamb MSS.. (1765–1766). The society at Baltimore was well organized. *New York Gazette,* March 24, 1766. Leake (*Life of John Lamb,* 19) prints a letter from New York to Baltimore which I did not find in the Lamb papers. At Annapolis an organization was effected April 10. *New York Gazette,* April 24, 1766.

[106] Undated letter from Sons of Liberty at New York to Boston; Lamb MSS., (1765–1766.) *Cf.* Same to Providence, April 2, 1766; *ibid.*

[107] Statement made in *Mem. Hist. of New York,* **2**: 379. I have found no contemporary authority for it. In 1774, abolition of the post office was broached. William Goddard to John Lamb, March 23, 1774; Lamb MSS., (1774–1775).

[108] The Lamb papers contain no minutes or records of meetings. *Cf.*, however, "These heroes of liberty keep an office and enter minutes and record them and all their correspondence," etc. *Montressor Journals,* 357.

[109] Montressor, quoted in *Mem. Hist. of New York,* **2**: 379.

[110] The last, that is, for this period. The Lamb papers contain a few letters dated 1774, and some documents relating to the later society of Federal Republicans.

[111] *Montressor Journals,* 378.

annually to celebrate the repeal of the stamp act.[112] The club was apparently never formed;[113] but the leaders did hold together in a fashion,[114] and every March for some years the repeal was celebrated by a public dinner on which occasion patriotic toasts were listened to.

It is sometimes said that the society of the *Sons of Liberty* was formed for the purpose of resisting the stamp act;[115] it is sometimes asserted, that it was a continuation of the Whig club of 1752.[116] The latter statement is wholly unfounded; the former is misleading. It is a curious fact that the Society whose *raison d'etre* is said to have been the nullification of the stamp act was not formally organized until after the stamps had been safely lodged in the town house. The fact is, simply, that no organization like the *Sons of Liberty* was necessary to nullify the stamp act, because practically every class in the province was openly determined that it should not take effect. The stamp act was opposed by John Cruger and James De Lancey, who were leaders in the old court party; by Livingston, William Smith, and John Morin Scott, who founded the Whig club and were leaders of the popular party; by John Lamb, Isaac Sears, and Marinus Willett, who had hitherto taken but little part in the politics of either party. But as opposition developed, it became clear that there was a wide difference of opinion as to the proper method of procedure; the use of mob violence, the in-

---

[112] Nicholas Ray to the Sons of Liberty at New York, July 28, 1766; **Lamb MSS.**, (1765-1766).

[113] Leake says that the society replied to Ray, October 10, 1766, *Life of John Lamb*, 36. I have found no reply in the Lamb Papers.

[114] Leake, *Life of John Lamb*, 37.

[115] "The association of the Sons of Liberty was organized in 1765, soon after the passage of the Stamp-Act, and extended throughout the Colonies from Massachusetts to South Carolina." Leake, *Life of John Lamb*, 3.

[116] The sources of this notion are Colden and Galloway. "So early as the year 1754 there were men in America . . . who held independence in prospect. . . . These men when the Stamp-Act was passed, made a . . . screen of the gentlemen of the law in every part of America to sound the trumpet of opposition against government . . . When the Tea act passed they made the same use of the merchants." *Examination of Joseph Galloway*, 5. *Cf.* Colden to Hallifax, February 22, 1765; *Letter-Book* 1: 469. Colden to Lords of Trade, April 7, 1762; *ibid*, 187. Colden to Hallifax, April 27, 1765; *ibid.*, 479. Colden to Conway, September 23, October 26, 1765; *ibid.*, 2: 35, 49. Dawson gives currency to the idea. *Westchester County*, 40.

creasing activity of the unfranchised classes, the attempt to encourage the transaction of business without stamps, gradually separated sincere fanatics like Lamb, and vain carpet-knights like Sears, from long-headed men of conservative temper like Robert Livingston and John Cruger. Thereupon the radical leaders drew together, depended more and more upon the unfranchised classes whose poverty made them radical, and finally organized themselves under the name of the *Sons of Liberty*. The society was thus the result of conservative opposition to radical methods of resisting the stamp act. The radical leaders, finding themselves in a minority, identified conservative opposition to their policy with royal oppression, and came to regard themselves, therefore, as the only true patriots—as preëminently the *Sons of Liberty*. Surrounded by "inveterate enemies," both at home and abroad, they thought to increase their own efficiency, first by organizing in their own province, and finally by turning for support to kindred spirits in neighboring colonies. The society of the *Sons of Liberty* represents, in fact, the protest of the unfranchised classes, guided by leaders partly sincere and partly interested, against the determination of the privileged classes to retain an exclusive control of political affairs, and to settle the stamp act quarrel by methods that appeared to them to be entirely adequate.

While the conservative and radical parties were being differentiated on these lines, steps were being already taken to repeal the law which had created all the trouble. The resolution to repeal the stamp act gave occasion for the first serious discussion of the American situation that Parliament had listened to. For the first time, there was presented to it a clear exposition of the colonial commercial system, and of the effect upon that system of the sugar act and the stamp act;[117] petitions from English merchants supported American demands;[118] statistics and logic combined to prove beyond a doubt that the system of Grenville was an economic blunder. Opposition to the repeal was grounded

---

[117] For the debates, see *Parl. Hist.*, **16**: 133, ff. Summarized in *Annual Register*, 1766, p. 32 ff.

[118] *Parl. Hist.*, **16**: 133.

on political considerations, which, happily, did not prevail, and the law was repealed March 18, 1766.[119] The sugar act was so far modified at the same time, by the reduction of the duty on molasses to one penny,[120] as to remove one of the objections to that law; and certain other acts were passed which greatly facilitated the trade of the colonies.[121] The mutiny act and the currency act were, however, left unmodified, with what results shall presently be seen.

The general result of the stamp act episode was thus to create a broad, ill-defined distinction between the conservative and the radical elements in the population, and to give to the latter a taste for political agitation.[122] Of the radicals, the *Sons of Liberty* constituted the most extreme and the most active portion. Associated with them, however, was a considerable body of the merchant class—men who still saw more clearly the danger to trade from British taxation than the danger to property from violent methods. In the first enthusiasm they were not strongly opposed to the measures of the *Sons of Liberty,* the society, indeed, numbering many merchants among its members. With the conservatives belong all those who were opposed to the stamp act as a specific measure, but who were even more opposed to violent methods of all kinds, and jealous also of the presumption of the unfranchised classes. These were the large property owners—land owners, merchants of wealth and political influence—and all essentially conservative and temperate men. The issue between the two parties was two-fold: first, whether the resistance to British measures should be directed by the whole people, or by the legal voters only; second, whether resistance should consist in a mere evasion of the law, or in an open violation of it.

Of these two questions, the first was not so prominent at this

---

[119] 6 *George III.,* ch. 11.

[120] *Ibid.,* ch. 52.

[121] *Ibid.,* ch. 3. 7 *George III.,* ch. 4.

[122] The stamp act agitation, said Governor Moore, led the people to think that any conduct "which had the appearance of resisting government might be undertaken with impunity." The rent riots and the so-called "leveller" movement, which appeared in Dutchess and Westchester counties in April, 1766, were doubtless in some measure the outgrowth of the stamp act agitation. Moore to Conway, April 30, July 14, 1766; *New York Col. Doc.,* 7: 825, 845.

time as it became later, while the repeal of the stamp act disposed of the second for the time being. But the Townshend acts raised the same question once more, though in a slightly different form. The Townshend acts furnished, however, only one of the points in dispute which, during the next three years, contributed to party development; of equal importance were the difficulties arising from the mutiny act and the currency act. With respect to the alignment of parties, the history of these years is far from simple. It can have little meaning for those who regard the Revolution as a spontaneous uprising of the colonies in defense of a political principle, or for those others who can see in it nothing but the achievement of a deliberately planned independence. There was at first a certain reaction from the violence of the stamp act period; purely local issues not infrequently confused party lines altogether; but toward the close of the year 1769, and during the winter of 1770, a combination of various influences, almost wholly economic, contributed to differentiate once more, and more clearly than the stamp act had done, the radical and conservative elements of the population; and in this differentiation both parties gained something—the conservatives, by attaching to themselves the whole body of merchants; the radicals, by identifying themselves with a policy that ostensibly bore the stamp of disinterestedness. These general tendencies we shall attempt to trace in some detail in the next chapter.

CHAPTER III

THE ECONOMIC CRISIS OF 1768–1770: THE MORE COMPLETE DIFFERENTIATION OF RADICALS AND CONSERVATIVES

The tranquillity which was confidently expected to follow the settlement of the stamp act controversy was not altogether realized. The repeal of the stamp act and the act of indemnity[1] were highly appreciated; and the loud rejoicing with which they were greeted deadened somewhat the rather ominous sound of the declaratory act.[2] The New York assembly complied, though with some reluctance, it was thought, and not in entire good faith, with the demand for compensation for the sufferers in the November riots.[3] But a new difficulty at once arose with respect to the mutiny act. Grenville's colonial policy involved not only the raising of a revenue from the colonies, but also the establishment in them of a part of the British army. Early in 1765, accordingly, a law was passed extending the ordinary regulations of the mutiny act to the colonies, establishing barrack and billeting regulations, and requiring the

---

[1] 6 *George III.*, ch. 51.

[2] *Ibid.*, ch. 12. Grenville thought the Americans should rejoice at the repeal since "they are thereby exempted forever from being taxed by Great Britain for the public support even by themselves." *Grenville Papers,* 3: 250.

[3] It was first proposed to "recommend" this measure to the colonial governments, but the word "require" was afterwards substituted. *Grenville Papers,* 3: 358. When the government laid the resolution before the assembly, the "upland counties opposed it, saying that the Yorkers did the damage, and ought to bear the expense; on the first division 11 for the bill, against 10. On the second division, 13 to 10." Whately to Grenville, July 29, 1766; *ibid.,* 282. Two laws were passed: one, December 19, 1766 appropriated about 2000 £ for the losses of James Gautier, Mallet, and H. Van Schaack; the second, June 6, 1767, appropriated 123 £, 13sh., 9½d., for Philip Martin. *Col. Laws of New York,* 4: ch. 1302, 1320. Colden, whose losses amounted to 195£, 3 sh., was never compensated. *New York Col. Doc.,* 7: 832, 886, 994.

colonial assemblies to furnish "fire, candles, vinegar and salt, bedding, utensils for dressing victuals, and small beer, cyder, or rum."[4] To the establishment of troops in the colony there was little objection at this time, but the requirement that the colony should provide for their support was deemed to be a direct tax under the guise of a requisition.[5] It was not until July 3, 1766, after the governor had sent two messages to the assembly, and nearly a fortnight after the arrival of the troops themselves, that a law was finally passed making provision for all the articles mentioned in the mutiny act with the exception of salt, vinegar, beer or cyder.[6] The omission of these articles, which was destined to create no little difficulty, was justified on the ground that they were not required to be furnished to troops in English barracks.[7]

When the Parliament assembled towards the close of the year, the government was, accordingly, far from satisfied with the conduct of New York. The provision bill was regarded generally as little better than an open refusal to comply with the law.[8] Indeed, the governor had already been instructed to refuse his assent to all bills until proper provision for the troops was made;[9] but in December the assembly was apparently unan-

---

[4] *5 George III.,* ch. 33. Considerable care was taken to bring these laws within the provisions of the Petition of Rights. *Cf. Grenville Papers,* **3:** 11, 12, 13. For a curiously inaccurate statement of this matter, see Walpole, *Mem. George III.,* **2:** 318.

[5] *Cf.* Speech of Pownall, *Parl. Hist.,* **16:** 331. *Cor. of Wm. Pitt,* **2:** 186, 191.

[6] *Col. Laws of New York,* **4:** ch. 1296. Moore to Conway, June 20, 1766; *New York Col. Doc.,* **7:** 831.

[7] *New York Col. Doc.,* **7:** 831.

[8] "A spirit of infatuation has taken possession of New York; their disobedience to the mutiny act will *justly* create a great ferment here, open a fair field to the arraigners of America, and leave no room to any to say a word in their defense." Chatham to Shelburne, February 3, 1767. *Cor. of Wm. Pitt,* **3:** 188. Shelburne replied that the general feeling was that the government ought to assert itself in the matter of New York. Two difficulties he foresaw: (1) The danger of creating a precedent for oppressive action; (2) The colonies may resist, and France and Spain are only waiting an opportunity to break the peace. February 16, 1767; *ibid.,* 209. *Cf.* Sackville to Irwin, February 13, 1767; *Hist. MSS. Com.,* **9:** Pt. 3, p. 26.

[9] "No bill will pass here in consequence of the late instructions sent over, on account of the suspending clause." Moore to the Lords of Trade, November 15, 1766; *New York Col. Doc.,* **7:** 878.

imous in its refusal to make any further concession,[10] and in April, 1767, the king vetoed the provision bill that had been passed in July.[11] In other matters the conduct of New York, and of the colonies generally,[12] was no less unsatisfactory. The same packet which brought letters from Moore regarding the conduct of the assembly carried a petition from the merchants praying for relief in certain specific points from the trade acts,[13] a request which was regarded as a highly inappropriate method of expressing gratitude for the repeal of the stamp act, and which, to say the least, was most inopportune.[14] The recompense to the sufferers from the November riots was thought to have been granted with an ill grace generally,[15] and, in the case of New York, it was not complete. More especially, the practice of sailing without letter-passes and the illegal trade with Holland, which had been inaugurated in the one case and greatly increased in the other during the stamp act period, had not only not ceased after the repeal but was reported to have stead-

---

[10] In reply to the governor's message an address was presented in which the assembly refused. "The House was unanimous in their opinion, and I am fully persuaded that they not only have given their own sentiments, but those of their constituents also." Moore to Shelburne, December 19, 1766 ; *ibid.*, 883.

[11] *Col. Laws of New York*, 4: ch. 1296.

[12] "New York has drunk deepest of the baneful cup of infatuation, but none seem to be quite sober." Chatham to Shelburne, February 3, 1767 ; *Cor. of Wm. Pitt*, 3: 193. "At present the devil seems to have taken possession of their understandings." Bedford to Chatham, April 29, 1767 ; *ibid.*, 251. "The colonies are growing worse and worse." Sackville to Irwin, February 13, 1767 ; *Hist. MSS. Com.*, 9: Pt. 3, p. 26. *Cf. Parl. Hist.*, 16: 492.

[13] Moore forwarded the petition. Being sick, he neglected to examine it, but later acknowledged that it was an "improper representation." *New York Col. Doc.*, 7: 920. "A petition is come from New York signed by 240 persons." *Cor. of Wm. Pitt*, 3: 186. "A petition just arrived from New York praying relief from the chief points in the act of Navigation." Sackville to Irwin, February 13, 1767 ; *Hist. MSS. Com.*, 9: Pt. 3, p. 26.

[14] "The petition of the merchants of New York is highly improper : in point of time, most absurd ; in the extent of their pretensions, most excessive ; and in the reasoning, most grossly fallacious and offensive." Chatham to Shelburne, February 3, 1767 ; *Cor. of Wm. Pitt*, 3: 188. "The merchants here unanimously disavow the New York petition, and say that a Mr. Kelly has . . . kindled this fire." Shelburne to Chatham, February 6, 1767 ; *ibid.*, 191.

[15] Sackville to Irwin, February 13, 1767 ; *Hist. MSS. Com.*, 9: Pt. 3, p. 26.

ily increased.[16] This condition of affairs, we are told, "has soured the minds of the people here, and occasions a great deal of distress among the ministers, who must perceive how ill they are requited for that extraordinary indulgence with which they treated the last year these undutiful children. These affairs must come into Parliament, and will afford matter of triumph to those who foretold the fatal consequences of yielding to riot and ill-grounded clamour."[17]

The Parliament proceeded, accordingly, during the winter of 1767, to pass three acts, two of which were the direct outcome of the conditions just mentioned. The first was a law authorizing the king to place the collection of colonial customs in the hands of "commissioners," who were to reside in the colonies.[18] The second was the so-called Townshend act, laying certain duties on the importation of glass, lead, painters' colors, tea, and paper, the proceeds of which were to be applied to the administration of justice and the support of the civil government within the provinces, and the enforcement of which was to be secured by writs of assistance issuing from the supreme court in each colony.[19] The third was the restraining act, which suspended the legislative privileges of the New York assembly until "provision shall have been made for furnishing the King's troops with all the necessaries required by law."[20] The Townshend act was to become operative November 20, and the restraining act, October 1, 1767.

While all of these laws were unpopular in the colony, their effect on all classes was not the same. The notion of resident

---

[16] Moore to the Lords of Trade, January 14, 1767; *New York Col. Doc.*, **7:** 891. "I am well assured that a greater quantity of goods has been run without paying duties since the repeal of the stamp act than had been done in ten years before. Whole cargoes from Holland and shiploads of wines has [sic.] been run, besides what is done in the usual way of smuggling." Colden to Shelburne, November 23, 1767; *New York Col. Doc.*, **7:** 995. "Almost the whole trade of America is illicit." Hood to Grenville, August 8, 1767; *Grenville Papers*, **4:** 335.

[17] Sackville to Irwin, February 13, 1767; *Hist. MSS. Com.*, **9:** Pt. 3, p. 26.

[18] **7** *George III.*, ch. 41.

[19] *Ibid.*, ch. 46.

[20] *Ibid.*, ch. 59. Pownall opposed this act. *Parl. Hist.*, **16:** 331. The compilers of the *Annual Register* regarded it as a "moderate measure." *Annual Register*, 1767, p. 48.

commissioners acted upon the minds of the radical leaders much as the prospect of stamp distributors had done formerly. The smugglers were not likely to relish the thought either of commissioners or of writs of assistance; the fair traders were naturally opposed to the duties. From a broader point of view, all classes were united in regarding the Townshend duties as a revival of the stamp tax in a different form. Taken by itself, there was little ground for opposition; when viewed in connection with the mutiny act and the restraining act there was perhaps some justification for the fear that taxation was merely preliminary to the total suppression of legislative independence.

The conduct of the assembly, and of the people generally, was quite different, nevertheless, from that which had prevailed two years before. The assembly had already made further provision for the troops before the restraining act became effective, before, indeed, the news of the restraining act had reached America. June 6, 1767, an act was passed which, without mentioning any of the articles required by the mutiny act, ordered 3000£ to be paid to the commander-in-chief for the purposes in question.[21] The governor signed the bill with hesitation, but afterwards appears to have regarded the measure as satisfactory;[22] and when the assembly met, November 18, it was accordingly declared to have operated as a repeal of the restraining act. The assembly proceeded, therefore, to perform its ordinary functions, passing several laws, among others one making a further appropriation of 1500£ for the king's troops.[23] Altogether the assembly had now voted, within the year, the sum of 4500£, a larger sum by 500£ than was ever granted subsequently during twice that period. On this point at least, it was supposed that nothing but commendation could be forthcoming

---

[21] Col. Laws of New York, 4: ch. 1320.
[22] In August Moore wrote that he had about determined to veto the act. It was at best, he thought, an "evasive proceeding." New York Col. Doc., 7: 948. In October he wrote that "the troops are supplied with all the articles mentioned in the act of Parliament in as full and ample a manner as if they had been particularly specified in the Bill." Ibid., 980. In December, after the second grant by the assembly, he expressed his great satisfaction with the assembly. Ibid.
[23] Col. Laws of New York, 4: ch. 1328.

from the government.   The supposition proved well founded.[24]
The Board of Trade decided[25] that New York had made a satisfactory provision for the troops, and that the acts of assembly
passed after October 1, 1767, were valid.   In due time the decision of the king was communicated to Governor Moore[26] in a
letter from Hillsborough, who had already expressed his cordial
appreciation of the conduct of the assembly.[27]

The readiness of the assembly to grant so large a sum was
equaled only by the indifference with which the entire episode
had been regarded by the people.   The same indifference .char-
acterized the period when the Townshend duties became operative.
While the merchants of Boston were forming a non-importation association before the new law went into effect,[28] the New
York merchants took no step whatever in the matter until the
spring of the following year.   Even the *Sons of Liberty* were
not stirred to the rioting fever either by the mutiny act or the
Townshend act.   The prospective appearance of the customs'
commissioners alone seemed to arouse them.   Late in December
hand bills signed *Pro Patria* were circulated about the city urging "every votary of that celestial goddess Liberty" to take the
same "glorious stand" against "a set of gentry called commissioners" that had formerly been taken against "a set of miscreants under the name of stamp masters."[29]   Nothing came of
the affair, however, and as late as January 23, 1768, although
the *Farmers'* letters were running in the *Mercury*,[30] Watts could
write to Monckton that the colony had "grown the quintessence

---

[24] Grenville, nevertheless, could not see how "giving a sum of money to the
crown, but refusing to take the least notice of the Mutiny Act, can be called
a submission to that act." *Grenville Papers*, 4: 260.

[25] Report of the Lords of Trade, May 7, 1768; *New York Col. Doc.*, 8: 63. *Cf.
ibid.*, 91.

[26] Hillsborough to Moore, August 13, 1768: *New York Col. Doc.*, 8: 87.

[27] Hillsborough to Moore, April 15, 1768; *ibid.*, 55.

[28] The agreement was adopted at Faneuil Hall, October 27, 1767; manufactures were to be encouraged; the dutied articles were to be neither imported
nor consumed; certain superfluities were to be consumed in the smallest
quantities possible. *Annual Register*, 1768, p. 67. *Cf. Mem. Hist. of New York*,
2: 389.

[29] *Doc. Hist. of New York*, 3: 523.

[30] The seventh letter appeared January 25, 1768. *New York Mercury*, January 25, 1768.

of moderation—all its neighbors are writing inflamatory papers."[31] Such was the situation at the beginning of 1768, when the assembly, having sat for seven years, was dissolved February 6, and writs were issued for a new election.[32]

The election of 1768 has been touched upon in another connection,[33] and here it will be sufficient to point out its importance in the development of parties in the revolutionary period. From this point of view, it reflected two main tendencies; the rising importance of the mercantile interest, and the reaction of the conservative classes from the violence of the stamp act period. Ostensibly the old party divisions reappeared; on one side the Livingston or popular party, on the other the De Lancey or court party. Since the last election, in 1761, when the Livingston faction had carried the day, the issue had so far shifted that Livingston was now deserted by many of his former supporters. One of the main elements of strength in the popular party had always been the legal profession. But the lawyers were now regarded with suspicion, at least by three classes of people. The conservative property owners charged them with having instigated the riotous proceedings that had troubled the city since the passage of the stamp act.[34] And in a measure the charge was true. The leaders of the Livingston party were at first identified with popular resistance to that law, and John Morin Scott, who was now a candidate on the Livingston ticket, had gone so far as to assert that if measures like the stamp act were essential to the welfare of the mother country, then the connection between the colonies and England "ought to cease,

[31] Chalmers' MSS., 3. Hillsborough spoke of the "repeated testimonies which the Assembly of New York has lately given of a disposition cheerfully to comply with his majesty's orders." New York Col. Doc., 8: 55.

[32] Moore to the Lords of Trade, February 26, 1768; New York Col. Doc., 8: 14.

[33] Cf. Chapter I.

[34] Colden to Conway, February 21, 1766; New York Col. Doc., 7: 813. Colden to Hillsborough, April 25, 1768; ibid., 8: 61. "The apprehensions which every person of property was under during the late commotions from the licentiousness of the populace are not yet forgotten and I believe they would not willingly see those scenes of disorder renewed." Moore to Hillsborough, July 7, 1768; New York Col. Doc., 8: 80.

and sooner or later it must inevitably cease."[35]   The mercantile interest felt very strongly that lawyers could not properly represent a commercial city,[36] while the Church was opposed to them because they were identified with the Dissenters.[37]   Even the *Sons of Liberty,* now sided with De Lancey; for while the conservative men of property charged the lawyers with having incited the stamp act riots, the extreme radicals charged them with having basely deserted the cause of liberty by opposing the plan of carrying on business without stamps.[38]   We may infer also, although there is no direct evidence that such was the case, that they were not pleased with the action of the assembly in granting money for the troops with so lavish a hand.   The result was that the De Lancey-mercantile-Church combination was easily successful; three of its candidates were elected, Philip Livingston alone of the old members retaining his seat.

It was some weeks after the election, which was held the second week in March, that the merchants began at last to exhibit some interest in the Townshend act.   Towards the end of the month, a letter was received from the Boston "Committee of Merchants,"[39] and a number of meetings were held in the early weeks of April.   One of them, at Bolton and Sigel's tavern, April 8, 1768, resulted in the foundation of the New York Chamber of Commerce, an association of twenty-four men engaged in foreign trade, whose object was the "encouraging commerce, supporting industry, adjusting disputes relative to trade and navigation, and procuring such laws and regulations as may be found necessary for the benefit of trade in general."[40]   A

---

[35] Quoted in Dawson, *Westchester County,* 70.   The assertion was made in a series of articles signed *Freeman,* which ran in *The New York Gazette,* 1765.

[36] *Lenox Broadsides,* 23, 24.

[37] Colden to Hillsborough, April 25, 1768; *New York Col. Doc.,* 8: 61.   Alexander McCrady to Sir Philip Francis; quoted in *Mem. Hist. of New York,* 2: 466.

[38] To the Freeholders, etc., February 26, 1768; a broadside bound with the Lenox Library copy of the *New York Journal,* 1768.   Cf. *Lenox Broadsides,* 23, 24.   Leake, *Life of John Lamb,* 41.

[39] *New York Journal,* March 31. 1768.   *New York Col. Doc.,* 8: 69.

[40] From resolutions quoted in *Mem. Hist. of New York,* 4: 516.   Cf. *ibid.,* 2: 390.   The original twenty-four members were: John Cruger, Elias Desbrosses, James Jauncey, Jacob Walton, Robert Murray, Hugh Wallace, George Folliot, William Walton, Samuel Ver Planck, Theophylact Bache, Thomas White, An-

non-importation agreement was evidently regarded as one means of attaining that object. In any case, a committee that had been appointed at one of the meetings of the merchants to ascertain the sentiments of the inhabitants, found all but unanimous approval of such an agreement; and by the middle of April, so we are told, "most of the merchants and importers of goods have already subscribed to a voluntary engagement to each other that they will not sell on their own account or on commissions, nor buy nor sell for any person whomsoever, any goods (save a very few enumerated articles) which shall be shipped from Great Britain after the first day of October next, . . . provided Boston and Philadelphia adopt similar measures by the first of June."[41] These measures unaccountably alarmed Governor Moore, who feared they would lead to "fresh commotions." He twice laid the matter before the council, but that body was of the opinion that no danger whatever threatened the city, since the principal men concerned were men of character who were, moreover, perfectly free to dispose of their own property as they liked. The governor, nevertheless, believing that those who signed the association from fear were not disposing of their property as they liked, publicly proclaimed his intention of supporting "any one in his situation who should refuse to subscribe to it."[42]

Meanwhile, the first of June passed, and no word came from Boston. The Boston merchants had entered into a non-importation agreement as early as October, 1767, which was much less comprehensive than the one they were now asked to sign; and not until August did they formally accept the New York proposal.[43] From Philadelphia the only reply was an objection:

thony Van Dam, Miles Sherbrooke, Walter Franklin, Robert R. Waddle, A. Thompson, Lawrence Kirtright, Thomas Randall, William McAdam, Isaac Low. Probably more than half of these men became loyalists.

[41] *New York Journal,* April 14, 1768.

[42] Moore to Hillsborough, May 12, 1768; *New York Col. Doc., 8: 69.* Moore added that "The association has since been adopted by some and rejected by others."

[43] The Boston agreement was entered into August 1, 1768. The preamble recited the difficulties of trade, scarcity of money, trade acts, new duties, taxes for late war, bad corn crop and poor prospect for whale fisheries; "by which our principal sources of remittance are likely to be greatly reduced, and we thereby

the New York plan, it was said, would serve to create a monopoly by enabling the merchants with capital to lay in a large stock of the proscribed commodities before the agreement became effective.[44] Such, obviously, was the case. Doubtless it is not necessary to assume that the leading importers deliberately used the non-importation policy for the sole purpose of filling their pockets at the expense of the people; the motives of individulas are rarely so simple as that, the motives of classes, never. The public spirit of the merchants was doubtless as genuine as that of any other class. But it is a rare public spirit which does not ultimately draw its nourishment from some stratum, however deep down, of sub-conscious self-interest. It can hardly be supposed that the policy of non-importation appealed to the shrewd merchants of New York any the less strongly as a patriotic policy, because there was bound up with it the possibility of monopoly. They doubtless reasoned that since the chief burden of supporting such a policy fell to themselves (which was only half true) they were justified in taking advantage of whatever recompense the situation offered. Unquestionably, therefore, many importers found it expedient to enlarge their orders considerably during the six months that intervened between March and October.[45]

It was perhaps for the purpose of meeting this objection half

---

rendered unable to pay the debts we owe the merchants in Great Britain, and to continue the importation of goods from thence." The resolutions were in substance as follows: (1) To import no goods from Great Britain during the Fall, save what had already been ordered; (2) to import none from Great Britain from January 1, 1769, to February 1, 1770, except salt, coals, fish-hooks and lines, hemp, duck, bar-lead and shot, wool-cards and card-wire; (3) to purchase no goods imported by any one else contrary to (2); (4) to purchase no tea, glass, paper, or other goods commonly imported from Great Britain, which were brought in to Massachusetts from any other colony during the year 1769; (5) to import no tea, glass, paper, or painters' colors from Great Britain after January 1, 1769, until the duties were withdrawn. *Annual Register*, 1768, p. 235.

[44] *New York Journal*, April 21, 1768.

[45] "Expecting the non-importation which ensued, they purchased a double quantity of goods." Lord North in Parliament; *Parl. Hist.*, **16**: 855. The statistics do not bear this out. Imports from England into New York for the years 1766, 1767, 1768, were 330,829£, 417,957£, and 482,930£, respectively. McPherson, *Annals of Commerce*, **3**: 456, 475, 476, 487; if the association became operative November 1, 1768, these figures show that the increase was more than normal, but by no means double.

way, although Philadelphia did not accept their proposal, that the New York merchants met once more late in August, and subscribed to a new agreement, somewhat more elaborate than the old one, to take effect in some respects at once. The new association, which bears the date August 27, 1768, was said to have been signed by "nearly all the merchants and traders in town." It contained the following stipulations: (1) not to import, either for themselves or on commission, any more goods, with certain trifling exceptions, from Great Britain directly, until the duties were repealed, and to countermand all orders since August 16 by the first conveyance; (2) nor indirectly by way of any colony or the West Indies after November 1; (3) not to import any more goods from Hamburg or Holland, directly or indirectly, except files and brick; (4) to store in warehouses all goods imported contrary to the agreement, there to remain until the repeal of the duties; (5) to treat as enemies those who violated the agreement.[46] September 5, the retailers subscribed to a separate agreement neither to buy nor to sell any goods imported contrary to the merchants' agreement, and to boycott publicly any retailer who should do so.[47] If the provision making the agreement effective in part from August 16 was designed to meet the charge of monopoly, the provision regarding the Dutch trade was probably designed to prevent, in part at least, the smuggling from Holland. Thus early the two-fold weakness of the non-importation policy was manifest: if sufficiently comprehensive, it gave a monopoly to those who inaugurated it; if limited to England, it enriched the smuggler. For the present merchant and mechanic acted in unison, but within a year and a half the question of monopoly *versus* smuggling had hopelessly divided the mercantile interest.

Meanwhile, the new assembly convened in November. The opening address to the governor expressed sentiments sufficiently cordial to satisfy not only Sir Henry himself but even the much

---

[46] *New York Journal,* September 8, 1768. *New York Mercury,* September 12, 1768. *Cf. Grenville Papers,* 4: 366, 369.

[47] *New York Journal,* September 15, 1768. *Annual Register,* 1768, p. 236.

more exacting Earl of Hillsborough.[48] From the latter's point
of view, the main business of the new assembly was the annual
grant for supplying the troops; and the attitude of the preceding assembly, and, until the middle of December, the attitude of
the present one, gave no occasion to suppose there would be any
difficulty on that head.[49] But late in December the temper of
the deputies changed. The provision bill was dropped.[50] December 17, a petition was addressed to the House of Lords com-
plaining that the laws of trade were destroying commerce, that
the jury system was threatened, that New York was about to
lose its legislative independence.[51] December 31, a series of
resolutions was passed which declared in the strongest terms
the illegality of the restraining act, and the right of the assembly
to "correspond and consult with any of the neighboring colonies,
or with any other of his Majesty's subjects . . . whenever
they conceive the rights, liberties, or privileges of this House or
its constituents to be affected."[52] In support of the last contention, a committee of correspondence was appointed for the
purposes expressed in the resolution.[53] The conduct of the assembly surprised Moore and astounded Hillsborough,[54] and there
was on the surface some justification in the latter case if not in
the former. The restraining act had never operated for a day;
the provisioning of the troops may well have been considered
settled; the jury system was as safe as at any time since the
sugar act;[55] the right of correspondence was hardly, at this time,
of first rate importance for New York; the Townshend duties had

---

[48] Moore to Hillsborough January 4, 1769; *New York Col. Doc.*, 8: 143. Hillsborough to Moore, March 24, 1769; *ibid.*, 155.

[49] *New York Col. Doc.*, 8: 143, 155.

[50] Moore to Hillsborough, January 20, 1769; *New York Col. Doc.*, 8: 147.

[51] *Hist. MSS. Com.*, 14: Pt. 10, p. 69. *Parl. Hist.* 16: 603, 604.

[52] Quoted in *Mem. Hist. of New York*, 2: 396.

[53] *Mem. Hist. of New York*, 2: 396.

[54] "Very extraordinary proceedings and resolutions of the assembly." Hillsborough to Moore, March 1, 1769; *New York Col. Doc.*, 8: 154. "I am at a
loss to conjecture what could be the cause of so extraordinary an alteration
in the course of six weeks when no new event whatever had happened." Hillsborough to Moore, March 24, 1769; *ibid.*, 155.

[55] The reference to the jury system doubtless was to the recommendation
of the Lords relative to the revival of the old statute of Henry VIII. *Cf. Parl.
Hist.*, 16: 479. *35 Henry VIII*, ch. 2.

been collected for over a year without the slightest difficulty—
almost without complaint.[56] To understand the assembly's
sudden change of front, which so disconcerted Hillsborough, it
will be necessary to touch upon some matters that were scarcely
appreciated at their true value by the colonial secretary.

The truth is that the full effects of Grenville's economic and financial legislation were now beginning to be felt. During the
eighteenth century, the trade of New York had on the whole steadily increased.[57] The character of that trade, and the routes by
which it was carried, which changed but little during the century,
were in their most important aspects as follows: From England
there was imported all kinds of manufactured goods; from Ireland, linen and canvas; from other European countries, salt.
In return, the province exported to England naval stores, furs,
and commodities secured from the West Indies, mainly cocoa,
indigo and logwood; to Ireland, flax seed and staves; to the rest
of Europe, grains, hides, lumber, and West Indian products.
To the West Indies the principal exports were flour and all kinds
of provisions, lumber, horses, and goods secured from England.
In return, the foreign islands sent to New York rum, molasses,
sugar, cocoa, indigo, logwood, cotton-wool, tobacco, while the
British plantations sent enumerated commodities, rum, pimento,
sulphur, hides, mahogany, and ebony.[58] The value of English
imports was always greatly in excess of the exports to England,
while the value of the exports to the islands and to Europe ex-

---

[56] "The obstructions complained of by Commissioners of his Majesty's customs
. . . have never been occasioned by any thing which has happened in
this province, nor has there been the least subject of complaint from the behavior
of any person here, on account of the late duties imposed." Moore to Hillsborough, August 18, 1768; *New York Col. Doc.,* 8: 96.

[57] From 1724 to 1728, the imports from England ranged between 63,000 £ and
84,000£ in value. *New York Col. Doc.,* 5: 897. From 1764 to 1768, between
330,000£ and 515,000£. McPherson, *Annals of Commerce,* 3: 410, 435, 456,
457, 486.

[58] Cornbury to Hedges, July 15, 1705; *New York Col. Doc.,* 4: 1150. Hunter
to Lords of Trade, August 11, 1720; *ibid.,* 5: 556. Colden's account of the
Trade of New York, January 18, 1737; *ibid.,* 685 ff. Kennedy on the Trade of
New York, January 18, 1737; *ibid.,* 6: 127. Same for 1747; *ibid.,* 393. Clinton
to Lords of Trade, May 23, 1749; *ibid.,* 511. Tryon's report, June 11, 1774;
ibid., 8: 434.

ceeded the value of the imports from those places.[59] The English
balances were paid in bills of exchange on London and in the
silver. that was being constantly remitted, particularly from
Curocoa and Jamaica, in return for flour which these islands
took for the Spanish trade.[60]   With the exception of a few
Lyon dollars, pieces of eight made up the bulk of the metal
money in the province.   The readiness of the colonists to buy
goods from England, even beyond their ability to pay for them,
resulted in a steady drain of this silver specie to Europe.[61]   To
maintain a medium for local trade and at the same time pay
the English balances was therefore always a serious problem in
New York; and this problem was solved satisfactorily during
most of the century by the issue of bills of credit, which were
made legal tender.[62]   Paper money was necessary not only to
furnish a local medium of exchange but to prevent the decline
of foreign trade as well; for when money became scarce, the
resulting high rates of interest induced merchants to withdraw
their capital from commerce and put it out at loan.[63]   The
necessity of paper had been recognized by the government, and
the   success of the colony in keeping the bills of credit

---

[59] Statistics on imports and exports are in Anderson, *History of Commerce,* **4,**
and McPherson, *Annals of Commerce,* **3,** under the different years. *Cf. New
York Col. Doc.,* **5: 897; 8: 434.** *New York Mercury,* May 21, 1770. Almon,
Remembrancer, **1: 117.** "The trade of the West Indies is wholly to the ad-
vantage of this province, the balance being everywhere in our favor." Colden's
Account, 1723; *New York Col. Doc.,* **5: 685 ff.**

[60] Cornbury to Lords of Trade, July 1, 1708; *New York Col. Doc.,* **5: 55 ff.**
Burnet to Lords of Trade, November 31, 1724; *ibid.,* **738.** Clarke to Lords of
Trade, June 2, 1738; *ibid.,* **6: 116.** Clarke to Newcastle, February 28, 1741;
ibid., **179.** "But whatever advantage we have by the West Indian trade, we
are so hard put to it to make even with England, that the money imported
for [from] the West Indies seldom continues six months in the province before
it is remitted for England, the current cash being wholly in Paper Bills of the
Province and a few Lyon dollars." Colden's Account, 1723; *ibid.,* **5: 685 ff.**

[61] *New York Col. Doc.,* **5: 557, 685, 738; 6: 116, 179.** *Cf. Annual Register,*
1765, pp. 18, 19, 20, 21, 22. Examination of Benjamin Franklin; *Parl. Hist.,*
16: 130. Petition of London Merchants, January 17, 1766; *ibid.,* **133.** Resolutions of the Stamp-Act Congress; Niles, *Princ. of the Rev.,* 163.

[62] Burnet to Lords of Trade, November 21, 1724: *New York Col. Doc.,* **5: 735 ff.**

[63] Clarke to Lords of Trade, June 2, 1738; *New York Col. Doc.,* **6: 116.** *Col.
Laws of New York,* **2: ch. 666.**

on a par with silver had not infrequently been a subject for special commendation.[64]

Such was the situation when Grenville's new policy was inaugurated. The sugar act of 1764 placed important restrictions upon the West Indian trade: the importation of rum was forbidden, the new duties on sugar and molasses were still, probably, prohibitive, and new duties were laid on indigo, coffee, wine, and silks; the duties were required to be paid in silver.[65] In so far as the duties were prohibitory, they destroyed the principal market for New York flour—the chief export of the colony. The European market was still open, but the export of grain to England was burdened by heavy duties. All of the duties, whether prohibitive or not, operated to decrease the supply of silver money, at the same time that new demands for it were created by Grenville's legislation. These restrictions, it was asserted, would destroy colonial commerce.[66] In 1766 the English merchants stated that orders for goods were ceasing, and in Parliament the claim that the American merchants were already indebted to the English merchants upwards of 4,000,000£ was unchallenged.[67] There was doubtless some exaggeration in these assertions;[68] but it is unquestionable that the economic legisla-

---

[64] *New York Col. Doc.*, **5**: 514. In 1719 the merchants petitioned against any further issue of paper, claiming that depreciation would result. The Lords of Trade thought that, on the contrary, "if the credit of the bills is maintained according to the tenor of the act, the trade of the province will be greatly encouraged . . . thereby, as it appears to have been since the first bills were issued." *Ibid.*, 522, 525. In 1723, Burnet wrote that paper was equal to silver in New York. *Ibid.*, 700, 736, 738. In 1766 Moore wrote: "They have always kept up the credit of their paper currency." *Ibid.*, **7**: 885.

[65] *4 George III.*, ch. 15.

[66] *Cf.* Thatcher, quoted in Tyler, *Am. Rev.*, **1**: 55. Resolutions of the Stamp-Act Congress; Niles. *Prin. of the Rev.*, 163. *Annual Register*, 1765, pp. 18–22. *Parl. Hist.*, **16**: 133.

[67] *Parl. Hist.*, **16**: 133, 205. Walpole, *Mem. of Geo. III*, **2**: 210. The debt to the English merchants of "Several millions sterling," the Americans "Absolutely refused to pay, pleading in excuse their utter inability; which plea, it appears the merchants admitted to be reasonable." *Annual Register*, 1766, p. 32. *Cf. ibid.*, 46.

[68] It is difficult to see how the trade of the colonies could have been destroyed by the sugar act; and the statement that the American debt was upward of 4,000,000 £ sterling seems excessive. For the English trade, the

tion of Grenville would have required a very considerable readjustment of colonial commerce, at least in the middle and northern colonies. This readjustment was in fact greatly facilitated by the English government itself, when the situation was once

figures, gathered from McPherson, *Annals of Commerce*, **3:** 339, 351, 365, 410, 435, 456, are, in round numbers, as follows:

		New Eng.	New York.	Pa.	Md. and Va.	Carolinas.	Ga.	Totals.
1760	Exports.....	£37,000	£21,000	£22,000	£504,000	£162,000	£12,000	£758,000
	Imports.....	599,000	480,000	707,000	605,000	218,000	....	2,609,000
1761	Exports.....	46,000	48,000	39,000	455,000	253,000	5,000	846,000
	Imports.....	334,000	289,000	204,000	545,000	254,000	24,000	1,650,000
1762	Exports.....	41,000	58,000	38,000	415,000	181,000	6,000	739,000
	Imports.....	247,000	288,000	206,000	417,000	194,000	23,000	1,375,000
1763	Exports.....	74,000	53,000	38,000	642,000	282,000	14,000	1,103,000
	Imports. ..	258,000	238,000	284,000	555,000	250,000	44,000	1,629,000
1764	Exports.....	88,000	53,000	36,000	559,000	341,000	31,000	1,008,000
	Imports.....	459,000	515,000	435,000	515,000	305,000	18,000	2,247,000
1765	Exports.....	145,000	54,000	25,000	505,000	385,000	34,000	1,149,000
	Imports.....	451,000	382,000	363,000	383,000	334,000	29,000	1,942,000
1766	Exports.....	141,000	67,000	26,000	461,000	293,000	53,000	1,041,000
	Imports.....	409,000	330,000	327,000	372,000	296,000	67,000	1,861,000
Totals.	Exports.	....	....	....	....	....	....	£6,644,000
	Imports.	....	....	....	....	....	....	13,253,000

Total imports in excess of exports, £6,809,000.

The entire English balance, excluding the West Indian trade, and the trade to Europe outside of Great Britain, was thus about seven millions for the seven years. The British West Indian trade, and the European trade must have reduced this considerably. Further, the southern colonies imported from England less than they exported, and this excess would have opened a market for the northern colonies. The trade of the northern colonies might have been adjusted to the sugar act, it seems, without great difficulty even without the aid which the government in fact gave them by the legislation of 1766, at least if some satisfactory solution of the paper money difficulty had been found. On the other hand, there is some indication that the official statistics of imports were too low, which may in part explain the alleged debt of the American merchants. In 1774, Tryon wrote: "If the brokers in Great Britain employed as shippers of goods were for one year obliged to give in the value of the goods when they apply for cockets, the exact amount of what the inhabitants of each colony take from thence would be easily ascertained . . . As the amount of the goods never appears on the cockets, no judgment can be formed of their value from the quality or number of pieces. Silks, for in-

clearly presented to it.[69] Aside from the repeal of the stamp
act, the duty on molasses was reduced to $1d$,[70] the duty on grain
sent to England was removed,[71] and some laws were passed encouraging colonial manufactures.[72] These measures must have
relieved the situation greatly, since the imports from England,
so far from ceasing, were greater than before.[73] After 1766,
therefore, the trade acts were scarcely a serious burden, save in
so far as they constituted a drain upon the colony's metal money.

The importance of the trade acts can be appreciated, indeed,
only in connection with Grenville's paper-money policy. Other
colonies had been less successful than New York in preventing depreciation, and in 1764 an act was passed by Parliament "to

---

stance, come out from 25f. to 2sh. per yard, and in general the other articles
differ in the same proportion . . . When no particular stop is put upon
the trade with Great Britain, it is generally estimated here that the annual
imports from thence to this Colony amount on an average to five hundred
thousand pounds sterling." Tryon's Report, *New York Col. Doc.,* 8: 440.

[69] The commercial system of the colonies was described clearly in Parliament,
probably for the first time, in the debate on the repeal of the stamp act.
Cf. Parl. Hist., **16.**

[70] 6 *George III.,* ch. 52.

[71] *Ibid.,* ch. 3.   7 *George III.,* ch. 4.

[72] Bounties were offered for the importation of flax, hemp and lumber.   4
George III., ch. 36.   5 *George III.,* ch. 45.

[73] The figures for the years 1767-1770 are as follows:

		New Eng.	New York.	Pa.	Md. & Va.	Caro-linas.	Ga.	Totals.
1767	Exports......	£128,000	£61,000	£37,000	£437,000	£395,000	£35,000	£1,093,000
	Imports......	406,000	417,000	371,000	437,000	244,000	23,000	1,898,000
1768	Exports......	148,000	87,000	59,000	406,000	508,000	42,000	1,250,000
	Imports......	419,000	482,000	432,000	475,000	289,000	56,000	2,153,000
1769	Exports......	121,000	73,000	26,000	361,000	387,000	82,000	1,050,000
	Imports......	207,000	74,000	199,000	488,000	316,000	58,000	1,342,000
1770	Exports......	148,000	69,000	28,000	435,000	278,000	55,000	1,013,000
	Imports......	394,000	475,000	134,000	717,000	146,000	56,000	1,922,000
Totals.	Exports.	....	....	....	....	....	....	4,406,000
	Imports..	....	....	....	....	....	....	7,316,000

Total imports in excess of exports, £2,910,000.

The decline in imports for 1769 was the result of the non-importation agreements. McPherson, *Annals of Commerce,* **3:** 475, 476, 486, 495, 508.

prevent paper bills of credit, hereafter to be issued in any of his Majesty's colonies . . . from being declared to be a legal tender in payment of money; and to prevent the legal tender of such bills as are now subsisting, from being prolonged beyond the periods limited for calling in and sinking the same.'"[74] So far as New York was concerned, there was little need for such a law;[75] in fact, there was every reason against it. Practically, however, the prohibition did not become effective until November, 1768, since the issues of 1758, 1759, and 1760, together amounting to 260,000£, were to run until that time.[76] But the difficulty that would then arise was clearly foreseen. As early as 1766, Governor Moore presented the situation to the Board of Trade.[77] The Board of Trade, however, went no further than to recommend that New York be permitted to issue 260,000£ in accordance with the provisions of the act of 1764—that is, without making the bills a legal tender.[78] The assembly felt that such a privilege was no privilege at all,[79] and, as there was reason for thinking that the government might make a proper concession before the present currency was sunk,[80] nothing further was done in the matter for some months.

Early in 1768, when nearly all the paper money, except the 260,000£ which was to expire in the following November, was

---

[74] 4 *George III.*, ch. 34.

[75] The only complaint I have found was that bills paid into the treasury to be cancelled were sometimes fraudulently reissued. *New York Col. Doc.*, 6: 699.

[76] *Col. Laws of New York*, 4: ch. 1059, 1082, 1120. *New York Col. Doc.*, 7: 828.

[77] "All the present bills will be sunk next year, and the country left without any medium of commerce, for there has been very little silver to be met with since the interruption of the trade with the Spaniards, and at present the province is greatly distressed for want of a paper currency." Moore to Lords of Trade, March 28, 1766; *ibid.*, 820. Moore was mistaken in the date. The paper was not to be called in until November, 1768.

[78] Even this required special permission, since the governor was instructed to assent to no paper money bill whatever except in case of invasion. *New York Docs.*, 7: 827, 843.

[79] It was thought that an issue of 130,000£ legal tender, to run five years would be the last that was necessary. Moore to Lords of Trade, November 15, 1766; *ibid.*, 878.

[80] The Lords of Trade had written to Moore that before November, 1768, "The further sense of Parliament in respect to the American currency and the propriety of allowing it a legal tender, may be obtained." *Ibid.*, 844.

sunk,[81] and the Townshend duties having been operative for two months, the money stringency began to yield its proper fruit. The poorer classes were in distress. December 29, 1767, at a meeting in New York city, there was appointed a committee "to consider the expediency of entering into measures to promote frugality and industry and employ the poor."[82] In January the committee reported in favor of using various home-made articles, discouraging useless expense in wearing apparel and at funerals; and during the winter there were further meetings and reports on the same subject.[83] The foundation of the Chamber of Commerce, and the merchants' first non-importation association, which have already been mentioned, were doubtless partly the result of the same conditions. Property declined in value, and the merchants could with difficulty find the means of paying the duties or of meeting their obligations in England. Under these circumstances, the currency problem was again broached by the governor. Aside from the economic need for a new issue of legal tender paper, he suggested that the permission to pass such an act would have an excellent effect in bringing the colony to a cordial support of the mutiny act.[84] Hillsborough replied that the New York assembly should prepare a bill and present it to the king for his decision.[85] When the assembly met in November, the very month in which the entire paper money of the colony was to be called in, the prospect for relief was, therefore, as remote as ever.

Meanwhile, the customs' commissioners at Boston had recently issued an order that was little likely to increase the prospect of a liberal supply bill for the troops. During the summer, Elliot, collector of customs at New York, was instructed for the future

---

[81] The issue of 1737 was sunk in four parts, one each in April of the years 1765, 1766, 1767, 1768. *Col. Laws of New York*, 4: ch. 1214.

[82] *New York Mercury*, January 18, 1768.

[83] *Lenox Broadsides*, 23.

[84] "Commerce here, as well as the ordinary services of government must very shortly be exposed to great inconvenience." A compliance with the wishes of the assembly "would be attended with such returns of duty and submission," etc. Moore to Shelburne, January 3, 1768; *New York Col. Doc.*, 8: 1.

[85] Hillsborough to Moore, February 20, 1768; *ibid.*, 13.

to accept nothing but silver in payment of the duties. Hitherto Elliot had granted the merchants very liberal terms, allowing them a week or ten days in which to settle. Not only had he never lost a cent by this procedure, but no practical opposition had yet been made to the duties themselves. It was now impossible to pay in silver because there was no silver in the province. The governor was of opinion that the order would "certainly occasion very great uneasiness here . . . and serve no other purpose than that of furnishing those who are inclined to be riotous with some pretense of complaint, and lay the foundation for future disorders."[86] Hillsborough agreed, after the evil was done, that the order was unwise, but it was a matter for the treasury board, to which accordingly it was referred.[87]

In this same month of August another difficulty of some importance, personal and trivial as it appears on the surface, had reached a climax: the dispute between Governor Moore and General Gage over the question of precedence. It appears that the instructions to the commander-in-chief had rather vaguely given him precedence over the governors and other officials in the colonies on occasions when he presided at any general council of colonial officials. The governor's instructions, on the other hand, quite clearly placed him at the head of his own colony, and gave him precedence over all other officials in all civil functions. In March, 1768, Moore wrote requesting an interpretation;[88] and in May, Hillsborough replied that he trusted the matter would be amicably settled without official interference, and requested to know the occasion which had given rise to the dispute.[89] From Moore's reply in August it appears that the breach began on the occasion of the celebration of the king's birthday in June, 1767, and that it was completed in February, 1768, on the occasion of a military ball at which Gage had been given precedence by certain military officials who made the arrangements.[90] The importance of the episode was that, taken

---

[86] Moore to Hillsborough, August 18, 1768; *ibid.*, 96, 97.
[87] Hillsborough to Moore, October 12, 1768; *ibid.*, 100.
[88] Moore to Shelburne, March 15, 1768; *ibid.*, 15.
[89] Hillsborough to Moore, May 14, 1768; *ibid.*, 73.
[90] Moore to Hillsborough, August 19, 1768; *ibid.*, 97.

in connection with the mutiny act, the restraining act, and the
Townshend act, it confirmed the fear, which was already present
in many minds, that the government had nothing less in view
than the substitution of arbitrary military rule for the existing
civil government.[91] That nothing could be "more foreign to his
Majesty's intentions" was, as Hillsborough assured Moore,[92] undoubtedly quite true, but the effect was none the less unfortunate
for all that. Throughout the year there was, in any case, an observable change in the attitude of the people towards the soldiers,
many public amusements in which they had heartily joined for
the last thirty years being now given up.[93]

These conditions, it seems, might have prepared Governor
Moore at least for the resolutions which the assembly passed in
December, and which, as we have already seen, so astonished
Hillsborough. If one recalls the economic distress resulting
from the financial stringency, and the popular suspicion and
dislike of the soldiers resulting from the quarrel between Gage
and Moore, the renewal of radical agitation against the mutiny
act seems quite the most natural consequence. Shortly after
the assembly met, the *Sons of Liberty* in fact formed the design
of parading the streets with effigies which in due course were to
be burnt. Several times the magistrates frustrated the design,
but ultimately it was accomplished. This expression of popular
sentiment was followed by the promulgation of a set of instructions to the representatives which were signed, apparently, by
many people, though the governor assures us that most people
of any account refused.[94] Outside pressure of this sort, which

---

[91] "The suspension of the legislative powers here was a measure which very
much alarmed the people . . . They were made to believe that this was
only the first step toward the total abolition of the civil power in order to
introduce a military government . . . These mistaken notions are again
revived . . . upon the present claims of the Commander in Chief of the
forces." Moore to Shelburne, March 15, 1768 ; *New York Col. Doc.*, 8: 18.

[92] *New York Col. Doc.*, 8: 73.

[93] "The inhabitants . . . have already begun to behave toward them
(the soldiers) with a coldness and distance too visible not to be remarked."
New York Col. Doc., 8: 99. Such quarrels were not confined to New York. *Cf.*
Parl. Hist., 16: 994.

[94] Moore to Hillsborough, January 4, 1769, *New York Col. Doc.*, 8: 143.

was not wholly confined to the city,[95] eventually gave to the radicals the control of the assembly;[96] in the words of the governor,
it "intimidated" many members who would otherwise have
voted for different measures. Intimidated is, however, hardly
the word. Pressure from the *Sons of Liberty*, who, it must be
remembered, had helped to elect the city members, came as the
climax of a series of events which in themselves must have been
nearly sufficient to give the radicals a majority. At least the
merchant members, of whom there were many, must have been
extremely susceptible to intimidation of this sort when they re-
called the scarcity of money, the new duties, the recent order
of Collector Elliot, the "commissioners," and the writs of assistance. The truth is that the resolutions of December registered a
protest against an economic situation that was rapidly becoming
intolerable, and expressed a very genuine concern, which appear-
ances to some extent justified, for the security of the colony's
political privileges. Nevertheless, the resolutions were considered seditious,[97] and on January 2, 1769, the assembly was dissolved.[98]

The new election, which was held before the month was out,
registered the popular approval of the conduct of the assembly,
for the old members were returned almost to a man.[99] Curiously
enough, perhaps, the only one of the four city representatives
who supported the resolutions without reservation, that is Livingston, was not returned, while the other three, who had voted
for a substitute resolution, were elected. De Lancey had made
an effort to cut out the resolution with respect to the right of
correspondence, by substituting a resolution of protest against
the restraining act only.[100] It was a distinction of little pop-

---

[95] *Cf. Instruction from Queens County.* Onderdonck, *Queens County in Olden
Time,* 42.

[96] "The assembly is composed of plain well-meaning men, whose notions from
their education, are extremely confined, their fears of being . . . pointed
out as enemies of their country, engaged them in measures which they never
wished to see adopted." Moore to Hillsborough, January 4, 1769; *New York
Col. Doc.,* 8: 143.

[97] Hillsborough to Moore, March 24, 1769; *ibid.,* 8: 156.

[98] The council voted 4–4 on dissolution. *Ibid.,* 8: 143.

[99] *New York Mercury,* January 30, 1769.

[100] *Mem. Hist. of New York,* 2: 396.

ular interest. The matter of correspondence had arisen as a result of the Massachusetts circular letter issued nearly a year before,[101] the consideration of which the governors were instructed to regard as sufficient ground for dissolution.[102] Dropping the provision bill was the main thing in the eyes of the people, and the re-election of De Lancey and his colleagues was a confirmation of the assembly's conduct as a whole.[103] Livingston's defeat followed upon his refusal to become a candidate with the three old members.[104] In joining his fortunes with John Morin Scott, he encountered the opposition to the lawyers and the Dissenters; both the merchants and the *Sons of Liberty* voted the De Lancey ticket; and Livingston, encumbered by his own colleagues, was defeated by a large majority.[105]

Two months later the merchants who had subscribed to the non-importation agreement found it desirable to appoint a committee of inspection.[106] Whether the association had been operative since September it is impossible to say. If it had, it is dif-

---

[101] February 11, 1768. Cushing, *Works* of *Samuel Adams,* **1:** 184.

[102] Hillsborough to the Governors, April 21, 1768 ; *New York Col. Doc.,* **8:** 58. *Cf. Parl. Hist.,* **16:** 476 ff.

[103] De Lancey had astonished the government in January, 1769, by refusing a council appointment. *New York Col. Doc.,* **8:** 148.

[104] *New York Mercury,* January 9, 1769. Sedgwich, *Life of Livingston,* 146.

[105] *New York Mercury,* January 9, 16, 23, February 6, 1769. John Chew to William Johnson, January 11, 1769 ; Johnson MSS., **17:** 34. Lossing, *Schuyler,* **1:** 236. *Lenox Broadsides,* 24, 25. *Broadsides,* **1.** Watts to Monckton, February 6, 1739 ; Chalmers' MSS., **3.** *New York Col. Doc.,* **8:** 170. Van Schaack, *Life of Van Schaack,* 10.

[106] *New York Journal,* March 9, 16, 1769. The names of the committee are not given. De Lancey, in his edition of Jones' *History of New York,* (**2:** 438) gives a list of twenty-four names, with a reference to the *New York Journal,* September 8, 1768. I do not find in the *Journal* of that date, any indication that a committee was appointed at that time, nor any list of names. Further, the statements in the *Journal* of March 9, 16, 1769, indicate that no committee had been appointed up to that time. The list given by De Lancey is as follows : Isaac Low, James Desbrosses, John Alsop, John Broome, William Neilson, Theodorus Van Wyck, Walter Franklin, John Murray, Jacob Walton, Theophylact Bache, Thomas Franklin, Jr., Samuel Ver Planck, Isaac Sears, Peter Van der Voort, Th. W. Moore, Henry Remsen, Jr., J. H. Cruger, John Thurman, Jr., Thomas Walton, P. T. Curtenius, Herbert Van Wagenen, Joseph Bull, Edward Laight, Charles McEvers. This list is undoubtedly the correct one, for in June, 1770, "The Committee of Inspection," published some resolutions which were signed by the members of the committee ; there were twenty-one names, one member was out of town, two had resigned ; and this list is identical with that of De Lancey. De Lancey's list probably being copied from it. *New York Journal,* July 5, 1770.

ficult to understand why a committee was not appointed at that time. Besides, the importations from England in 1768 exceeded those of 1767 by 65,000£. On the other hand, the association definitely declared that the direct importation of English goods was to cease at once, and the indirect importation from November 1; and the increase in importations for the year 1768, may very well have represented the extent to which the merchants had stocked up in view of monopoly prices. In any case, the appointment of a committee was quite in harmony with the assembly resolutions of December, and the victory of the merchants in the January election. The composition of the committee shows that the mercantile interest was still undifferentiated into radicals and conservatives. There was, for instance, on the committee list, the name of Isaac Sears, one of the most hot-headed radicals who ever disturbed the peace of New York,[107] coupled with that of Theophylact Bache, who afterwards became a loyalist.[108] The contrast is, indeed, typical, though there were more of the latter sort than of the former on the committee. In truth, the rough differentiation of classes into radical and conservative factions, which had been effected by the stamp act episode, had largely disappeared; from 1766 to 1769 the issues had been so various, and in some cases so disparate, that distinct party alignment can hardly be said to have existed. But during the year 1769, and the winter of 1770, conditions were preparing for a more definite and a more lasting separation of radical and conservative elements. The non-importation agreement brought prominently to the front the old issue of the stamp act period, the issue taking, in this instance, the form of monopoly *versus* smuggling; while the currency question ultimately produced a renewal of mob violence which served to unite once more those who had property rights and political privileges to protect. We shall now trace the events that led to the accomplishment of this result.

The new assembly was soon summoned by the governor, who

---

[107] Besides Sears, the principal radicals were Van der Voort, Remsen, and Curtenius.

[108] Others who became loyalists were: Low, Alsop, Laight, McEvers.

hoped that a better temper might characterize its deliberations.[109] The hope was realized, if at all, only to a very slight extent.[110] The new assembly confirmed the resolutions of December,[111] and instructed the speaker to thank the merchants for the non-importation agreement.[112] Its opposition to the lawyers was registered in a resolution to exclude the judges from sitting in the assembly,[113] and the determination to secure relief from the currency stringency was reflected in a proposed bill to emit 120,000£ in bills of credit.[114] On the other hand, the wishes of the governor were met with respect to provisioning the troops, 1,800£ being granted for that purpose.[115] This measure, as Moore assured the colonial secretary, was nevertheless intimately associated with the prospect of a paper currency;[116] it was a preliminary concession in return for which the king's approval of the bills of credit act was confidently expected. Colden, who succeeded upon the death of Moore in September,[117] assured the government, indeed, that the grants to the troops would be regularly made in future only on condition that the financial stringency be relieved.[118] Meanwhile the proposed bill was sent over for the inspection of the king; unaccountably delayed, it was not received until November,[119] and at the close of the year it was still awaiting the decision of the Privy Council.[120]

This delay was unfortunate in the highest degree. For when the assembly met again in November, whereas it might justly

---

[109] First Tuesday in April. *New York Col. Doc.*, 8: 157.

[110] Moore complains of the stubborness of the assembly and the supineness of the council. *New York Col. Doc.*, 8: 157.

[111] Hillsborough to Moore, July 15, 1769; *ibid.*, 176.

[112] *Ibid.*, 176, 194.

[113] *Ibid.*, 8: 194. *Col. Laws of New York*, 5: ch. 1435.

[114] *New York Col. Doc.*, 8: 195. Moore strongly urged the policy of allowing the bill. "The miseries of the people increasing to such a degree as to be past credibility." *Ibid.*, 169.

[115] *Col. Laws of New York*, 4: ch. 1386.

[116] A paper currency would be "of infinite advantage to the province, by enabling it to grant the proper supplies." Moore to Hillsborough, July 11, 1769; *New York Col. Doc.*, 8: 175. *Cf. Ibid.*, 169.

[117] *Ibid.*, 187, 188, 189. *New York Mercury*, September 18, 1769.

[118] Colden to Hillsborough, October, 4, 1769; *New York Col. Doc.*, 8: 189.

[119] *New York Col. Doc.*, 8: 176, 190.

[120] Lords of Trade to the Privy Council, December 28, 1769; *New York Col. Doc.*, 8: 195.

have been expected that the king's decision would be known, all that Colden could communicate was Hillsborough's acknowledgment that the bill had been received. There was, therefore, no prospect of a paper currency during the present session, and the possibility of a provision bill was correspondingly remote. But, unknown to the assembly, concessions on another point had been promised. In May, Hillsborough had written to Moore that "his Majesty's present administration have at no time entertained a design to . . . lay any further taxes upon America for the purpose of raising a revenue, and . . . it is at present their intention to propose in the next session of Parliament to take off the duties upon glass, paper, and colors, upon consideration of such duties having been laid contrary to the true principles of commerce."[121] Colden was bent upon securing a provision bill at any cost, and contrary to his instructions, he communicated this intelligence to the assembly in his opening address.[122]

But the provision bill was now too inseparably bound up with the currency act for this intelligence to have much effect upon the assembly. Nearly a month passed without so much as a discussion of the subject.[123] Colden was privately given to understand that no supply bill could be passed unless he promised to sign a paper money bill without waiting for the king's approval.[124] Meanwhile, Hillsborough had written again stating that there were objections to the bill that had been sent over, from which its rejection by the council was the most likely inference.[125] Under these circumstances, Colden, supported by the council, resolved to violate his instructions a second time; on condition that the new law should not become effective till the following June, which would give the king ample time to pass upon it, he promised his signature.[126] Both bills were then

---

[121] Hillsborough to the Governors, May 13, 1769; *ibid.*, 164. May 1, the Cabinet, by a vote 5–4, had authorized the Secretary of State to make this statement "in his correspondence and conversation." Duke of Grafton's MSS. memoirs; Mahon, *History of England,* 5: Appendix, 37.

[122] Hillsborough to Colden, January 18, 1770; *New York Col. Doc.,* 8: 201.

[123] Colden to Hillsborough, December 16, 1769; *ibid.,* 193.

[124] Colden to Hillsborough, January 6, 1770; *ibid.,* 199.

[125] Hillsborough to Colden, December 9, 1769; *ibid.,* 193.

[126] Colden to Hillsborough, April 25, 1770; *ibid.,* 212. *Cf. ibid.,* 198.

passed by the assembly.[127]   The currency act nevertheless contained the same features to which Hillsborough had objected in the former bill, and the provision bill, although it provided that one-half of the sum granted should be paid out of the new paper currency, received a bare majority.[128]   All that the lieutenant-governor received for his pains was a scathing letter from Hillsborough,[129] and both currency bills received the king's veto,[130] which was published in New York in April.[131]

The economic situation had now reached a crisis. For over a year the colony had been without any legal tender money save the Lyon dollars, now rarely seen.[132]   Spanish silver, which had never been a legal tender, was wholly insufficient to serve as a medium, even if freely accepted, as it undoubtedly was.[133]   To the business stagnation which everywhere prevailed, the non-importation agreement, the enforcement of which was doubtless greatly helped by the lack of money, contributed much.[134]   The demands of creditors resulted in the sale of property at a half or a third of its value,[135] the prisons were filling up, and, for the first time in many years, it was necessary to pass a law for the relief of imprisoned debtors.[136]   Under the circumstances the provision bill, safeguarded as it was, and the failure of the currency act, inevitably precipitated a tumult. Once more the leaders of the *Sons of Liberty* resorted to mass-meetings and mobocracy; rioting and effigy-burning became the order of the

---

[127] January 5, 1770. *Col. Laws of New York*, **5:** ch. 1422. The preamble of the currency act gives the reasons for its passage. The amount was 120,000 £. receivable at the Loan Offices for 14 years, and at the Treasury for 15 years. *Ibid.*, 1423.

[128] *New York Col. Doc.*, **8:** 199.

[129] February 17, 1770; *ibid.*, 205.

[130] *Ibid.*

[131] Colden to Hillsborough, April 25, 1770; *ibid.*, 212.

[132] Moore to Hillsborough, May 14, 1768; *ibid.*, 72.

[133] Moore to Lords of Trade, March 28, 1766; *ibid.*, **7:** 820.

[134] The imports from England dropped from 482,000 £ in 1768 to 74,000 £ in 1769. McPherson, *Annals of Commerce*, **3:** 486, 495. The lack of specie undoubtedly helped to enforce the non-importation agreement. *Cf.* Colden to Hillsborough, October 4, 1769; *New York Col. Doc.*, **8:** 189.

[135] "All our funds are exhausted, and the scarcity of money so great that a farm of sixty acres of land with a dwelling house and . . . improvements . . . shall be sold . . . for ten pounds." Colden to Hillsborough, July 11, 1769; *New York Col. Doc.*, **8:** 175. *Cf. ibid.*, 169.

[136] *Col. Laws of New York*, **5:** ch. 1463, ch. 1480.

day; and for two months the long-gathering hostility to the soldiers, and to those who had voted to furnish them with supplies, was hardly to be restrained.

The introduction of the provision bill was the signal for the outbreak.[137] December 16, 1769, there appeared the famous handbill entitled *To the Betrayed Inhabitants of the City and Colony of New York,* signed *A Son of Freedom.*[138] The highly inflammatory tirade charged the representatives with having betrayed the liberties of the country; De Lancey in particular was denounced for having formed a coalition with Colden for the purpose of maintaining his influence in the assembly. "What I would advise to be done," the author said in conclusion, "is to assemble in the fields, on Monday next where your sense ought to be taken on this point; notwithstanding the impudence of Mr. Jauncey in his declaring in the House, that he had consulted his constituents and that they were for giving money. After this is done, go in a body to your members and insist in their joining with the minority to oppose the bill; if they dare refuse your just requisition, appoint a committee to draw up a state of the whole matter, and send it to the speakers of the several Houses of Assembly on the continent and to the friends of our cause in England, and publish it in the newspapers that the whole world may know your sentiments." Almost simultaneously, probably on the 17th, a second sheet, entitled *To the Public,* made its appearance, which also urged the people to assemble in the Fields.[139] By 12 o'clock on that day, some 1,400 people had collected, and, having appointed John Lamb to propound the necessary questions, it was decided by a large majority that money should be voted to the troops under no circumstances whatever.[140] The resolution was presented to the city representatives by a committee of ten, but De Lancey and his colleagues replied that "they were of opinion that a majority of the inhabitants were disposed to give money to support the troops."[141]

---

[137] *New York Col. Doc.,* 8: 199.

[138] *Broadsides,* 1.   *Lenox Boradsides,* 27.   *Doc. Hist. of New York,* 3: 528. Dawson, *The Park and its Vicinity,* 25.

[139] *Broadsides,* 1.   *Doc. Hist. of New York,* 3: 534.

[140] *New York Mercury,* December 25, 1769.

[141] *Ibid.*

This event did much in itself to revive the enthusiasm of the *Sons of Liberty;* but far more was effected to that end by the attitude which the government thought necessary to assume in the matter. Proclamations were issued offering rewards for the apprehension of the author of the broadsides, and information furnished by James Parker resulted in the arrest of Alexander MacDougall, who, refusing to give bail which he might easily have obtained, remained in jail eighty-one days, when he was dismissed without trial.[142] Among the radicals, MacDougall at once became the hero of the hour. From the vantage point of the New Gaol, he wrote letters to the public,[143] appointed special hours for receiving the crowds that came to see him,[144] and consciously posed as the Wilkes of America.[145]

Colden assured the Earl of Hillsborough that the meetings of the *Sons of Liberty* were small and disappointing to their leaders, but that the provisioning act was nevertheless extremely unpopular, and that strong measures in the case would doubtless cause more harm than good.[146] However that may have been, the newly aroused ardor of the *Sons of Liberty* found further vent in the final struggle with the soldiers over the liberty pole. The liberty pole had been erected in 1766 to commemorate the repeal of the stamp act. It proved an eye-sore to the soldiers, who cut it down several times only to see it as often restored.[147] January 16, 1770, the *Sons of Liberty* issued a broadside criticising those who employed the soldiers instead of the poor who needed work,

---

[142] *Ibid. Doc. Hist. of New York,* **3:** 532, 534, 535. Thomas, *Hist. of Printing,* **2:** 260–262.

[143] MacDougall to the Freeholders, etc., December 22, 1769, and January 26, 1770; *Broadsides,* **1.**

[144] Quoted in Dawson, *The Park and its Vicinity,* 32.

[145] "Could easily have found the bail required . . . but he chose to go to jail and lies there imitating Mr. Wilkes in Everything he can." Colden to Hillsborough, February 21, 1770; *New York Col. Doc.,* **8:** 208. The Assembly resolutions were copied at page 45 of the Journals, and "No. 45," became the watch word of the *Sons of Liberty* as it was of the friends of Wilkes. Dawson, *The Park and its Vicinity,* 31. The address of Wilkes to the freeholders of Middlesex was reprinted in New York. *New York Gazette,* June 11, 1770. *The Case and Trial of John Peter Zenger* was also reprinted. *New York Mercury,* March 26, 1770.

[146] *New York Col. Doc.,* **8:** 199, 206, 212.

[147] *Cf.* Dawson, *The Park and its Vicinity,* 21 ff. Dunlap, *Hist. of New York,* **1:** 433.

and calling a meeting at the liberty pole the next day. That night the soldiers again destroyed the pole. On the night of the 18th, some soldiers, while posting some broadsides entitled *Sixteenth Regiment of Foot*, were seized by Isaac Sears and others, and taken to the mayor's office; an attempted rescue resulted in the affair of Golden Hill, in which, it is sometimes claimed, the first blood of the Revolution was shed.[148] Colden reported a "few bruises" on either side.[149]

The renewal of mob-violence on the part of the *Sons of Liberty*, accompanied as it was by some meetings of the same faction for the purpose of instructing the representatives on certain measures then before the assembly,[150] resulted in a closer union of property owners and conservative men of all classes. The position of Colden was strengthened, and many who had opposed the supply bill came to regard that measure with less disfavor.[151] Broadsides appeared supporting the granting of money to the troops,[152] ridiculing the *Sons of Liberty*, and satirizing MacDougall as a noisy Irish upstart.[153] The growing conservatism was fairly voiced in a four-page hand bill entitled *The Times*, which came out in January.[154] "May it not be," says the author, "that the frequent notices to meet at Liberty pole, the violent rage and resentment which some people have endeavored generally to excite against soldiers, pretended to proceed from

---

[148] *Broadsides,* **1.** *Lenox Broadsides,* 27, 28. *New York Gazette,* February 5, 1770. *Cf.* Leake, *Life of John Lamb,* 54, 55, 58, 59. *Magazine of Am. Hist.* New Series, **5: 1** ff. A new pole was finally erected on private ground. *New York Mercury,* February 5, 1770. *New York Journal,* February 8, 1770.

[149] *New York Col. Doc.,* **8:** 208.

[150] *New York Mercury,* January 8, 22, 1770. Advertisement, January 5, 1770; *Broadsides,* **1.** *Cf.* above Chapter I.

[151] "A disappointed faction . . . have drawn upon themselves a general detestation." Colden to Hillsborough, April 25, 1770; *New York Col. Doc.,* **8:** 213. "The principal inhabitants are now heartily united in favor of Government." *Ibid.,* 217. After the affair of Golden Hill, "a very respectable number of the principal citizens publicly met together, and sent 42 of their number to the mayor, to assure the magistrates of their assistance." Colden to Hillsborough. February 21, 1770; *ibid.,* 208.

[152] A Citizen's Address, December 18, 1769; *Broadsides,* **1.** *Lenox Broadsides,* 27.

[153] News from the Liberty Pole; *Lenox Broadsides,* 27. *Cf. The Douglead,* a series of articles satirizing MacDougall, *New York Mercury,* April 9, to June 25, 1770.

[154] Signed, A Merchant, not dated. *Broadsides,* **1.** *Lenox Broadsides,* 28.

a love of liberty and a regard for the interests of the poor: do
all tend to the same end . . . may not—no money to the
troops—who-raw for balloting—employ no soldiers—all mean
the same thing . . . ? If we cannot bring a disturbance and
kick up a dust in one way, we must in another, and if we cannot render Mr. Colden's Administration odious and breed dissen-
tion and animosities . . . all our hope in a future election
will be blasted and the commercial interest—O terrible calamity!
will prevail against the ambitious lawyer and keep him out of
the . . . assembly.''

In this conservative reaction the majority of the merchants
were now ready to take part. During the stamp act period,
some of the leading merchants had opposed the violent action of
the *Sons of Liberty* as well as the plan of carrying on business
without stamps; as a class they were, however, largely identified
with the radicals, and neither the elections of 1768 and 1769,
nor the formation of the non-importation association, had revealed any hostility between fair trader and smuggler, or between merchant and mechanic. But by the spring of 1770, the
unity of the industrial interest had disappeared; the merchants
and importers of wealth and standing were prepared to take a
frankly conservative attitude; the mechanics and artisans, the
merchants and importers whose profits were largely identified
with smuggling, held fast to the radical program, and constituted
the rank and file of the *Sons of Liberty*. This breach was formally complete in July, 1770, when the merchants voted to modify
the non-importation agreement which they had signed in August, 1768, and the stand which they then took was partly due to
the fact that they were losing all sympathy with the violent
and spectacular methods of the radicals—methods which had been
so strikingly exhibited in December and January. But that was
not the only consideration that determined their conduct; the
principal cause of the modification of the non-importation association was the failure of the non-importation policy.

The association of 1768, it will be remembered, prohibited
importations either from England or Holland, with certain unimportant exceptions. If the agreement were enforced it would

operate beneficially for those who possessed sufficient capital
or credit to provide themselves with a large stock of goods before the date at which the agreement became effective;[155] if it
were only partially enforced it would of course operate beneficially for those who were willing to break it. So far as the importation of goods from England was concerned, the association
was observed more rigidly in New York than in Pennsylvania or
New England.   The value of New York imports for the year
1768, was approximately 482,000£; for the year 1769, approximately 74,000£. A comparison of values for several years previous to 1768, and subsequent to 1769, shows no such differences,
but generally a slight increase from year to year.[156] The drop
in 1769 can have had but one cause—the association.[157] With
respect to the Holland trade, it is unquestioned that smuggling
was not seriously interfered with by the association.[158]   The
vagabond trader, who regarded neither the association nor the
British trade acts, found the association a source of great profit. For the time being, the fair trader who had goods on hand
in August, 1768, found it a source of profit also. The difference was this: the fair trader's monopoly was temporary, and
even while it lasted was weakened by the prevalence of smuggling, but the smugglers' advantage was permanent, and it became greater than ever when the fair trader was sold out. Before the year was out the association had ceased to be an advan-

---

[155] "You have had one trial of a non-importation agreement . . . Were
the prices of goods raised on you then? . . . The honor of the merchants
. . . obliged you to take old, moth-eaten clothes that had been rotting
in the shop for years. and to pay a monstrous price for them." Seabury, *Free
Thoughts*, 10. *Cf. Freeman of Connecticut; New York Gazette*, August 6, 1770.
Lord North made the same charge. *Parl. Hist.*, 16: 855.

[156] *Cf.* McPherson, *Annals of Commerce*, 3: 339, 351, 365, 385, 410, 435,
456, 475, 486, 495. Almon, *Remembrancer*, 1: 117.

[157] I find few instances of the seizure of goods imported contrary to the
Association. *Cf. New York Col. Doc.*, 8: 222, 225. *New York Journal*, July 5,
1770.

[158] *Cf.* Barre on export of Tea. *Parl. Hist.*, 16: 873. "There never was imported more tea than in the last year, either directly from Holland or by way
of the Dutch West India islands." Pownall's speech, April, 1769; *Parl. Hist.*,
16: 619. "It is well known that little or no tea has been entered at the Customs
House for several years. All that is imported is smuggled from Holland, and
the Dutch Islands in the West Indies." Seabury, *Free Thoughts*, 10. "In New
York they import scarce any other than Dutch teas." *Cal. Home Office Pap.*,
1770–1772, No. 827. *Cf.* also *New York Col. Doc.*, 8: 446, 487.

tage to the fair trader, but the profits of the smuggler were daily increasing.

For those merchants who observed the association, there was another source of dissatisfaction with the non-importation policy. Before signing the agreement of 1768, a point had been made of securing the cooperation of Boston and Philadelphia; but as time passed it became clear that in neither place were the restrictions being satisfactorily observed. There is considerable contemporary evidence, mostly prejudiced it is true, that Boston in particular was more active in "resolving what it ought to do than in doing what it had resolved."[159] The value of New England imports from England for 1768 was approximately 419,000£, for 1769, approximately 207,000£.[160] The Pennsylvania figures for the same years are 432,000£, and 199,000£ respectively.[161] Nothing is more certain than that the laxness with which the association was observed at Boston was one of the principal considerations in inducing the New York merchants to take the first step in its abolition. That laxness, however, was of no disadvantage to the Holland smuggler; indeed, it gave him additional opportunities for plying his trade without detection. The New York merchants were convinced, to use their own words, that the association no longer served "any other purpose than tying the hands of honest men, to let rogues, smugglers, and men of no character, plunder their country."[162]

The coming breach between radicals and conservatives in the matter of the importation policy was clearly forecast in March, 1770, on the occasion of the annual celebration of the repeal of

---

[159] *New York Journal*, August 30. 1770. *New York Gazette*, supplement, reprinted from the *Mercury*, August 13–27, 1770. Defections at Boston led to special efforts to improve matters. *New York Journal*, February 1, 8, 15, March 1, 1770. *Cf.* also, *New York Mercury*, September 3. 1770. *Hist. MSS. Com.*, 10: Pt. 1, p. 422. *Grenville Papers*, 4: 485.

[160] McPherson, *Annals of Commerce*, 3: 485, 495. Almon, *Remembrancer*, 1: 117.

[161] McPherson. *Annals of Commerce*, 3: 486, 495.

[162] *New York Mercury*, August 30, 1770. Tryon speaks of the difference in sentiment expressed "by good citizens and fair traders, by men of cool sense and just discernment, on the one hand, by fraudulent dealers, artful smugglers, inflammatory politicians and patriots on the other." *New York Col. Doc.*, 8: 407.

the stamp act. Previous to 1769,[163] there had been a cordial cooperation of all classes in this event; merchant, mechanic, lawyer, and land owner alike had assumed for the day the title of *Sons of Liberty*.[164] But in 1770, there were two celebrations, and the political significance of the division is obvious. As the day approached, the radical leaders posted a notice calling a meeting of the *Sons of Liberty* at Montagnie's as usual, but without consulting that gentleman.[165] Montagnie had, however, already engaged his house to the other party, a fact which he publicly announced in the *Journal;*[166] and in the same issue there appeared a notice that ''the Friends of Liberty and Trade, who formerly associated at Bardins . . . to celebrate the . . . repeal . . . are requested to meet . . . at the home of Mr. Abram de la Montagnie.''[167] The radicals, thus excluded from the usual place, finally secured the ''corner house on the Broadway, near Liberty Pole, lately kept by Mr. Edward Smith,''—a fact which was publicly announced ''to all the *Sons of Liberty*.''[168] Both dinners were well attended, though a war of words ensued on that point,[169] and each party claimed to be the genuine *Sons of Liberty*. A comparison of the toasts reveals the difference between them very clearly. With three or four exceptions the two lists were identical: the *Sons of Liberty* drank a toast to Mac Dougall and visited him at New Gaol, while the *Friends of Liberty and Trade* did neither; the *Sons of Liberty* drank to ''a continuance of the non-importation agreement until the revenue acts are repealed,'' while the *Friends of Liberty and Trade* drank to ''trade and navigation and a speedy removal of their embarrassments.''[170] A list of those who at-

---

[163] There was a division in 1769, but it appears to have been the result of rivalry between the radical leaders, particularly Sears and MacDougall. *New York Journal,* March 1, 1770.

[164] *Cf. New York Mercury,* March 9, 16, 23, 1767.

[165] *Ibid.,* February 5, 1770.

[166] *New York Journal,* February 8, 1770. Dawson, *The Park and its Vicinity,* 42.

[167] *New York Journal,* February 8, 1770.

[168] *Ibid.,* February 15, 1770.

[169] *Ibid.,* March 29, April 5, 12, 1770.

[170] *New York Mercury,* March 26, 1770. *Cf. New York Journal,* March 29, 1770.

tended at Montagnie's, which has fortunately been preserved,[171] shows that the *Friends of Liberty and Trade* were the leading merchants and property owners of the city. Obviously, they differed from the *Sons of Liberty* in two respects; they had no sympathy with the spirit of agitation which the "Wilkes of America" represented; and they felt that trade was being unduly sacrificed to the zeal for liberty. They were friends of trade as well as of liberty, and for the future they were determined to search for a formula that would make for their interests without surrendering their principles.[172]

The event was now approaching which was to furnish the occasion for taking some practical action. It had long been known that the ministry was considering the repeal of the principal parts of the Townshend duties; Hillsborough had written as much to Moore in May, 1769, and in November, Colden had communicated this intelligence to the assembly.[173] In April, 1769, Pownall had in fact moved the repeal of all the duties, but the ministry had secured a postponement until the next session.[174] It is not surprising, therefore, that a letter from Boston to the New York merchants in December, 1769, "exhorting them to enter into a new resolution of not importing any British manufactures," was "passed over without the least notice."[175] In March, 1770, the matter of repeal again came up in Parliament. Pownall, who expected to renew his previous motion, gave way to the ministry, who thought themselves "pledged, by the Earl of Hillsborough's letter, to move for a repeal."[176] Accordingly, March 5, 1770, Lord North moved the repeal of all the duties

---

[171] The writer who denied that there were 300 at Hampden Hall, gave a list of 233 who met at Montagnies. The list includes the names of: John Cruger, Thomas Jones, Oliver De Lancey, John Alsop, John H. Cruger, William Walton, Theo. Bache, George Folliot, Isaac Low, Leonard Lispenard, James Beekman, Gabriel Ludlow, Peter Van Schaack, Edward Laight. There were some who afterwards joined the extreme radicals: Leonard Lispenard, Daniel Dunscomb, being examples. *New York Journal* April 12, 1770.

[172] The controversy as to which faction was the true *Sons of Liberty* was carried on in May. *Cf. New York Journal*, May 3, 10, 1770.

[173] See above, notes 121, 122.

[174] *Parl. Hist.*, **16**: 608, 610, 618.

[175] *New York Col. Doc.*, **8**: 191.

[176] *Parl. Hist.*, **16**: 855.

save those on tea.[177] The attempt of Pownall to include the tea duty failed by a vote of 240–142,[178] and, in April, the measure of Lord North was passed to take effect December 1.[179] At the same session a special act was passed permitting New York to issue 120,000£ in bills of credit receivable at the Loan Offices and at the Treasury.[180] These measures gave great satisfaction at New York, and the consideration of the non-importation agreement at once assumed a practical character.[181] Aside from other reasons for modifying the agreement, it was felt that concession on the part of Great Britain called for concession on the part of the colony. The merchants, therefore, hoped to restate the association in such a way as to relieve the commercial situation while still registering a protest against the principle of taxation.

The New York merchants were at first not alone in desiring this change. Before the middle of May they had been informed by the Philadelphia merchants that the latter would be under the necessity of breaking the agreement,[182] and May 10, Nathaniel Rogers, a Boston importer, came to New York for the precise purpose, it was alleged, of inducing the merchants to give up their association.[183] As soon as it was known that the repeal had been effected, the New York merchants ''sent to Philadelphia that they might unitedly agree to a general importation of every thing except tea.''[184] They received a favorable reply: since England had repealed part of the duties, the merchants ought now to show their loyalty by relaxing the agreement; May 14, a meeting had in fact been held at Philadelphia,

---

[177] *Journals of the House of Commons,* March 5, 1770. *Parl. Hist.,* 16: 852. *Annual Register,* 1770, p. 73. Sedgwick to Weston, [February ?] 6, 1770; *Hist. MSS. Com.,* 10: Pt. 1, p. 421. The date of this letter should properly be March 6.

[178] *Parl. Hist.,* 16: 855, 874.

[179] 10 *George III.,* ch. 17.

[180] *Ibid.,* ch. 35.

[181] The repeal act reached the colony before the middle of May. *New York Col. Doc.,* 8: 214, 216. The act authorizing the currency law reached the colony probably late in June. *Ibid.,* 215. It was understood that such permission would be given, however, as early as February. *Ibid.,* 205.

[182] *New York Journal,* August 16, 1770. *New York Mercury,* August 13, 1770.

[183] *New York Mercury,* May 14, 1770.

[184] *New York Col. Doc.,* 8: 217. *Cf. ibid.,* 214.

but it was agreed to determine nothing until June 5, in order to arrive at some precise agreement with New York, Boston, Rhode Island, and Maryland; meantime a committee had been appointed to propose to the meeting of June 5, a list of articles that might be imported.[185] Before the end of the month, the association had been set aside by the Newport merchants,[186] and the Albany merchants had asserted their determination to import everything except tea.[187]

Meanwhile the radicals were not idle. May 10, Rogers, the Boston importer, was hanged in effigy, and he escaped severer treatment only by remaining away from his lodgings during the day and leaving for Boston at two o'clock in the morning.[188] The next day the committee of the *Sons of Liberty* wrote to Philadelphia stating that a great majority of the New York merchants were determined to keep the association.[189] They were encouraged by letters from other colonies urging unanimity.[190] They indignantly rejected the suggestion that the question was one to be settled by the merchants alone, or even by the legal voters. They asserted that the mechanics, "and the virtuous of all other ranks," should "conspire, as it were with an oath, to brand with public infamy and public punishment, the miscreants who, while the odious Power of Taxation by Parliamentary authority, is in one single instance exercised, even dare to speak of the least infraction of the non-importation agreement."[191] May 30, when the radicals learned of the Rhode Island infraction, a series of resolutions was drawn up, denouncing the Rhode Island merchants, declaring them enemies of their country, proposing to boycott them, and once more asserting the adherence of the New York merchants to the original

---

[185] *New York Mercury*, August 13, 1770. *New York Journal*, August 16, 1770.

[186] *New York Mercury*, June 11, 1770. Resolutions, May 30, 1770; Lamb MSS., (1765–1706).

[187] *New York Journal*, August 30, 1770.

[188] *New York Mercury*, May 14, 1770. *Cf. Lenox Broadsides*, 28.

[189] Committee at New York to Philadelphia, May 11, 1770; Lamb MSS., (1765–1766).

[190] Letter to the Sons of Liberty, April 25, 1770; *New York Journal*, May 17, 1770.

[191] Brutus to the Free . . . Inhabitants; *Lenox Broadsides*, 28.

association.[192] A meeting was called for June 5,[193] to confirm these resolutions, and on that day "a considerable number of inhabitants" did assent to them by a large majority.[194] The committee of inspection had met the evening before,[195] however, and, after the radical meeting of June 5, it formally disapproved of the resolutions, and declared that the matter in question had been satisfactorily disposed of at the meeting of June 4.[196]

Precisely what the committee of inspection did on the evening of June 4 is not known; but it probably took steps to secure a formal modification of the association. At least on Monday, June 11, a number of individuals waited on the committee (a measure probably arranged by the committee at its meeting of June 4,) and requested it to "take the sense of the city, by subscription to determine whether an alteration should not be made in our non-importation agreement."[197] The committee responded readily, for that same evening a meeting was held, and persons were appointed to go through the wards proposing to each of the inhabitants the following questions: "Do you approve of a general importation of goods from Great Britain except teas and other articles which are or may be subject to an importation duty? Or do you approve of our non-importation agreement continuing in the manner it now is?"[198] The subscription was apparently not limited to the legal voters, but in spite of that fact the conservatives had a majority. According to Colden, 1,180 persons were in favor of importing, about 300

---

[192] Lamb MSS., (1765-1766). *New York Mercury*, June 11, 1770. *New York Journal*, June 7, 1770.

[193] *New York Mercury*, June 11, 1770.

[194] *Ibid.*

[195] *Ibid. New York Journal*, June 7, 1770.

[196] The committee of inspection resigned on this occasion, but was re-elected at a public meeting. *New York Mercury*, June 4, 1770.

[197] *New York Mercury*, June 18, 1770. *New York Journal*, June 21, 1770. *New York Col. Doc.*, 8: 219.

[198] *New York Mercury*, June 18, 1770. The following day a paper was published giving the new agreement in precise terms: (1) No goods imported that were taxed "in America:" (2) All of the dutied goods were excluded until December 1, the date at which the repeal act became effective; after December 1, tea only was excluded so long as the duty was retained; (3) goods imported contrary to this agreement were to be reshipped. *New York Journal*, June 21, 1770. *Cf.* Brutus account of the Reception of the Tea; 4 *Am. Arch.*, 1: 252, note.

"were neutral or refused to declare their sentiments, and few of any distinction declared in opposition to it."[199]

The committee did not, however, make a formal declaration in favor of importation at this time, nor did the merchants begin to import. The delay was doubtless due to the fact that an effort was being made to secure more cordial support in the neighboring colonies. Encouraged by the Philadelphia letter of May 15, the New York committee had already, June 2, dispatched a letter to Philadelphia and to several towns in New Jersey, proposing a conference of deputies at Norwich, Connecticut, to formulate an inter-colonial agreement in order that "no one colony may be liable to the censure of others."[200] June 6, a second letter was sent to Philadelphia urging an immediate reply, and stating that Boston had determined to modify the agreement if New York failed to maintain it,[201] and June 16, the result of the New York canvass was also communicated to Boston and Philadelphia.[202] But the replies, some of which came in during the month of June, were chilling. The Boston merchants claimed that their position had been grossly misrepresented.[203] The New Jersey towns were in favor of strengthening the association.[204] A scathing letter was received from Albany.[205] Even the merchants of Philadelphia, upon whom the New York committee had counted most confidently, faced about, as the result it was said of letters from England,[206] and voted to maintain the association.[207]

---

[199] *New York Mercury*, June 18, 1770, *New York Col. Doc.*, 8: 217. It was denied that there was a majority for importing. *New York Journal*, June 21, 1770.

[200] *New York Journal*, August 16, 1770. *New York Mercury*, August 6, 1770. The New Jersey towns were Newark, Elizabeth, and Perth Amboy. The proposal was for "six deputies" to meet a similar number from Boston, New York, Connecticut, "and other such places as may choose to send any."

[201] *New York Journal*, June 21, 1770.

[202] *New York Col. Doc.*, 8: 218. *New York Journal*, June 21, 1770.

[203] *New York Journal*, June 21, 1770. *New York Mercury*, July 16. 1770.

[204] *New York Mercury*, July 23, August 6, 13, October 8, 1770. The youthful enthusiasm of James Madison was reflected in a letter from Princeton, where the students burnt the New York letter. *Works of James Madison*, 1: 4.

[205] *New York Mercury*, August 20, 1770. *New York Journal*, August 23, 1770.

[206] *New York Col. Doc.*, 8: 216, 218.

[207] *New York Mercury*, July 16, 1770.

But neither protest nor denunciation sufficed to turn the New
York merchants from the plan upon which they had fixed. In
spite of "riots, clamours, and threats," with which the radicals
disturbed the city, it was felt that the majority of the inhabitants would support them.[208]   The economic pressure for importation was strong precisely because the association had been reasonably well kept during the past year.[209]   The radicals, who
were daily bringing discredit upon themselves by lawless actions,
were further weakened by the arrival, sometime in June, of the
law permitting New York to issue bills of credit.[210]   July 5, accordingly, the merchants met and publicly resolved to send orders by the next packet for all commodities except tea.[211]   Saturday morning, a broadside appeared denouncing these resolutions, and calling the inhabitants to assemble at 12 o'clock at
the city hall.   The meeting was presided over by Sears and
MacDougall, the former of whom made a characteristically radical speech, and a resolution against importation was easily carried.   Meanwhile the merchants had again assembled at the
Coffee House.   They were willing to decide the matter by ballot, offering to give up importation if a majority of the inhabitants were opposed to it.   It was requested that the packet,
which was to have sailed Sunday morning, be delayed until the
subscription could be taken.[212]   Two subscriptions were prepared, and persons of note on both sides of the question went
through the wards from house to house, taking the vote of every

---

[208] *New York Col. Doc.*, 8: 218.   *Cf. ibid.*, 216.

[209] "Many families must starve if an importation of goods from Great Britain
did not soon take place, for many could not subsist their families, especially
mechanics." Alexander Colden to Anthony Todd, July 11, 1770; *New York
Col. Doc.*, 8: 219. The clause. "especially mechanics," is significant, as it
was from this class that the radicals ordinarily received strong support. The
weakness of the *Sons of Liberty* at this time was undoubtedly due in part
to the economic pressure on the lower classes.

[210] Some goods taken by the committee of inspection, were forcibly seized
by a mob and destroyed.   Resolutions of censure were passed by the Committee,
whereupon Sears and Van den Voort resigned. *New York Journal,* July 5, 1770.
Dawson, (*The Park and its Vicinity*, 48.) and Leake, (*Life of John Lamb,* 67.)
speak of a Committee of One Hundred at this time.   I was myself misled by
them.   *Cf. Am. Hist. Rev.*, 7: 70.

[211] *New York Col. Doc.*, 8: 218, 219.

[212] *Ibid.*, 219.

inhabitant.[213]   The canvass, which was finished Monday evening,
July 9, resulted in a victory for the merchants.[214]   The same
evening, the committee of inspection formally "resolved to import,"[215] and the Wednesday following the packet sailed for
England carrying orders for goods not taxed.[216]

In the face of this second defeat, some of the radicals proposed
that a new committee of inspection should be formed, since the
other colonies would no longer correspond with the old one.[217]
But it was a forlorn hope.   Radical merchants themselves took
advantage of the new agreement;[218] and before the year was out
Philadelphia and Boston followed the lead of NewYork.[219]   For
the time being the *Sons of Liberty* were discredited, and in the
autumn elections for city magistrates the faction was defeated
by a large majority.[220]

The separation of the merchants from the *Sons of Liberty*
greatly strengthened the conservatives in numbers, but the radicals derived an advantage from the episode in the matter of
party policy.   Both factions had opposed the British measures,
and both factions continued to oppose them.   But hitherto the
radicals had advocated methods of resistance that could with difficulty bear the light of day.   They proposed to resist British
law by violating it and it was mainly in this that they were distinguished from the conservatives.   From now on, they stood
for absolute non-intercourse as distinguished from the conservative policy of modified non-intercourse.   And for this new

---

[213] *New York Journal*, July 19, 1770.   *New York Col. Doc.*, 8: 219.

[214] *New York Journal*, July 19, 1770.   *New York Col. Doc.*, 8: 218.

[215] *Broadsides*, 1.   4 *Am. Arch.*, 1: 252, note.

[216] *New York Col. Doc.*, 8: 221.

[217] *New York Journal*, July 19, 26, 1770.

[218] "Have, notwithstanding, sent themselves orders for large quantities of
goods."   Colden to Hillsborough, August 18, 1770; *New York Col. Doc.*, 8: 245.
Cf. Protest of *Sons of Liberty* against being considered enemies of their country
for importing.   Probably satirical.   *New York Mercury*, July 30, 1770.

[219] Philadelphia merchants resolved to import September 20, 1770.   *New York
Journal*, September 27, 1770.   The Boston resolution was taken October 11.
Ibid., Oct. 18, 1770.   *Cf.* Letter from Boston to Philadelphia, September 15.
Ibid., Oct. 11, 1770.

[220] "It gave me particular satisfaction to find this party entirely defeated last
week in a violent struggle to turn out such of the elected magistrates of the
city as had distinguished themselves any way in favor of government."   Colden
to Hillsborough, October 15, 1770; *Letter-Book*, 2: 229.

policy of the radicals much could be said: it was the policy which could easily be made to appear the only patriotic and unselfish policy—a policy which had broken down in other colonies only through the selfishness of the New York merchants. This advantage was to prove of great service to the radicals in the time of the first Continental Congress. Meanwhile, the tea episode once more raised the old question of violent methods in much the same fashion as the stamp act had done.

CHAPTER IV

THE TEA EPISODE

The years that immediately followed the repeal of the Townshend duties were exceptionally quiet and peaceful in New York.[1] The trade acts had been modified in a manner that was satisfactory.[2] The currency difficulty was settled. Early in 1771 the assembly took advantage of the permission granted by Parliament, and passed a law issuing 120,000£ in bills of credit, of which the first tenth was not to be sunk until 1776 and the remainder in the nine succeeding years.[3] The provisioning of the troops gave no further difficulty. In 1769 an act of Parliament modified the mutiny act in some of its most objectionable features;[4] and while the arrears occasioned by the veto of the provision bill of 1770 were never specifically made up,[5] beginning with 1771, the assembly made annual grants for the support of the troops until 1775.[6] The exclusion of judges from the as-

---

[1] The question of the New Hampshire grants created difficulty, but was without effect on the political situation. Colden gave place to Dunmore, and with characteristic misfortune, was forced, contrary to custom, to surrender part of his rightful salary. *New York Col. Doc.,* 8: 249. Dunmore was soon transferred to Virginia, and Tryon of North Carolina, became Governor of New York, arriving July 7, 1771. *Ibid.,* 278.

[2] Complaint of the tea duty ceased; the duty was avoided by smuggling. In 1771 imports from England reached 653,000£, dropping in the two following years to 343,000£, and 289,000£. Illicit trade, the growth of manufactures, and indirect importation through New England and the southern Colonies, furnish the explanation. See McPherson, *Annals of Commerce,* 3: 518, 533, 550. Weeden, *New England,* 2: 737. Tryon's Report, June 11, 1774; *New York Col. Doc.,* 8: 434 ff.

[3] *Col. Laws of New York,* 5: ch. 1472.

[4] 9 *George III.,* ch. 18.

[5] Dunmore to Hillsborough, March 9, 1771; *New York Col. Doc.,* 8: 264.

[6] *Col. Laws of New York,* 5: chs. 1474, 1513, 1596, 1647. The grant was 2000£, each year, save in 1773 when 1000£ was the sum.

sembly was of slight importance.[7] Neither the city elections nor
the celebrations of the repeal of the stamp act occasioned any
factional conflicts; the lower classes were prosperous and con-
tented; the *Sons of Liberty* were no longer heard of. In the
summer of 1773 as cordial relations as had ever existed between
colony and mother country seemed in a fair way to be established, when the half-forgotten 3*d* duty on tea resulted in events
that led directly to the Revolution.

In the year 1773 Parliament passed a law giving the East
India Company permission to export tea then stored in its warehouses free of all duties, but bearing the tax in America.[8] In
the colonies this measure was at once denounced as a political
trick, wholly designed to force the colonists to pay the tax which
they claimed was unconstitutional;[9] and American historians
have generally regarded it in that light. To determine how
much justification there may be for such an assertion, it will be
necessary to consider briefly the position of the East India Company and the Parliamentary legislation with respect to it.

After 1763 the East India Company occupied a peculiar position. Chartered as a private trading corporation, it had come
virtually to represent the English government in the exercise of
a growing political control in India. This control was not really
in the hands of the company, however, but in that of its servants,
upon whom no effective restraints were placed. The situation
offered unusual opportunities as well as unusual temptations
for official corruption and private plunder. Both the company
and the natives suffered. While individuals returned to England
with fat purses, the conditions in India were every year becoming more intolerable, and the company itself was falling into
bankruptcy.[10] As early as 1766 the Indian question became
prominent in England. Certain concessions which were pur-

---

[7] The exclusion act was vetoed. *New York Col. Doc.*, **8:** 215. *Cf. Ibid.*,
207, 209, 210.

[8] 13 *George III.*, ch. 44.

[9] A clear statement of the colonial view of this act is in the first of a series of
articles entitled *The Alarm. New York Journal*, October 14, 1773. *Cf. The
Monitor*, No. IV. ; *4 Am. Arch.*, **3:** 1725.

[10] This statement is based upon Lecky, *England*, **3:** 513 ff.

chased by the company for an annual payment of 400,000£,[11] improved matters very little, or not at all. Unsuccessful wars, famine in Bengal, high dividends in the company, and, as was thought by some,[12] the loss of the American tea trade, brought matters to a crisis. In 1770 the company's stock fell 60 per cent.[13] In 1772 its debts were upwards of a million pounds. The government annuity could not be paid, and in 1773 the directors came to Parliament for relief.[14] The first minister might well say: "I found it necessary for something to be done to save the company from a situation little short of absolute bankruptcy."[15]

But already larger issues were involved than mere solvency. In November, 1772, a secret committee had been appointed to inquire into the company's affairs,[16] and its startling reports forced Parliament to take up the broader question of Indian government. For days at a time, and throughout the entire session, the subject was exhaustively debated.[17] Ultimately the proposals of the government were embodied in the law "For establishing certain regulations for the better management of the affairs of the East India Company, as well in India as in Europe."[18] The title, however, scarcely indicates the scope of the act. The company's charter was virtually annulled, and the government of India was vested in a governor general, a council, and judges, under the direct control of the crown. Aside from the proposed loan to the company, and the matter of the supervisors, the long debates were concerned with the principal points of the regulation act. Nowhere in the proposals of the ministers nor in the debates is there any indication that the Indian question was in any way related to American affairs.

It was apparently wholly aside from the main theme that, on

---

[11] For legislation with respect to the company in the years 1767-1769, see 7 *George III.* chs. 48, 49, 56, 57. 9 *George III.*, ch. 24.

[12] *Annual Register*, 1772, p. 151. Palmer's Plan; Drake, *Tea Leaves*, 207.

[13] Lecky, *England*, **3**: 524.

[14] *Parl. Hist.*, **17**: 799. *Annual Register*, 1773, p. 210.

[15] *Ibid.*, 802.

[16] *Ibid.*, 453, 527.

[17] *Ibid.*, 227-383, 453, 464-475, 527-537, 559-568, 646-686, 799-837, 855-880, 890-914. Summarized in *Annual Register*, 1773, p. 63 ff.

[18] 13 *George III.*, ch. 63.

April 27, 1773, Lord North arose and "observed, that throughout the whole examination which the House had made of the East
India business, nothing could possibly have been more attentive
to their interests [the company's] than his motions . . .; that
it was evident the public would suffer from the faulty way in
which the company had conducted their affairs, even to the loss
of 400,000£ a year; and now instead of that receipt, were obliged
in policy to lend the company nearly four times that sum; . .
that he had now in pursuance of these favorable ideas of the
company a proposal to make, which would be wholly to their
advantage."[19]   This proposal, which the minister explained
briefly, was more precisely embodied in two resolutions which
were read, and which were substantially as follows: (1) That
after May 10, 1773, all teas sold at the company's sales or imported under license may be exported to any of the American
plantations free of the customs duties paid upon importation
into England; (2) that the commissioners of the treasury be
permitted to grant licenses to the East India Company to export teas to America or to "foreign parts," free of all customs duties "paid upon the importation of such teas," and with
an "exemption of the inland duties charged thereupon," provided only that there be left in the company's warehouses a
quantity of tea not less than ten million pounds weight.   Without further comment, and without opposition of any kind, the
resolutions "were agreed to."[20]   The incident was closed, and
Parliament proceeded to the consideration of other business.
Thus casually was enacted the law involving consequences of
such tremendous moment for America.

Not only was this the only East India measure to which there
was no Parliamentary opposition, it was the only one to which
the company itself was not opposed.[21]   It is true that over a year
later Governor Johnstone stated that the directors were not in

---

[19] *Parl. Hist.*, **17**: 840.

[20] *Ibid.*, 841.   *Cf. Annual Register,* 1773, p. 100.

[21] The Company wanted assistance without regulation. Its attitude is expressed in the petitions which it presented from time to time.   *Annual Register,* 1772, p. 201 ; 1773, p. 210 ff.   *Parl. Hist.,* **17**: 889, 921.

favor of the resolution,[22] but I can find no contemporary evidence that such was the case;[23] and if the directors were opposed to the resolution, the question naturally arises, why did they immediately take advantage of it? The only answer to this question is given by Almon, who is at the same time the sole English authority for the assertion that the whole affair was a political trick, played by the king to force the issue of taxation in America. The tea which was sent to America, says Almon,—the statement was made many years after the event—was Bohea tea, the most saleable tea, whereas it was the inferior Singlo tea with which the company was overstocked. But, in spite of the wishes of the directors, "it was the resolution of the cabinet to send the most saleable, presuming that the temptation to purchase being greater by the offer of good tea . . . some . . . might be thereby induced to barter liberty for luxury." The directors explained the differences: "It was again objected at the minister's home. To the last application Lord North, being perhaps wearied with repetition on the subject said 'It was to no purpose making objection, for the ———— would have it so.' These were his lordship's words; and he added 'that the————meant to try the question with America.'" Furthermore, Almon concludes that Boston was selected as the place where the test should be particularly made, since it was only at Boston that the officials refused to issue clearance papers for the return until the cargo was landed.[24]

Almon's *Anecdotes of Chatham,* from which these assertions

---

[22] *Parl. Hist.,* 18: 178.

[23] The *Annual Register,* in 1774, mentions the opposition of some active members of the company to the bill "as rather calculated for the establishment of the revenue law in America, than as a favor . . . to the Company" p. 47. This was probably a reflection of Johnstone's speech in parliament, as the *Register* makes no mention of such an idea in 1773. The king, in his correspondence with North, had many occasions to mention the affairs of the Company; but there is no hint anywhere that the legislation was designed to force the tax. *Cf.* Donne, *Correspondence of George III.,* 1: 113, 115, 117, 124, 132, 133, 134, 135, 137, 141. The letter of March 9, 1773, is typical of the king's attitude. *Ibid.,* 124. The Company was of course desirous of securing the repeal of the 3d duty. *Cf. Hist. MSS. Com.,* 14: Pt. 10, p. 114.

[24] Almon, *Anecdotes of William Pitt,* 2: 105-109.

are taken, is not an authority of great value in general,[25] and the facts do not confirm his statements in this particular case. The evidence indicates that the directors came to a resolution, in the ordinary way, to export tea to America;[26] and, as the law did not require them to do so, it is difficult to understand how a cabinet resolution could have forced the measure upon them. It is true that the company was overstocked with Singlo tea, and desired to create a market for it;[27] but it is certain that the directors were not prohibited from exporting Singlo since the American shipment did in fact include such tea.[28] Indeed, it seems that the amount and kind of tea to be shipped was determined by the directors on purely economic grounds. The new law was scarcely passed before they began to inquire into the state of the American tea trade, and the best information which could be secured[29] was as follows: (1) The consumption

[25] Almon strongly supported the colonial contentions and in his *Remembrancer* much space is given to American affairs. The *Anecdotes* was published in 1792, fourteen years after Chatham's death and nineteen years after this particular event is related to have occurred. The source of many of the anecdotes was Lord Temple. *Cf. Grenville Papers*, 3: 366, note. In the preface he says the anecdotes were "all of them in their day very well known." He says he kept a diary. Preface, Doublin Ed., p. v.

[26] "In consequence of this measure, the company . . . adopted the new system, of becoming its own exporter." *Annual Register*, 1774, p. 47. "We are informed that you have come to a resolution to ship tea to America." Greenwood and Higginson to the Directors, May 4, 1773; Drake, *Tea Leaves*, 208. "Being informed that you intend to export teas," etc., *ibid.*, 208. "The candid intimation given by you of an intention to export them [teas] to the colonies," etc., *ibid.*, 209. "Being informed of your resolution to export a quantity of tea," etc., *ibid.*, 212. "Being informed that you have it in contemplation to export teas," etc., *ibid.*, 213.

[27] Drake, *Tea Leaves*, 242.

[28] *Ibid.*, 245.

[29] "It appears that the company . . . consulted some of the most eminent persons in the tea trade upon the subject. By some of the most intelligent of them it was represented as the wildest scheme that could be imagined." *Annual Register*, 1774, p. 47. It is true that the merchants engaged in the tea trade would be inclined to represent the scheme as a wild one. But the statement in the *Register* was made after the scheme had in fact proved to be "the wildest . . . that could be imagined." A considerable correspondence with merchants in the tea trade has been published by Drake, (*Tea Leaves*, 189 ff), and in this correspondence there is no suggestion that the scheme was a wild one; on the contrary it is generally represented as entirely practicable. One unsigned memorial rather discourages the venture, but even this one goes on to suggest a plan. *Ibid.*, 218. Information on the state of the American trade was given by Mr. William Palmer, Gilbert Barkly, Thomas Walpole, Watson and Rashleigh, etc. *Ibid.*, 189–203, 205, 211, 216, 222.

of tea in America was very great,[30] and at present the trade was
supplied almost wholly from Holland;[31]   (2) Almost the only
tea used was Bohea; but a demand for Singlo might be developed gradually, and it would be well to include a small amount
in the first shipment to test the matter;[32]   (3) There was strong
opposition to the 3d tax; but ''mankind in general are bound by
interest,'' and ''the company can afford their teas cheaper than
the Americans can smuggle them from foreigners, which puts the
success of the design beyond a doubt.''[33]   With this information
at hand, the directors applied to the treasury for the necessary
license, which was granted August 19 without specification of

[30] Estimates of the annual consumption in the colonies ranged from five
and a half to six million pounds. Cf. Drake, Tea Leaves, 192, 193, 197, 200.
Cal. Home Office Pap., 1773-1775, No. 447. Hist. MSS. Com., 11: Pt. 5, p. 346.
It was reported that even the Indians drank tea twice a day. Hist. MSS.
Com., 14: Pt. 10, p. 131.

[31] Drake, Tea Leaves, 191, 192, 193, 195, 201. Letter from Boston stated
"We are confident that not one chest in five hundred has been seized in this
province for two or three years past. . . . At New York, we are told it
is carted about at noon day." Ibid., 194. By smuggling "there is a regular
and sufficient supply of tea, and has been for several years, equal to the demand of this whole country." Reed to Dartmouth, December 23, 1774; Hist.
MSS. Com., 11: Pt. 5, p. 346.

[32] Bohea was reported as "the species of tea already consumed here." Drake,
Tea Leaves, 197. Mr. Palmer proposed to send besides Bohea, "Congo, Souchong, and Hyson, but more particularly the several species of Singlo . . .
from a conviction that, by degrees, the consumption of . . . Singlo tea
might be introduced into America." Ibid., 190. Cf. Ibid., 242. "The consumption of Bohea tea through the continent increases every year." Ibid., 192.
In Nova Scotia the proportion was "20 chests Bohea, and 3 or 4 of good common green." Ibid., 202. At Boston, 400 Bohea, 50 green. Ibid., 203. Walpole advised the Company to send to Philadelphia "five hundred chests of
black teas, one hundred half chests of green teas, and seventy-five chests of
Congo and Souchong teas." Ibid., 203. Mr. Palmer proposed sending "chests
of Bohea tea, chests of each species of Singlo tea, together with a smaller assortment of Hyson, Souchong, and Congo teas." Ibid., 206. The New York
agents thought that in New York 1500 to 2000 chests of Bohea might be sold,
but with respect to other sorts, they were "not well informed." Cal. Home
Office Pap., 1773-1775, No. 47.

[33] Barkly to the Chairman, June 29, 1773; Drake, Tea Leaves, 216. "Nothing
will be effectual short of reducing the price in England equal to that in Holland. If no other burthen than the 3d duty in the Colonies, to save that
alone would not be sufficient profit, and the New Yorkers, etc., would soon
break through their solemn engagements not to import from England." Letter
from Boston, September 11, 1772; ibid., 193. Cf. ibid., 219.

any sort as to the kind of tea to be exported.[34]   An assortment had in fact already been made up by Mr. Palmer, a London merchant engaged in American trade, consisting of 1,586 chests of Bohea, 290 of Singlo, 70 of Congo, 70 of Hyson, and 35 of Souchong.[35]

To dispose of the tea in America, it was suggested that a branch of the company be established,[36] but it was thought wiser for the present to intrust the business to well-recommended American merchants.   June 1, Frederick Pigou informed the directors that he had established a firm in New York under the name of Pigou and Booth, and requested "the favor of that house having a share in the consignments."[37]   July 5, William Kelly recommended the firms of Abram Lott and Co., and Hugh and Alexander Wallace.[38]   Henry White applied for a consignment, and was supported by John Blackburn of Scots Yard, who stated that "his consequence as a merchant of fortune" will enable him to advance "the interest of the company . . . as well as silencing any prejudices from the mode of its introduction."[39]   Acting on these recommendations, the directors designated as the New York agents the three firms of Abram Lott and Co., Henry White, and Pigou and Booth.[40]   The merchants who recommended the consignees also informed the directors that they had a "ship, river built, called the *Nancy*, commanded by

---

[34] The petition of the Company for a Treasury license is given in Drake. *Tea Leaves,* 246, with the date April 19, 1773.   This must be an error as the resolution of Lord North was not introduced until Apr'l 27, 1773.   The license is given in Drake, 248, with the date August 20, 1773.   It is possible that the proper date for the petition is August 19, instead of April 19, but in that case the reply from the treasury was unusually prompt.

[35] These figures are given in Drake, *Tea Leaves,* 245, under the heading, *Mr. Palmer's Assortment of Teas for America.*   The assortment for New York was as follows: Bohea, 568 chests; Congo, 20; Singlo, 80; Hyson, 20; Souchong, 10; total 698.   As there were exactly 698 chests entered for freight charges on account of the *Nancy,* I have assumed that Mr. Palmer's assortment was the one actually used by the Company.   There is the same correspondence between the freight charges and Palmer's assortment for the other colonies, save Boston.   Palmer's list gives 398 chests for Boston, the freight charges only 384.   Drake, *Tea Leaves,* 256, 257.

[36] Memorial of Gilbert Barkly; Drake, *Tea Leaves,* 199.

[37] Drake, *Tea Leaves,* 208.

[38] *Ibid.,* 226.

[39] *Ibid.,* 228.

[40] *Ibid.,* 305; *New York Mercury,* December 6, 1773.

Captain Colville, completely fitted and ready to receive the tea for New York."[41] The offer was accepted, and the *Nancy* was accordingly freighted with 698 chests of tea, exported on account of the East India Company.[42]

From the readiness of the American merchants to act as consignees, it seems clear that the later violent opposition to the company's new venture was not so clearly foreseen as it is sometimes represented to have been. As late as November there appeared in New York a series of able articles, signed *Popliocola*, which dwelt upon the benefits of commerce, and advocated the reception and purchase of the tea.[43] And there were some who believed that there would have been little opposition had the New York cargo arrived before the tea was destroyed at Boston.[44] But such views were too sanguine. The new law was disliked by all classes:[45] by the fair trader because it gave a virtual monopoly to an English corporation;[46] by the smuggler because it threatened to destroy the lucrative Holland trade.[47] If the measure was not a political trick, it did in fact cut the ground from under the non-importation policy of the conservatives, and force the issue as it had not been forced since the stamp act. Even the policy of modified non-intercourse could be maintained only by resorting to one of two methods: non-consump-

---

[41] Drake, *Tea Leaves*, 254.

[42] *Ibid.*, 257.

[43] To The Worthy Inhabitants, etc., *Broadsides*, 1. *Rivington's Gazetteer*, November 18, 1773. *Lenox Broadsides*, 29.

[44] Tryon to Dartmouth, January 3, 1774; *New York Col. Doc.*, 8: 407. *Cf Cal. Home Office Pap.*, 1773–1775 No. 498. *Parl. Hist.*, 17: 1165.

[45] "There is a general and spirited opposition to its being sold." The Agents to Tryon, December 1, 1773; Drake, *Tea Leaves*, 306. *Cf. Ibid.*, 270.

[46] The Alarm, No. 1.; *New York Journal*, October 14. 1773. *Hist. MSS. Com.*, 14: Pt. 10, p. 176. *Cf.* Tryon to Dartmouth, November 3, 1773; *New York Col. Doc.*, 8: 400.

[47] "The introduction of the East India Company's tea is violently opposed here by a set of men who shamefully live by monopolizing tea in the smuggling way." Merchant in New York [Abram Lott] to William Kelly, November 5, 1773; *Cal. Home Office Pap.*, 1773–1775, No. 399. Drake, *Tea Leaves*, 269. *Cf.* Tryon to Dartmouth, January 3, 1773; *New York Col. Doc.*, 8: 407. Mr. Barkly's proposal to establish a branch house in the colonies was "in order to put a final stop to that destructive trade of smuggling." Drake. *Tea Leaves*, 199. The opposition, according to Tryon, was "calculated . . . to make popular the cause of those who are deepest concerned in the illicit trade of foreign countries." *New York Col. Doc.*, 8: 400.

tion agreements or forcible resistance to the landing of the tea. A non-consumption agreement which distinguished between the company's tea and Holland tea was scarcely practicable,[48] while one which included Holland tea would destroy the smugglers' profits, besides requiring a degree of self-sacrifice not to be counted on.[49] On the other hand, a resort to lawless methods of resistance was contrary both to the principles and to the interests of the conservatives. It was, for the moment, no longer a question of absolute or partial non-importation; the question was whether the conservative policy could be maintained without resorting to radical methods. The situation gave a distinct advantage to the radicals: for them the way was clear, but the conservatives halted between the desire to maintain the non-importation of English tea on the one hand, and the dislike of giving countenance to lawlessness on the other.

The radicals were not slow to take advantage of the situation. October 6, 1773, there appeared in the *Journal* the first of a series of articles denouncing the new law as an obvious political trick, which would undermine the commerce of the colony by giving to the company a monopoly of trade, and threaten the liberty of the people by forcing them to pay an unconstitutional tax.[50] Other writers compared the tea agents to stamp commissioners, and called upon them to resign under threats of personal violence.[51] October 15, "most of the merchants and many other inhabitants," voted an address of thanks to the London captains who had refused to carry the Company's tea.[52] Early in November Colden wrote that if the tea came bearing the duty it would be opposed as a tax, while if it came without the duty it would be opposed as a monopoly.[53] Abram Lott, one of the consignees, believed that the tea would not be safe if it came sub-

---

[48] "For it was easily seen that if the tea was once landed and in the custody of the consignees, no associations, nor other measures, would be sufficient to prevent its sale and consumption." *Annual Register*, 1774, p. 48.

[49] "The cry then was that there was not virtue enough in the city to prevent the tea from being bought and sold." Seabury, *The Congress Canvassed*, 22.

[50] *New York Journal*, October 14, 1773.

[51] *Ibid.*, Oct. 14, 21, 1773.

[52] *Ibid.*, October 21, 1773. *New York Mercury*, October 25, 1773.

[53] November 3, 1773; *New York Col. Doc.*, 8: 400.

ject to the duty ''as almost every body in that case speaks against the admission of it,'' and even if it could be landed ''there will be no such thing as selling it.''[54] November 24, the consignees were requested to declare that they would neither receive nor sell any of the Company's tea.[55] and on December 1, having learned in the meantime that the tea would come bearing the duty, they publicly ''declined receiving or selling it under that predicament.''[56] The same day the agents addressed a memorial to Governor Tryon requesting him to take measures ''for the preservation of the said tea.''[57] The governor at once applied to Captain Asycough of the royal ship *Swan* ''to take the vessel when arrived under his protection until the tea can be landed.''[58]

But steps had already been taken to prevent the landing, or at least the consumption of the tea. November 29, 1773, the leading radicals prepared a document entitled *The Association of the Sons of Liberty of New York*. The preamble recited the history of the tea duty, and the recent legislation of Parliament with respect to the company. ''Therefore, to prevent slavery . . . we, the subscribers, being influenced from a regard to liberty and disposed to . . . transmit to our posterity those blessings of freedom which our ancestors have handed down to us, . . . do, . . . agree to associate together under the name and stile of the *Sons of Liberty of New York,* and engage . . . to observe . . . the following resolutions.'' The resolutions were in substance as follows: (1) Those aiding or abetting the introduction of dutied tea to be treated as en-

---

[54] Abram Lott to William Kelley, November 5, 1773; Drake, *Tea Leaves,* 269; *Cal. Home Office Pap.,* 1773-1775, No. 399.

[55] *Brutus on the Reception of the Tea* in *4 Am. Arch.,* **1:** 253, note.

[56] *New York Mercury,* December 6, 1773. *Brutus,* etc., in *4 Am. Arch.,* **1:** 253, note.

[57] Drake, *Tea Leaves,* 305.

[58] Tryon to Dartmouth, December 1, 1773; *New York Col. Doc.,* **8:** 402. *New York Mercury,* December 6, 1773. It was this order, doubtless, that led the compiler of the *Annual Register* to say, "At New York it was indeed landed under the cannon of a man of war." *Annual Register,* 1774, p. 50. The sentences which immediately follow indicate that the writer has confused the disposal of the tea at New York with that made at South Carolina, an error copied by Anderson, *History of Commerce,* **4:** 165, and also by McPherson, *Annals of Commerce,* **3:** 546.

emies; (2) Those who buy or sell or aid or abet the purchase or sale of dutied tea to be treated as enemies; (3) Whether the duty is paid in England or America is immaterial; (4) Those who transgress these rules "we will not deal with, or employ, or have any connection with him."[59] The association was circulated for signatures, and a fortnight later, it had been signed, we are told, by "a great number of the principal gentlemen of the city, merchants, lawyers, and other inhabitants of all ranks."[60]

It is likely, however, that the number of signers was not as great as could be desired. In any case, the radicals decided to strengthen their position by the familiar device of a mass-meeting. Accordingly, on Thursday, December 16, the "committee of the association" called a meeting for the following day at the city hall to which was invited every "friend of the liberty and trade of America."[61] In spite of bad weather, a "very numerous and respectable number of citizens" met at the appointed time and place.[62] Letters from Boston and Philadelphia were read by John Lamb, and a committee of fifteen chosen to answer them and to institute a correspondence with other colonies. The resolutions of November 29 were then read, and when the chairman put the question "whether they agreed to these resolutions? it passed in the affirmative *nem. con.*" At this point the mayor and recorder came in with a message from the governor, who proposed that the tea should be put into the fort at noonday, there to remain until the council or the king or the proprietors should order it delivered. "Gentlemen," said the mayor, "is this satisfactory to you?" The thrice repeated negative, which was shouted back, left no doubt that it was not. The chairman then put the question, "Is it then your opinion, gentlemen, that the tea should be landed under the circumstances?" So general was the negative reply that there was no call for a

---

[59] *The Association of the Sons of Liberty of New York*, November 29. 1773; *Broadsides*, 1. *New York Journal*, December 6, 1773.

[60] *New York Journal*, December 16, 1773. *Brutus on the Reception of the Tea* in *4 Am. Arch.*, 1: 254, note.

[61] Advertisement, December 16, 1773; *Broadsides*, 1. *New York Journal*, December 16, 1773.

[62] Advertisement, etc.; *Broadsides*, 1. A radical account estimated the attendance at 2,000. *Brutus, etc.*, in *4 Am. Arch.*, 1: 254, note.

division. The association, together with an account of the meeting, was ordered printed and sent to the neighboring colonies,[63] and the meeting was adjourned until the arrival of the tea ships.

The leaders of this movement were undoubtedly the ultra-radicals like Lamb, Sears, and MacDougall. Nevertheless, they had so worded the association as to alienate the conservatives as little as possible. The association said nothing about using force to prevent the landing of the tea; it merely declared that the subscribers would have nothing to do with the landing of the tea, and that they would boycott any one who did. If the great majority of the inhabitants subscribed to the agreement and kept it, the boycott would prove an effective weapon, but otherwise it would prove to have been a useless measure. After all, therefore, the vital question was, did the association tacitly authorize the use of force to prevent the landing of the tea if the simple boycott proved insufficient? It was to the advantage of the radicals to leave this question unanswered, but the conservatives were anxious to have a more definite understanding in the matter.

Accordingly, on Monday, December 20, Jacob Walton and Isaac Low solicited subscriptions to the following statement:[64] "Whereas an association has been lately entered into . . . and a doubt has arisen, whether it is the general sense of the subscribers, and the rest of the inhabitants, that the landing or storing of the said tea should be opposed by force? We, the subscribers, to remove the said doubt, as far as concerns our respective sentiments, do declare and resolve as follows: (1) That we do concur with the parties to the said association, that the said tea ought not, on any account, to be suffered to be sold or purchased while it remains subject to a duty. . . . (2) That to carry this resolve into execution, a firm and vigorous opposition ought to be given to all persons who shall attempt to betray our liberties, either by purchasing or vending the said tea. (3) That we are determined to have no agency in landing or storing the said tea. (4) That as our liberties . . . must effectually be

[63] Advertisement, etc.; *Broadsides*, 1: *Cf. Leake, Life of John Lamb*, 77–79.
[64] *Brutus on the Reception of the Tea* in *4 Am. Arch.*, 1: 254, note.

secured by a strict adherence to the preceding resolves, we do
not conceive it necessary or expedient to hazard the peace of the
city, by opposing the landing or storing the said tea with force.''
What success this effort met with is not known. Nothing further
is heard of it; and some months later a radical writer stated that
but few subscriptions were obtained, and that on Tuesday the
attempt was abandoned.[65] The failure at least served to define
the position of the radicals: if force was found necessary, force
would be used. Such, at least, was the opinion of the agents.
December 27, they wrote to Captain Lockyear a letter to be delivered upon his arrival at Sandy Hook, stating that they could
neither receive the tea nor pay the duty, and advising him ''for
the safety of your cargo, your vessel, and your person, . . .
to return, as soon as you can be supplied with such necessaries
as you may have occasion for.''[66]

Such was the situation in January, 1774; and in that month
even the assembly registered a protest against the tea measure
by appointing a standing committee of correspondence.[67] But it
was not until April 18 that the *Nancy,* having been driven
southward by adverse winds, finally arrived at Sandy Hook.[68]
The letter from the consignees was there delivered to Captain
Lockyear, who, following the advice contained in it, informed
the committee that he desired to come up to the fort to secure provisions for his return, promising to leave the ship at Sandy Hook.
To this the committee agreed, but it assured the public, by means
of a broadside published April 19, that ''when ever he comes up
care will be taken that he does not enter the Custom House, and
that no time be lost in dispatching him.''[69] Wednesday, April
20, the captain came up to the city and informed the consignees by
letter that he was ''ready to deliver the said cargo according to

---

[65] *Ibid.*

[66] Drake, *Tea Leaves,* 358. For Governor Tryon's opinion of the situation *cf.*
Tryon to Dartmouth, January 3, 1774; *New York Col. Doc.,* 8: 407.

[67] *Ass. Jour.,* January 20, 1774. *Rivington's Gazetteer,* January 27, 1774.

[68] ''The long expected tea ship arrived last night at Sandy Hook.'' To the
Public, April 19, 1774; *Broadsides,* 1. The accounts of these proceedings are
in *New York Journal,* April 28, 1774; *New York Mercury,* April 25, 1774; *Rivington's Gazetteer,* April 21, 1774. An account from the *Gazette,* and Colden's
account are in *Am. Arch.,* 1: 248, 249.

[69] To the Public, April 19, 1774; *Broadsides,* 1.

the bill of lading." The consignees replied at once that they could not "take charge of the same, or any part thereof."[70] The captain thereupon promised to return, and his departure was fixed for the morning of Saturday, April 23, at 9 o'clock.[71] "Every friend of his country" was summoned to attend at Murray's Wharf at that time, in order that he might see "with his own eyes, their detestation of the measures passed by the ministry to enslave the country."[72]

Meanwhile, advices had been received of the sailing of Captain Chambers, whose ship, the *London*, it was positively learned on Wednesday, contained a private shipment of the East India Company's tea.[73] On a previous voyage, Chambers had taken credit to himself for being the first to refuse to carry the company's tea, and it was with difficulty believed that he would now sail into the harbor with any on board.[74] The *London* arrived at Sandy Hook on Friday,[75] and two members of the committee of observation, a sub-committee appointed to watch the tea ships,[76] at once went on board and examined the cockets. Chambers denied that he had any tea, and no cockets were found. At four o'clock, when the ship came up to the harbor, a "number of citizens" nevertheless threatened to examine every package on the ship, whereupon the captain admitted that he had tea and delivered the cockets. He was at once ordered before the general committee at Fraunces' Tavern, where it was further learned that he was the sole owner of the tea. The whole matter was then communicated to the people assembled near the ship; and although the agreement provided for the reshipment of all dutied tea, nothing less than its destruction appears to have been thought of in the present case, so great was the resentment against Chambers for his duplicity. "The Mohawks," we are told, "were prepared to do their duty at a proper hour," but

[70] Drake, *Tea Leaves*, 359, 360.
[71] *4 Am. Arch.*, **1**: 248, 249. To the Public, April 21, 1774; *Broadsides*, **1**.
[72] To the Public, April 21, 1774; *Broadsides*, **1**.
[73] *4 Am. Arch.*, **1**: 250. *New York Journal*, April 28, 1774. *Rivington's Gazetteer*, April 28, 1774.
[74] Colden to Dartmouth, May 4, 1774; *4 Am. Arch.*, **1**: 249.
[75] *4 Am. Arch.*, **1**: 250.
[76] *Rivington's Gazetteer*, April 21, 1774. *4 Am. Arch.*, **1**: 254, note.

the people were too impatient, and at 8 o'clock a number of men boarded the ship and dumped the tea into the harbor. No damage was done to the ship or to the remainder of the cargo, and at ten o'clock the crowd dispersed quietly.[77]

Next morning bells were rung, and at eight o'clock a great crowd assembled at the Coffee House. An hour later the committee came out of the inn with Captain Lockyear, who was forthwith escorted by the people to Murray's Wharf, where he embarked while the band, a little incongruously perhaps, played *God save the King*. Sunday evening the committee of observation returned to the city and reported that Captain Lockyear had that day put to sea. With him there sailed, as a passenger, Captain Chambers, whose ship still lay at Murray's Wharf. "Thus to the great mortification of the secret and open enemies of America, and the joy of all friends of liberty and human nature, the union of these colonies is maintained."[78]

The destruction of the tea was accomplished quietly and, if the expression is permissible, in good order. Colden wrote that the great part of the town was perfectly quiet.[79] Nevertheless, the event aroused the old conservative fear of mob-violence, and the old opposition to the intrusion of the un-privileged classes in political affairs. A letter appeared in *Rivington's Gazetteer*, protesting against the "out-rage," in which, it was maintained, not a twentieth part of the people shared. The author asked by whose authority the committee of observation acted; he denied that the sense of the city had been taken, and denounced the trial of Chambers as a ridiculous farce; signing himself a friend to the constitution, he declared himself a sworn foe "to *Cobblers and Tailors* so long as they take upon their everlasting and immeasurable shoulders the power of directing the loyal and sensible inhabitants of the city and province of New York."[80] Once more the *Sons of Liberty*, the mechanics, the "Cobblers

---

[77] *4 Am. Arch.*, **1:** 250, 251, note. *Cf. ibid.*, 249.

[78] *Ibid.*, 250.

[79] There was a "pretty large number of spectators." Colden to Dartmouth, May 4, 1774; *Ibid.*, 249.

[80] *Rivington's Gazetteer*, April 25, 1774. Quoted in *4 Am. Arch.*, **1:** 251, note. This letter called out the elaborate reply of *Brutus*. *Rivington's Gazetteer*, May 12, 1774; reprinted in *4 Am. Arch.*, **1:** 254, note.

and Tailors,'' had proved too radical,—and, in any case, if the particular matter had been satisfactorily settled, there was no reason why the unfranchised classes should have assumed the task of settling it.

If the tea episode had for the moment united conservatives and radicals in some respects, its ultimate effect was to bring out more sharply than ever the essential differences between them. The coercive acts at once revived the old issue of absolute *versus* modified non-importation. And another issue, which had always distinguished the two factions to some extent, was destined to play a much more prominent part in future contests: as the direction of affairs fell more and more under the control of extra-legal committees, the question of whether the unfranchised should properly share in the election of such committees became of vital importance. The conservatives were coming to realize that if the policy of the colony was henceforth to be directed by moderate men of property rather than by the mob, a policy of holding aloof on their part would no longer suffice. The organization of the *Sons of Liberty*, which was now controlled by the radicals, whether it really represented the city or not, was in fact grounded in a wide popular support. It was the essential political institution of the hour, and the conservatives realized that it would be wiser to get control of it than to oppose or ignore it. To this end, therefore, they now directed their energies.[81]

---

[81] "After the destruction of Captain Chamber's tea and some other violent proceedings of the pretended patriots, the principal inhabitants began to be apprehensive and resolved to attend the meetings of the inhabitants when called together by hand bills. The consequence is that Scott, MacDougall, Sears, and Lamb are all in disgrace, and the people are now directed by more moderate men." Colden to Conway, September 23, 1774; *Letter-Book*, 2: 361.

CHAPTER V

THE ELECTION OF DELEGATES TO THE FIRST CONTINENTAL CONGRESS

The tea episode was hardly closed before the coercion acts opened the way for a determined effort to carry out the conservative policy. The Boston port act reached New York from England on Thursday, May 12,[1] and was at once re-printed and circulated about the city in the form of handbills.[2] The conservatives were determined to take the initiative, and within the next two days, probably on Friday, May 13, a notice was posted at the Coffee House, inviting the merchants to meet at the "house of Mr. Samuel Fraunces, on Monday evening, May 16."[3] About the same time, very likely after the above notice was posted, the radicals held a meeting composed, it was said, of "a number of respectable merchants and the body of mechanics," at which there was named a committee of twenty-five, which included the leading members of the old committee of the as-

---

[1] "Last Thursday Captain Couper arrived from London in 27 days. By him we have received . . . Act of Parliament, that shuts up your Port the first of June." New York Letter, May 14, 1774; *Boston Gazette,* May 23, 1774. *Cf. 4 Am. Arch.,* **1:** 289, note.

[2] It appears to have been printed twice. One broadside contained the act alone. The Alarming Boston Port Act, etc.; *Broadsides,* **1.** Another, probably printed on Saturday, contained the act together with some London letters. *4 Am. Arch.,* **1:** 289, note.

[3] *4 Am. Arch.,* **1:** 293. It is sometimes implied that this meeting was called by the merchants as a result of a letter written to Boston promising hearty support by New York. *Cf.* Leake, *Life of John Lamb,* 87. The letter in question was, however, not written till May 14. It was published in the *Boston Gazette* May 23, and the merchants in New York learned of it, for the first time apparently, from the *Boston Gazette* towards the end of the month. *Cf.* Colden to Tryon, May 31, 1774; *Letter-Book,* **2:** 343. *New York Mercury,* June 6, 1774. The view of Leake is derived from a New York letter dated May 31. *Cf. 4 Am. Arch.,* **1:** 299, note.

sociation of the *Sons of Liberty*, and a number of conservatives.[4] From the sequel, and from the composition of this committee, it is to be inferred that the radicals were preparing to check-mate the conservative move by offering this committee at the meeting on Monday. The wide-spread indignation which had been aroused by the Boston port act, doubtless led them to suppose that there would be no serious opposition to the appointment of such a committee, or, indeed, to a return to the radical policy of absolute non-importation.

In any case, both parties were present at the meeting on Monday, which, it appears, was so large as to make an adjournment to the Exchange necessary;[5] and the central point of interest was the contest between them over the nomination of the new committee. The conservatives appear to have had a majority. Isaac Low was made chairman, and it was agreed, probably without opposition, that a new committee should be nominated that evening, to be confirmed at a future meeting called for that purpose. The radicals then evidently proposed that the committee should be limited to twenty-five, and presented the ticket which they had already prepared at an earlier meeting. To oppose this ticket, upon which 'the radicals had very shrewdly placed representatives of both factions, would put the conservatives in a bad light; to accept it without modification would place the movement in the hands of the radicals. The conser-

---

[4] "A Committee of Twenty-Five: The following are nominated by a number of merchants and the Body of Mechanics of this city to be a Committee of Correspondence for it with the neighboring Colonies. John Alsop, Theophylact Bache, P. V. B. Livingston, Isaac Sears, David Johnston, Alexander MacDougall, Thomas Randall, Leanard Lispenard, Jacobus Van Zandt, Thomas Pearsall, Richard Yates, John Broome, Nicholas Hoffman, Abram Walton, Henry Remsen, George Browne, Peter T. Curtenius, Abram P. Lott, John Aspinwall, Gerard W. Beekman, Abram Duryee, Joseph Bull, Richard Sharp, Thomas Marston, Francis Lewis." *Broadsides,* 1.

[5] The meeting was called to meet at Fraunces Tavern. The minutes of the Committee state that certain persons "did accordingly appear at the time and place appointed, and then and there," etc., 4 *Am. Arch.,* 1: 294. On the other hand, the official account of the meeting, printed in a broadside, is headed, "At a Meeting at the Exchange, May 16, 1774." *Broadsides,* 1. In other places the minutes of the Committee also assert that the meeting was held at the Exchange. 4 *Am. Arch.,* 1: 293, 295. The *Mercury,* May 23, 1774, also gives the Exchange as the place. A New York Letter says the meeting was at the Coffee House. 4 *Am. Arch.,* 1: 299, note.

vatives refused to do either; they accepted the ticket substantially, but rejected the plan of limiting the committee to twenty-
five.   To the radical ticket of twenty-five the conservatives consequently opposed a ticket of fifty, consisting of twenty-three
members of the radical slate, and twenty-seven others.   When
the question was put, "Whether the committee of fifty be appointed, or twenty-five?" it was carried for the fifty.[6]

The committee thus nominated had yet to receive the "approbation of the public;" that is, it had, in some manner, to be
elected.   But if the work of the conservatives was thus not
fully accomplished, the radicals had at least been disarmed.
Since twenty-three of the candidates were of their own choosing, they could not well oppose the election of the fifty without
laying themselves open to the charge of acting from interested
motives.   The fifty might, with more truth than was ordinarily
the case, be considered as representing the will of the people;
and it was precisely as representing the will of the people that
the radicals had always claimed authority for the actions of
their own committees.   The conservatives quickly followed up
the advantage they had thus gained.   On Tuesday handbills
were circulated which announced that in order to observe all
the necessary formalities for constituting "a committee duly
chosen," a second meeting would be held at the coffee house on
Thursday, May 19, at one o'clock.   Not the merchants merely,

---

[6] At a meeting at the Exchange, May 16, 1774; *Broadsides,* 1. The account
is a very brief one, and gives no indication of rivalry except the sentence
quoted in the text. The names of the fifty are given. They include all of the
twenty-five, except John Aspinwall and Francis Lewis. Lewis was afterwards
added. Besides these, the Committee of Fifty consisted of the following: Wil-
liam Bayard, Philip Livingston, Charles McEvers, Charles Nicoll, John Moore,
Isaac Low, James Duane, Edward Laight, Elias Desbrosses, William Walton,
John De Lancey, Miles Sherbrook, John Thurman, John Jay, Benjamin Booth,
Joseph Hallet, Charles Shaw, Alexander Wallace, James Jauncey, Gabriel
H. Ludlow, Gerardus Duychinck, Peter Van Schaack, Hamilton Young,
Peter Goelet, Abram Brasher, David Van Horn, William McAdam,
Broadsides, 1. "In spite of all that could be done by the old committee, which
consisted of eight or ten flaming patriots without property, or anything else
but impudence, a new committee was chosen, consisting of 50 members, most
of them men of sense, coolness, and property." New York Letter, May 31, 1774;
4 *Am. Arch.,* 1: 299, note. For other accounts of the election, see *ibid.,* 293.
Colden, *Letter-Book,* 2: 340. *New York Col. Doc.,* 8: 433. The broadside
is reprinted in Lamb, *Hist. of the City of New York,* 1: 769, 770.

but "the inhabitants of the city and county," were requested to attend for the purpose of approving "of the committee nominated," or of appointing "such other persons as in their discretion and wisdom may seem meet."[7] Yet, as if to deprecate as far as possible any tendency to act upon this last suggestion, a second handbill was circulated a few hours before the time appointed for the meeting, setting forth the wisdom and discretion of supporting those who had been nominated in a more or less legitimate way.[8] Whatever may have been the result of this appeal, at one o'clock "a great concourse of the inhabitants" met at the Coffee House.[9] As before, both parties were present. They may very likely have appeared, as Bancroft says, "in array; on the one s:de men of property, on the other tradesmen and mechanics"; but it is questionable whether the mass of the people were ready to "found a new social order."[10] The men of property seem rather to have been in the majority; in any case they again named Isaac Low chairman, who presently made a speech in which there was little hint of a new social order. Men were urged to act according to the "dictates of calm reason only," and to set aside "all little party distinctions, feuds and animosities."[11] The names of the fifty were then proposed, and confirmed by the meeting, "and Mr. Francis Lewis was added to the latter by unanimous consent."[12]

That the Committee of Fifty-One, nominated and elected in

---

[7] *Am. Arch.*, 293, 294.

[8] " 'Tis therefore hoped that . . . the choice [will be] confirmed without any sinister opposition from narrow and ungenerous sentiments." *4 Am. Arch.*, 1: 293, note.

[9] *Ibid.*, 293, 294.

[10] Bancroft, *Hist. of the United States*, 4: 10. These statements are based upon the letter of Gouverneur Morris to Mr. Penn, May 20, 1774. "Yesterday I was present at a grand division of the city, and these . . . my fellow citizens . . . fairly contended about the future forms of our government, whether it should be founded upon aristocratic or democratic principles. I stood in the balcony, and on my right hand were ranged all the people of property, with some few dependents, and on the other all the tradesmen." The entire letter is well worth consulting for those who wish to understand the situation at this point. Printed in full in *4 Am. Arch.*, 1: 343. *Cf.* Dawson, *Westchester County*, 12, note.

[11] *4 Am. Arch.*, 1: 294, 295. *New York Mercury*, May 23, 1774. Quoted in Dawson, *The Park and its Vicinity*, 57.

[12] *4 Am. Arch.*, 1: 295. "And Francis Lewis added *Nem. Con.*" *New York Mercury*, May 23, 1774. Lewis was one of the twenty-five.

this manner, represented a victory for conservative ideas is clear enough:[13] the movement from first to last was in the hands of conservative leaders, while the committee, as finally composed, included only twenty-four of the slate prepared at the radical caucus, with twenty-seven added by the merchants. But the majority, thus numerically stated, fails in a signal manner to express the real force with which the committee was to stand for moderation and conservatism, not to say hesitation. Possible though it is to speak broadly of the two factions of merchant and mechanic, of conservative and radical, it is yet necessary to remember that by no means was there perfect homogeneity within either of these two factions. Of the twenty-four members taken from the committee nominated by the mechanics, not all were radical *Sons of Liberty* like Isaac Sears or Alexander MacDougall;[14] of the remaining twenty-seven members, not all certainly were ready, like Peter Van Schaack, to stand for the king in the face of steady and unrelieved persecution, when the appeal to arms finally came. These were the two extremes: there were perhaps eleven men in the committee who might be classed with Sears and MacDougall,[15] nearly twice that number remained loyal to the king.[16] Between these extremes

---

[13] A letter to Boston, ascribed by Thomas Young to James Rivington, says: "You may rest assured no non-im. nor non-exportation will be agreed upon, either here or at Philadelphia. The power over our crowd is no longer in the hands of Sears, Lamb, and such unimportant persons. . . . their power . . . expired instantly upon the election of the . . . Fifty-one, in which there is a majority of inflexibly honest, loyal, and prudent citizens." Quoted in Thomas Young to John Lamb, June 19, 1774; Lamb MSS., (1774–1775). It was the general opinion. *Cf. 4 Am. Arch.,* 1: 299, note, 372. Colden, *Letter-Book,* 2: 242, 433. *New York Col. Doc.,* 8: 433.

[14] The radical committee of twenty-five was composed partly of conservatives, probably in order that it might be more readily accepted at the meeting of May 16. Alsop, Bache, Richard Yates, Sharp. were of this sort.

[15] July 8, eleven members formally withdrew from the Committee. They may be taken as the extreme radicals. They were: Lewis, Hallett, MacDougall, P. V. B. Livingston, Sears, Randall, Lott, Lispenard, Broome, Brasher, Van Zandt. See below, note 43. All of these but Hallett and Brasher were members of the twenty-five.

[16] Flick, *Loyalism in New York,* 22, note 4, says that "no less than twenty-one members of the Committee later became avowed loyalists." He makes James Duane a loyalist, however, which is of course an error. I have found only nineteen of the committee who can be called loyalists. They are: Alsop, Bayard. Bache, Nicoll. Moore, Low, Laight. Pearsall. Wm. Walton. Abr. Walton. Yates, De Lancey, Sherbrooke, Thurman, Wallace, Jauncey, Van Schaack, Young, McAdam.

stood the remaining members of the committee: unlike those who ultimately became loyalists, they were ready for forcible resistance when that seemed to them the only alternative; unlike the *Sons of Liberty*, they believed in negotiation and compromise, they feared the growing political influence of the unfranchised, the "levelling spirit of New England."[17] For the moment, therefore, the middle group worked with the more extreme conservatives for the accomplishment of two main objects—the settlement of the quarrel with England along conservative lines, and the exclusion of the unfranchised classes and their leaders from further political influence.

The new committee met for the first time on Monday, May 23. An organization was effected by the election of Isaac Low as chairman and John Alsop as deputy chairman.[18] A subcommittee was immediately appointed to answer an important letter from Boston, which stated that the port act had been met in that city by resolutions of complete non-intercourse, and requested the support of New York in the passage of a similar measure.[19] The merchants of New York, however, had already voted down complete non-intercourse, and had declared for the

---

[17] Philip Livingston was one who "seems to dread New England, the levelling spirit," etc. *Works of John Adams*, 2: 351. "Mr. MacDougall gave a caution to avoid every expression here which looked like an allusion to the last appeal. He says there is a powerful party here who are intimidated by fear of a civil war . . . another party, he says, are intimidated lest the levelling spirit of New England should propagate itself into New York. Another party are prompted by Episcopalian prejudice against New England. Another party are merchants largely concerned in navigation, and therefore afraid of non-importation . . . agreements. Another party are those who are looking up to government for favors." *Ibid.*, 350. *Cf.* Flick, *Loyalism in New York*, 30, 31.

[18] *4 Am. Arch.*, 1: 295. *New York Mercury*, May 30, 1774. Duane, Jay, and Van Schaack were appointed a committee to draw up a set of rules for the regulation of the committee's procedure. One week later, May 30, rules were reported and adopted. Among others were rules providing that the secretary should not be a member of the committee; that no question once determined by a majority should be reconsidered except with the consent of a majority; that the committee should meet on adjournment and if special meetings were called a printed notice must be left at each member's house; that the meetings were to be secret, free access to the records being granted to the public only in the presence of a member; and that absences should be punished by fines. *4 Am. Arch.*, 1: 298, 299.

[19] *4 Am. Arch.*, 1: 296, 297. For proceedings in Boston *cf. ibid.*, 331. Thomas Young to John Lamb, May 13, 1774; Lamb MSS. (1774-1775).

non-importation of such commodities only as were now or might in the future be taxed by the English government. But such a policy, while it might be serviceable in resistance to taxation, was scarcely applicable to the situation in which the port act would place Boston on the first of June. The question that now faced the conservatives was consequently a serious one. Of three possible answers, one must be returned: to refuse the request of Massachusetts and maintain the conservative policy of modified non-intercourse; to grant the request of Massachusetts and identify themselves with the radicals; or to suggest some new method of procedure. The port act had aroused popular sympathy to such an extent as to make the first impracticable for the moment, even had the committee itself wished to leave Massachusetts without support. The second was out of the question, since it would be virtually equivalent to a surrender of all the ends gained in the long struggle with the *Sons of Liberty.* A new method of procedure was therefore suggested: the committee proposed a continental congress, to which all quest.ons involving the relations of the colonies to the mother country should be referred.[20] The sub-committee accordingly prepared a carefully worded letter, dated May 23, in reply to the Boston correspondence; the offering of sympathy with which the letter opened was chilled by the reminder that no action could

---

[20] Bancroft is authority for the statement that the old committee of the *Sons of Liberty* "Were the first to propose a general congress. These recommendations they forwarded through Connecticut to Boston, with entreaties to that town to stand firm." *History of the United States,* 4: 9. Roberts, *New York,* 2: 389, says that a recommendation for a congress was sent to Boston, dated May 14, and signed by Sears and MacDougall. It is certain that a letter, dated May 14, was sent to Boston, for extracts of such a letter were published in the *Boston Gazette,* May 23, 1774. The letter is obviously from a radical source, and may very well have been written by MacDougall, but there is no suggestion in it, so far as published, for a continental congress. I have had the Boston newspapers, for this period examined, but without finding in them any letter from New York signed by Sears and MacDougall, or any earlier than that of the Fifty-One suggesting a general congress. When the *Boston Gazette* containing the extracts mentioned above reached New York towards the end of the month, the committee made a strict enquiry "to find out the author and have in particular called upon the late committee to answer whether or not they had wrote, or know anything of the writing of that letter—which all deny." Colden to Tryon, May 31, 1774; *Letter-Book,* 2: 343. The next number of the *Mercury* contained a formal disclaimer of the letter. *New York Mercury,* June 6, 1774.

be of permanent benefit which did not express the united voice
of the colonies; the committee could, therefore, return no answer with reference to the "expedient" suggested by the Boston letter, but emphasized the necessity of immediately assembling a general congress.[21] The plan was favorably received
in many colonies, and ultimately Massachusetts also agreed to
it.[22]

But by referring the matter to a general congress the conservatives had by no means rid themselves of the troublesome
question of non-importation. A congress once determined upon,
it became necessary to elect delegates to it, and in this election the old issues reappeared: were the delegates to be conservatives or radicals, and in either case were they to be instructed to work for absolute non-importation or for modified
non-importation? The possession of the committee of Fifty-One
doubtless gave the conservatives a great advantage. The committee did in a sense represent the city, and to it fell the important function of taking the initiative. But after all the committee was extra-legal, and it had no authority except the authority
of popular support. It could, therefore, duly propose questions
which must be decided by the people; and in these decisions
there inevitably arose the important question, who were the
people, and how were their wishes to be known. Were the legal

---

21 "The alarming measures of the British Parliament relative to your
. . . town . . . fill the inhabitants of this city with inexpressible
concern. As a sister Colony . . . we consider your interests as a common cause, to the redress of which it is equally our duty and our interest to
contribute. But what ought to be done . . . is very hard to be determined.
We lament our inability to relieve your anxiety by a decisive opinion. The
cause is general, and . . . we foresee that no remedy can be of avail,
unless it proceeds from the joint act and approbation of all . . . Upon
these reasons we conclude that a congress of deputies from the Colonies in
general is of the utmost moment; that it ought to be summoned without delay
and some unanimous resolutions formed . . . not only respecting your
deplorable circumstances, but for the security of our common rights. Such being
our sentiments it must be premature to pronounce any judgment on the expedient you have suggested." *4 Am. Arch.*, **1:** 297, 298. *New York Mercury*,
June 27, 1774. *Rivington's Gazetteer*, June 30, 1774. Dawson ascribes this
letter to James Duane. *Westchester County*, 17. But it is usually ascribed
to John Jay. *Cf.* Johnson, *Jay Papers*, **1:** 13, note. The judicial coldness
and the excessive caution that pervade it point to Jay as the author.

22 The Fifty-One received a letter from Boston dated May 30, which appears
to have been a reply to the radical letter of May 14. *Cf. 4 Am. Arch.*, **1:** 303.

voters alone to act as the people, or were the unfranchised also to
be included? Were the decisions to be by ballot or by mass-
meeting demonstrations? The radicals saw clearly enough that
the conservatives, under the lead of the Fifty-One, would work
for conservative candidates, for modified non-importation instructions, and for a limitation of the franchise to the freemen and freeholders. On these issues they prepared for the contest. Their only hope of success lay in securing recognition for
the unfranchised classes, and, in order to give weight to the
claims of these classes, a committee was formed, known as the
"Committee of Mechanics," which was virtually a continuation
of the organization of the *Sons of Liberty*. Ostensibly representing the mechanics only, this committee was in fact the chief
instrument through which the radical leaders made their determined fight for the election of delegates to the first Continental
Congress.[23]

Not unnaturally the radicals took the initiative by raising
the question in the committee of Fifty-One. June 27, Mac-
Dougall made a motion relative to the "most eligible mode of
appointing deputies,"[24] but it was voted to postpone the mat-

---

[23] At its first meeting, May 23, the Fifty-One received a letter from the "Body
of the Mechanics, Signed by Jonathan Blake, their Chairman," which expressed
their concurrence in the election of the Fifty-One. *Ibid.*, 295. Leake states
that the committee of the Sons of Liberty did not dissolve upon the election
of the new committee. *Life of John Lamb*, 92. As the Mechanics Committee
took its place, this was virtually true but the term Sons of Liberty is seldom
or never heard of after the election of the Fifty-One. *Cf. 4 Am. Arch.*, 1: 307.

[24] The question of the method of electing deputies gave rise to some discussion
outside of the committee. A proposal to leave the matter in the hands of
the assembly's committee elicited a broadside signed "A Citizen," dated June
30. The author (probably MacDougall. *Cf.* To the Public, June 30, 1774,
Broadsides, 1,) considers that the election of deputies calls for all the wisdom
in the province. This end will fail if the assembly's committee name the
deputies, for the committee has not the wisdom of all the freeholders. But
"the city members, assert the assembly's committee . . . are authorized
. . . to appoint the deputies. . . . The people never gave the committee this power. Therefore if they have any such auhority it must have
been delegated them by the assembly." The author demonstrates that the
assembly *did* not give this power and *could* not have done so legally, since the
people alone have the right. Delay is opposed; "if the city committee does
not without delay devise a plan for electing the deputies by votes of the people,
I submit it to you whether each ward should not be called together, and the
votes taken for Deputies by opening a poll in the manner observed in choosing
aldermen." *Ibid.* A more elaborate scheme was advocated in a Philadelphia

ter until the next meeting. June 29, the radicals forced the issue by a motion which revealed the object at which they were aiming. Assuming that the committee of mechanics was of coordinate authority with the Fifty-One, it was proposed that a ticket of five persons to be named by the letter should be referred to the former for its concurrence, and then to the freeholders and freemen. Confident, however, in the strength of their position, the conservatives felt that it should be no part of their program to recognize any other organization as sharing with the Fifty-One the right to act for the city and county.[25] At the next meeting of the committee, July 4,[26] the proposition of MacDougall was accordingly voted down,[27] and an essentially similar motion, without the objectionable clause, was made by Mr. Bache.[28] Defeated at this point, the radicals allowed the motion of Mr. Bache to pass without a division; but they at once assumed the offensive again by offering a ticket which they doubtless believed the conservatives might accept, but which, they nevertheless felt confident, would as a whole repre-

---

paper under the date of June 22. It was reprinted in a New York broadside, entitled, "To the Inhabitants of the City and Colony of New York." The author proposes that in each province those qualified to vote for assemblymen should proceed in the usual manner to elect deputies to a provincial convention, which should in turn elect from its own number delegates to the congress. The deputies from each county might then act as a county committee, and the provincial convention appoint a standing central committee. The author urges above everything that the election should be by some method which would secure the "actual, not the virtual" representation of the people. It was urged in other words, that extra-legal, far more than legal, activity needs to be broadly based in order to be efficient. *Ibid.* This article without heading or signature, is printed in *4 Am. Arch.,* **1:** 441.

[25] It was again voted to postpone. *4 Am. Arch.,* **1:** 307.

[26] When the committee met there was awaiting it a letter from the Mechanics' committee, dated July 4. I have not found the letter. *Cf.* however, advertisement, July 6, 1774; *Broadsides,* **1.**

[27] The following voted against MacDougall's motion: Bayard, Alsop, Marston, Young, Sharp, Bull, Ludlow, Sherbrooke, Beckman, Shaw, Wallace, Goelet, Duychinck, Laight, Booth, Wm. Walton, McAdam, Bache, De Lancey, Yates, Nicoll, Remsen, Sherman, McEvers. The following voted for it: Curtenius, Lewis, Sears, P. V. B. Livingston, Lispenard, Van Zandt, Brasher, Moore, Lott, Randall, Hallett, Broome, MacDougall. *4 Am. Arch.,* **1:** 308.

[28] "To nominate five persons to meet in a general congress . . . ; and that the freeholders and freemen . . . be summoned to appear at a convenient place to approve or disapprove of such persons." Carried without a division. *Ibid.*

sent radical views. The ticket proposed consisted of Isaac Low, James Duane, Philip Livingston, John Morin Scott, and Alexander MacDougall. The first two were preëminently of the conservative party; the last two were in an equal sense radicals. But Philip Livingston was neither the one nor the other; and certainly no one could have been named more likely to win the support of the conservatives for the ticket, and at the same time secure a virtual representation for radical views in the congress.[29] The conservatives were, however, too confident of their position to accept any doubtful compromises—indeed, they were probably too much opposed to the last two names on the ticket to accept it in any case—and the names of Scott and MacDougall were presently replaced by those of John Alsop and John Jay.[30]

The nomination thus made was to be presented to the "inhabitants" of the city and county for confirmation or rejection on Thursday, July 7, at the city hall.[31] While the conservatives perhaps expected to meet with some opposition in the election of their ticket,[32] it does not appear that they gave themselves

[29] Philip Livingston was the fourth son of Philip, second lord of the manor. He took an active part in the Revolution, and was a signer of the Declaration of Independence. His whole career makes it clear that he was by no means inclined to submit to British restrictive measures. On the other hand, he was connected with the colonial aristocracy, and was known to be opposed to the growing influence of the unfranchised classes. "Seems to dread New England, the levelling spirit, etc. Hints were thrown out of the Goths and Vandals; mention was made of our hanging the Quakers, etc." *Works of John Adams,* **2:** 351.

[30] The division on the radical ticket was 25-12, being the same as on MacDougall's motion save that Lewis voted with the conservatives. De Lancey then moved that the committee proceed to nominate five candidates, "when the following had . . . the greatest number of voices, . . . viz.: Philip Livingston, John Alsop, Isaac Low, James Duane, John Jay." 4 *Am. Arch.,* **1:** 308. "I am told a violent effort was made in the committee to have John Scott, an eminent lawyer, and Alex. MacDougall, the Wilkes of New York, named in place of Jay and Alsop." Colden to Dartmouth, July 6, 1774; *New York Col. Doc.,* **8:** 469: *Letter-Book,* **2:** 346.

[31] 4 *Am. Arch.,* **1:** 308, 309. Advertisement, 5th July, 1774; *Broadsides, 1.* To The Inhabitants, etc., July 5. 1774; *ibid.*

[32] A broadside writer hoped that the "voice of the committee will be the voice of the people." Nevertheless, in view of the existence of "turbulent tempers," and the late attempt to appoint a committee of twenty-five, he fears objections may be raised on Thursday, and a demand be made for a "poll." Against the latter, he counsels resistance. To the Inhabitants, etc., July 5, 1774; *Broadsides,* 1.

much concern about the matter. The radicals, on the other hand, were far from idle during the three days from Monday to Thursday. On Tuesday, July 5, the Committee of Mechanics met at Edward Bardin's tavern, and, having taken into consideration the ticket nominated by the Fifty-One, rejected the names of Duane and Alsop, which they replaced by the names of Leonard Lispenard and MacDougall.[33] The next day a broadside was circulated announcing that this ticket would be proposed at the meeting on Thursday in opposition to the ticket of the Fifty-One. Candidates had thus been nominated; a platform was necessary. Tuesday, July 5, a broadside was accordingly circulated by the radical leaders, calling a meeting "in the fields" for six o'clock the following evening.[34] This meeting was presided over by MacDougall, who announced that the principal business of the evening was to counteract, as far as possible, the "vile arts" of their enemies in "distracting the councils of America." For this purpose a series of resolutions was twice read, "and the question being separately put on each of them, they were passed without one dissentient." In essence, these resolutions asserted that, since the liberties of America could best be preserved by a policy of absolute nonintercourse, the New York delegates should be empowered (and were thereby empowered) to bind the province to such a policy. The committee of correspondence was formally instructed to carry out these resolutions, which were printed and sent to all of the colonies as expressing the well-considered sentiments

[33] "Advertisement. At a general meeting of the Committee of Mechanics, at the home of Edward Bardín, yesterday evening, the nomination of the Committee of Merchants, of deputies . . . was taken into consideration, and . . . a negative was placed upon Messrs. Duane and Alsop, and Mr. Leonard Lispenard and Mr. Alexander MacDougall were nominated in their stead. And as the Committee of Merchants did refuse the Mechanics a representative on their body, or to consult with their committee, or offer the names of the persons nominated to them for their concurrence, the mechanics . . . and every other friend to the liberty of his country, are . . . requested to attend at the general meeting at the City Hall tomorrow (being Thursday) at 12 o'clock . . . to give their voices for the five following persons, or to choose such others as they may think proper. Isaac Low, Philip Livingston, John Jay, Leonard Lispenard, Alexander MacDougall. Wednesday, July 6, 1774." *Broadsides*, 1.

[34] Advertisement, July 5, 1774; *Ibid. Dawson. The Park and its Vicinity*, 61.

of the city.[35] The radicals now had a ticket and a platform; with these in hand they were ready, like any modern party, to "go before the people" on the following day.

The proceedings of the meeting at the city hall on Thursday, July 7, are known only imperfectly. Ostensibly, both factions attended with no other purpose than the election of deputies. No election, however, for reasons which can only be conjectured, took place. It is possible that the vote was indecisive; or it may be that the conservatives prevented the question from coming to a vote at all, foreseeing, from the result of the meeting in the Fields the day before, that a mass-meeting vote, from which the unfranchised could not well be excluded, would probably defeat their ticket. Whatever the reason, the fact is that a new method of election was determined upon, so vaguely defined, nevertheless, that both factions evidently regarded it with favor. The new method amounted substantially to this: The Committee of Fifty-One and the Committee of Mechanics, acting together, were to canvass the city and county for votes on the candidates already nominated by the two factions.[36] That this plan might be carried out with no unneces-

---

[35] It was at this meeting that Alexander Hamilton is alleged to have made an enthusiastic speech. *Cf.* Hamilton, *Works of Hamilton,* 1: 22, 23. I have found no contemporary reference to the fact. *Cf.* also, Dawson, *Westchester County,* 25, note. The resolutions adopted were in substance as follows: (1) Port Act unconstitutional; (2) An attack on one colony is an attack on all; (3) Closing of any port unconstitutional; (4) General non-importation agreement will result in repeal of Port Act; (5) New York delegates to be instructed for general non-importation agreement; (6) This meeting will abide by all measures of congress for above objects; (7) A provincial convention would be a proper method of choosing deputies to congress; counties requested to appoint delegates to such a convention if they appprove of it; (8) Subscription to be circulated to aid people in Boston suffering from Port Act; (9) Committee of Correspondence for the city instructed to carry out their resolutions, which are to be printed and sent to other colonies. *New York Mercury,* July 11, 1774. *Rivington's Gazetteer,* July 14, 1774. *4 Am. Arch.,* 1: 312, 313. Dawson, *Westchester County,* 61. Hamilton, *Works of Hamilton,* 1: 21-23. Leake gives the date of this meeting incorrectly. *Life of John Lamb,* 93.

[36] The proceedings of this meeting are related in the Minutes of the Committee of Fifty-One as follows: " . . . it was unanimously agreed that this committee appoint a committee of their body to attend with the Committee of the Mechanics at Mr. Fraunces' at 10 o'clock to-morrow morning, in order to appoint two or more persons in each ward . . . to take with them a list of the five persons nominated by this committee, and also a list of the five persons nominated by the Committee of the Mechanics . . . and exhibit to the

sary delay, the Fifty-One assembled at six o'clock the same evening, and appointed a sub-committee to meet with a similar committee from the Mechanics at Fraunces' Tavern on the following day. The sub-committee was instructed to offer to the Mechanics the following plan for carrying out the agreement made at the city hall:[37] (1) that the two sub-committees should appoint two or more persons in each ward; (2) that the persons so appointed should take the ticket nominated by the Fifty-One and the ticket nominated by the Mechanics, and present both of them to the "freeholders, freemen, and such of the inhabitants who pay taxes;" (3) that each voter should be permitted to sign either ticket. This plan, while conceding something in the matter of suffrage, made individual selection impossible. It was very likely designed by the Fifty-One for the express purpose of defeating MacDougall, since it forced those who might be willing to sacrifice Duane *or* Alsop for Mac-Dougall (and the popularity of MacDougall made it probable that there were many such) to sacrifice *both* of them. So, in any case, the sub-committee of the Mechanics interpreted it. Consequently they objected to the plan, and proposed in its stead that the seven candidates should be offered as a single list, from which each voter should choose any five, the five receiving the highest number of votes to be declared elected.[38] To this

---

freeholders, freemen, and such of the inhabitants who pay taxes, both lists, leaving it to their election to sign either, for the five names nominated by the committee, or for the five nominated by the Committee of Mechanics." *4 Am. Arch.*, 1: 309. This purports to be an exact statement of the resolution entered into at the City Hall; it is impossible to say whether it is so, or whether it is merely the Fifty-One's interpretation of that agreement. The latter supposition is borne out by a letter of MacDougall's, published two days latter, in which he announces his resignation as a candidate. "When I consider the manner in which the Committee of Correspondence have determined to carry the resolution at the City Hall into execution, I conceive your votes cannot be properly taken. They have determined that the papers containing the names of the five persons nominated by the Committee of Correspondence, and the five nominated by the Committee of Mechanics shall be presented to the voters, and that they must vote for one or other of the five . . . or not be allowed to vote at all. This deprives the people of voting for any five of the seven." MacDougall to the Freeholders, July 9, 1774 ; *Broadsides,* 1.

[37] *4 Am. Arch.,* 1: 309. The committee consisted of: Hallett, Shaw, Sears, Goelet, Lewis, Curtenius, Sharp, Laight, Bull. *Ibid.,* 310.

[38] "That seven columns should be ruled, one for each of the persons nominated, and that the elector's name should be put down and the persons in respective columns for whom he should vote." MacDougall to the Freeholders, July 9, 1774 ; *Broadsides,* 1.

it appears that the conservatives in turn refused to agree, for on Saturday MacDougall resigned as a candidate on the ground that the plan of the Fifty-One was unfair.[39]   There is no evidence that the canvass was ever made.

So far as the election of delegates was concerned, the situation was now precisely what it had been; the Fifty-One had nevertheless been forced to recognize the Committee of Mechanics, and had found it impossible to limit the suffrage to freeholders and freemen.   It was not the Mechanics' Committee, however, which particularly sharpened the edge of conservative resentment, but the fact that the radical members of the Fifty-One used every effort outside of the committee to defeat the execution of measures which they were unable successfully to resist within the committee.   The meeting of the Fields, July 6, which had contributed more than anything else to the fiasco at the city hall, had been presided over, and very likely instigated and called, by a member of the Fifty-One, without its sanction, in his mere private capacity.   Such proceedings could not pass without notice.   Accordingly, at the meeting of the committee in the evening of July 7, Mr. Thurman introduced a resolution of censure, disavowing the meeting in the Fields and its proceedings, on the grounds, first, that no individual had authority to call a meeting of the city, and second, that no series of resolutions should be agreed to by the city, until well considered by the committee and presented by it to the public in the regular manner.[40]   This resolution, which passed by a vote of twenty-one to nine,[41] was followed by a motion to publish the minutes of the committee relating to it, which was also carried, by a vote of thirteen to nine—eight members apparently

---

[39] *Ibid.*

[40] *4 Am. Arch.*, **1:** 310.   Extracts of the Proceedings, July 7, 1774; *Broadsides*, **1.**   *Rivington's Gazetteer*, July 14, 1774.   *New York Mercury*, July 11, 1774.

[41] *Affirmative:* Bull, Remsen, Alsop, McEvers, Beekman, Sharp, Young, Booth, Wallace, Thurman, Nicoll, Bache, Laight, Wm. Walton, Shaw, Goelet, Moore, Hoffman, Sherbrook, Bayard, Ludlow. *Negative:* Lewis, P. V. B. Livingston, Lispenard, Sears, Randall, Curtenius, MacDougall, Lott, Hallett. *4 Am. Arch.*, **1:** 311.

having left the chamber before the vote was taken.[42] If a conservative account is to be believed, eight of the nine members who opposed these resolutions immediately ordered their names to be erased from the membership roll, and on the following day, July 8, published a formal resignation, in which they were joined by three other members, absent the evening before.[43] The eleven who thus resigned included the leading radicals. Whether they only awaited a favorable opportunity to withdraw cannot now be known; it is certain that the small minority in which they found themselves, and the uncompromising temper exhibited by the majority, must have convinced them of the uselessness of remaining longer on the Committee of Fifty-One. Their resignation was justified on the ground that the right of the people to assemble and adopt resolutions was not conditioned by the will of any committee whatever, while the printing of the resolution of censure was an unusual and unnecessary procedure, calculated to encourage the English government, and destructive of the ends for which the committee had been elected.[44]

---

[42] *Ibid.*, 312. The radicals claimed that the motion to publish was made after the adjournment had been moved, when "some members were gone, and one going down stairs." *Ibid.*, 314. In any case, eight of those voting on the previous motion did not vote on the resolution to publish. Whether they did not vote because they had left, or whether they left because they did not wish to vote, does not appear. "Let those who quitted the chamber in a rage, ordering their names to be struck off, and afterwards bawling along the street '*The Committee is dissolved, the Committee is dissolved!*' . . . be answerable for the consequences of a division." One of the committee, etc., July 9, 1774 ; *Broadsides,* **1.** *Rivington's Gazetteer,* July 14, 1774. *4 Am. Arch.,* **1:** 314.

[43] The three members who resigned but were not present at the meeting of July 7, were Brasher, Van Zandt, and Broome. Of the nine who voted against Thurman's motion to disavow the meeting of the Fields, all resigned save Curtenius. *Rivington's Gazetteer,* July 14, 1774. *4 Am. Arch.,* **1:** 314.

[44] In the letter of resignation it was stated that "printing the proceedings of the committee has been agitated several times, and judged inexpedient." According to the rules, proceedings were secret. *4 Am. Arch.,* **1:** 299. At first the minutes were not published, though accounts of what was done were reported to the papers. "This day they will assemble again. Afterwards it is hoped their proceedings will be published for the information of their constituents." *New York Mercury,* June 13, 1774. Mr. Thurman's motion appears to have been the first of the minutes to be published *in extenso.* It was not mere personal spite, as suggested in the letter of resignation, that led the Fifty One to publish its proceedings in this instance contrary to custom. The resolutions of July 6, which they were now disavowing, had been "held up to the world" as the well-

No serious attempt was made to induce the dissatisfied members to withdraw their resignation.[45] The event, therefore, marks the failure of the effort to direct the opposition to Parliamentary legislation through an extra-legal organization representing both factions. It was inevitable that the minority should secede and form a committee of its own. From this time the struggle no longer centered in the rivalry between conservatives and radicals within the Fifty-One: the contest was now between the two committees, each representing a faction, each in a position to compel recognition from the other. The conservatives had attempted to give to the Fifty-One, in some measure, the character of a government; the radicals had forced it to take, without qualification, the position of a party organization. The time was not yet ripe for the transformation of either party organization into a government.

While both parties thus organized had fixed upon candidates, the radicals had in addition formulated (in their resolutions of July 6) the policy for which those candidates stood—a policy which was clear-cut and well understood. Hitherto the conservatives had given no more definite indication of what their candidates stood for than might be gathered from the noncommittal letter to the Boston committee; the aggressiveness of their opponents now forced this question to the front. Having disavowed, in a formal manner, the radical resolutions

---

considered views of the city and county, when, as a matter of fact, they constituted a party program merely; the conservatives wished them to be understood as such. "You are told that 'The people have an undoubted right to convene themselves and come to whatever resolutions they shall think proper.' . . . This is granted . . . ; but you would think me a very impudent fellow . . . if I, as a member of that committee, was to call you together this evening by an anonymous advertisement and propose a set of resolves . . . of the last importance, without . . . consulting your committee upon that occasion. This was the ground of the committee's conduct." One of the committee, etc., July 9, 1774; *Broadsides*, 1. *4 Am. Arch.*, 1: 314. *Rivington's Gazetteer*, July 14, 1774. *Cf.* William Smith to Philip Schuyler, July 19, 1774; Lossing, *Schuyler*, 1: 282. [Lossing has incorrectly dated this letter July 9.] The resignation was published in a broadside. To the Inhabitants, etc., Broadsides, 1. Also in *Rivington's Gazetteer*, July 14, 1774; and *4 Am. Arch.*, 1: 313, 314.

[45] *Cf.*, however, A moderate man, to the Freeborn citizens, etc., July 11, 1774; *Broadsides*, 1. *Lenox Broadsides*, 30. His proposition that the seceders should return was ridiculed by Agricola, To the Inhabitants, July 12, 1774; *ibid.*

of July 6, the Fifty-One was left with no alternative but to publish resolutions that it would avow; a course of mere negation could win the conservatives nothing, while it left their candidates with no other strength than their own personal influence and their individual reputations for a more or less extreme conservatism.

On the evening of July 7, a sub-committee was accordingly appointed to draw up resolutions to be proposed to the people, "expressing their sense of the Boston Port Act, and our concurrence with such of the neighboring colonies as have declared what may . . . be done for . . . the redress of American grievances."[46] A subterfuge lurked in some measure, in these directions, since a square meeting of the issue required a statement of the instructions which the conservatives believed should govern their candidates if they were sent to Philadelphia. The resolutions themselves, which were reported at the next meeting of the committee, laid the conservatives open, only the more flagrantly, to the charge of evasion and insincerity. On the direct questions they asserted that it was premature to instruct the delegates, who ought nevertheless to be in a position to pledge the colony to any policy which might be deemed expedient. As to what that policy should be, the resolutions went only so far as to suggest that if a non-importation agreement were entered into, it should be "very general, and faithfully adhered to," otherwise such an agreement could serve no good purpose.[47] While these resolutions of the Fifty-One lacked the

---

[46] 4 *Am. Arch.*, 1: 312.

[47] These resolutions are not included in the minutes as published in the *American Archives*. Under date July 13, the editor has the following in brackets: "The committee appointed on the 7th instant, presented a set of resolutions to be presented to the city." 4 *Am. Arch.*, 1: 315. This is not strictly correct. Three members of the committee appointed on the 7th had resigned from the Fifty-One. The remaining members, doubting their authority to draw up resolutions, appeared on the 13th and referred this matter to the general committee. A new sub-committee was then appointed, and this committee presented a series of resolutions which in substance were as follows: (1) Loyalty to George III fully asserted; (2) Port Act unprecedented and arbitrary, and (3) not the result of the destruction of the tea merely; (4) vengeance separately directed is the most dangerous; therefore it is the duty of all the colonies to give every "reasonable assistance" to Massachusetts; (5) the proposed congress is the most advisable method of procedure; (6) premature to instruct delegates; (7) only the direst necessity would justify measures injurious to the English mer-

clear-cut positiveness of the radical resolutions of July 6, it is doubtful if they were so constructed for any mere vote-catching purpose, since they certainly added nothing to the influence and reputation of the candidates themselves. It may be supposed rather that they were truly expressive of the hesitation and uncertainty which characterized the views of so many of the committee at this time. However this may be, the resolutions were accepted by the Fifty-One, which ordered them published, and directed that the people should be assembled to act upon them. And, since the two parties had failed to agree upon the method of canvassing the city for votes on the delegates, the committee now fell back upon the original method of election by mass-meeting; it was accordingly ordered that the conservative candidates should be offered to the people at the same time as the resolutions. The date fixed upon for this meeting was the 19th.[48]

It is clear enough, even in the absence of documents, that the radicals accepted the challenge to a popular election on the 19th; for they controlled the meeting from first to last,[49] though it is difficult to determine in all respects just what they succeeded in doing. It appears that the conservative, rather than the radical, ticket and resolutions were presented to the people for their decision—perhaps because the meeting had been called by the Fifty-One, perhaps because (and the sequel bears this

chants; (8) a non-importation agreement only partly observed, like the last, would be worse than none; (9) delegates should be so chosen as to be able to pledge themselves for the colonies they represent; (10) thanks due to friends in England. Proceedings of the Committee of Correspondence in New York July 13, 1774; *Broadsides*, 1. *Hist. MSS. Com.*, 14: Pt. 10, p. 223. These resolutions were afterwards slightly modified by the committee; as modified they appear in the minutes. *4 Am. Arch.*, 1: 316.

[48] Proceedings of the Committee, July 13, 1774: *Broadsides*, 1. *4 Am. Arch.*, 1: 315.

[49] There appears no record of any formal organization of the radicals preparatory to this meeting; but it is not to be doubted that they were well agreed as to what should be done. The influence of men like MacDougall and Scott was very great with the people, and street-corner caucuses were the order of the day. One broadside writer, in speaking of the former, mentions "his eloquence so liberally bestowed at the corner of every street where he can find . . . people to be his auditors." To the Public, July 20, 1774; *Broadsides*, 1. In any case the radicals were sufficiently well organized to elect J. M. Scott chairman, though he himself denied any knowledge that such was the intention. To John M. S——, Esq., July 23, 1774; *Broadsides*, 1.

out) the radicals desired to reject the conservative ticket and resolutions without, for the moment, confirming their own.[50] The decision of the people with reference to the delegates was apparently affirmative in character, though by no means decisive, for on the following day a card appeared, signed by Low, Alsop, and Jay, stating that "notwithstanding the proceedings of yesterday at the Coffee House," the sense of their fellow-citizens "remains so uncertain" that they cannot consider themselves or any others as duly elected.[51] As for the resolutions, it is certain that, having been subjected to a severe criticism by the chairman, they were rejected.[52] It seems, however, to have been no part of the radical plan to present their own resolutions of July 6 to the meeting for its decision. After the action of the meeting on the conservative candidates, they doubtless saw clearly that no decisively affirmative result could be obtained for any proposition to which there was any serious objection; from the very nature of a mass meeting a decision must be useless unless unanimous, or nearly so. The radicals could scarcely hope, therefore, to gain anything by presenting their resolutions of July 6. But if compromise was necessary, they were unwilling to intrust the duty of arranging it to the committee of Fifty-One. The meeting accordingly proceeded to name a new committee, composed of five conservatives and ten radicals, which was instructed to draw up a fresh set of resolu-

---

[50] "They [the Fifty-One] have since published resolves, and today the town meets to approve or disapprove of them. Those who know the populace say nothing will be done, but a motion be made to amend them." Smith to Schuyler, July 19, 1774 ; Lossing, *Schuyler*, **1**: 282.

[55] To the Respectful Public, July 20, 1774 ; *Broadsides*, **1**. *New York Mercury*, July 25, 1774. *Rivington's Gazetteer*, July 21, 1774. *4 Am. Arch.*, **1**: 317. The same idea is expressed in the minutes of the committee ; "the sentiments of the majority still remaining uncertain," etc. *4 Am. Arch.*, **1**: 315.

[52] "Certain resolves having been proposed . . . at the Coffee House yesterday and rejected," etc. To the Respectful Public, July 20, 1774 ; *Broadsides*, **1**. A letter from New York to Boston states that the resolutions "were rejected as destitute of vigor, sense, and integrity." *4 Am. Arch.*, **1**: 317, note. "It was he [J. M. Scott] who harangued the people, and prevailed upon them to discard the resolutions of their Committee of Fifty-One, as void of vigor, sense, and integrity." *Works of John Adams*, **2**: 346. *Cf.* to John M. S——, Esq., July 23, 1774 ; *Broadsides*, **1**.

tions to be presented at a future meeting.[53]   The conservatives, defeated at every step, still refused, nevertheless, to surrender the initiative.   On the morrow, when the new committee of fifteen was summoned to meet at Mr. Doran's, only the ten radical members responded in person to the call.[54]   The conservative members sent a letter in which they stated their refusal to serve on a committee which, in their opinion, was too irregularly elected to draw up authoritative resolutions: in any case, their own views being expressed in the modified resolutions of the Fifty-One, they could be of no service in the present instance.[55]   Having read this letter, the ten members proceeded to draw up a series of thirteen resolutions, which were at once less vague than those of the Fifty-One, and less extreme than those adopted at the radical meeting of July 6.   The rights of the colonies were more vigorously asserted than in the former, while, on the other hand, without instructing the delegates in any way, it was agreed that the province should consider itself bound by the decision of the congress.[56]

Certainly these resolutions conceded much to the conservatives —so much, indeed, that the two factions no longer had any serious grounds for difference, especially as the Fifty-One had at

[53] The committee was composed of five of the radicals who had resigned from the Fifty-One; P. V. B. Livingston, Lispenard, MacDougall, Sears, Randall: and of five who had never been on the Fifty-One; J. M. Scott, James Van Varck, Wm. Goforth, John Lamb, Theo. Anthony; and of five conservatives from the Fifty-One; Low, Moore, Remsen, Jay, and Duane. At this time, Duane was out of the city. *New York Mercury,* July 25, 1774.

[54] *Ibid.*

[55] To the Respectful Public, July 20, 1774 ; *Broadsides,* 1. *New York Mercury,* July 25, 1774. *4 Am. Arch.,* 1: 317.

[56] These resolutions may be summarized as follows: (1) allegiance to the king; (2) allegiance entitles to protection and equal rights; (3) the common inheritance of all British subjects to be free from taxes not laid personally or by representatives; (4) taxes on colonies unconstitutional; (5) Port Act unparalleled in rigor and destructive to liberty; (6) and is more dangerous than if directed against all colonies alike; (7) duty of all to oppose Port Act; (8) minds of all should be as one; (9) therefore we approve the congress; (10) and will abide by its decision; (11) best method of electing delegates by provincial congress; (12) thanks due to our agent in England; (13) approve conduct of Committee of Fifty-One relative to Boston poor.   These resolves were ordered printed and a meeting was called at the city hall, July 25, to act upon them. *New York Mercury,* July 25, 1774. For criticism of Democritus, Remarks upon the Resolves of the New Committee, July 22, 1774 ; *Broadsides,* 1.

the same time taken measures to strengthen their own resolutions somewhat.[57] This substantial agreement in respect to resolutions was possible, however, only on condition that the real question at issue should be left out of consideration; in waiving the question of instructions, the resolutions became of secondary importance, and all interest once more centered in the delegates.[58] At its meeting on the evening of the 19th, the Fifty-One had, indeed, again brought forward its scheme of canvassing the city for the votes of the "freeholders, freemen and such others who pay taxes" on the candidates whom they had nominated.[59] On the other hand, the committee of fifteen (or of ten, since the conservative members refused to act) had, in its resolutions of the 20th, suggested a provincial convention, and meanwhile had called a meeting of the city for the 25th, to receive its report. So far as is known, nothing came of the proposition of the Fifty-One. In response to the call issued by the committee of fifteen, a number of persons did, indeed, come together on the 25th, but as to what was done, one must needs be content with the statement that "nothing decisive was resolved upon."[60]

At this point, after more than two weeks of practically fruitless maneuvering, the Fifty-One finally came forward with a plan which was carried out so swiftly and smoothly that the inference of a previous arrangement is all but imperative. A singular lack of information for the period from July 20 to July 25, and the meagre account of the meeting on the latter date, make it entirely possible that such an arrangement was

---

[57] The conservatives were not unwilling to change their resolutions, and public criticisms pointed out the way. *Cf.* To the Freemen, July 16, 1774; *Broadsides*, 1. On the evening of July 19, after the meeting at the Coffee House, certain amendments were ordered in the resolutions of July 13. *4 Am. Arch.*, 1: 315. Article 2 was changed to express a more vigorous opposition to the Port Act. Article 3 was made to state that the main object of the Port Act was to subject the colonies to taxation. Article 7 was made to express greater solicitude for the liberties of the country, and less for the welfare of the English merchants. *Ibid.*, 316. Proceedings of the committee, July 19, 1774; *Broadsides*, 1.

[58] *Cf.* To the Respectful Public, July 25, 1774; *Broadsides*, 1. *Lenox Broadsides*, 30.

[59] *4 Am. Arch.*, 1: 315.

[60] "Last Monday, a large number of the inhabitants . . . attended at the City Hall, but nothing decisive was resolved upon." *Rivington's Gazetteer*, July 28, 1774. *New York Mercury*, August 1, 1774.

entered into at that time; while the fact that the plan was proposed at a meeting of the Fifty-One on the evening of the 25th
(the very day on which the general meeting called by the committee of fifteen was held) tends strongly to confirm such a
supposition.[61] The plan in question, which was moved by Mr.
Remsen, was substantially as follows: (1) that the polls be
opened at the usual places in each ward on Thursday, July 28,
at nine o'clock in the morning, to elect "five deputies for the
city and county of New York;" (2) that, "in order that the
same may be conducted in the most unexceptionable manner,"
the election be supervised in each ward by the aldermen, common council and vestry, by two persons appointed by the Mechanics Committee and by two persons appointed by the Fifty-
One; (3) that freeholders, freemen and persons "who pay
taxes" be deemed qualified to vote.[62] This plan, which required
a distinct concession from the conservatives, did not differ essentially from the proposal which the radicals had previously
made, and they were found quite willing to settle the matter in
this way.[63] But instead of adhering to their own ticket, as one
might expect them to do in view of the steady gains lately made
at every point, the radicals at once took steps for withdrawing
that ticket in favor of the conservative candidates. On the 26th
a meeting was held at Mr. Mariner's, which sent a letter by committee to the conservative candidates stating that, if the latter
would agree to work sincerely in the congress for a complete
non-importation agreement, the radical ticket would be withdrawn, otherwise not.[64] To this letter four of the conservative

---

[61] The editor of the *Lenox Broadsides,* 30, asserts that the hand bill of Remsen
was sent out by the meeting, at the city hall. I have found no evidence supporting this contention, but think it very likely the true one. The resolutions
of Remsen were carried in the committee in the evening, and ordered printed
in hand bills. I have not found the hand bill, which would perhaps throw
some light on the action of the meeting. *4 Am. Arch.,* 1: 318. *New York Mercury,* August 1, 1774. *Rivington's Gazetteer,* July 28, 1774.

[62] *4 Am. Arch.,* 1: 318.

[63] *Ibid.,* 320.

[64] "Whether . . . you will engage to use your utmost endeavors at the
proposed congress, that an agreement not to import goods from Great Britain
until the American grievances be redressed, be entered into by the Colonies
. . . If you will so engage, the body by whom we are nominated will
support you, if not that body have a set of candidates who will." *4 Am. Arch.,*

candidates replied on the following day that they would use their "utmost endeavors to carry every measure into execution at the proposed congress, that may then be thought conducive to the general interests of the colonies; and, at present, are of opinion that a general non-importation agreement, faithfully observed, would prove the most efficient means to procure a redress of our grievances.''[65]   This reply was found satisfactory by the meeting at Mr. Mariner's, and it was then unanimously resolved to confirm the nomination of the conservative candidates.[66]   The election now became a mere matter of form. On July 28 the poll was opened; the election passed off quietly, and in the evening the Fifty-One, having duly examined the lists, had the satisfaction of recording that Philip Livingston, Isaac Low, John Jay, John Alsop, and James Duane, "the persons nominated by this committee,'' were unanimously elected.[67]

Whether prearranged or not, this agreement between the two factions is somewhat difficult to understand. It is not strange perhaps that the Mechanics should have made the proposal, for they may have been informed of the willingness of the conservative candidates to accede to it; nor strange perhaps that those candidates should have entertained such demands favorably, for they may have despaired of winning in any other way an election upon which they were determined at any cost.   The curious part of it is that the radicals at Mr. Mariner's should have been satisfied with the reply which was returned to them, for in no essential respect did the conservative candidates pledge themselves to carry out the radical program; they merely said they were *at present* in favor of a non-importation agreement *faithfully observed*, and at the congress would work for whatever seemed *then* for the best interests of the country.   The conservatives had said as much as this before.[68]   It was far from

---

1: 319. *New York Mercury,* August 1, 1774. *Rivington's Gazetteer,* August 4, 1774. The members of the sub-committee were, Brasher, Theo. Anthony, Francis Van Dyck, Jer. Platt, and Christian Duychink. *New York Journal,* July 28, 1774.

[65] 4 *Am. Arch.,* 1: 319.

[66] *Ibid.*

[67] *Ibid.,* 320.

[68] *Cf. ibid.,* 316.

saying (what the radicals had demanded of them) that they would "use their utmost endeavors" to secure a non-importation agreement. As a matter of fact, the influence of the New York delegates in the congress was exercised along conservative lines.[69]   It is difficult, therefore, to see why the conduct of the conservative candidates should call for particular comment, not to say censure; it is rather the conduct of the radicals which seems inexplicable.

Meanwhile, the committee of Fifty-One had not confined its attention exclusively to the election of the city delegates; it was also seeking for support in the rural counties. That the committee should have expected to receive such support was perhaps not unreasonable, since the country population was strongly conservative, the stamp act and the Townshend act having created but little excitement outside of the city.[70]   It is no way remarkable, therefore, that one of the first acts of the committee of Fifty-One should have been directed to the formation of similar committees throughout the colony.   Although the rural districts may not have had the same interest in opposing absolute non-intercourse as the merchants of New York, it was indisputable that the conscious conservatism of the great landowners, and the instinctive conservatism of the small farmers, would lead them to support the Fifty-One rather than the Mechanics. The vital question was, could this conservative majority be induced to take any positive action at all, or would it remain passively aloof, thus leaving the field open for the radical minority?[71]   Without seeing, or without fearing, this danger, the Fifty-One, at its second meeting, May 30, appointed a sub-com-

---

[69] Not only did they work for conservative measures, but the general feeling at the time of the election was that they would do so. *Cf. ibid.*, 953. Colden, *Letter-Book*, 2: 350, 352, 360. *Cf.* also, Seabury, *What Think Ye of Congress Now?* 18.

[70] *Cf.* Dawson, *Westchester County*, 26, 27. Lossing, *Schuyler*, 1: 288. Albany was active in the stamp act period. *New York Mercury*, January 27, 1766. *New York Gazette*, January 23, 1766. *Cf.*, also, Colden, *Letter-Book*, 2: 97. *New York Col. Doc.*, 7: 825, 845.

[71] *Cf.*, nevertheless, Colden to Dartmouth, November 2, 1774; 4 *Am. Arch.*, 1: 957. "I am afraid the business in the counties will be left to a few forward and intemperate men, who will undertake to speak for the whole." Colden to Tryon, June 2, 1774 ; *Letter-Book*, 2: 344.

mittee to draft a circular letter to all the counties in the province.[72] The letter, which was reported on the following day,
acquainted the counties with the appointment of the Fifty-
One, and suggested that each county should appoint a similar
committee to correspond with it.[73] Of the three hundred
letters which were ordered printed, a certain number was sent
to the treasurer of each county, who in turn was instructed to
distribute them to the supervisors.[74]

This appeal met with no general response. So far as is known
positively, only three counties took any action in the matter.
These were Suffolk, Orange, and Cumberland.[75] The earliest
action was taken by the "inhabitants of the parish of Southhaven," in Suffolk County, who met on June 13, appointed
William Smith moderator, voted resolutions in favor of absolute non-intercourse, and appointed a standing committee of
seven to correspond with the committee "in New York city and
others."[76] Eight days later a "town meeting" of Huntington
passed similar resolutions and appointed a committee "to act,
in conjunction with the other towns in the county, as a general
committee of the county, to correspond with the committee of
New York."[77] Resolutions of some sort were drawn up at Shel-
ter Island and Easthampton also, while it is possible that the
"general committee" spoken of in the Huntington resolutions
may have been formed.[78] Only one town in Orange County appears to have responded to the letter of the Fifty-One. On

---

[72] 4 *Am. Arch.*, **1**: 299. *Cf.* Van Schaack to Silvester, May 21, 1774; Van
Schaack, *Life of Van Schaack*, 17.

[73] 4 *Am. Arch.*, **1**: 300.

[74] *Ibid.*, 301.

[75] The Fifty-One received a letter from Tryon County dated June 22, one
from Albany dated June 29, and one from Dutchess dated June 29. 4 *Am.
Arch.*, **1**: 308, 309. It is likely that these letters were replies to the request
of the committee; it is even likely that some favorable action was taken in
the case of Albany, for the letter was signed by Jacob Lansing. who was chairman of an Albany committee in August. *Cf.* Lossing, *Schuyler*, **1**: 289. Onderdonck, *Documents and Letters . . . of Queens County*, 14. In the
case of Tryon County this letter was probably from the supervisors stating that
Tryon County would take no part whatever in the dispute with the mother
country. 4 *Am. Arch.*, **2**: 151.

[76] *New York Mercury*, June 27, 1774.

[77] Resolutions strongly favored non-importation. 4 *Am. Arch.*, **1**: 453.

[78] *Ibid.*, 307, 308.

July 4 the freeholders and inhabitants of Orange town passed resolutions favoring non-intercourse, and appointed a committee of five to correspond with the city of New York.[79] In Cumberland County it appears that the supervisors refrained from laying the letters before the towns, with the intention of saying nothing and doing nothing about it. But in September it became known that such letters existed, and a delegation from Rockingham and Westminster waited upon the supervisors and insisted that the directions of the Fifty-One should be carried out. This was finally done, however reluctantly, and on October 19 and 20 a "county congress" was held at Westminster, consisting of eighteen delegates from twelve towns, which passed a series of resolutions and appointed a committee of five to correspond with New York.[80]

It will thus be observed that, with the exception of Cumberland (and its action was not taken until long after the New York delegates had been elected), none of the counties responded to the letter of May 31 by what could in any sense be called an authoritative action. Not only so, but the individual towns which did reply must have disappointed the committee, since every one of them, so far as there is record, declared for complete non-intercourse. This meant merely—what the Fifty-One had perhaps failed to foresee—that the conservative spirit of the counties was first expressed, as it had, indeed, been expressed in New York City itself, negatively and not positively—that is, by refusing or neglecting to take any part whatever in the movement. The effort of the Fifty-One to strengthen its own position by appealing to the rest of the province had, therefore, no other immediate practical result than that of encouraging the radicals to hope for support where they had probably never expected to find any; in the light of the resolutions from Suffolk and Orange, it is not difficult to understand the proposal for a provincial convention, which was incorporated in the radical resolutions of July 6, and again in those of July 20.

But the Fifty-One did not despair in the face of one defeat.

---

[79] *Ibid.*, 506.
[80] *Ibid.*, 2: 218, 1064, 1065.

If the conservative elements in the counties failed to appoint
committees for a general purpose, it was hoped that they would
at least see the necessity of making their influence felt in the
specific matter of electing delegates to congress. On July 29,
accordingly, a second circular letter was prepared by the Fifty-
One, and sent to all the counties in the province. Each county
was urged either to elect delegates of its own or to authorize,
in explicit terms, the New York delegates to act for it.[81] The
result was, nevertheless, but little less discouraging than before.[82]
Three counties only sent delegates of their own—Kings, Orange,
and Suffolk—and in none of them can it be said, certainly, that
the election was a representative expression of the county's
wishes.[83] In Orange County, Henry Wisner and John Haring
were chosen, on August 16, by "a meeting of the several committees of the County of Orange."[84] The term "several committees" indicates that this was a delegated county meeting; if
so, it may have been fairly representative of the county. On the
other hand, Colden understood it to be a primary rather than a
delegated meeting, for he speaks encouragingly of the fact that
out of one hundred freeholders in the county "not twenty persons" attended.[85] Of the election of William Floyd from Suffolk, still less is known; he was present at the congress on the
first day and presented credentials which were considered satisfactory.[86] The election in Kings County, as related by Galloway, recalls the oft-repeated story of old Sarum. Two persons
assembled; one was made chairman, the other clerk; and the

---

[81] *Ibid.*, **1**: 322.

[82] "Seven counties . . .   neither appointed delegates for themselves, nor
concurred in the choice made by the city." Colden to Dartmouth, September 7,
1774; *Letter-Book,* **2**: 360.

[83] "In the counties that have joined in the measures of the city I am informed
that the business has been done by a very few persons, who took upon themselves to act for the freeholders." Colden to Dartmouth, October 5, 1774;
Letter-Book, **2**: 367; *4 Am. Arch.,* **1**: 819; *New York Col. Doc.,* **8**: 493.

[84] *4 Am. Arch.,* **1**: 322, note.

[85] Colden, *Letter-Book,* **2**: 367. *4 Am. Arch.,* **1**: 819. *New York Col. Doc.,*
8: 493.

[86] *4 Am. Arch.,* **1**: 893. Bayles, *Suffolk,* 107.

latter certified to the congress that the former, Mr. Simon Boerum, was unanimously chosen for the county of Kings.[87]

Four counties, in a more or less authoritative way, authorized
the New York delegates to act for them. These were Albany,
Westchester, Dutchess, and Ulster.[88] Albany certainly elected
delegates of its own,[89] but for some reason the New York delegates were ultimately authorized to act in their stead.[90] The
action of Westchester was the most representative of any of the
four. Meetings were held in the individual towns of Bedford,[91] Mamaronee,[92] Rye,[93] and Westchester,[94] and on August
22 a general county meeting, which authorized the New York
delegates to act for Westchester, was assembled at White
Plains.[95] The action of Dutchess County is not very clear, and
certainly was not representative.[96] At least three meetings were

---

[87] *Examination of Joseph Galloway,* 11. Galloway stated that he had the
story from "almost all the delegates of New York." *Ibid.,* 61. However elected,
Kings was certainly not enthusiastic, for it was one of the counties which, as
late as September 29, were urged to send delegates, and Boerum did not take
his seat until October 1. *4 Am. Arch.,* 1: 326, 906.

[88] Ulster is not usually included with Albany, Dutchess, and Westchester because congress received no credentials from that county authorizing the New
York delegates to act for it. *Ibid.,* 896. But action was taken in Ulster quite
as authoritative as in Dutchess, and it was one of the four to send a deputation to New York to authorize the delegates of the latter county to act. To
the Public, January 18, 1775; *Broadsides,* 1. *4 Am. Arch.,* 1: 1188.

[89] The action of Albany County is not clear. A meeting in Albany on August
13 resolved that Robt. Yates, Peter Silvester, and Henry Van Schaack should
be the delegates if "approved by the majority of the delegates from the several districts at a general meeting for the county." *4 Am. Arch.,* 1: 322, note.
But on August 23, Jacob Lansing, chairman of the Albany committee, wrote
to Colonel Schuyler informing him that he, Schuyler, had been appointed a delegate. Lossing, *Schuyler,* 1: 284. This is confirmed. "The county of Albany
have chosen Philip Schuyler, Esq., to represent them as a delegate at the general congress." *Rivington's Gazetteer,* September 1, 1774. *Cf. New York Mercury,* September 5, 1774.

[90] *4 Am. Arch.,* 1: 326, 896.

[91] *Ibid.,* 325.

[92] *Ibid.*

[93] Meeting on August 10. Committee of five, and five resolutions agree'ng
to abide by decisions of congress. *New York Mercury,* August 15, 1774. *Rivington's Gazetteer,* August 18, 1774. Baird, *Rye,* 219. There was opposition to
these measures. *4 Am. Arch.,* 1: 703, 803.

[94] *New York Mercury,* August 29, 1774. *4 Am. Arch.,* 1: 703.

[95] *4 Am. Arch.,* 1: 1188, 1189. Dawson, *Westchester County,* 31, 32.

[96] August 10, a meeting of freeholders at Poughkeepsie, of which Z. Platt was
chairman, decided not to appoint delegates. Resolutions were passed favoring
action through the assembly. No mention was made of congress or of the New

held in Ulster County at which the New York delegates were authorized to act for those present, if not for the whole county.[97] The remaining six counties were apparently entirely unresponsive to the appeal of the Fifty-One.[98]

Thus, after a long and bitter conflict, the conservatives succeeded in electing their ticket, with instructions that were in no way prejudicial to conservative feeling. They did not succeed, however, in ignoring the radical organization, or in excluding the unfranchised classes from taking an effective part in the conflict. It remained to be seen what action the continental congress would take: whatever that action might be, it was certain to affect profoundly the future course of provincial politics.

York delegates. 4 *Am. Arch.*, **1:** 702. Yet on August 20 Platt informed the Fifty-One that his precinct authorized the New York delegates to act for it. *Ibid.*, 324. Later the Fifty-One received another letter from Poughkeepsie, dated August 31, "approving the resolves and delegates of New York." *Ibid.*, 326. Whether other meetings were held is not known, but in any case both the New York delegates and the congress were informed of the wish of Dutchess to be represented through the New York delegates. To the Public, Janaury 18, 1775; *Broadsides,* **1.** 4 *Am. Arch.*, **1:** 896. Smith, *Dutchess County*, 340.

[97] Kingston and New Winsor approved "of the delgates adopted for the city and county of New York." 4 *Am. Arch.*, **1:** 325. "Wednesday last (August 31) a great number of inhabitants of Ulster County had a meeting and agreed in sentiment with their brethren in New York, and did not intend sending any delegates to . . . Philadelphia." *New York Mercury.* September 5. 1774. The New York delegates were informed of Ulster's wishes by committee (To the Public, January 18, 1775; *Broadsides,* **1.**) but no authorization was sent to congress.

[98] In Tryon County the Palatine district was active in approving the New York delegates. 4 *Am. Arch.*, **1:** 740. But apparently a majority of the county was in favor of taking no part in the congress. *Ibid.*, **2:** 151. Seabury voiced the feeling of the extreme conservatives in saying that the delegates did not represent a hundredth part of the people. "It is notorious that in some districts only three or four met and chose themselves to be a committee on this most important occasion." *The Congress Canvassed,* 9. The fact probably is, however, that many conservatives who, like Seabury, denounced the congress after it adjourned, were at this time passive supporters of the movement, because they hoped that it might promote conciliation. Seabury was himself such a supporter of the congress. That the delegates were elected by a very small minority in New York is, however, absolutely certain.

CHAPTER VI

THE FIRST CONTINENTAL CONGRESS

In sending delegates to a general congress, the two factions in New York virtually agreed to throw the burden of formulating a policy of resistance upon a power outside the colony; consciously or unconsciously they thereby greatly increased the difficulty of ever again having a policy of their own. If congress formulated a definite policy of any sort, that policy would represent the position of the colonies as against Great Britain, and from that moment any local faction could dissent from the measures of congress only at the risk of appearing to countenance, to that extent, the measures of Parliament.[1] And if, in addition to formulating and recommending a policy of resistance, Congress should take steps to enforce its recommendations upon all individuals alike, the effect would be to raise an altogether new issue—the issue of allegiance. In order to understand the further development of parties in New York, it will be necessary, therefore, to know rather precisely what the first Continental Congress did.

When Congress assembled, September 5, 1774, representative men of all factions were looking to it for the accomplishment of ends which they had most at heart. From the instructions to the delegates, the conservatives were encouraged to hope that a conciliatory policy would prevail.[2] The radicals, on the other

---

[1] In October Colden wrote: "I am certain a majority of the most considerable [merchants] are convinced it [non-intercourse] is a wrong measure, and wish not to come in to it, but whether they will have resolution enough to oppose the sentiments of all the other colonies, can only be known when they are put to the trial." *New York Col. Doc.,* 8: 493.

[2] The instructions, almost without exception directed the delegates to work for reconciliation. Ford, *Journals,* 1: 15 ff. "The hopes of all moderate . . . persons . . . were long fixed upon the general American Congress."

hand, were determined upon the more vigorous measure of non-intercourse.[3] And finally, there were many moderates, of whom Jay and Duane were typical, who were aiming to hold the balance between the extremes of both groups; without precipitating rebellion, they hoped for a firm union of the colonies in measures that were free from any charge of undue submissiveness.[4]

The first question to arise was one of jurisdiction. Before the formal opening, delegates were asking each other whether Congress was an informal body with power of advice only, or a government with power to enforce its recommendations. The conservative feeling was expressed by Rutledge. "We have no legal authority," he said, "and obedience to our determinations will only follow the reasonableness, the apparent utility and

---

Chandler, *A Friendly Address*, 30. "We ardently expected that some prudent scheme of accommodating our unhappy disputes . . . would have been adopted." Seabury, *Free Thoughts*, 3. *Cf.* Seabury, *What Think Ye of Congress Now?* 6, 11 ; *The Congress Canvassed*, 8, 13. "It was the general expectation that decent petitions would be presented to Parliament." Galloway, *Hist. and Pol. Ref.*, 66.

[3] Galloway asserts that there at once appeared two parties, one for petition and one for independence. *Hist. and Pol. Ref.*, 66. Low said, "We have too much reason to suspect that independence is aimed at." *Works of John Adams*, **2**: 394. R. H. Lee told Adams that the congress should demand the repeal of every revenue act and the coercion acts, and the removal of the troops. *Ibid.*, 362. "The Boston commissioners are warm, and I believe wish for a non-importation agreement, and hope the colonies will advise and justify them in a refusal to pay for the tea until their grievances are redressed. They are in their behavior and conversation very modest, and yet they are not so much so as not to throw out hints, which like straws and feathers, tell us from which point in the compass the wind comes." Letter from one of the Delegates [Galloway], September 3, 1774 ; 1 *New Jersey Arch.*, **10**: 475. "The Virginians and Carolinians, Rutledge excepted, seem much among the Bostonians. . . . The gentleman from New York has as little expectation of much satisfaction from the event of things as myself." *Ibid.*, 477.

[4] Jay and Duane supported Galloway's plan, but afterwards signed the association. *Works of John Adams*, **2**: 389. They were inclined to oppose the selection of Charles Thompson, who was regarded as "the Sam Adams of Philadelphia," as secretary. *Ibid.*, 358, 365; *Cf.* Galloway's version, 1 *New Jersey Arch.*, **10**: 477. Duane was much interested in inserting in the resolutions an acknowledgment of the right of Parliament to regulate trade. *Works of John Adams*, **2**: 397. Duane was considered by some as a "violent supporter of Congress," while a recent historian has dubbed him "loyalist." *Cf. Hist. MSS. Com.*, **14**: Pt. 10, p. 237. Flick, *Loyalism in New York*, 34, note 1. Adams himself stated : "We have a delicate course to steer between too much activity and too much insensibility." *Familiar Letters*, 40. The moderate view is well expressed by Washington in a letter to Robert MacKenzie, October 9, 1774 ; *Works of George Washington*, **2**: 443.

necessity of the measures we adopt."[5]   The New York delegates undoubtedly held this view.[6]   On the other hand, there were those who believed with Patrick Henry that "Government is dissolved. Fleets and armies and the present state of things show that government is dissolved:"[7]—a statement of which the obvious corollary was that Congress possessed *de facto* the authority which had ceased elsewhere. The question thus raised was of more than academic importance, because with it was bound up the practical question of the means that Congress could use in maintaining the rights of the colonies. The value of the non-intercourse measures, which Massachusetts wished to carry,[8] depended upon the possibility of enforcing them upon the colonies, and the New York delegates and some others[9] questioned the propriety of such measures because they could not be carried out. This objection the radicals could meet by asserting either that the people would voluntarily keep such agreements—which all experience disproved—or that Congress should assume sufficient governmental authority to enforce its recommendations upon all alike. Thus early did the question of policy raise the profounder question of power, and the question of power bring the Congress face to face with the question of revolution.

With the instinct of true Britons, the delegates kept the theoretical question in the background, and ultimately avoided it altogether. Before the close of the third day, a committee was appointed to state the rights and the grievances of the colonies, and to suggest means of redress.[10] The committee sat daily for some time, and the questions referred to it were undoubtedly fully discussed.[11] As a result of these discussions, the cautious Jay came to the conclusion that there were only three means of securing redress: "Negotiation, suspension of commerce, and war." War, he is reported to have said, was "by general con-

[5] *Works of John Adams,* 2: 344, 367.

[6] *Ibid.,* 368.

[7] *Ibid.,* 366.

[8] *Cf. Letter from Galloway,* September 3, 1774 ; *1 New Jersey Arch.,* 10: 475.

[9] Hutchinson's *Diary,* 1: 296. *1 New Jersey Arch.,* 10: 474, 476, 477.

[10] Ford, *Journals,* 1: 26. *4 Am. Arch.,* 1: 899.

[11] *Works of John Adams,* 2: 374.

sent to be waived at present.''[12] Low's suspicions[13] to the contrary notwithstanding, there appears to have been no deliberate intention of precipitating war; and the alignment of parties in the Congress was made on the question of non-intercourse *versus* negotiation. There is indirect evidence that the non-intercourse proposal was once voted down, and that, a petition having been drawn up, the Congress was on the point of adjourning when certain events turned the drift of sentiment toward more radical measures.[14] However this may be, it is certain that for the first fortnight the radicals had no advantage at least.[15] Toward the end of September, however, two influences contributed to weaken the conservatives and leave the radicals in control. These were the events at Boston and the letters from England.

From first to last, indeed, the predicament of Boston was of prime importance in shaping the action of Congress. It was the Boston Port Bill that had brought about the Congress in the first instance, and since the Massachusetts delegates were keen for non-intercourse it was difficult to oppose that policy without incurring the charge of unfriendliness.[16] Nevertheless, had any kind of accommodation between Gage and the Bostonians been reached during the first weeks of September, the action of Congress might easily have been different than it was. But no accommodation seemed possible; on the contrary, with every hour

---

[12] *Ibid.*, 385.

[13] "We have too much reason . . . to suspect that independence is aimed at." *Ibid.*, 394.

[14] Hutchinson reports this on authority of Pownall, who claimed that every step in congress was reported by correspondence. "The New York and New Jersey men were determined against non-importation . . . and others came in and carried a vote against it; and they agreed to present a Petition to the King which Adams drew up; . . . and they expected to break up, when letters arrived from Dr. Franklin, which put an end to the Petition, and obtained a vote for non-importation." Hutchinson's *Diary*, 1: 296.

[15] *Cf.* Galloway, *Hist. and Pol. Ref.*, 67.

[16] Quincy told Lord North that the Congress would undoubtedly adopt non-importation, as "otherwise, the delegates from Massachusetts Bay would be much dissappointed." Hutchinson's *Diary*, 1: 301. Seabury reflected the later extreme opposition to congress in saying that the conduct of the radical party of Boston was timed to influence congress. *The Congress Canvassed*, 12. 13. Galloway asserts that the radicals sought to use the events at Boston to create sympathy for radical action. *Hist. and Pol. Ref.*, 67.

almost, the situation became more tense. The very day that Congress assembled, Gage began to fortify Boston Neck, and the next day the Suffolk County convention drew up those famous resolutions which placed Massachusetts in a state of rebellion. Rumors were current that Boston was being bombarded,[17] and within a fortnight the Suffolk resolutions were placed before Congress for confirmation. The position of Congress was a difficult one.[18] To countenance the Suffolk resolutions and then to stick at non-intercourse was, indeed, to strain at the gnat after the camel was already down. Yet even those conservatives who believed the conduct of Massachusetts rash and impolitic naturally found it difficult not to confirm its resolutions. It was now a question of accomplished fact: it was one thing to believe that the Suffolk resolutions were too radical, quite another deliberately to strengthen the government in its contest with a neighboring colony. The Congress was in the dilemma of countenancing rebellion or striking at that unity of action of the necessity of which Congress was itself the chief expression.[19]

Meanwhile the letters from England strengthened the feeling that it would be most inpolitic, whatever the merits of the controversy might be, to take any step that would indicate lack of unity in the colonies. The belief was gaining ground, chiefly through the letters of Franklin,[20] that the opposition in England was wholly in sympathy with the colonial contentions, and that a few months at most would witness the fall of the ministry and the inauguration of a policy of conciliation. If the Congress be unanimous for non-importation, wrote Franklin, "you cannot well fail of carrying your point. If you divide you are

---

[17] Adams, *Familiar Letters,* 31.   Seabury, *The Congress Canvassed,* 12, 13.
[18] Adams, *Familiar Letters,* 40.
[19] The Suffolk resolutions were regarded as of vital importance in England. Hutchinson regarded them as more alarming than anything that had yet occurred. *Diary,* 1: 272.   Dartmouth was "Thunderstruck." *Ibid.,* 273.   The king said that New England was in rebellion. Donne, *Correspondence of George III.,* 1: 215.   The conservatives in America thought the same. *Cf.* Seabury, *What Think Ye of Congress Now?* 21.
[20] Hutchinson, *Diary,* 1: 296, 359.   "Many letters were written from Great Britain recommending it." [Non-importation.] Galloway, *Hist. and Pol. Ref.,* 63.   Without union, says one correspondent, "Any expedient they may think proper to adopt will, I fear, avail little." London Letter, July 30, 1774; *New York Journal,* September 29, 1774.   *Cf. ibid.,* October 20, 1774.

lost."[21] As a result of these considerations, the delegates were turning from the theoretical to the practical question; from the question of the precise demands they were justified in making to the question of the probable effect of whatever demands might be made.[22] The colonies, no less than the home government, were possessed of the fatal delusion that the other side would back down.

Such was the situation when the Suffolk resolutions were laid before Congress, September 17, 1774. These resolutions declared that the coercion acts were a gross violation of the constitution; that, therefore, "no obedience is due from this province to either or any part of the acts above mentioned," but that they be regarded as the "attempts of a wicked administration to enslave America." An absolute non-importation agreement was recommended. The inhabitants were urged to arm themselves. Provision was made for a provincial congress. Finally, they were "determined to act merely upon the defensive, so long as such conduct may be vindicated by reason and the principles of self-preservation, but no longer."[23] When the issue was presented in this definite fashion, a sufficient number of conservatives joined the radicals to confirm the resolutions. If they were passed "unanimously," as the journals officially declare, and Adams and others asserted, it could only have been a formal unanimity. We cannot suppose that all of the delegates were willing to vote for them. It is safe to say that the crucial contest of the congress was over the confirmation of these resolutions, and

---

[21] Franklin to Timothy, September 7, 1774; *Works of Benjamin Franklin,* 8: 132.

[22] This attitude was in evidence from an early date. R. H. Lee favored a bold stand because he thought it would result in immediate redress, otherwise "he should be for exceptions." *Works of John Adams,* 2: 362. *Cf.* Hutchinson's *Diary,* 1: 296, 297, 555. On the other hand, Low pointed out that Parliament might not back down; therefore, it would be wise "to provide ourselves with a retreat or a resource." *Works of John Adams,* 2: 394. Dartmouth thought the congress was not prepared to back up its declarations, but would "wait to see how it was received." Hutchinson's *Diary,* 1: 251. White wrote to Tryon that congress was confident the non-importation would make Britain tremble. *Hist. MSS. Com.,* 14: Pt. 10, p. 237. And that the association was only "hung out *in terrorem* to Great Britain." *Ibid.,* 232. Hamilton expressed this attitude exactly in his reply to Seabury; the conduct of congress was justified partly because it would probably succeed. *A Full Vindication,* 12.

[23] Ford, *Journals,* 1: 31, 32. 4 *Am. Arch.,* 1: 901-904.

there is reason to think that the division, in this as in other matters of importance, was not permitted to appear in the journals.[24] However that may be, the Suffolk resolutions were officially declared to have passed unanimously, and the people of Boston were recommended to perserve "in the same firm and temperate conduct that had hitherto distinguished them."[25]

The approval of the Suffolk resolutions was the decisive event of the first Continental Congress: it was equivalent to a declaration for the policy of non-intercourse, and it disposed of the policy which the conservatives had first advocated—that of confining the action of Congress to the presentation of a petition.[26]

---

[24] According to the *Journals,* "Congress resolved unanimously." Ford, *Journals,* **1:** 39. Adams makes the statement without qualification. *Works of John Adams,* **2:** 380 ; *Familiar Letters,* 39. But Galloway states that "long and warm debates ensued between the parties," and, when the vote carried, "two of the dissenting members presumed to offer their protest against it in writing which was negatived. They next insisted that the tender of their protest and its negative should be entered on the minutes ; this was also rejected." *Hist. and Pol. Ref.,* 69. In the examination before Parliament in 1779, Galloway stated that he and Duane protested against the resolution of October 8, and tried to get their protest recorded, but were refused. *Examination of Joseph Galloway,* 58. It is quite possible that there was only one protest, and that in one or the other of these statements Galloway was mistaken. If there was but one protest, it is difficult to understand why it should have been against the resolution of October 8, when the Suffolk resolutions, which were more important, had already been passed. This is, however, a minor point. It is certain that the only sense in which the Suffolk resolutions were passed unanimously is that a majority of delegates from every colony voted for them. No matter how strong the opposition was, if every colony voted for a measure it was entered *Nem. Con.* or *Unanimously. Examination of Joseph Galloway,* 56. Seabury says, that it was agreed at the beginning that "neither protest nor dissent should appear upon their minutes." *Free Thought,* 24. Since the vital contest in the congress was whether non-intercourse measures or petitions only should be carried, it is impossible to suppose that there was no opposition to the Suffolk resolutions. Besides, we know perfectly that the minutes were falsified in respect to Galloway's Plan, and that a protest either to the Suffolk resolutions, or to the resolution of October 8, was denied. There is every reason to suppose, therefore, that whatever opposition there may have been to the Suffolk resolutions was suppressed precisely as in other instances. It may be concluded that while the Suffolk resolutions were passed unanimously as to colonies, there was a strong opposition as to individual delegates. The only indication which the *Journals* give of opposition to any measure is that some resolutions are recorded *Resolved Unanimously,* and others *Resolved, etc.*

[25] Ford, *Journals,* **1:** 39. *4 Am. Arch.,* **1:** 904.

[26] The vote on the Suffolk resolutions laid "the foundation of military resistance." *Hist. and Pol. Ref.,* 69. Seabury thought it put reconciliation out of the question. *The Congress Canvassed,* 13. "From that time every moderate man . . . has despaired of seeing any good produced by the Congress." Chandler, *A Friendly Address,* 31.

Accordingly, the radicals at once began to work out the details of an effective non-intercourse scheme. September 22, a resolution was carried requesting the merchants to send no more orders to England, and to cancel such as had not been filled.[27] Five days later more precise form was given to this recommendation: it was resolved that after December 1 no goods should be imported directly or indirectly from Great Britain or Ireland, and that no goods so imported should be purchased or consumed in · any colony.[28] But the conservatives were not yet ready to renounce all hope of defeating radical measures. They prepared a counter-move, and September 28 Galloway introduced his plan for a British-American Parliament.[29] It was a serious and practicable proposal for permanent reconciliation.[30] The motion of Galloway was seconded by Duane,[31] and a second motion was then made to enter the plan upon the minutes and to refer it for further consideration. Upon this motion "long and warm debates ensued." The conservatives, including Jay and Rutledge, supported the motion, and it was carried by a majority of one colony.[32] Further consideration for the plan could not be secured, however. The news from Boston was daily more alarming,[33] the con-

---

[27] Ford, *Journals,* **1:** 41. *4 Am. Arch.,* **1:** 904.

[28] Ford, *Journals,* **1:** 42. *4 Am. Arch.,* **1:** 905.

[29] Ford, *Journals,* **1:** 43. Galloway had come to the congress with the idea of proposing representation in Parliament. Governor Franklin to Dartmouth, September 5, 1774 ; *1 New Jersey Arch.,* **10:** 474. *Cf.* Letter of Galloway, September 3, 1774 ; *ibid.,* 476. The feeling that representation was impracticable doubtless led to the change. *Ibid.,* 474.

[30] "Greatly approved of by some of the most sensible men in that city" [New York]. Governor Franklin to Dartmouth, December 6, 1774 ; *1 New Jersey Arch.,* **10:** 503. Rutledge was of opinion that it was almost a perfect plan. *Works of John Adams,* **2:** 390. Dartmouth was much in favor of some such constitutional union. Dartmouth to Colden, Jaunary 7, 1775 ; *New York Col. Doc.,* **8:** 529. "How amazing it is my Lord that when a rational mode of proceeding, evidently tending to a reconciliation, was introduced and supported by men of the best judgment, the Congress should prefer a method big with wickedness." Colden to Dartmouth, the December 7, 1774 ; *ibid.,* 513.

[31] *Works of John Adams,* **2:** 389.

[32] "Warm and long debates ensued on the question whether it should be entered on the proceedings of Congress or be referred to further consideration. All the men of property, and most of the ablest speakers supported the motion while the republican party strenuously opposed it. The question was at length carried by a majority of one colony." Galloway, *Hist. and Pol. Ref.,* 81. *Cf. Works of John Adams,* **2:** 387 ff. *1 New Jersey Arch.,* **10:** 504.

[33] *Cf.* Ford, *Journals,* **1:** 55–58.

servatives lost their majority, and ultimately, probably October 21,[34] it was voted to expunge the plan, and all resolutions referring to it, from the minutes.[35]

Meanwhile, the policy of non-intercourse was worked out. September 30 the non-exportation resolution was passed.[36] A few days later, in reply to a communication from Boston, it was resolved that "this Congress approve of the opposition by the inhabitants of Massachusetts Bay, to the execution of the late acts of Parliament; and if the same shall be attempted to be carried into execution by force, in such case, all America ought to support them in their opposition."[37] The reports of the committees on the association, on the addresses, and on the petition, were now presented in rapid succession and adopted, with what opposition cannot be learned. Probably there was but little. The radical policy was a foregone conclusion, and even Galloway and Duane signed the Association.[38] October 26, having carried through radical measures by a bare majority, rather than with that cordial unanimity which the journals reported, the congress was dissolved.[39]

It is usually maintained that the first congress carried through a conservative policy. The explanation of this fact is that an altogether excessive attention has been given to the addresses and the petitions. Of these, certainly, there was a sufficient number: the Petition to the king, the Address to the People

---

[34] "Met, dismissed the plan for a union." *Ward's Journal*, October 22. 1774: *Mag. of Am. Hist.*, 1: 442. It seems certain that the plan was not expunged until after October 20, the date of the signing of the association, for Galloway says he was induced to sign the association in the expectation that the rule referring his plan for further consideration "would have been regarded." Galloway, Candid Examination, etc.; quoted in *Works of John Adams*, 2: 387.

[35] "Rejected it, without suffering it to be discussed . . . and ordered it to be expunged from the minutes." Galloway, *Hist. and Pol. Ref.*, 82. "But, though a plan . . . was proposed . . . and even entered on their minutes, with an order referring it to further consideration, yet they not only refused to resume the consideration of it, but directed both the plan and the order to be erased from their minutes, so that no vestige of it might appear there." Governor Franklin to Dartmouth, December 6, 1774; 1 *New Jersey Arch.*, 10: 504.

[36] Ford, *Journals*, 1: 51.

[37] *Ibid.*, 58.

[38] *Ibid.*, 80.

[39] *Ibid.*, 114.

of Great Britain, the Memorial to the Inhabitants of the British Colonies, the Address to the Inhabitants of Quebec.[40] That these addresses were frank and able expositions of the colonial position, there is no question. They were, on the whole, moderate and conservative enough, and they represented well enough the ideas of the conservative delegates. Had the work of Congress been limited to the formulation of these addresses, it would be quite true that "the conservative policy carried the day and restricted the proceedings to statements of the grievances and appeals for relief."[41] But that is precisely what did not happen : the proceedings were not restricted to statements of grievances and appeals for relief. Nothing is clearer than that the vital contest throughout was over the adoption of the non-intercourse measures; and these measures were forced through in spite of conservative opposition. The addresses were mere side issues, designed undoubtedly to conciliate the conservatives in America and secure the aid of the opposition in England.[42] The fact is that the results of the first Continental Congress would have been the same had these able and lengthy papers never been penned. It was the Association that gave the congress the importance which it had;[43] it is upon the Association, therefore, that attention must be fixed if one would understand what that importance was.

The Association[44] was divided into fourteen articles, for the most part unsystematically arranged. Article one provided for the exclusion, after December 1, 1774, of all goods directly or indirectly imported from Great Britain or Ireland; of East India tea imported from any part of the world; of certain specified

---

[40] *Ibid.*, 81, 90, 105, 115.

[41] *Ibid.*, 6.

[42] "An intercepted letter from one of the Congress—Harrison to Yates—opened their intention in the Petition to the King, to be only to prevent their friends in opposition here from giving up their cause." Hutchinson's *Diary*, 1: 557.

[43] It was the Association that alienated so large a group of conservatives in New York. *Cf.* Seabury, *What Think Ye of Congress Now?* 27 ff. Hutchinson affirms that Lord North would have strained a point as regards the Petitions "if it had not been for the extravagant resolves, Associations, and Addresses." *Diary*, 1: 330. Dartmouth said that signing the Association was equivalent to an act of treason. *Ibid.*, 324.

[44] The Association is in Ford, *Journals*, 1: 75, and *4 Am. Arch.*, 1: 913.

commodities imported from the British plantations and Dominica; of wines from Madeira and the western islands; and of foreign indigo. Article three provided for the non-consumption after March 1, 1775, of commodities mentioned in article one. Article four provided for the non-exportation to Great Britain and the West Indies of all commodities whatever, except rice, after September 10, 1775, unless the laws mentioned in the statement of grievances were repealed before that date. These articles, together with article two, which referred to the slave trade, constituted that part of the Association which was directed primarily against Great Britain: they embodied the measures of non-intercourse which, by striking at the material interests of the English people, it was hoped would force concession from Parliament. There was nothing striking, certainly nothing new, in these measures. Such measures, less sweeping in extent but similar in principle, had been tried by almost every colony at different times during the preceding ten years. The superiority of the measures of Congress lay in the thoroughness with which it was proposed to apply the non-intercourse principle, in the nationalization, if one may so speak, of a policy that had hitherto been purely local. But the superiority of the congressional measures brought to the front, only the more prominently, the practical difficulty of carrying them into execution: their strength would turn to weakness if they could not be rigidly enforced. The question of measures to be taken against England was thus not more important than the question of the means to be employed in enforcing obedience to these measures in the colonies. It was to the solution of this problem that the remainder of the Association was mainly devoted. For the development of parties it is this part of the Association that gives to the work of Congress its immense significance.

The means employed to secure obedience to the non-intercourse agreement were directed equally against colonies and individuals within the colonies. ''We will have no trade, commerce, or intercourse whatsoever, with any colony or province in North America, which shall not accede to, or which shall hereafter violate, the Association, but will hold them as unworthy of the rights of freemen, and inimical to the liberty of this country." Obedience to the Association was to constitute the test of loyalty to America: for each colony the question of allegiance was thus raised, and loyalty to America was rapidly becoming incompatible with adherence to the laws of the Empire.

It was probably not anticipated, however, that there would be serious difficulty with individual colonies. In any case, the hold of Congress upon a colony as such was slight; it was only by leaving the enforcement of its recommendations to the radicals within each colony that its ends could be accomplished. The Association, therefore, defined with greater precision and at greater length the measures that were to be taken for securing individual obedience. In one sense there were two classes of individuals to deal with; those who signed the Association, and those who did not. Legally, the distinction would doubtless disappear; but practically there would be less objection to enforcing the Association upon those who signed it than there would be to enforcing it upon those who did not. Whatever the distinction was worth, little account was made of it, for in articles ten, eleven, and twelve, provisions were formulated for enforcing the Association upon all classes alike.

To this end article eleven provided: "That a committee be chosen in every county, city, and town, by those who are qualified to vote for representatives in the legislature, whose business it shall be to observe the conduct of all persons touching the Association; and when it shall be made to appear to the satisfaction of a majority of any such committee, that any person within the limits of their appointment has violated the Association, that such majority do forthwith cause the truth of the case to be published in the *Gazette*, to the end that all such foes to the rights of British America may be publicly known, and universally condemned as enemies of American liberty; and henceforth we respectively will break off all dealings with him or her." By this article the Association became virtually a law of Congress, to be enforced on all alike. The penalty, it is true, was only boycott by the members of the congress. But the nature of the penalty scarcely affects the principle involved, and as a matter

·of course the radicals who supported Congress would support
the boycott. Nevertheless, the real significance of article eleven
can be appreciated only in connection with articles ten and
twelve. The latter directed the local committee to inspect the
customs' entries frequently, while the former authorized them
to seize all goods imported contrary to the Association, and to
dispose of them according to the recommendations of Congress
and largely irrespective of the owner's wishes.[45]   The effect
of these articles was to change what would otherwise have been
a voluntary association to do certain things, into a general law
to be enforced upon all persons by boycott and the confiscation
of property.

The first Continental Congress thus did essentially two things:
it resolved that a certain line of conduct ought to be maintained against Great Britain; it provided that those who refused to follow this line of conduct should be punished by social
ostracism, commercial boycott, and confiscation of property.
These were the bald facts, however much their baldness may
have been concealed by the non-mandatory character of the language in which they found expression. For the delegates to
sign, and to recommend others to sign, an agreement not to buy,
sell, or consume certain goods was, if not in the nature of negotiation, at least in the nature of peaceable resistance. But when
an attempt was made to force those who signed the agreement to
keep it, and those who did not sign it to act precisely as if they
had, a step was taken in the direction of revolution; private
persons were aiming to compel individuals to carry out a con-

---

[45] "In case any merchant, trader, or other person, shall import any goods
or merchandise, after the first day of December, and before the first day of
February next, the same ought forthwith, at the election of the owner, to be
either reshipped or delivered up to the committee . . . to be stored
at the risque of the importer until the non-importation agreement shall cease,
or be sold under the direction of the committee aforesaid: and in the last
mentioned case, the owner or owners of such goods shall be reimbursed out of
the sales, the first cost and charges, the profit, if any, to be applied towards
relieving and employing such poor inhabitants of the town of Boston, as are
immediate sufferers by the Boston port-bill; and if any goods . . . shall
be imported after the said first day of February, the same ought forwith to be
sent back again, without breaking any of the packages thereof." Ford, *Journals,*
1: 78, 79.

tract for the enforcement of which neither the existing government nor the law made any provision; an agreement not to do
certain things which the law did not compel any one to do, became an agreement to do certain things which the law prohibited.
It was one thing for two men to agree not to buy goods of
English merchants; quite another to agree that if a third did so
they would seize the goods and dispose of them as they pleased.
That is precisely what the congress proposed to do, and in making these recommendations, it was transformed from a peaceable assembly into a revolutionary organization. While proclaiming in words its allegiance to the king, it tacitly announced
that the acts of the king's government no longer bound the
colonists; while proclaiming the Association a voluntary agreement, measures were taken to clothe its provisions with the force
of law. One of two things had happened: either the colonies
were subject to Great Britain, in which case Congress was engaged in systematic robbery, or the colonies had ceased to be subject to Great Britain, in which case Congress was something
very like a *de facto* government enforcing its own law.

A careful reading of the Association makes it difficult, certainly, to characterize the work of the first congress as conservative. The friends of the colonists in England did not so regard it.[46] In America it was thought by many to have precipitated a rebellion. If it did not precipitate a rebellion, it at
least marked a most important turning point in the history of
parties. As a result of the action of the first congress, the question of allegiance stood prominently forth for the first time, and
henceforth it remained, under various disguises, the central fact
in political history until the Declaration of Independence. With
increasing distinctness a new process is clearly observable: the
old factions, based upon differences of opinion as to how and by
whom the resistance to English measures should be conducted,
gradually gave place to parties asserting allegiance to different
authorities. In the eyes of a large group of conservatives, prac-

---

[46] "There is no doubt," Dartmouth is reported to have said, "that every one
who had signed the Association was guilty of treason." Hutchinson's *Diary,*
1: 324.

tical identification with Congress and its committees was equivalent to rebellion; while the ultra-radicals, although asserting
in words their allegiance to Great Britain, were more and more
inclined to regard any refusal to submit to the decrees of Congress as a treasonable desertion of the American cause. As the
question of allegiance became the dominant one, therefore, the
radical party organization tended more and more to be transformed into a government claiming the right to exact obedience,
while those who denied this right, those who repudiated all allegiance save to the crown, however much they may have opposed
the British measures, identified themselves with the home government in its effort to suppress what they regarded as open rebellion.

In the measure that allegiance became the principal issue,
there ceased to be any proper function for the old conservative
faction. In New York at least, this faction had hitherto embraced the great majority of the inhabitants, most of whom
however had taken no active part in the political agitation of
the time. They had opposed, with varying degrees of intensity,
the measures of Parliament; they had favored, with varying degrees of earnestness, a peaceable settlement of the quarrel; they
had believed that such a settlement was possible through calm
discussion and reasonable compromise, and that it ought to be
conducted through the assembly or through extra-legal organizations controlled by men of property with political privileges
to lose rather than by men of no property who had at best only
political privileges to gain. Throughout the next two years,
the failure of the conservative program and the dissolution of
the conservative party was steadily accomplished. With increasing sharpness, there was presented to the conservative group
the alternative of adhering to Congress even if it meant rebellion and independence, to which they had always been opposed,
or of adhering to Great Britain even if that meant submission to
those parliamentary measures to which they were also opposed.[47]

---

[47] Seabury gave exact expression to the loyalist attitude towards this alternative: "If I must be enslaved, let it be by a king at least, and not by a
parcel of upstart, lawless committeemen." *Free Thoughts*, 18.

For them the question of allegiance meant a choice between two evils. To some, the lesser evil was an unquestioning adherence to Congress; to others, an equally unquestioning adherence to the mother country; many could never decide, and remained as neutral as possible, awaiting patiently the course of events.

This process was, of course, a very gradual one, not fully completed until the Declaration of Independence. Yet, in so far as any definite date can be given, it may rightly be said that the Association of the first congress gave birth to the loyalist and revolutionist parties. The term loyalist, if it is to convey any useful meaning, must be confined to those who were prepared to side with England when for them it became a choice between submitting to Parliament or to Congress, just as the term revolutionist must be confined to those who were prepared to side with Congress under the same conditions. Some conservatives made this choice directly the resolutions of the first congress were published. The great majority of the old conservative group, however, was not yet convinced that opposition to British measures necessarily involved forcible resistance, much less independence. An effort was made, consequently, to maintain the old conservative organization, through which it was hoped to secure a conservative interpretation of the Association. When this proved hopeless, through the growth of radical influence in the organization, many still sided with the radicals in the hope of sufficiently moderating radical action to prevent hostilities. Of this group many were carried half-consciously or deliberately into revolution, some withdrew with the outbreak of war to become loyalists or neutrals, and some remained until the Declaration of Independence banished all hope of conciliation.

CHAPTER VII

THE RISE OF THE LOYALIST PARTY AND THE COMMITTEES OF THE ASSOCIATION

In New York the most striking direct result of the first Continental Congress was the appearance of active loyalist opposition. We are told that even before the Congress assembled certain Episcopal clergymen were "engaged night and day writing letters and sending dispatches to the other colonies and to England," for the purpose, it was supposed, of forming "an union of the Episcopal party through the Continent in support of ministerial measures."[1] While this supposition was largely groundless, the congress had not yet closed before the more extreme conservatives began to take an active interest in the political situation. Pamphlets and broadsides and sermons appeared in great numbers, expressing, with a freedom hitherto unknown, the reasons for opposing all measures "which must be offensive to Parliament."[2] What may be called distinctively loyalist literature now made its appearance, and it performed the functions of expressing the views of that party and of directing the conduct of its members.

The writers who have left us the clearest and fullest expression of the loyalist position were mainly Episcopalian clergymen —Seabury, Chandler, Cooper, and Inglis—who had never taken any active part in resistance to British measures, and whose

---

[1] Told to Adams by P. V. B. Livingston. *Works of John Adams,* **2**: 348. An Episcopal convention was held in New York, May 18, 1774, which may have been the origin of Livingston's story. *Cf. Hist. MSS. Com.,* **14:** Pt. 10, p. 219.

[2] "Men now speak and publish sentiments in favor of government . . . with much greater freedom . . . than has been known here for some years past." ' Colden to Dartmouth, September 7, 1774; *New York Col. Doc.,* **8:** 488. *Cf. ibid.,* 493.

creed doubtless predisposed them to submit more readily than
other men to the constituted authorities in church and state.
Even these extreme conservatives had passively supported Congress, had looked to it to effect a permanent reconciliation, or
at least to throw the weight of its influence against all measures
looking toward rebellion.[3] But when the Suffolk resolutions
were approved and Galloway's plan expunged they believed
that nothing but evil could longer be expected of Congress,[4]—
a belief which was confirmed by the Association, in which they
could see nothing but the erection of a rebellious government.[5]
In a series of pamphlets—notably those of Seabury[6]—in which
the whole question was discussed with remarkable ability and
incisiveness, the congress was accordingly denounced as having
betrayed America.[7] The writers of these pamphlets accepted the
challenge of the Association, which branded them as enemies
of liberty, and in turn branded the supporters of Congress with
the same epithet. They maintained that the conduct of Congress
was inexpedient, illegal, and tyrannical. It was inexpedient because non-intercourse would injure America more than it would
injure England,[8] and because it would be quite impossible ''to

---

[3] Seabury, *The Congress Canvassed*, 5, 13. Seabury, *Free Thoughts*, 3. Chandler, *A Friendly Address*, 30.

[4] Chandler, *A Friendly Address*, 31. Seabury, *What Think Ye of Congress
Now?* 6, 21. Seabury, *The Congress Canvassed*, 5.

[5] Congress has spent its time ''in exercising an assumed power of government.''
''Every article in this instrument was intended by them to have the force of
a law.'' Seabury, *The Congress Canvassed*, 13, 14. Seabury, *What Think Ye
of Congress Now?* 27. Chandler, *A Friendly Address*, 35.

[6] The principal pamphlets appearing at this time on the loyalist side were:
The American Querist, probably written by Cooper; *A Friendly Address*, prob-
ably written by Chandler; *What Think Ye of Congress Now?* probably written
by Seabury; and a series of four pamphlets signed A. W. Farmer, written by
Seabury. They were in order of apppearance: *Free Thoughts*, etc., *The Congress
Canvassed*, etc., *A View of the Controversy*, etc., *An Alarm to the Legislature
of the Province*, etc. All of these pamphlets appeared between July, 1774, and
February, 1775. There is an excellent summary of the Farmers' pamphlets in
Tyler, *American Revolution*, **1:** 334 ff.

[7] ''They have taken no one step that tended to peace; they have . . .
either ignorantly misunderstood, carelessly neglected, or basely betrayed the
interests of all the colonies.'' Seabury, *Free Thoughts*, 3.

[8] This was the main theme of Seabury's first pamphlet, *Free Thoughts*. The
merchants were charged with desiring non-importation for monopoly prices.
''The proof that prices will rise is that they have already risen.'' *Free
Thoughts*, 12, 13.

bully and frighten the supreme government of the nation" into making concessions.[9] It was illegal because in the Association Congress had assumed powers of government; and in assuming the powers of government a tyranny far more oppressive than the alleged tyranny of Parliament had been established.[10] "If I must be enslaved," wrote Seabury, "let it be by a king at least, and not by a parcel of upstart, lawless committeemen."[11]

In defining their position the loyalists were strong; it was in giving practical effect to their views that they were weak. They never had any party organization worthy cf the name, and in the nature of the case it was difficult for them to have one. Their position was essentially one of negation: they denied the authority of Congress; they denied the expediency of non-intercourse; their organization was the English government itself, and upon it they relied to do whatever was necessary. To attempt to suppress the extra-legal committees by force would involve the very illegal methods against which they protested. It was open to them to express their opposition to the radical program by taking part in the election of delegates or committeemen. This they usually did whenever there was an opportun-

---

[9] "Can we think to threaten and bully and frighten the supreme government of the nation into a compliance with our demands?" Seabury, *ibid.*, 6. "It will greatly distress a country which I love, and it will not answer the purpose." Chandler, *A Friendly Address,* 35.

[10] In spite of soft words "they have solemnly bound themselves and their constituents, by whom they effect to mean every inhabitant in the Colonies, . . . to adhere firmly to the Association . . . they have appointed their officers to carry it into execution—and they have ordained penalties upon those who shall presume to violate it." Seabury, *The Congress Canvassed,* 14. "To talk of being liege subjects of King George while we disavow the authority of Parliament is another p¹ece of Whiggish nonsense." Seabury, *A View of the Controversy,* 10. That Congress could bind its constituents was nonsense. "Not one person in one hundred, in th's province at least, gave his vote for their election." Seabury, *Free Thoughts,* 23. *Cf. What Think Ye of Congress Now?* 18. Chandler, *A Friendly Address,* 31.

[11] "Will you be instrumental in bringing the most abject slavery on yourselves? Will you choose such committees? Will you submit to them should they be chosen by the weak, foolish, turbulent part of the country people? . . . I will not. No. If I must be enslaved," etc., Seabury, *Free Thoughts,* 18. "They are making us the most abject slaves that ever existed." *Ibid.,* 22. Having boasted that no British Parliament should ever dispose of a penny of your money, "you suffer yourselves to be bullied by a Congress and cowed by a committee." Seabury, *The Congress Canvassed,* 16, 17. *Cf.* Chandler, *A Friendly Address,* 31.

ity to vote for or against the appointment of any committee or of any delegates whatever. But this opportunity was rarely offered; most frequently it was merely a question of voting for one set of delegates rather than another; to vote for either set would be to recognize the extra-legal program, and the refusal to recognize that was precisely what distinguished the loyalists from the conservatives. In thus withdrawing from the extra-legal movement altogether, the loyalists, in so far as they sought redress from British measures or the suppression of the radical organization, were forced to rely upon the assembly and ultimately upon the British army. The proper conduct for all true Americans was clearly outlined in the pamphlets of Seabury: they were counseled to renounce congresses, ignore committees, and prevent their election whenever possible, and for the future to rely upon their constitutional representatives in the assembly.[12] Henceforth the loyalists, in so far as they constituted a party, followed this advice, the practical effect of which was to strengthen the radicals by weakening the conservatives.

If the loyalists regarded Congress as having betrayed America, the extreme radicals naturally felt that it marked a victory for themselves.[13] The Association was a more thorough-going expression of their policy than they could reasonably have expected, or at least a more nearly perfect realization of it than they had ever achieved, or could ever achieve, perhaps, without intercolonial support. In one point only the Association did not satisfy them: the exclusion of Holland tea threatened to destroy

---

[12] "Renounce all dependence on Congress and committees. They have neglected or betrayed your interests. Turn then your eyes to your constitutional representatives. They are the true, and legal, and have been hitherto the faithful defenders of your rights and liberties. . . . Address yourselves to them. . . . Present petitions to them, entreating them to take the matter into their own hands." Seabury, *Free Thoughts,* 22. *Cf.* Seabury, *What Think Ye of Congress Now?* 42, 43, 47. The last pamphlet of Seabury was itself a petition to the assembly to save the colony from revolution. *Cf. An Alarm to the Legislature,* etc.

[13] Cooper asked "whether it be not time for our farmers and mechanics and laborers to return to their business, and the care of their families." *The American Querist,* 29. But from the mechanics' point of view, now was precisely the time to advance their political fortunes. The mechanics were at some pains to thank the delegates for their services. *Rivington's Gazetteer,* November 24, 1774.

a very profitable smuggling trade.[14]   But generally speaking,
the policy of Congress was precisely that of the radicals in New
York, and they were prepared to give to it the most loyal support,—the more so, as only through the congress, expressing the
will of all the colonies, was it possible to secure an effective realization of that policy in New York, ánd thus of assuring for themselves political supremacy in their own colony.[15]

The leaders of the faction, accordingly, began at once to interest themselves in the enforcement of the congressional recommendations.   While the proceedings of Congress were in the
main withheld from the public until its adjournment, the published resolutions of September 22 and 27 were sufficient to indicate the stand that would ultimately be taken.[16]   It was perhaps in response to these recommendations that a meeting was
called at Mr. Mariner's to consider the case of some merchants
who were reported to have furnished the troops at Boston with
supplies.[17]   September 27, a committee was appointed to "wait
on these gentlemen   .   .   .   and obtain their answer in writing."   "All the friends of liberty" were requested to attend
the following evening at Bardin's to "adopt such measures as
the exigency of th's alarming occasion may require."[18]   What
the committee reported does not appear.   But that it attempted
to carry out its instructions is evident, for the Fifty-One was
shortly petitioned to assemble a meeting to inquire into the af-

---

[14] White wrote to Tryon that the Association was disliked by smugglers. *Hist.
MSS. Com.,* **14**: Pt. 10, p. 237.   "The non-importation Association effects smugglers as well as fair traders   .   .   .   The smugglers expect large quantities
of Dutch tea.. and insist that it shall be exempt from the effects of the Association.   Others declare that the fair traders shall not be the only sufferers."
Golden to Dartmouth, December 7, 1774 ; *New York Col. Doc.,* **8**: 512.

[15] *Cf.* William Smith to Tryon, November 25, 1774 ; *Hist. MSS. Com.,* **14**: Pt.
10, p. 235.   Smith to Schuyler, November 22, 1774 ; Lossing, *Life of Schuyler,*
1: 288.

[16] Ford, *Journals,* **1**: 41, 43.   These were the initial non-importation resolutions.   After the Suffolk resolutions were approved, the non-intercourse was
generally regarded as inevitable.   *Cf. Hist. MSS. Com.,* **11**: Pt. 5, p. 362.

[17] To the Public September 28, 1774 ; *Broadsides,* **1**.   The Mechanics Committee had recently received a letter from Boston relative to the attempt of Gage
to employ New York workmen.   *4 Am. Arch.,* **1**: 803.   *Cf.* To the Public, October 5, 1774 ; *Broadsides,* **1**.

[18] To the Public, September 28, 1774 ; *Broadsides,* **1**.

fair.[19] The Fifty-One was quite willing to maintain its position as the only authoritative city committee, and on the 30th a meeting was assembled at the city hall. When Acting Chairman Remsen attempted to present the matter to the people a disturbance was created which made it necessary to adjourn to the Coffee House. Here two questions were put: whether those now assembled had authorized the alleged committee to inquire into the private affairs of citizens, and whether in any case they approved of its action. Both questions were negatived "by a very great majority."[20]

While the loyalists were denouncing Congress in unsparing terms and the radicals were preparing to secure a vigorous execution of its recommendations, the conservatives, with characteristic caution, were slow to commit themselves. The arrival of the non-exportation resolution towards the middle of October, we are told, "alarmed the good people here very much," the utility of such a measure being "flatly denied."[21] Colden wrote that "a large majority of the people wish that a non-importation agreement may not be proposed; and were very much surprised on finding that such a measure would probably be resolved on by Congress."[22] These resolutions, when finally published, he was convinced, "do not meet with rapid applause here." The farmers did not like the prospect of non-exportation, while "the merchants seem to disrelish the non-importation Association;" they are "at present endeavoring to sift out each other's sentiments . . . a sure sign, I take it, that they wish to avoid it."[23]

Sifting out each other's sentiments was, in fact, the most vital matter for the conservatives at this moment. The line of conduct for them to follow was not clearly discernible. One solution

[19] Petition of a Number of Inhabitants, September 29, 1774; *Broadsides*, **1.** *New York Mercury*, October 3, 1774. *Rivington's Gazetteer*, October 6, 1774. 4 *Am. Arch.*, **1:** 326, 327.
[20] Petition of a Number of Inhabitants, September 29, 1774; *Broadsides*, **1.** *Cf.* Colden to Dartmouth, October 5, 1774; *New York Col. Doc.*, **8:** 493.
[21] Peter Van Schaack to John Jay, October 12, 1774; Van Schaack, *Life of Van Schaack*, 21.
[22] Colden to Dartmouth, October 5, 1774; *New York Col. Doc.*, **8:** 493.
[23] Colden to Dartmouth, November 2, 1774; *New York Col. Doc.*, **8:** 510.

was to follow the advice of Seabury and go over to the loyalists. A few, doubtless, took that step. But most of them were
not convinced of the wisdom of such a procedure, for the practical result would be to leave the control of affairs in the hands
of the radicals. A conservative policy was still believed to be
practicable. The Association might be rejected, if not, its enforcement might be intrusted to the old committee of Fifty-
One; if a new committee was indispensable, the conservatives,
by taking an active part in its election, might still control the
situation. It was felt to be far better for the conservatives to
control the execution of an Association of which they did not
approve than to withdraw, as the loyalists advised, and leave its
execution to the radicals. These were the considerations, undoubtedly, which had led the conservative delegates, Jay, Duane,
and Low, to sign the Association which they had opposed during
the proceedings of Congress; they were the considerations which
now influenced the committee of Fifty-One, a large majority of
whose members were still opposed to it.[24]

---

[24] "You know what spirit prevailed in the Committee of Fifty-One before
the Congress had published their resolves, letters, etc. Their delegates have
become converted to the prevailing sentiments of the Congress. The true
motives I cannot as yet pronounce . . . I have a little clue. Suppose
some of them who were once opposed to the liberty boys should have reasoned
thus at Philadelphia: 'The government favor we have already lost and the
question only is whether we shall court the continent or the merchants of New
York. From the last we have less to fear. There is an approaching election,
and with part of the trade, part of the church, all of the non-Episcopals, and
all of the liberty boys, we may secure places in the Assembly and laugh at the
discontented.' You'll not wonder therefore to learn that by the interest of the
delegates the committee of Fifty-One is to be dissolved and a new committee
to be appointed to execute the decrees of Congress, which is to consist of the
Delegates and such a set as the most active of the Liberty Boys approve, and
had (through the mechanics, who were consulted) chosen in conjunction with
the Fifty-One, from which a set who formerly dictated all their movements,
have retired, outwitted and disgusted, and, as they think, betrayed." Smith
to Schuyler, November 22, 1774; Lossing, Life of Schuyler, 1: 288. "I was
surprised to find such men joining with the committee, whose design is to execute the plan of the Congress. I have at length discovered that they act
with a view to protect the city from the ravages of the mob. For this purpose,
they say, they are obliged to support the measures of the Congress; that if
they did not, the most dangerous men among us would take the lead: and
under the pretence of executing the dictates of Congress would immediately
throw the city into the most perilous situation." Colden to Dartmouth, December
7, 1774; Letter-Book, 2: 372; New York Col. Doc., 8: 513; 4 Am. Arch., 1:
1030.

November 7, accordingly, the committee, without expressing any opinion in the matter whatever, resolved that, inasmuch as Congress had seen fit to draw up the Association and had recommended the appointment of committees to enforce it, the freemen and freeholders should be assembled at the usual place of election on November 18 to choose eight persons in each ward to act as a committee of inspection.[25] It was doubtless intended that the suffrage should be confined to the legal voters, as Congress had recommended.[26] There was, besides, nothing in the announcement that implied the dissolution of the Fifty-One; it is likely, indeed, that the new committees were intended to serve as ward committees under the supervision of the Fifty-one. If the conservatives, therefore, took the first step in response to the recommendations of Congress, it was only that they still hoped to exercise a controlling influence in a situation with which they had little sympathy, and for which they were not responsible.

The radicals no doubt clearly perceived the end which the old committee had in view. But they were far too much encouraged by the conduct of Congress, and by the dilemma in which the conservatives were placed by it, not to take advantage of their opportunity.[27] On Sunday, November 13, the Mechanics Committee published a broadside calling for a special meeting of that body at 4 o'clock and a general mass-meeting of all radicals at 5 o'clock on the following day, presumably for the purpose of discussing the questions raised by the resolutions of the Fifty-One.[28] It is not known precisely what was done at either of these meetings, but it is obvious that the proposals of the conservative committee were found unsatisfactory. The Fifty-One on the evening of the same day addressed to the Mechanics Committee a letter requesting a conference on the day following, in order that a "mode that shall be agreeable to their fellow citizens in general" might be arranged.[29] This conference resulted

---

[25] 4 *Am. Arch.*, **1**: 328, 329. Moved by Duane.
[26] The Association, Art XI.; Ford, *Journal*, **1**: 79.
[27] The radicals were encouraged by letters from Boston. *Cf.* Letters of Thomas Young, October 4, November 19, 1774; Lamb MSS., (1774-1775).
[28] Daniel Dunscomb, To the Mechanics, November 13, 1774; *Broadsides*, 1.
[29] 4 *Am. Arch.*, **1**: 329.

in the adoption of a plan widely different from the original proposition of the conservatives. Instead of ward committees, there was to be a general committee of inspection of not more than seventy or less than sixty members. It was to be elected by the freemen and freeholders, not in ward elections, but at the city hall, under the supervision of the vestrymen. Finally, it was understood that the election of the new committee should be followed by the immediate dissolution of the Fifty-One.[30]

If this arrangement is to be regarded as a compromise, it was a curiously one-sided one. There were two points which it was of serious importance for the conservatives, if they wished to remain conservative, to hold to—the limitation of the suffrage, and the continued existence of the Fifty-One. Virtually, both points were given up. It is true the suffrage was not technically extended, but the method of election was so changed that the suffrage ceased to be a matter of any importance: to say that the committee should be elected by the freemen and freeholders, at the city hall, under the supervision of the vestrymen, was only crudely to conceal the fact that the decisive method of election by ballot was to be replaced by the indecisive method of election in general mass-meeting. The second point was given up without reservation, and this was, after all, the matter of vital importance. Its importance consisted in the fact that in losing the Fifty-One the conservatives were losing their independent organization. The new committee, nominated by both factions, could not represent the conservatives as the Fifty-One had represented them. On the contrary, it would stand quite as much (more, indeed, as the sequel proved) for radicalism as for conservatism. There was, consequently, no more inherent reason for the dissolution of the old conservative Committee of Fifty-One than there was for the dissolution of the old radical

---

[30] *Ibid.*, 330. "Each Committee to interchange one hundred names out of which the Committee is to be nominated." *Ibid.* The printed agreement says nothing about the dissolution of the Fifty-One. But it was one of the stipulations, since the Fifty-One stated in a later announcement: "This committee . . . having consulted with many of their fellow citizens. and also conferred with the committee of Mechanics . . . and having agreed to dissolve their body as soon as the new committee shall be appointed," etc. *Ibid.*

Committee of Mechanics. But by the present arrangement, after both parties had united in the formation of a new joint organization, one party was required to dissolve its old special organization, the other was not.

We are told that the new plan was carried through by the delegates, who were to be included in the new committee together with "such a set as the most active of the Liberty boys approve," and that when the ticket was made up a minority of the old committee, "who formerly dictated all their movements, retired, outwitted and disgusted, and, as they think, betrayed."[31] That the old committee was not unanimously in favor of the compromise, we can well believe, and some of its members doubtless made this event the occasion for identifying themselves with the loyalists. There was, however, no open rupture. November 15, the Fifty-One issued a second notice, pointing out the changes which had been made, and the election was now fixed for the 22nd of November.[32] On that day "a respectable number of freeholders and freemen" appeared at the city hall, and the ticket prepared by the two old committees was elected without a dissenting voice.[33]

The election of the Committee of Sixty was a victory for the radicals. It is true that all shades of opinion were represented in it, just as all shades of opinion had originally been represented in the Fifty-One. But there were fewer men on the Sixty than there had been on the Fifty-One who ultimately became loyalists, and more who advocated a radical policy. Twenty-nine members of the original Fifty-One found places on the Sixty. Of these not more than eight became loyalists; eleven were radicals from the *Sons of Liberty* camp; the rest were moderates who gave an active or passive support to the Revolu-

---

[31] *Cf.* Letter of William Smith, quoted above, note 24.

[32] 4 *Am. Arch.,* **1**: 330.

[33] This is the committee's announcement of the result of the elections. 4 *Am. Arch.,* **1**: 330. *Rivington's Gazetteer,* November 24, 1774; *New York Mercury,* November 28, 1774. Colden assured Dartmouth, on the other hand, that "About 30 or 40 citizens only appeared at the election and chose the 60." 4 *Am. Arch.,* **1**: 1030; *New York Col. Doc.,* **8**: 512.

tion.[34] Of the twenty-two members of the Fifty-One who were now excluded from the Sixty, a majority became loyalists, and only three or four ever became active supporters of the Revolution.[35] The thirty-one members of the Sixty who were not members of the Fifty-One included not more than five or six loyalists, and about ten who became active radicals.[36]

The election of the new committee thus offered no consolation to those who hoped that the Association would be rejected outright; while those who expected that its enforcement would be merely nominal[37] were fated to disappointment. The non-intercourse agreement was rigidly enforced by the new committee. In October the importers themselves took the lead by publicly declaring that they would not increase their stock of goods before the first of December, or raise prices after that date, and they agreed to boycott any one who should do either.[38]

[34] The following were on both the Fifty-One and the Sixty; those in italics ultimately became loyalists; those in small capitals represented the radical wing. *Isaac Low,* Philip Livingston, James Duane, *John Alsop,* John Jay, P. V. B. LIVINGSTON, ISAAC SEARS, David Johnson, *Charles Nicoll,* ALEXANDER McDOUGALL, THOMAS RANDALL, LEONARD LISPENARD, *Edward Laight, William Walton,* JOHN BROOME, JOSEPH HALLETT, Charles Shaw, Nicholas Hoffman, *Abram Walton, Peter Van Schaack,* Henry Remsen, PETER T. CURTENIUS, ABRAM BRASHER, ABRAM P. LOTT, Alexander Duryee, Joseph Bull, FRANCIS LEWIS, *John De Lancey,* G. H. Ludlow.

[35] The following are the names; those in italics became loyalists, or neutrals with loyalist sympathies. *William Bayard, Theophylact Bache,* Jacobus Van Zant, Thomas Pearsall, *Elias Desbrosses,* Richard Yates, *Miles Sherbrook, John Thurman, Benjamin Booth, Alexander Wallace, James Jauncey, Gerardius Duychink, Hamilton Young, George Browne, Peter Goelet, David Van Horn,* Gerard W. Beekman, *William McAdam, Richard Sharpe.* Thomas Marston, *Charles McEvers, John Moore.*

[36] The names follow: those in italics became loyalists; those in small capitals became prominent radicals: JOHN LASHER, *John Roome,* Joseph Totten, *Samuel Jones,* FREDERICK JAY, W. W. Ludlow, George Janeway, *Rudolphus Ritzema, Lindlay Murray,* Lancaster Burling, Thomas Ivers, Hurcules Mulligan, JOHN ANTHONY, Francis Bassett, Victor Bicker, John White, THEOPHILUS ANTHONY, William Goforth, WILLIAM DENNING, ISAAC ROOSEVELT, Jacob Van Voornees, JEREMIAH PLATT, William Ustic, COMFORT SANDS, ROBERT BENSON, W. W. Gilbert, John Berrien, NICHOLAS ROOSEVELT, EDWARD FLEMING, Lawrence Embree, J. B. Moore.

[37] In December Colden wrote that the Association would be kept in appearance only since the smugglers were affected. Colden to Tryon, December 7, 1774; *Letter-Book,* 2: 375. That the smugglers were affected was an incentive on the part of the fair traders to keep it rigidly, however.

[38] Declaration signed by Henry Remsen, by "order of a large number of importers met at the Exchange." *New York Journal,* October 13, 1774.

Shortly after December 1, the Sixty appointed two sub-committees to superintend the sale of two cargoes that had arrived contrary to the Association, and several parcels of goods were sold accordingly.[39] In January, 1775, the committee resolved that after February 1, all goods imported contrary to the agreement should be sent back as directed by article 10 of the Association, and appointed a sub-committee to observe the movements of vessels entering the harbor.[40] Some cargoes which arrived in February and March were forced to depart,[41] and the attempt of two New York merchants to sell nails to the British troops was summarily suppressed.[42] Smugglers apparently fared no better than fair traders;[43] and Colden himself admitted that the non-importation agreement "is ever rigidly maintained in this place."[44] The profits arising from the sale of goods imported in violation of the Association amounted to 375£, 4sh., 1d., and the money was remitted to Boston by order of the committee.[45]

Meanwhile the Association had been circulated in the counties by the Fifty-One.[46] What action the rural counties would take, no one could say. That they were strongly conservative was generally admitted; but whether the conservative element would remain passive and leave the field open to a small radical minority was the vital question. This had generally been the case in the election of delegates to the first Congress, but even then in but few counties was there a sufficient radical interest to take

[39] Ibid., December 15, 1774.

[40] Ibid., February 2, 1775.

[41] Neither master nor owner of these ships asked for any assistance of the government in landing the cargoes. These events gave the radicals "great spirits," according to Colden. Colden to Dartmouth, March 1, 1775; New York Col. Doc., 8: 543. Cf. Hist. MSS. Com., 14: Pt. 10, p. 289. New York Journal, March 23, 1775.

[42] William and Henry Ustic, the former of whom was a member of the S'xty. New York Journal, April 13, 1775. 4 Am. Arch., 2: 282. To the Inhabitants, April 13, 1775; Broadsides, 1.

[43] The committee resolved that the third article of the Association prohibited the sale of tea after March 1, 1775, irrespective of the time of its importation. New York Journal, March 30, 1775. Philip Lott wrote that there was no sale for Dutch tea in New York. Lott to Elphinstone of Copenhagen. May 3, 1775; Hist. MSS. Com., 14: Pt. 10, p. 297.

[44] New York Col. Doc., 8: 543.

[45] New York Journal, April 27, 1775.

[46] 4 Am. Arch., 1: 328, 329.

any action in the matter. On the other hand, the rise of loyalist opposition to the congress might very well result in positive conservative action which would defeat the Association in many counties.

The result, in fact, was not materially different than that which attended the election of delegates to the first congress. Three counties at most can be said to have given the Association a favorable reception on its first appearance: Albany, Suffolk, and Ulster. The Albany committee, which had now become a permanent organization, ratified the proceedings of Congress December 10, 1774, although the delegates were asked to explain why they voted to allow the exportation of rice from South Carolina.[47] It was asserted that the committee was almost evenly divided on the question,[48] but it appears that the division occurred with respect to instructing the representatives in assembly to vote for approval of the congress.[49] The action of the committee appears not to have been publicly opposed save in King's district. December 24, "five of the King's justices of the county of Albany and a great number of the people belonging to the said district" resolved to resist all associations to obstruct the courts of justice or to obstruct the offices of the law.[50]

The Suffolk county committee met November 15, at the county hall, and resolved "that we do fully approve of the proceedings of the late continental Congress, and recommend it to the several towns to see that the Association . . . be strictly observed."[51] In February a meeting of several town committees confirmed these resolutions, and instructed the representatives of Suffolk County to vote for any motion made to appoint delegates to the second congress. The conduct of Benjamin Floyd in signing a loyalist paper was censured, and all publishers and circulators of papers tending to create dissentions were denounced as enemies of the country. It was asserted that most of the towns and districts in Suffolk have "fully adopted the

---

[47] Albany Committee to the Delegates, January 5, 1775. *Ibid.*, 1098.
[48] *Ibid.*, 1097.
[49] *Ibid.*, 1097, 1098.
[50] *New York Mercury*, February 6, 1775. 4 *Am. Arch.*, 1: 1063.
[51] 4 *Am. Arch.*, 1: 1258.

measures recommended by Congress, and determined upon a strict observance of the Association.''[52]

Next to Suffolk, the most radical county appears to have been Ulster. January 6, 1775, freeholders from five towns assembled at Hurley, approved the Association, and recommended the towns to appoint committees to enforce it.[53] Such committees were forthwith appointed in Kingston,[54] New Windsor,[55] Hanover,[56] Showangnuk,[57] and Wallkill.[58] Loyalists, of whom there were many, were threatened with tar and feathers. But the loyalists in Showangnuk, finding that reason was insufficient, bore public testimony to their loyalty by erecting, on the 10th of February, ''a royal standard on a mast seventy-five feet high,'' bearing an inscription which asserted their determination to help enforce the laws in opposition to any congress or committee whatever.[59]

Certain counties appear to have been about evenly divided, loyalist activity being sufficient practically to nullify the Association. In Tryon County the influence of the Johnsons was sufficient to counteract the radical sentiment in the German districts. March 16, 1775, the Grand Jury and the magistrates and some others, thirty-four in all, issued a declaration opposing the Association, and affirming their loyalty to the king.[60] Committees were nevertheless subsequently appointed in four districts, but they did not meet as a county committee until June 6, 1775, when the situation had very materially changed.[61] In Dutchess County a loyalist Association was signed by a number

---

[52] Huntington, Smithtown, Islip, Southhaven, "and some of the principal inhabitants of the town of Brookhaven," February 23, 1775. *Ibid.*, 1257.

[53] Kingston, Hurley, Marbletown, Rochester, and New Paltz. Shoonmacher, *Kingston*, 164. 4 *Am. Arch.*, **1**: 1100.

[54] Committee of seven chosen April 7, 1775. *New York Mercury*, April 17, 1775. 4 *Am. Arch.*, **2**: 298. *Cf.* Schoonmacher, *Kingston*, 164.

[55] Committee of six chosen March 14, 1775. 4 *Am. Arch.*, **2**: 131–133.

[56] Committee of seven chosen January 27, 1775. *Ibid.*, **1**: 1191.

[57] Meeting of freeholders in January occasioned by the circulation of Seabury's *Free Thoughts*. A committee of five chosen. *Ibid.*, 1183.

[58] Committee of five chosen January 30. *Ibid.*, 1201.

[59] *Ibid.*, 1230.

[60] *Ibid.*, **2**: 151. Campbell, *Annals of Tryon County*, 33.

[61] The districts were: Palatine, Conajoharie, German Flatts, Mohawk. Campbell, *Annals of Tryon County*, 44. Benton, *History of Herkimer County*, 66, 67.

of inhabitants, who agreed to "support each other in the free exercise of our undoubted right to liberty in eating, drinking, buying, selling, communing . . . with whom we please, consistent with the laws of God and the laws of the land, not withstanding the Association entered into by the Continental Congress."[62] No public approbation of Congress appears to have been declared in this county.

Both parties were very active in Queens County. A town meeting at Jamaica, December 6, approved the measures of Congress, thanked the delegates, and resolved to use "constitutional and prudent" measures for carrying out the Association, for which purpose a committee of nine was appointed.[63] But January 27, 1775, one hundred and thirty-six men, including, it was claimed, ninety-one of the one hundred and sixty freeholders in the town, signed a resolution abjuring Congress and denouncing the Association.[64] At Flushing, a loyalist report tells us, one-seventh of the freeholders appointed a committee of twelve to enforce the Association.[65] At New Town the supervisors advertised a town meeting for December 10, when a "great number of the most respectable freeholders" assembled and appointed a committee of seventeen,[66] which passed resolutions in support of the Association.[67] A number, it is said, refused to serve on the committee, which was soon reduced to seven,[68] while the resolutions themselves were repudiated by fifty-six persons, who resolved not to recognize any authority but the general assembly.[69] In Oyster Bay the freeholders were assembled December 30, 1774, to consider the resolutions of Congress, but "there being present but a small part of the freeholders, the meeting was adjourned."[70] Another report has it, however, that there were ninety freeholders present, and

---

[62] 4 *Am. Arch.*, 1: 1164.
[63] *Ibid.*, 1027.
[64] *Ibid.*, 1191.
[65] Onderdonck, *Doc. and Letters of Queen's County*, 21.
[66] 4 *Am. Arch.*, 1: 1035.
[67] *New York Mercury*, January 9, 1775.
[68] Ricker, *New Town*, 175.
[69] *New York Mercury*, January 16, 1775.
[70] Onderdonck, *Doc. and Letters of Queen's County*, 20.

that the meeting was adjourned because a majority considered the object of the meeting to be illegal.[71]

In seven counties the Association was either ignored entirely or easily suppressed until after the events of April, 1775. A committee was appointed at White Plains in Westchester County, but forty-five freeholders denounced the Association, and the committee did nothing.[72] In the counties of Kings, Orange, Richmond, Charlotte, Cumberland, and Gloucester, there is no record of any action on the Association until after the battle of Lexington. Meanwhile, there was another question of greater interest than the Association, but closely connected with it, which was engaging the best efforts of loyalists, conservatives, and radicals alike during the winter and spring of 1775—the election of delegates to the second congress, which was to assemble in May.

---

[71] *New York Mercury,* January 9, 1775. *Rivington's Gazetteer,* January 5, 1775. 4 *Am. Arch.,* 1: 1076, 1077.

[72] *New York Mercury,* January 16, 1775. *Cf.* Dawson, *Westchester County,* 36 ff. Baird, *History of Rye,* 220. Two loyalist associations circulated in Westchester, one of which originated in Dutchess. They are given in Dawson, *Westchester County,* 43, note 1, 44.

CHAPTER VIII

ELECTION OF DELEGATES TO THE SECOND CONTINENTAL CONGRESS.

Early in the year 1775, the assembly, which had been prorogued to meet January 10,[1] became the center of interest. Its deliberations were certain to be concerned with the double question of confirming or refusing to confirm the action of the first Continental Congress, and of appointing or refusing to appoint delegates to the second. Even the best informed could not foretell which answer the assembly would give to either of these questions;[2] and the result was that all parties, save perhaps the extreme radicals, were hoping to make use of it for the purposes which they had in view.

The old *Sons of Liberty* were not much interested. If the assembly should confirm the Association, it would doubtless appoint delegates to the second congress, and such an event, besides securing for New York a conservative delegation, would lessen the importance of the extra-legal machinery which they were now in a fair way to control. The conservatives, on the other hand, saw in the assembly the best hope for maintaining their policy. The second congress was a foregone conclusion; if the assembly could be induced to take part in the popular movement, the conservatives, by their double representation on the Sixty and in the assembly, would have an excellent chance to exercise the same influence which they had formerly exercised

---

[1] Colden to Dartmouth, December 7, 1774; *New York Col. Doc.*, **8:** 513.

[2] "Many people think there is a probability that they will go upon conciliatory measures . . . The event is uncertain." Colden to Dartmouth, December 7, 1774; *New York Col. Doc.*, **8:** 513. Smith thought the assembly would approve of Congress. Smith to Tryon, December 6, 1774; *Hist. MSS. Com.*, **14:** Pt. 10, p. 236. *Cf. ibid.*, 232.

through the committee of Fifty-One. Finally those who, like Seabury and Chandler, were taking a frankly loyalist position, looked to the assembly to confirm their decision. "To you, gentlemen," wrote Seabury, "the good people look for relief . . . from this intolerable state of slavery. . . . If laws made and decrees passed at Philadelphia, by the enthusiastic republicans of New England and Virginia, are to bind the people of this province, why, gentlemen, do you meet? . . . Your duty requires you to . . . break up this horrid combination of seditious men."[3] The assembly was petitioned to censure Congress, and take measures to secure a redress of grievances from the king directly.[4] Aside from these groups, doubtless the majority throughout the colony was waiting to follow any lead which the established government might take. Colden himself turned to the assembly as the least of evils: fearing that it might approve Congress, he believed that it could not make matters worse than they were, while it might at least thwart the attempt "to convene a Provincial Congress."[5] The meeting of the assembly in the winter of 1775 was, therefore, of considerable importance: opposing interests were hoping to make use of it; the result would serve to crystalize sentiment and clear the way for future action.

The members began to assemble January 10, 1775,[6] but two weeks passed before any serious business was broached. The principal loyalist leaders were Isaac Wilkins and Colonel Philipse, who were ably seconded by the four city members. They were determined to ignore Congress altogether, and to take into their own hands the matter of grievances.[7] The con-

---

[3] Seabury, *An Alarm to the Legislature,* January 17, 1775; quoted in Tyler, *American Revolution,* **1**: 347.

[4] To The Freeman, January 19, 1775; *Broadsides,* **1.**

[5] "I do not apprehend there is any danger that the Assembly will make matters worse than they are." Colden to Dartmouth, December 7, 1774; *New York Col. Doc.,* **8**: 513. "If I find there will not be a majority for prudent measures, I shall incline to prorogue them . . . On the other hand there is room to fear, that if the Assembly do not meet, an attempt will be made to convene a provincial Congress." Colden to Dartmouth, January 4, 1775; *New York Col. Doc.,* **8**: 528.

[6] Colden to Dartmouth, February 1, 1775; *New York Col. Doc.,* **8**: 531. Proceedings of the assembly are in *4 Am. Arch.,* **1**: 1281 ff.

[7] Colden to Dartmouth, March 1, 1775: *New York Col. Doc.,* **8**: 543.

servatives, on the other hand, of whom the principal leaders were Philip Livingston, Philip Schuyler, and Abram Ten Broeck, were determined to secure a formal expression of opinion on the work of the first congress, and, if possible, the election of delegates to the second congress, which was to meet in May.[8] To this end three separate resolutions were introduced and pressed to a vote. The first one, January 26, was a motion to consider the work of the first congress.[9] The second, February 21, looked toward a vote of thanks to the merchants for maintaining the non-intercourse agreement.[10] The third, February 23, was introduced immediately after the committee on grievances made its report, by Mr. Thomas, who moved that a vote be taken on the necessity of appointing delegates to the second congress. All three resolutions were defeated by increasing majorities—the last by a vote of 17–9[11]—but they made it impossible for the loyalists to ignore the work of the first congress and the appointment of deputies to the second. The motion of Mr. Thomas was debated at length,[12] and the loyalist position was clearly stated, especially by Brush and Wilkins, whose speeches have been preserved.[13] Technically, the assembly ignored the extra-legal movement altogether; practically, it

---

[8] "Every machination that restless spirits can devise, will in the meantime be exerted to secure an approbation of the proceedings of Congress which is the grand point they aim to carry." Colden to Dartmouth, January 21, 1775; *Letter-Book,* **2:** 380. That this was the main d fference between the parties is evident from the fact that the resolution to petition was moved by Livingston and carried unanimously. *4 Am. Arch.,* **1:** 1288.

[9] Motion was lost by 11–10. *4 Am. Arch.,* **1:** 1286, 1287. The small majority of the loyalists was due to the fact that a number of the deputies had not yet arrived. "These ten are . . . the whole strength of that party. The nine members which have not yet appeared . . . it is well known will join the eleven." Colden to Dartmouth, February 1, 1775; *New York Col. Doc.,* **8:** 532. The assembly refused even to thank the delegates. *4 Am. Arch.,* **1:** 1289.

[10] Moved by Livingston; voted down 15–10. *4 Am. Arch.,* **1:** 1290.

[11] *Ibid.*

[12] *Ibid.*

[13] Brush maintained that the action of Congress was not a subject to come before the assembly, that the assembly could not delegate its authority to a body of men unknown to the constitution, that, if the conduct of Congress were considered, it should be condemned because it had assumed power "to enact laws," and had erected itself into the "Supreme Legislature of North America." *4 Am. Arch.,* **1:** 1291, 1292. Wilkins' speech presented more clearly the precise issue: it was better to desert the neighboring colonies than to desert Great Britain. *Ibid.,* 1293.

expressed its disapproval of the first congress, and refused to appoint deputies to the second.

Having disposed of these matters, the assembly proceeded to the report of the Committee on Grievances.[14] On the question of grievances the conservatives were practically in accord with the loyalists. They contested some unimportant points in the report, and succeeded in introducing some slight modifications;[15] but the resolutions as adopted may be taken as representing the views of both factions in so far as the issue was one between the colonies and Great Britain.[16] The report on grievances was substantially as follows:[17] (1) the colonies owe to the king the same allegiance as other Englishmen; (2) the colonies owe obedience to acts of Parliament that are not contrary to the rights of Englishmen; (3) it is a right of Englishmen that no tax be laid save by consent, given personally or through representatives in assembly; (4) certain acts of Parliament are subversive of the rights of the colonists—e. g., the raising of revenue in America for the administration of government, the extension of the admiralty jurisdiction, etc.; (5) jury trial is essential to the rights of Englishmen. On the basis of these resolutions the assembly formulated a petition to the king,[18] a memorial to the Lords,[19] and a remonstrance to the Commons.[20] From the loyalist point of view, all had now been done that could rightfully be done; the issue rested with king and Parliament. Accordingly, having appointed a standing committee of correspondence composed of both factions, the assembly was adjourned to the 3rd of May.[21]

---

[14] The committee was appointed January 31, and consisted of: De Lancey, Schuyler, Clinton, Brinkerhoff, Gale, Wilkins, Brush, Billopp, Rapalje, Kissam, and Nicoll. *Ibid.*, 1288.

[15] *Ibid.*, 1301. *Cf.* Colden to Dartmouth, March 1, 1775; *New York Col. Doc.*, 8: 543.

[16] Even MacDougall said that the resolutions represented the sentiments of New York. *4 Am. Arch.*, 2: 283, 284.

[17] *Ibid.*, 1: 1302.

[18] *Ibid.*, 1313.

[19] *Ibid.*, 1316.

[20] *Ibid.*, 1318.

[21] The committee: Cruger, De Lancey, J. Walton, Benjamin Seaman, Wilkins, Philipse, Daniel Kissam, Zebulon Seaman, Jno. Rapalje, Simon Boerum, Samuel Gale, George Clinton. The adjournment was voted April 3. *Ibid.*, 1324. *Cf. Hist. MSS. Com.*, 14: Pt. 10, p. 285.

The action of the assembly was regarded by the English government as a serious blow to the union of the colonies and the policy of Congress.[22] By many of the friends of Congress, it was regarded in the same light.[23] The conservatives especially, clearly perceived that the withdrawal of the assembly from the extra-legal movement would tend to place the control of Congress in more radical hands. The loyalists and conservatives were essentially at one in the matter of grievances; but to the loyalists the extra-legal movement had already become illegal and revolutionary, and rather than be in any way connected with it, they preferred not to secure any redress of grievances at all.[24] The conservatives were, however, either not convinced that the extra-legal movement was revolutionary, or else inclined to consider the redress of grievances of more importance than the preservation of allegiance to England. Failing to draw the assembly into the movement, they therefore turned to the Committee of Sixty.[25] In the assembly they had worked in vain for the appointment of any delegates whatever; they were now to work, for the most part in vain also, for the appointment of delegates who would stand for moderate rather than for radical measures in the congress.

The radicals had, indeed, taken up the question of the delegates as soon as it was known that the assembly would not appoint any. February 27, four days after the defeat of Mr. Thomas' motion, P. V. B. Livingston, at a meeting of the Com-

---

[22] In Dartmouth's circular letter to the governors the clause "which has already shown so good a disposition towards a reconciliation with the mother country," was inserted in the New York letter after the word assembly. 4 Am. Arch., 2: 27, 28. New York Col. Doc., 8: 545–547. Cf. Dartmouth to Colden, March 4, 1775; Ibid., 547. For the effect of the assembly's conduct in England generally, see 4 Am. Arch., 2: 29, 252. Hist. MSS. Com., 14: Pt. 10, p. 276.

[23] Assembly's conduct strongly disapproved by South Carolina. 4 Am. Arch., 2: 29. A Virginia letter speaks of the "polluted members of the Assembly." Ibid., 153. Cf. Ibid., 123. After the vote against appointing delegates, eighteen anonymous, threatening letters were delivered to the speaker and those who voted against the measure. Deane Papers, 5: 538, 539.

[24] Cf. Speech of Wilkins, 4 Am. Arch., 1: 1293.

[25] "They are now gone home to get fhat done by the election of the people which they could not effect in the House." Colden to Tryon, April 5, 1775; Letter-Book, 2: 398, 399. Cf. New York Col. Doc., 8: 566.

mittee of Sixty, moved to consider "the ways and means of causing delegates to be elected to meet the delegates of the other colonies . . . in general Congress."[26]   On March 1, when the question was again taken up, the committee, concluding that it had no power to elect the delegates itself, decided to refer the matter to the freeholders and freemen.[27]   A notice was accordingly published summoning the freemen and freeholders to meet at the Exchange on March 6 to "signify their sense of the best method of choosing such delegates, and whether they will appoint a certain number of persons to meet such deputies as the counties may elect for that purpose, to join with them in appointing out of their body delegates for the next Congress."[28] Whether consciously worded or not, the fact is that the two purposes expressed in this resolution are somewhat inconsistent. It is not clear why the committee should express a desire to refer the question of method in the election of delegates to the freemen and freeholders, and then, before there could be any decision of that point, thrust their own definite plan so intrusively in their faces.   In truth it would be quite superfluous for the freemen and freeholders to consider the first question (the question of the best method) if they were expected in any case to consider the second question (the question of a particular method); and, under the circumstances, a refusal to adopt the committee's plan would be very nearly equivalent to an expression of hostility to Congress.   It is clear, therefore, not only that the radicals were in favor of sending delegates to Congress, but also that they wanted those del-

---

[26] Extract of the Committee's Proceedings, February 27, 1775; *Broadsides,* **1.** Samuel Jones alone dissented.

[27] Extract from the Committee's Proceedings, February 27, 1775; *Ibid.*

[28] *Ibid.; Rivingston's Gazetteer,* March 9, 1775; *New York Mercury,* March 6, 1775; 4 *Am. Arch.,* **2:** 4.   A provincial convention had been urged in connection with the election of delegates to the first Continental Congress, by the radicals in New York city in their resolutions of July 6, 1774 (*New York Mercury.* July 11, 1774), and again in their resolutions of July 20, 1774 (*Ibid.,* July 25, 1774.)   In connection with the second Continental Congress the earliest suggestion appears to have come from Suffolk County.   A county meeting on February 23, 1775, resolved that if the assembly refused to appoint delegates, "the Committee of Correspondence for . . . New York be desired . . . in that case to call a provincial convention for that purpose." 4 *Am. Arch.,* **1:** 1257.

egates to be chosen by a provincial convention composed of
deputies from all the counties in the colony. Such a method of
choosing delegates would almost necessarily diminish the relative influence of New York city in the congress; it is, consequently, necessary to understand why the radicals in the city
were in favor of a provincial convention.

The answer to this question is simply that the radicals were
now bent on bringing New York more nearly into line with
New England and the South. If the old method of election was
adopted, this could be done in one of two ways—either by electing a new and radical delegation from the city or by electing
sufficiently large and radical delegations from the counties to
outvote and, what was more important, to outweigh in influence
the old delegation from the city. Neither plan was practicable.
The old city delegates were men of the highest standing and of
wide influence. While they had opposed the action of the first
Continental Congress, they had not refused to support the Association. With two exceptions[29] they represented at its best
that part of the conservative faction which was ultimately prepared to join the revolutionists. But they had not as yet gone
very far in that direction. Without being sufficiently radical
to suit the Committee of Sixty, they were not sufficiently conservative to be in any sense out of the race. To defeat these men
was probably impossible; to attempt to do so was, in any case,
impracticable. On the other hand, it was unwise to depend on
the election of large radical delegations from the counties; the
action of the counties on the Association had been all but decisive on that point. The alternative was a new method of election which would enable the Sixty at once to support the old
city delegates and to neutralize their influence. A provincial
convention would enable the Sixty to do this, because the city
delegation to a convention might properly be made sufficiently
large to leave the old delegates in a minority, whereas it would
be out of the question to send so large a delegation from the
city directly to the congress. In the same way the convention
could easily form a delegation for the province as a whole in

---

[29] Isaac Low and John Alsop.

which the old delegates should find a place, but in which they could no longer exercise a determinative influence; and this could most probably be done equally well whether the rural counties took an active part in the convention or not.[30]

The conservative element, in the committee and out of it, divined the purposes of the Sixty and made an ineffectual attempt to defeat them. A meeting was held at Montagnie's on March 3, presided over by John Thurman. The proposals of the Sixty were disapproved of, first, because there was not time enough before March 6 to settle so important a question; second, because the method of taking the vote "by collecting the people together" was inexpedient, since it permitted of no distinction between freeholders and freemen, who had a right to vote, and "such as were collected on purpose to make a show of numbers;" third, because a provincial convention tended directly to the introduction of a provincial congress. It was accordingly suggested that the whole matter be postponed until the reply of the English government to the assembly's proposals should have been received; if nothing could be effected in this way, then let the poll be opened in the usual places for the election of delegates to a convention by freemen and freeholders only. The conservatives declared they were not necessarily opposed to Congress, or even to a convention, but to the haste with which the matter was being pushed through.[31] The protest was scarcely

---

[30] In reply to the charge that the convention would deprive the city of the old delegates, one writer says that New York cannot presume to elect delegates for the whole colony, and, on the other hand, it is improper to crowd the Congress with delegates from each county. In another broadside of the same date, March 14, the author, who signs himself "A Friend of the Congress," says that "the necessity of this mode of choosing the delegates for the colony arises from the counties having taken offense at the conduct of this city in choosing the last delegates without consulting the counties. . . . The tale that your late delegates are excluded, is a mere trick; for there is the highest probability that they will be chosen by the deputies of the counties as they are in the . . . nomination of the committee." *Broadsides, 1. Cf. 4 Am. Arch., 2:* 139.

[31] *4 Am. Arch., 2:* 48, 49. *Cf. A Freeman, etc., New York Mercury.* March 6, 1775; *4 Am. Arch., 2:* 44. A Burgher, March 6, 1775; *ibid.* To the Respectable Citizens, March 6, 1775; *ibid.*

heeded. An answering broadside appeared the next day,[32] and in the evening some radicals met and resolved to support the proposals of the committee.[33]

On Monday, March 6, the day fixed by the committee for the meeting, preparations began early. The vote was to be taken at noon. In mid-forenoon the radicals began to assemble at the liberty-pole, and by eleven o'clock they were on the way to the Exchange, carrying a banner on one side of which was the inscription, "George III Rex, and the liberties of America," and on the other, "The union of the Colonies, and the measures of Congress." About the same time the opposite party, strengthened, as was alleged, by royal officials, civil and military, began a similar procession from Montagnie's. When the processions met at the Exchange, a general mêlée was avoided with difficulty. Order having been restored, the chairman of the Sixty announced the questions upon which the vote was to be taken. The questions, as now announced, were not formulated as they had been by the committee in its handbill of March 1,—indeed, they were not the same questions at all. The first question announced by the chairman was whether deputies should be sent to a provincial convention; the second, whether the people then present would authorize the committee to nominate eleven deputies to a provincial convention. On the first question the conservatives demanded a poll in order that the matter might be decided by freeholders and freemen according to the recommendation of Congress. This was refused, and the sense of the meeting was taken *en masse*. According to the radical account, both questions were carried by a very great majority. The conserva-

---

[32] The author, who calls himself "A Tory," makes the following points: (1) The sense of the city can be taken Monday as well as any other time. (2) A convention is the plan used by the colonies of New Jersey, Virginia, Maryland, and North Carolina. (3) Little probability that the assembly will appoint delegates. "And as to the danger of their being influenced by the measure, I really can see no great harm in a Representative being influenced by his constitutents, 'on the contrary they ought to be." (4) As for waiting advice from England, "may as well wait for the conversion of the Pope as the arrival of the Packet." (5) "That whoever says the committee have prescribed rules for the counties, lies under a mistake, they mean only . . . to propose it to the counties and consult with them on the occasion." To the Learnea and Loquacious Chairman, March 4, 1775, *Broadsides*, 1.

[33] 4 *Am. Arch.*, 2: 48.

tives, on the other hand, claimed that it was impossible to say whether the questions were carried or lost: consequently, even granting the propriety of the method of voting, it could not rightly be considered either that the county was in favor of a provincial convention, or, if it was, that any power of nomination had been conferred upon the committee.[34]

Whether carried or not, the framing of the questions was such as to make it impossible to settle them on their merits. The wording of the questions shows, indeed, that the Sixty had taken a full step in advance since issuing the first of March handbill. The committee had called the freeholders and freemen together to ask them what they considered the best method of electing delegates to Congress, and whether they were in favor of a provincial convention; now that they, together with others, were assembled, the committee really asked, not the freeholders and freemen, but the inhabitants generally, whether they would send delegates to a provincial convention, and whether they would authorize the committee to nominate *eleven* delegates to that convention. On the first of March two inconsistent questions had been presented together in such a way that the real issue had been whether New York County should join in a provincial convention or not. On the sixth of March two questions somewhat different, but equally inconsistent with each other, were presented together in such a way that the real issue was whether the committee's method of sending delegates to a provincial convention should be adopted or not. The first alternative had been a convention or no Congress; within six days the alternative had become eleven deputies nominated by the committee or no Congress.

A little closer consideration of the two questions presented by the Sixty on March 6 will make this all but obvious. A negative vote on the first question was practically equivalent to opposing the second Continental Congress. Undoubtedly there were many men in favor of Congress but opposed to the convention as a

---

[34] Extracts from the Committee's Proceedings, March 6, 1775; *Broadsides,* 1. Two accounts, one radical, the other conservative, are given in *4 Am. Arch.,* 2: 48, 49. The only points in which they disagree are noted in the text. *Cf. Rivington's Gazetteer,* March 9, 1775.

method of electing delegates to the congress,—men who, nevertheless, if the convention were legitimately determined upon, were willing to send delegates to it rather than not take part in the congress at all. These men wanted a chance to vote against the convention and in favor of some other method. Yet the man who voted negatively on the first question said not, "I am not in favor of the convention as a method of choosing delegates," but, "I am not willing that New York County should join the other counties in sending delegates to the convention, and consequently to the congress:" such a vote, practically, would not have the effect of replacing the convention as a method by some other method, but merely of keeping New York County out of the movement altogether.[35] More incisively than ever and not altogether fairly, there was presented to the conservatives the alternative of supporting the convention or of seeming to refuse to support Congress; by a shrewd sort of political legerdemain it had come about that supporting or opposing the radical committee was apparently identical with the alternative of standing with the colonies or with the home government. The second question was equally treacherous. The convention once determined upon, many men not in favor of it in the first instance, but willing if delegates were to be sent to it that the committee should nominate them, were not willing that the ticket should consist of eleven members. Such men could not vote against nominating a ticket of eleven delegates without voting against allowing the committee to nominate the ticket at all.[36]

With questions presented in this fashion, those of the old conservative faction who were facing away from loyalism were likely to prefer to support the radical committee rather than give the appearance of refusing to support Congress: they

[35] "It has been artfully propagated that the citizens who assembled at Montagnie's on Friday had resolved to oppose the appointment of delegates," etc. A Burgher, March 6, 1775; 4 Am. Arch., 2: 44.

[36] This point was clearly stated in a letter of March 16, signed A Citizen. He says the great majority of those who voted for the delegates did so because there was no alternative. They trusted that the eleven knew the sentiments of the colony so well that they could not go astray. Had it been possible to vote for the five old delegates alone, they would have been elected almost unanimously. 4 Am. Arch., 2: 139.

thereby took a long step in the direction of revolution. Those of the old conservative faction who were facing away from revolution doubtless preferred to give the appearance of opposing Congress rather than place that body unreservedly in radical hands: they thereby took a long step in the direction of loyalism. The meeting on March 6 was thus another and an important stage in the disintegration of the old conservative party. Those who voted in favor of sending deputies to the convention, and in favor of permitting the committee to nominate a ticket of eleven members, whatever their motives may have been for so voting, found themselves in the company of men who voted in the same way precisely for the purpose of imparting to Congress a radical and revolutionary impetus. On the other hand, those who voted, for whatever reason, not to join with the counties in a provincial convention, and against the nomination of delegates by the committee, found themselves in the company of men who voted in the same way because they considered conventions and congresses illegal and treasonable.

The Sixty proceeded at once to nominate a ticket. Without any serious opposition apparently, the old delegates—Isaac Low, Philip Livingston, James Duane, John Alsop, and John Jay—were named, together with six others—Leonard Lispenard, Abram Walton, Francis Lewis, Isaac Roosevelt, Alexander Mac-Dougall, and Abram Brasher.[37] Of the new men, none was conservative like Duane or Low, none, perhaps, moderately judicious like Jay, none timid like Alsop. Five of them at least—Lispenard, MacDougall, Lewis, Brasher, and Roosevelt—were men who would speak and act effectively and unhesitatingly for radical measures. If the Sixty could get this ticket elected, it might well assume that without opposing the old delegates it had succeeded in neutralizing their influence.

The conservatives still had a fighting chance, perhaps, if they chose to use it; they might secede from the Sixty, as the radicals had done from the Fifty-One, and nominate a ticket of their own. But the radicals left the Fifty-One only after there was no more to be gained by remaining in it, and the conservatives

---

[37] Extracts from the Committee's Proceedings: *Broadsides,* 1.

had still something to gain by retaining a representation on the
Sixty—the limitation of the suffrage to freeholders and freemen. All that was accomplished, consequently, in respect to a
separate organization was an informal and vain effort at the
election to vote for the five old delegates without voting for the
six new ones. In respect to the limitation of the franchise, however, the conservative leaders were able to attain their end.
March 8, in committee meeting, John Jay moved that the election should be held on March 15 in the wards, under the supervision of the vestrymen and sub-committees of the Sixty, and
that the votes of freeholders and freemen only should be received.[38] The radicals felt the more safe in granting this, perhaps, since they would be able, now that a popular meeting
had decided the initial question of the expediency of sending
delegates at all, to force upon the voters the alternative of voting
for the committee's ticket as a whole, or not at all. On March
15 the election was held. Eight hundred and twenty-five freemen and freeholders were in favor of sending deputies, and
voted for the committee's ticket; one hundred and sixty-three
voted negatively on both points. Many, on the other hand, offered to vote for the old delegates only. They were refused.
The ticket of eleven members nominated by the Sixty was accordingly declared duly elected.[39]

Having thus succeeded in getting the support of the city for
its plan, the committee issued a circular to the counties on the
following day.[40] The question was referred to the counties in
much the same way as it had been referred to the city. The
counties were asked, first, to consider the advisability of a provincial convention; second, to send delegates to a convention
which was to meet (the Sixty took the liberty of fixing the day)
at New York, April 20. Practically it was quite as useless for
any individual county to consider the first question as it was

[38] Extracts from the Committee's Proceedings; *Ibid.*

[39] Extracts from the Committee's Proceedings; *Ibid.* *4 Am. Arch.*, **2:** 137.
138, 139. The vote by wards is in *New York Mercury*, March 20, 1775. The
total vote was about two-thirds of the voting population which, at that time
was over 1500. *Cf.* Dawson, *Westchester County*, 4, note 2.

[40] Letter from the Committee, March 16, 1775; *Broadsides*, **1.** *New York
Mercury*, March 20, 1775. *4 Am. Arch.*, **2:** 138. Almon, *Remembrancer*, **1:** 13.

impossible for the conservatives in the city to get an opportunity of doing so; the practical question before each county was whether it would send delegates to the convention, which, it appeared, was to meet in any case, or whether it would take no part in the convention. A refusal on the part of any county to send deputies to the convention would have no other practical effect than to leave that county without influence or voice in the second Continental Congress. In each county, therefore, the fight, where there was a fight, was virtually between those who were in favor of the second congress and those who were not—between those who were going the way of revolution and those who were going the way of loyalism. There was no place in the counties any more than in the city for those who, without being loyalists, were not in favor of Congress, or for those who, without being hostile to Congress, were opposed to a provincial convention. The result, for the moment, was a rather marked increase in radical activity. Eight counties, aside from New York, sent deputies to the convention, though in three of them there was strong opposition; one, at least, definitely refused to be represented; three, so far as is known, took no action.

In Albany County it was not primarily in response to the letter of the Sixty that delegates were elected. After the Albany committee had resolved, in December, 1774, to support the first Continental Congress, a new and more carefully organized county committee was established, which began to meet in January. It was composed of deputies from the three wards of the city and from the precincts of the county. March 1, 1775, at a meeting of this committee the chairman produced a letter from the Albany members of the assembly, which recommended that measures be taken for the election of delegates to Philadelphia. It was therefore resolved to request the sub-committees of the different districts in the county to assemble at Albany on March 21, "with full power to elect delegates."[41] Meanwhile the letter

---

[41] "A letter being produced by the chairman from Colls. Schuyler, Ten Broeck, and Livingston, members of the general Assembly, recommending the committee to appoint delegates to the intended Congress to be held at Philadelphia.

from New York reached Albany and gave a new direction to the activity of the committee. It is not known how this letter reached the various districts, but that it did reach them is evident from the fact that when the general committee met on March 21 all of the deputies had been authorized to elect delegates either to the congress at Philadelphia or to the convention at New York.[42] All of the committee except Henry Bogart were found to be in favor of sending delegates to the convention; and a ticket of five members was unanimously chosen for that purpose.[43] In Kings County representatives of four townships met at the county hall April 15 and unanimously appointed five deputies to attend the convention. The township of Flatlands remained neutral, neither supporting nor opposing the measure.[44] In Orange County the four precincts of Cornwall, Goshen, Haverstraw, and Orangetown held separate meetings and named deputies.[45] Of any opposition in these precincts, or of any action at all in others, there is no record. In Suffolk a county meeting was held at the county hall, April 6, and five delegates were chosen to represent the county.[46] Ulster County chose delegates in the same way. On April 7, thirty-nine

---

. . . It was unanimously resolved that letters be wrote to the committees of the different districts of this county requesting their meeting at the House of Richard Cartwright the 21st day of this month, at two o'clock . . . with full power to appoint delegates." Minutes of the Albany Committee, **1:** 10.

[42] "First the chairman put the question whether the members were fully authorized by their constitutents to elect Delegates or Deputies to meet the Deputies from the other counties it appeared that they were unanimously empowered to appoint either." Minutes of the Albany Committee, **1:** 12. The committee. at this meeting. consisted of fifteen members from the following districts: First Ward, 2; Second Ward, 1; Third Ward, 2; two districts of Rensselaerwyck, 2; Manor of Livingston, 1; Schaghchick district, 2; Claverack, 1; Scoharie and Duanesburgh, 2; Nestegarie and Halfmoon, 1; Saratoga, 1. *Ibid.*

[43] "A motion was made by Walter Livingston whether Deputies shall be appointed to represent the City and County of Albany to meet the 20 day of April . . . at the City of New York . . . Resolved, unanimously, that Deputies be appointed . . . Mr. Henry Bogart . . . dissented, he being for appointing delegates for the City and County of Albany to meet the intended congress at Philadelphia. Resolved by a majority that five persons be appointed. . . . Resolved unanimously that Abram Yates, Walter Livingston. Col. Schuyler, Colonel Ten Broeck and Col. Peter Livingston are appointed." *Ibid.,* 12.

[44] *Cal. of Hist. MSS.,* **1:** 41.

[45] *4 Am. Arch.,* **2:** 275, 352, 353: *Cal. of Hist. MSS.* **1:** 2, 3.

[46] *Cal. of Hist. MSS.,* **1:** 19.

deputies, from ten towns, assembled at New Paltz. Three delegates were named.[47] This action was approved by another town, Rochester, where a meeting was held on the same day. Opposition appears to have been confined to a letter signed by Cadwallader Colden, Jr., and Peter and Walter DuBois, protesting against the election as unlawful.[48]

In Dutchess, Queens, and Westchester there was strong opposition. Although Dutchess sent delegates in response to the New York letter, it is doubtful whether a majority of the inhabitants were in favor of doing so; it is certain that a majority of the precincts were not. The question was taken up first in the towns or precincts separately, although the meeting in Charlotte precinct is the only one of which a record has been preserved.[49] Of the eleven precincts in the county seven were opposed to sending delegates to the convention, four were in favor of doing so. The conservatives claimed that in the county as a whole there was a large majority opposed to the convention; the radicals claimed that there was a majority in favor of it.[50] On the strength of this claim a general meeting was held April 14, consisting of deputies from the four radical precincts, which named three delegates to represent the county.[51] Although it must be said, at the very least, that the wishes of Dutchess County were not ascertained in any satisfactory manner, the delegates were received by the convention. In Queens County the matter was taken up by the towns separately also. Three towns, Jamaica,[51] Hempstead,[53] and Oyster Bay,[54] voted not to send delegates; two

---

[47] George Clinton MSS., 1: 55; *Cal. of Hist. MSS.*, 1: 21, 22.

[48] *Cal. of Hist. MSS.*, 1: 22, 23. Schoonmacher, *Kingston*, 166.

[49] The meeting was held April 7. The vote stood 140–35 in opposition to delegates. About 100 more appeared after the poll closed, and offered to vote for "constitutional liberty," but the advocates of the Congress "gave up the contest." *New York Mercury*, April 17, 1775; *4 Am. Arch.*, 2: 304.

[50] *New York Mercury*, April 17, 1775; *4 Am. Arch.*, 2: 304.

[51] *Cal. of Hist. MSS.*, 1: 41. The four precincts were Rheinbeck, North East, Armenia, and Rumbout. Poughkeepsie was one of the seven opposed to the convention. It seems not unlikely that Dutchess was far from having a majority in favor of the convention.

[52] By vote of 94–82. *New York Mercury*, April 3, 1775; *Rivington's Gazetteer*, April 6. 1775; *4 Am. Arch.*, 2: 251, 838, 839.

[53] By resolution in town meeting. *Rivington's Gazetteer*, April 6, 1775; *Cal. of Hist. MSS.*, 1: 38, 39; *4 Am. Arch.*, 2: 273.

[54] By resolution in town meeting; vote, 205–42. Onderdonck, *Documents and Letters . . . of Queens County*, 26.

towns, Newtown[55] and Flushing,[56] appointed one delegate each. In Jamaica[57] and Oyster Bay[58] the radicals held subsequent meetings and appointed delegates to attend the convention as minority representatives. These four delegates (two representing two towns as such, two representing minorities in two other towns) attended the convention, but that body decided that Queens County was not entitled to vote on the measures which came before it.

In Westchester careful management on the part of the radicals was necessary to get the county represented. The New York letter appears to have been communicated—it is not clear just how[59]—to twelve gentlemen residing in four towns[60] in the southern part of the county. These twelve gentlemen met at White Plains, March 28, in order to devise means for "taking the sense of the county" on the subject of the convention. For this purpose a circular letter was issued by them and sent to the different districts, calling a general meeting of the freeholders and freemen at White Plains, April 11. As it was well known that the initiators of this movement were radicals, a letter was circulated by the conservatives, dated New York, April 6, urging all who were opposed to conventions and congresses and in favor of the assembly's measures to assemble at the time and place appointed for the radical meeting.[61] On April 11, accordingly, some two hundred and fifty persons met at White Plains, the two parties establishing their headquarters at different taverns

---

[55] By a popular meeting of freeholders. It is said that 100 freeholders, a majority of all the freeholders in the town, were present. Jacob Blackwell was elected unanimously. *4 Am. Arch.*, 2: 356; Onderdonck, *Documents and Letters* . . . *of Queens County*, 23; Ricker, *Newtown*, 179.

[56] John Talman, elected by "great majority" in town meeting. *4 Am. Arch.*, 2: 356; Onderdonck, *Documents and Letters*, 25.

[57] Joseph Robinson. *4 Am. Arch.*, 2: 356.

[58] Zebulon Williams (formerly Seaman) was given "full power and authority to act" in behalf of forty-two freeholders. *Cal. of Hist. MSS.*, 1: 39, 40.

[59] According to Dawson, there was no "vestage" of the old committee left in in Westchester, to which the letter might be sent. He thinks the letter was sent to Lewis Morris and communicated by him to the twelve men. Dawson, *Westchester County*, 65, 66.

[60] Theodosius Bartow, James Willis, Abram Guion, of New Rochelle; William Sutton, of Mamaronec; Lewis Morris, Thomas Hunt, Abram Leggett, of Westchester: James Horton, of Rye.

[61] *4 Am. Arch.*, 2: 282; Dawson, *Westchester County*, 67.

in the town.   About 12 o'clock the radicals assembled at the
court-house and were proceeding to the business of the day when
the other party, led by Isaac Wilkins and Colonel Philipse,
marched in from Hatfield's tavern.   Either from principle or
from a consciousness of inferior numbers, they made no attempt
to decide the question by ballot.   Isaac Wilkins, speaking for
the party, stated that they wished to have nothing to do with
congresses or deputies, that their sole purpose was to protest
against "such illegal and unconstitutional proceedings."   Giving three cheers, the party returned to Captain Hatfield's, "sing-
ing as they went the grand and animating song of God save
great George, our King."   Here, certainly, conservatism was
hardly to be distinguished from loyalism.   Without further opposition the radicals at the court-house proceeded to appoint
eight delegates to the convention.   As usual, each party claimed
a majority.[62]   The one county which definitely refused to send
delegates was Richmond;[63] those which apparently took no action
were Charlotte, Cumberland, Tryon, and Gloucester.

The Provincial Convention assembled at New York on April
20.[64] Credentials of election were presented by delegates from New
York, Albany, Ulster, Orange, Westchester, Kings, Suffolk, Queens,
and Dutchess.   The delegates from Queens were debarred from
voting,[65] but, even with this exception, a majority of the counties in the province were represented.   On the following day the

---

[62] The principal source of the meetings of March 28 and April 11 is the published statement made by Lewis Morris, who was chairman of the meeting of
April 11.   4 Am. Arch., 2: 314; Cal. of Hist. MSS., 1: 20, 21; New York
Mercury, April 17, 1775; Rivington's Gazetteer, April 20, 1775; Bolton, Westchester County, 2: 349; Dawson, Westchester County, 67.   The statement of
Morris should be checked by the conservative account of the meeting of April
11, in New York Mercury, April 17, 1775; 4 Am. Arch., 2: 321.   Cf. second
statement of Morris, May 7, ibid., 323.

[63] Meeting of April 11 opposed convention almost unanimously.   4 Am. Arch.,
2: 313.

[64] Minutes preserved complete.   Ibid., 351, 358.

[65] "That the gentlemen from Queens County, viz., John Talman, Joseph Robinson, Zebulon Williams, and Col. Jacob Blackwell, be allowed to be present
at its deliberations and will take into consideration any advice they may offer,
but cannot allow them a vote; with which those gentlemen declare themselves
satisfied."   Ibid., 356; Onderdonck. Documents and Letters . . . of Queens
County, 22.

old delegates,[66] with the exception of Isaac Low and John Haring,[67] together with five others—Peter Schuyler, George Clinton, Lewis Morris, R. R. Livingston, and Francis Lewis—were elected to represent New York province in the second Continental Congress. Of this delegation, the city's members were no longer a majority. One of the most conservative of the old city delegates, Isaac Low, had been replaced by an avowed radical, Francis Lewis. While the result was doubtless not wholly satisfactory to men like Alexander MacDougall and John Lamb, it represented a decided victory for radicalism. The conservative program was rapidly breaking down; and of the old members of the conservative faction, one part was becoming indistinguishable from the revolutionists, while the other was in part already identified with the loyalists.

---

[66] Isaac Low, James Duane, Philip Livingston, John Jay, and John Alsop, of New York city; Henry Wisner and John Haring of Orange; William Floyd, of Suffolk; Simon Boerum, of Kings.

[67] Haring gave satisfactory reasons for declining an election. Low was chairman of the Committee of Sixty, but he was not in sympathy with the radical policy of the committee. He was nominated, nevertheless, as one of the eleven deputies to the provincial convention. Before the election came off he announced that he would not attend the convention if elected. He was elected but did not attend. As the convention was limited to its own members in the choice of delegates to Congress, the secretary visited Low and asked him if he considered himself a member of the convention. He replied that he did not. 4 Am. Arch., 2: 355, 357.

CHAPTER IX

THE FIRST PROVINCIAL CONGRESS: THE REVOLUTIONARY GOVERNMENT ESTABLISHED

The Provincial Convention was dissolved on Saturday, April 22, and the next day, at four o'clock in the afternoon, news of the battle of Lexington reached New York.[1] At that time there was no naval force in the harbor, except the sloop *Kings Fisher*, and only one hundred men of the Royal Irish Regiment in the barracks of the city.[2] Governor Tryon was in England, and the administration had once more fallen to the experienced, but old and timid Colden.[3] Furthermore, it can readily be imagined that the story of Lexington had lost nothing in the many repetitions on the road from Boston.[4] It is not altogether surprising, therefore, that for nearly a week the city was ruled by the mob. Under the lead of hot-headed zealots like Lamb and Sears and Willett, the arsenal was forced open, and about six hundred muskets "distributed among the most active citizens, who formed themselves into voluntary corps and assumed the government of the city." The Customs House was closed. The public stores were seized. Business was at a standstill. Armed citizens paraded up and down the streets. Neither the governor nor the corporation made any effort to restore order, while the British regulars "confined themselves to their barracks."[5]

---

[1] Duane, *Diary of Marshall,* 18. Willett's *Narrative,* 54.

[2] *New York Col. Doc.,* 8: 571.

[3] Colden was fortunate or unfortunate enough to be in charge at the critical times: Stamp-Act, Tea Episode, and Battle of Lexington. He was never recompensed for his losses in 1765, and in 1771 Dunmore seized half his salary for a period of ten months. *Ibid.,* 257.

[4] "Published with horrid and aggravating circumstances." Colden to Dartmouth, May 3, 1775; *Ibid.,* 571.

[5] Willett's *Narrative,* 54, 55. *New York Col. Doc.,* 8: 571, 572. Capt. Montagu to Admiral Graves, April 26, 1775; *Cal. Home Office Pap.,* 1773-1775, No. 1020. 4 *Am. Arch.,* 2: 448, 459, 460.

The Committee of Sixty was no more prepared to deal effectively with this situation than the legal government. It had been chosen to enforce the Association, and that much of governmental authority it had exercised. But the time had now come for the extra-legal organization of the radicals to assume much more extensive governmental powers than there had ever been any occasion for before. What the Committee of Sixty could not do was done by the Committee of One Hundred and the Provincial Congress. Within a month after the Battle of Lexington, the radical party organization had been transformed into a virtual government which usurped the functions of the assembly and claimed to exact obedience by the authority of a popular mandate. How this transformation was effected, and by what means obedience was enforced, it will be worth while to trace in some detail.

Three days after the arrival of the news of Lexington, the Committee of Sixty published a circular letter stating that a new committee was necessary, and suggesting that it be composed of one hundred members of which thirty-three should constitute a quorum. It was proposed that the suffrage be limited to freemen and freeholders, that the vote be taken by ballot, in the wards, under the usual supervision. At the same time, so the circular ran, "it is highly advisable that a Provincial Congress be immediately summoned; and that it be recommended to the Freeholders and Freemen . . . to choose, at the same time that they vote for the new committee aforesaid, twenty deputies to represent them in the said Congress; and that a letter be . . . dispatched to all the counties requesting them to . . . appoint their deputies without delay, to meet at New York, on Monday, the twenty-second of May next." The election was fixed for Friday, April 28.[6]

No list of candidates, either for the committee or for Congress, was attached to this circular. On the following day, however, a second broadside appeared, containing a list of names for the

---

* Broadsides, 1. Cal. of Hist. MSS., 1: 3. New York Mercury, May 1, 1775.
4 Am. Arch., 2: 400.

committee and for Congress.[7]   This second broadside, which
it presently transpired was put forth by the Sixty, was unsigned,
in order, doubtless, to avoid the charge of having sought to influence the electors.   The committee's tickets at once aroused
opposition in extreme radical circles.   No record of these objections has been preserved, but from an answering broadside published by the Sixty in justification of its tickets, it appears that
the lists were opposed because they were too long and because
they contained the names of men whose loyalty to America was
doubtful.   In a broadside published Tuesday, April 28, the Committee acknowledged the tickets, and sought to justify them: a
large committe was desirable because all factions in the city
ought to be represented in it; men whose loyalty was questionable had been included for the very purpose of conciliating
them, and bringing them over to a hearty support of the patriot
cause.   In any case, the appointment of "some committee" was
the essential point.   Monday, instead of Friday, was now set for
the election, and the last word of the Sixty was to urge that
"a committee of 100" be appointed.[8]

In this apology of the Committee one can readily perceive
the influence of men like Jay, Duane, Low and Van Schaack;
and the growing influence of such men in radical councils is of
vital importance for understanding the future conduct of the
radical party.   While the radical party had won at every step
since the first congress, it had won because a considerable group
of the old conservative faction was always prepared in the end
to come over to the radical position rather than withdraw altogether from the extra-legal movement.   Conservatives had entered the Fifty-One in order to direct the popular movement
along moderate lines.   Conservative delegates had been elected
to the first congress for the same reason; while opposing the
radical program of Congress, they had nevertheless signed the
Association, had become members of the Sixty and delegates to
the second congress, with the same jurisdiction always at hand.

---

[7] Unsigned Broadside, April 27, 1775; *Broadsides*, 1.
[8] Broadside signed Isaac Low, April 28, 1775; *Broadsides*, 1; 4 *Am. Arch.*,
2: 427.

The radical policy was thus successful, but the radical party was steadily improving, as it were, in quality; it was now, at any rate, largely directed by men of conservative temper for whom the old conservative policy had ceased to be practicable. These far-seeing men realized fully that the crucial moment had arrived; if the radical party organization was to assume successfully the functions of a government it must proceed with extreme caution. If the new committee and the new congress were really the instruments of a party, the fact must be concealed; ostensibly at least, they must represent the whole people.

To secure an effective sanction for the new organization was, therefore, of fundamental importance. For this purpose a new association was prepared by Jay, Duane, and Van Schaack, and published on Saturday, April 29.[9] This important document was as follows: "Persuaded that the salvation of the rights and liberties of America depend, under God, on the firm union of its inhabitants .   .   . and convinced of the necessity of preventing the anarchy and confusion which attend a dissolution of the powers of government: We, the Freemen, Freeholders, and Inhabitants of the city and county of New York .   .   . do, in the most solemn manner, resolve never to become slaves; and do associate, under all the ties of religion, honour, and love to our Country, to adopt and endeavor to carry into execution whatever measures may be recommended by the Continental Congress, or resolved upon by our Provincial Convention, [Congress] for the purpose of preserving our Constitution and opposing the execution of the several arbitrary and oppressive Acts of the British Parliament, until a reconciliation between Great Britain and America, on Constitutional principles, (which we most ardently desire) can be obtained; and that we will, in all things, follow the advice of our General Committee respecting the purposes aforesaid, the preservation of peace and good order, and the safety of individuals and private property." In the enthusiasm of the hour the Association was signed by

---

[9] A General Asssociation, etc.: *Broadsides*, **1**. *4 Am. Arch.*, **2**: 471. Almon, *Remembrancer*, **1**: 61. Jones, *History of New York*, **2**: 505. (De Lancey's edition)

more than a thousand persons,[10] but within the month the signing, we are told, had "abated" somewhat, not more than a third
of those who might have signed having done so in fact.[11] For
the present, however, the document served the purpose for
which it was intended: it furnished an ostensible, if not a real,
popular sanction for the authority which the new organization
was preparing to exercise.[12]

The frank explanation of the Sixty, and the promulgation of
the Association, appear to have neutralized all further opposition to the committee's proposals, and on Monday, May 1, the
tickets which it had nominated were elected.[13] The new committee, certainly, so far as membership is concerned, did represent
the city. Fifty-five of the old Sixty were members of the One
Hundred.[14] Of these fifty-five, seven at least became loyalists,[15]
fifteen at least were prominent radicals,[16] the rest were men who
were likely to follow the lead of Jay, Duane, and Philip Livingston. The five members of the Sixty that were retired were
men of no special influence: three became loyalists,[17] one having
already been disciplined for a violation of the Continental Association.[18] Of the forty-five new members, seven had been members of the Fifty-One; of these seven, two became loyalists,[19]
one was a radical,[20] and the other four cannot be very definitely

---

[10] 4 Am. Arch., 2: 471. Duane, Diary of Marshall, 24. New York Mercury,
May 1, 1775. Almon, Remembrancer, 1: 61. Jones, History of New York, 1:
44.

[11] Colden to Dartmouth, June 7, 1775; Letter-Book, 2: 400.

[12] 4 Am. Arch., 2: 448. Adams, Familiar Letters, 50, 54.

[13] 4 Am. Arch., 2: 459. New York Mercury, May 15, 1775. New York Col.
Doc., 8: 600. Willett's Narrative, 57.

[14] The five of the Sixty who were excluded were: Charles Nicoll, Edward
Laight, Charles Shaw, John Roome, William Ustic. For the list of Sixty
see above chapter VII.

[15] Low, Alsop, Wm. Walton, Van Schaack, Ritzema, Murray, J. De Lancey.

[16] P. V. B. Livingston, Isaac Sears, Alexander MacDougall, Thomas Randall,
Leonard Lispenard, P. T. Curtenis, Abram Brasher, A. P. Lott, Francis Lewis,
Theo. Anthony, I. Roosevelt, Jer. Platt, Robert Benson, Comfort Sands, Nich.
Roosevelt.

[17] Edward Laight, Jno. Roome, Wm. Ustic.

[18] Wm. Ustic, who, with his brother, was disciplined in April for exporting
nails to Boston. Rivingston's Gazetteer, April 20, 1775.

[19] Yates, Young.

[20] Jacobus Van Zandt.

placed.[21] Thirty-eight members of the One Hundred had never been members of either the Fifty-One or the Sixty. Of these at least nine became loyalists;[22] three were among the most conspicuous radicals in the city, John M. Scott, John Lamb, and Daniel Dunscomb, the chairman of the Mechanics committee;[23] the rest reflected all degrees of loyalty, and were included doubtless precisely for that reason.[24]

But a consideration of membership alone will not suffice to determine what the committee represented in its actual conduct of affairs; it is equally important to know who were the active members, if the term may be used. The quorum was fixed at thirty-three, and, small as that seems, it was ultimately found necessary to reduce it to twenty-seven.[25] For the present a quorum was obtained without difficulty, but absences ranged from a fourth to nearly two-thirds of the whole membership. From May 1, to June 8, the total number of absences from seventeen meetings was approximately six hundred and fifty, or an average of over one-third.[26] Two members never attended;[27] twelve were present at less than half of the meetings;[28] thirty-five were absent from five to ten times;[29] fifty were absent not

---

[21] Thomas Marston, Richard Sharp, Gerardus Duychink. Peter Goelet.

[22] James Desbrosses, Augustus Van Horn, Benjamin Kissam, George Folliott, Abram Brinkerhoff, William Seaton, William Laight, Anthony Van Dam, Thomas Buchanan.

[23] Three other members of the Mechanics Committee were taken over from the Sixty: Brasher, Theo. Anthony, Jer. Platt.

[24] Jas. Beekman, Sam Ver Planck, David Clarkson, Thomas Smith, Garret Keteltas, Eleazer Miller, Cornelius Clopper, Jno. Reade, Jas. Van Cortlandt, Jno. Marston, Jno. Morton, Jacobus Leffertse, Benjamin Helme, Walter Franklin, David Beekman, Evert Bancker, Robert Ray, Nicholas Bogart, Sam Broome, David Phoenix, Jno. Finlay, Oliver Templeton, Lewis Pintard, Cornelius P. Low, Petrus Byvank, G. W. Ludlow.

[25] Not until January, 1776. 4 Am. Arch., 4: 693. In September, twenty new members were elected. Ibid., 3: 736.

[26] These statistics have been gathered from the lists given in Ibid., 2: 468–1645, passim.

[27] George Folliott and Sam. Jones. Their places were filled by William Bedlow and John Woodward. Ibid., 898, 933.

[28] Johnson, Embree, Ritzema, Murray, Ver Planck, Clarkson, Goelet, J. Marston, Morton, Franklin, Seaton, S. Broome.

[29] I. Low, P. V. B. Livingston, Sears, W. Walton, J. Broome, G. H. Ludlow, Abr. Walton, Van Shaack, Bassett, Bicker, White, I. Roosevelt, Van Vorhees, Platt, Benson, De Lancey, Burling, Yates, Smith, Desbrosses, Van Horn, Keteltas, Miller, Kissam, Scott, Van Cortlandt, Van Zandt, T. Marston, Leffertse, Sharpe, Young, D. Beekman, Laight, Phoenix, Pintard.

more than five times;[30] two were never absent.[31]   From this analysis it is clear that the committee of One Hundred, even during the first month, was largely dominated by those who had directed the Sixty, assisted by newly elected radicals; whatever it represented ostensibly, it was in fact the organ of that conservative—radical combination which was destined to inaugurate the revolution and achieve independence.

Meanwhile, the assembly, according to prorogation, was to meet May 3.[32]   The conciliatory resolution of Lord North had arrived,—unfortunately, one day after the news from Lexington, when the city was already in the hands of the mob.[33] The council, which advised the governor to prorogue the assembly for the present, prepared a statement of events since the beginning of hostilities: the "melancholy event in Masachusetts Bay," it was asserted, "has kindled a flame that renders it impossible for the Representatives of the people to give . . . attention to his Lordship's Letter . . . until the present ferment subsides;" nor would there be "the most distant hope of accomplishing his Majesty's intention, if there is any farther irritation by the movements of the army, and fresh effusion of blood."[34] Both the council and the lieutenant-governor were of the opinion that the government was "entirely prostrated;"[35] and a proclamation was issued proroguing the assembly till the seventh of June.[36] The action of the governor and council in some

---

[30] MacDougall, Randall, Lispenard, Hallett, Hoffman, Remsen, Curtenius, Brasher, Lott, Duryee, Bull, Totten, Ivers, Mulligan, J. Anthony, T. Anthony, Goforth, Denning, Sands, Gilbert, Berrian, G. W. Ludlow, N. Roosevelt, Flceming, F. Jay, W. W. Ludlow, J. B. Moore, Lasher, Janeway, J. Beekman, Clopper, Duychink, Brinkerhoff, Helme, Banker, Ray, Bogart, Lamb, Van Dam, Dunscomb, Finlay, Templeton, C. P. Low, Buchanan, Byvank, Duane, J. Jay, Alsop, P. Livingston, F. Lewis. The last five were in attendance until they left for the Continental Congress, which met May 10. The actual number of absences against these men were, in order: 13, 15, 14, 14, 10. Most of the deputies to the Provincial Congress were also members of the Committee. But as the Congress met in the day time and the Committee met in the evening, it was possible to attend both, as MacDougall did in fact.

[31] MacDougall and Goforth.

[32] *New York Col. Doc.*, **8:** 564.

[33] 4 *Am. Arch.*, **2:** 459, 460. Hutchinson's *Diary*, **1:** 467.

[34] 4 *Am. Arch.*, **2:** 459, 460.

[35] Colden to Dartmouth, May 3, 1775; *New York Col. Doc.*, **8:** 571. *Cf. Cal. Home Office Pap.*, 1773-1775, No. 1020. Hutchinson's *Diary*, **1:** 467.

[36] 4 *Am. Arch.*, **2:** 461. *New York Col. Doc.*, **8:** 571.

measure justified the Association; in any case, it left a clear field for the new committee.

The committee of One Hundred at once assumed the powers of a government; restored order in the city, and directed the province until the opening of the Provincial Congress.[37] At the first meeting, May 1, Isaac Low was chosen chairman, and rules of procedure were adopted.[38] It was resolved to offer the Association of April 29 to every inhabitant in the county, Colden only excepted, the names of those refusing to sign to be returned to the committee.[39] What attitude to assume towards such persons was of the very essence of the problem which the new organization had to solve. May 12, MacDougall moved that the committee of correspondence be instructed to report a resolution on that point, and meantime to direct that no person be treated as an enemy except on the direct authority of the Continental Congress or the One Hundred.[40] The further consideration of this delicate question, save for a resolution urging the people to "make their subscriptions as speedily as possible,"[41] appears to have been left to the Provincial Congress. The continential Association was, on the other hand, rigidly enforced,[42] and in this work the committee was assisted by several voluntary companies of citizens.[43] Besides securing its own position, the committee began at once to prepare for war. The port was opened, but no ships were permitted to clear for Boston or Halifax.[44] The mails were opened, and private messengers were used

---

[37] "Your honor cannot but see the sudden transition . . . from a state of tumult . . . to tranquility and good order, as the consequence of our appointment." Committee to Colden, May 11, 1775; *New York Col. Doc.*, 8: 585.

[38] 4 *Am. Arch.*, 2: 468. In absence of the chairman, all letters were to be opened by the first five on the roll who were in town. After the Continental delegates left for Philadelphia, these would ordinarily be: P. V. B. Livingston, Sears, Johnson, MacDougall, Randall.

[39] *Ibid.*

[40] *Ibid.*, 522.

[41] *Ibid.*, 605.

[42] *Ibid.*, 509, 727.

[43] *Ibid.*, 468, 604, 605.

[44] *New York Col. Doc.*, 8: 571. Almon, *Remembrancer*, 1: 61. *Hist. MSS. Com.*, 14: Pt. 10, p. 298. 4 *Am. Arch.*, 2: 530.

for the committee's correspondence.[45]   A night watch was established,[46] arms and ammunition were secured,[47] the sale of
necessary commodities was forbidden,[48] and the people were recommended to perfect themselves in military tactics.[49]   The committee justified its conduct to the lieutenant-governor in a public
letter in which it expressed its desire to strengthen the ''government in the due exercise of constitutional authority.''[50]

With the close of May the responsibility for the direction of
affairs passed largely from the One Hundred to the Provincial
Congress.   A provincial congress had long been desired by the
radicals and feared by the loyalists and more extreme conservatives.[51]   Not until the beginning of hostilities, however, was the
way open for the establishment of such a body.   April 28, the
Sixty sent circular letters to the counties requesting them to
choose deputies.[52]   Deputies were appointed in every county in
the province; but it is certain that in five at least only a very
small minority was at all concerned in the business; in some
others it seems that the deputies were fairly representative; in
others, it is impossible to say whether the representation was
virtual or merely nominal.   Even in the most conservative counties there was very little active opposition to the elections of
deputies, or none at all.   In many cases the election of deputies
was accompanied by a more complete systematization of the

---

[45] *New York Col. Doc.,* 8: 572.   *4 Am. Arch.,* 2: 482.   *Cal. Home Office Pap.,*
1773–1775, Nos. 985, 1037.
[46] *4 Am. Arch.,* 2: 636.
[47] *Ibid.,* 469, 529, 530, 531.
[48] *Ibid.,* 728.
[49] *Ibid.,* 470.
[50] *Ibid.,* 533, 534.   *New York Col. Doc.,* 8: 583, 585.   Almon, *Remembrancer,*
1: 101, 102.
[51] Colden had called the assembly early in the year in order to ward off the
Provincial Congress. *New York Col. Doc.,* 8: 528.   The Provincial Convention
had been opposed because it would lead to a congress. *4 Am. Arch.,* 2: 44.   A
letter from South Carolina, March 1, strongly urged the calling of a congress.
"This measure has given the greatest satisfaction here, and so firmly united
Town and Country, that we are thereby become one compact regularly organized body.   The enemies of American freedom are aware of the cementing tendency of such a step, and 'wherever they have influence, attempt to prevent it."
Ibid., 3.   The radicals had recommended a provincial convention for the election of delegates to the first Continental Congress.   See above chapter V.
[52] *Cal. Hist. MSS.,* 1: 4.   *4 Am. Arch.,* 2: 428.

committee system, the committees gradually assuming administrative functions under the direction of the Provincial Congress.

The most conservative counties in the province were Queens,
Tryon, Richmond, Dutchess, and Westchester. In the first two
there was some active opposition by the loyalists; in the last
three the elections were generally ignored altogether by the
loyalists and conservatives. In such counties the simplest method
of accomplishing the object which the radicals had in view was
the simple mass meeting. However few the radicals might be,
and whether widely scattered or confined to one or two towns,
they could all attend such a meeting without special authorization. Twenty or thirty men thus assembled could be represented
as "a respectable number of the freeholders of the county,"
and as such could assume to speak for the whole county. A
delegated county meeting, or a meeting of town committees, presented greater difficulties. Not unnaturally, therefore, the
former method generally prevailed in these five counties.

The New York letter and the Association were ignored in
Queens county for nearly a month; and about the middle of
May a second letter was dispatched to Jamaica, Hempstead, and
Oyster Bay.[53] The only reply from Oyster Bay was the public
declaration of three justices of the peace: "we pay no regard to
. . . any . . . matter contrary to the sacred oath we
have taken."[54] Three days later, May 22, a number of freeholders assembled at Jamaica, and unanimously elected ten deputies for the county.[55] One of the deputies, Thomas Hicks, who
had been appointed for the town of Hempstead, being assured
by leading citizens that the town did not wish to be represented,
refused to attend the Congress.[56] Four other deputies remained
away most of the time, one of them giving as his reason the belief that a majority of the county was opposed to the measure.[57]
In Tryon County, it is said, the people were terrified by the Johnsons, who had already dispersed one meeting in the Mohawk

[53] 4 *Am. Arch.*, **2:** 532.
[54] Onderdonck, *Documents and Letters* . . . *of Queens County*, 28.
[55] *Cal. Hist. MSS.*, **1:** 90.   *4 Am. Arch.*, **2:** 838.
[56] 4 *Am. Arch.*, **2:** 1114.
[57] *Jour. of Prov. Cong.*, **2:** 75.

district.[58] The county committee, however, resolved to support
Congress, and appointed two deputies on June 11,
nearly three weeks after the opening of Congress.[59] In Westchester County the circular letter was probably sent to Lewis
Morris,[60] and a general meeting was called at White Plains for
May 8. On that day some freeholders assembled and named a
committee of ninety persons, twenty being sufficient for a quorum. Twenty-three of the committee being there present, at
once named a ticket of deputies which was "unanimously"
elected by the meeting—the meeting doubtless being with difficulty distinguishable from the committee.[61] For Dutchess[62] and
Richmond[63] counties our information is limited to the official
credentials of the deputies, elected in each case at a "county
meeting."

In one county, Orange, the deputies were appointed in the
separate towns, two deputies being appointed by Orange Town,
two by Haverstraw, three by Cornwall, four by Goshen.[64] In
the remaining counties, deputies were appointed either by
county meetings of delegates elected especially for that purpose,
or by the town committees assembling at one place and acting
as a county convention or a general county committee. Few
details have been preserved, save in the case of Albany where
the procedure may be profitably contrasted with that at New
York.

The Albany committee did not wait for the appeal from New
York before acting on the news from Lexington. April 29 advertisements were sent to all the districts in the county stating
that "whereas the committee of correspondence do not conceive

[58] 4 *Am. Arch.*, **2:** 637.

[59] *Cal. Hist. MSS.*, **1:** 101. 4 *Am. Arch.*, **2:** 959. Only one of the deputies
attended ordinarily, and in September the number was reduced to one. *Ibid.*, **3:**
702.

[60] *Cf.* Dawson, *Westchester County*, 82.

[61] 4 *Am. Arch.*, **2:** 529, 832. *Cal. Hist. MSS.*, **1:** 64. Dawson says that not
more than twenty-four freeholders were present. *Westchester County*, 82.

[62] *Cal. Hist. MSS.*, **1:** 67. 4 *Am. Arch.*, **2:** 834. Rombout precinct alone
had no committee, but chose one in July. *Ibid.*, 1753.

[63] Election at Richmond town, May 1. *Cal. Hist. MSS.*, **1:** 42. 4 *Am. Arch.*,
2: 831, 509.

[64] *Cal. Hist. MSS.*, **1:** 42, 43. 4 *Am. Arch.*, **2:** 831, 832, 834

themselves fully invested with power to do every matter which
in this critical hour may become necessary," it would be well
for each district to appoint their old committeemen or others
in their places "to be a committee of safety, protection, and
correspondence with full power to transact all such matters as
. . . may tend to the welfare of the American cause." The
meeting of the new committee was fixed for May 10, and those
districts that had hitherto elected no members were assured that
no further opportunity would be given them to do so.[65] How
the district committees were elected is not known, save for the
city of Albany itself. May 1, the people were assembled at the
Market House, and requested to answer whether they were in
favor of appointing such a committee as was suggested in the
above advertisement, and "if yea, who are the persons you
choose to appoint?" Obviously the committee had a ticket already prepared, which was elected.[66] Besides Albany city,
seventeen districts elected committeemen. When the whole
committee met, May 10, the New York letter had meantime
arrived, and it was resolved to choose deputies by ballot from
the committee. Eleven deputies were accordingly chosen, six
being from the city of Albany, and one each from the manor of
Livingston, Saratoga, Claverack, Manor of Rensselaerwyck, and
Schenectady.[67] After the departure of the deputies, the committee was judged to be too small, and on May 25, two additional members were chosen from each ward in Albany city.[68]

In Cumberland County a "full meeting of delegates from
"several towns" approved the New York association and appointed deputies to Congress.[69] In Kings County the town of Brooklyn

[65] Minutes of the Albany Committee, 1: 18, 19.

[66] Ibid., 20, 21. Weise, Hist. of Albany, 355.

[67] Minutes of the Albany Committee, 1: 26, 32, 34. Cal. Hist. MSS., 1: 64.
The entire county committee so far as present on this occasion, consisted of
130 members, as follows: Albany 19. Great Impogt 2, Hosick 3, Bessington
8, Cambridge 8, Manor of Livingston 5, Schogtehoche 8, Kings District 3, German Camp 2. Cambridge District 3, Cochsahie and Katskill 5, Schoharie and
Duanesborough 6, Claverick 5, Kinderhook 4, Manor of Rensselaerwyck 22,
Saratoga 10, Schenectady 10, Half Moon 7.

[68] Minutes of the Albany Committee, 1: 45.

[69] Cal. Hist. MSS., 1: 97. 4 Am. Arch., 2: 918, 934; 3: 708.

named two deputies on May 20,[70] and three days later a meeting of township delegates confirmed the Brooklyn deputies and added six others.[71] In Suffolk the town committees met May 5, at the county hall and named deputies.[72] Brookhaven was the one town in the county that had no committee, but on May 16 and 17, Selah Strong was chosen to represent that town,[73] and June 8 a town committee was appointed.[74] In Ulster County a mass meeting, May 8, resolved to "bury in oblivion all past differences," and the Association was soon signed by nearly all the male inhabitants.[75] May 11, committees from eleven precincts met at New Paltz and unanimously appointed seven deputies.[76] In Charlotte County, committees from eight towns appointed two deputies on May 12, and a meeting at Fort Edward on June 29, confirmed the election and named three more.[77] Even Gloucester County, after receiving a letter from Congress, "formed a county committee, as also one in each town and precinct," and appointed one deputy.[78]

The most striking feature of this election was the absence of loyalist opposition. In view of the effect of the first Continental Congress, the choice of deputies from every county must have surprised the radical leaders as, on first sight, it does the historian. Judging from surface indications, one might suppose that the Battle of Lexington had thoroughly united all classes in the province.[79] That the beginning of hostilities profoundly affected the loyalists, there is no question. For the moment they were stunned, and in their confusion were unde-

---

[70] *Cal. Hist. MSS.*, **1**: 89. *4 Am. Arch.*, **2**: 837. Ostrander, *Brooklyn*, **1**: 208.

[71] *Cal. Hist. MSS.*, **1**: 89. *4 Am. Arch.*, **2**: 838.

[72] *Cal. Hist. MSS.*, **1**: 43. *4 Am. Arch.*, **2**: 831.

[73] *Cal. Hist. MSS.*, **1**: 44, 45, 46. *4 Am. Arch.*, **2**: 832, 835. The election in this precinct was by militia companies, May 16 and 17.

[74] Committee of 16, chosen by a "large majority" of the freeholders. The resolutions were published June 27. The committee apologized for "coming so late into Congressional measures," which was due to the fact that "opposition ran so high in some parts of this Town." *4 Am. Arch.*, **2**: 933, 934.

[75] *Ibid.*, 543.

[76] *Cal. Hist. MSS.*, **1**: 23. *4 Am. Arch.*, **2**: 832. For some difficulties in getting the association enforced, see *Ibid.*, 448, 548, 1659.

[77] *Cal. Hist. MSS.*, **1**: 65, 66. *4 Am. Arch.*, **2**: 833.

[78] *4 Am. Arch.*, **2**: 1668.

[79] The radicals so represented it. *Cf.* Adams, *Familiar Letters*, 50, 54. *4 Am. Arch.*, **2**: 547. *Hist. MSS. Com.*, **14**: Pt. 10, p. 298.

cided what course to pursue. The overthrow of legal government left them without support; unorganized, uncertain of their own strength, overawed by radical enthusiasm and violence, they were in no position to assert themselves. Many of them were thus led to sign the Association, which they hated, to parade in companies which only waited to welcome British troops, and to acquiesce at least in the organization of the new committees and the choice of deputies to the Provincial Congress.[80]

But aside from all this, the apathy of the loyalists was in part due to clever political maneuvering by the moderate radicals who carried the movement through. In nominating candidates for Congress, it was their policy, just as it had been in naming the committee of One Hundred, to select men from all factions in order to conciliate those who were undecided. Of the twenty-one deputies from New York city, seven became loyalists,[81] one of them, refusing to attend, being soon replaced by an avowed radical;[82] and some of the remaining fourteen were indifferents.[83] The same was true of other delegations, notably those of Queens, Richmond, and Westchester. Of the entire one hundred and thirteen deputies, no less than nineteen

---

[80] "The tories put to flight here . . .   such a spirit was never seen in New York." Adams, *Familiar Letters*, 54. "The tories there durst not show their heads." *Ibid.*, 50. "Whenever a sufficient protection appears, it will be found that his Majesty has many true and loyal subjects who are at present compelled to acquiesce in the plans of opposition. I have reason to believe that numbers now appear in Arms in the City, who have not the least intention to oppose government but will join to support legal authority when there is opportunity. I know of one company in particular who have associated to support government, but for the present appear and parade as others do." Colden to Dartmouth, June 7, 1775; *New York Col. Doc.*, 8: 582. "The firm friends of government here . . .   are now depressed by those who have taken the power into their hands possibly for deeper designs." Tryon to Dartmouth, July 4, 1775; *ibid.*, 589. "The city is almost cleared of Tories, and the few which remain are ashamed and afraid." New York Letter, May 10, 1775; 4 *Am. Arch.*, 2: 547. The treatment accorded to Rivington and Cooper was calculated to inspire fear. *New York Col. Doc.*, 8: 297, 581. *Cal. Home Office Pap.*, 1773–1775, No. 1020. *Hist. MSS. Com.*, 14: Pt. 10, p. 330, 334.

[81] I. Low, Hallett, Abr. Walton, Kissam, J. De Lancey, Yates, Folliott.

[82] Folliott was replaced by Isaac Sears by an election held June 8. 4 *Am. Arch.*, 2: 898, 933.

[83] The deputies from New York aside from the seven named above, were the following. Those in italics were prominent radicals. *P. V. B. Livingston, MacDougall, Lispenard*, Clarkson, Smith, *Brasher, I. Roosevelt, J. M. Scott*, John Van Cortlandt, J. Beekman, *Van Zandt*, Ver Planck, J. Marston, Walter Franklin.

were afterwards loyalists,[84] and a larger number were lukewarm. Many conservatives and loyalists were, therefore, still hoping that the Provincial Congress would lead New York out of revolution rather than into it, some of the loyalist deputies in fact attending regularly and working sincerely to that end.[85] But the Provincial Congress, following the lead of the Committee of One Hundred, led the province straight, though with great caution, into revolution; like the Committee of One Hundred, it represented the moderate-radical combination much more truly than its nominal membership would indicate. An analysis of its rules of procedure, and of the actual attendance, will make this abundantly clear.

A quorum of Congress was constituted by the presence of a majority of the counties.[86] What constituted a quorum of the county delegation is uncertain. Four counties, in the credentials of their delegates, determined the quorum by instruction; Richmond elected five deputies with three as a quorum;[87] Kings, eight with a quorum of three;[88] Suffolk, eight with a quorum of three;[89] Charlotte, five with a quorum of one.[90] These instructions were not in fact observed, however, the votes of Richmond and Kings being sometimes given by two deputies.[91] As for the other counties, the quorum seems to have ranged from one to four, except in the case of New York, but even there less than a majority was required.[92] The vote of each county was fixed irrespective of the number of deputies, New York having four votes, Albany three, and the other counties two each.[93]

---

[84] Besides the seven loyalists from New York, the following deputies became loyalists: G. Livingston, Abram Lent, Selah Strong, Philip Van Cortlandt, Richard Lawrence, Aaron Cortelyou, George Smith, Richard Stillwell, Daniel Rapalje, Zebulon Williams, Joseph French, Thomas Hicks.

[85] *Cal. Home Office Pap.*, 1773-1775, No. 1113.

[86] 4 *Am. Arch.*, **2:** 1242.

[87] *Cal. Hist. MSS.*, **1:** 42.

[88] *Ibid.*, 89.

[89] *Ibid.*, 43.

[90] *Ibid.*, 66.

[91] 4 *Am. Arch.*, **2:** 1244, 1308. In the case of Kings County, the two delegates who gave the vote of the county were the ones elected by the Town of Brooklyn.

[92] June 6, only ten of the twenty-one were present, but the county was counted as present. *Ibid.*, 1275.

[93] *Ibid.*, 1242.

The vote of each county was cast as a unit according to the majority of deputies present from that county, and every question was decided by a majority of votes so cast.[94]   It was thus possible for nineteen deputies, representing eight counties, to carry on the business of Congress, although that is a purely hypothetical case never in fact realized.

The question of attendance was, nevertheless, a pressing one, save perhaps for the first six weeks. The second day, May 23, the counties of New York, Albany, Dutchess, Ulster, Orange, Suffolk, Westchester, Richmond, and Kings were represented.[95] Delegates from Charlotte appeared May 24;[96] from Queens, May 25;[97] from Tryon and Cumberland, not until June 21 and 22;[98] while the delegates from Gloucester never attended. Some of the deputies from Queens neglected to take their seats on the ground that the county was not in favor of a congress; they were ordered to take their seats, however, inasmuch as the county of Queens "must necessarily be bound by the determinations of this Congress . . . and the dissent . . . is not to the persons chosen, but to the choice of any persons."[99]   The attendance of Congress steadily decreased, the average being, for May 78⅜, for June 63½, for July 48⅘.   The highest number appearing at any one time was 82, the least during these three months was 42.[100]   From the point of view of attendance, those who afterwards became loyalists may be divided into two groups; those who thought Congress might keep New York out of revolution and those who expected nothing from Congress. The former attended regularly and took an active part in the proceedings; such were Isaac Low, John De Lancey, Benjamin Kissam, Abram Walton, Joseph Hallett, and Philip Van Cortlandt, none of whom was absent more than nine times in forty-

---

[94] *Ibid.*, 1243, 1337.
[95] *Ibid.*, 1241.
[96] *Ibid.*, 1246.
[97] *Ibid.*, 1250.
[98] *Ibid.*, 1305, 1309.
[99] *Ibid.*, 1312, 1328.
[100] Based upon statements of attendance as given in *Ibid.*, 1241 ff. After July 28, the lists of members present is no longer given, except in one instance.

three.[101] On the other hand, George Folliott of New York,
Richard Stillwell of Kings, George Smith of Charlotte, and
Daniel Rapalje of Queens never attended; and Abraham Lent
of Orange, Selah Strong of Suffolk, Richard Lawrence of Rich-
mond, Zebulon Williams, Joseph French, and Thomas Hicks of
Queens, were absent from one-half to two-thirds of the time.[102]
Besides those who afterward became avowed loyalists, the absentees were mainly neutrals, or men of loyalist tendencies, such
as Marston and Franklin of New York, Robert Graham and
Dayton of Westchester, Thorne of Queens, Swart of Albany,
Watkins and Campbell of Charlotte, Seeley and J. Woodhull of
Orange.[103] The active members were the radicals and moderate
conservatives. From New York, MacDougall and Verplanck
were never absent, P. V. B. Livingston and Isaac Roosevelt
only once, Lispenard twice, Beekman three times, Brasher four
times, Sears eleven, and Scott twelve times. Gouverneur Morris
and Lewis Graham of Westchester, Jonathan Lawrence and
Joseph Robinson of Queens, Abram Yates, Peter Silvester, Walter
Livingston, Robert Van Rensselaer, and Henry Glenn of Albany,
Nathaniel Woodhull and John Sloss Hobart of Suffolk, were in
each case the men who were rarely absent.[104]

These were the conditions that prevailed in the best days of
the congress. From the middle of July it was increasingly difficult to secure a quorum either of the particular delegations or
of Congress itself. Cumberland County reduced its quorum to
one,[105] and Albany to four "by reason of the inconvenience attending the attendance of all the deputies."[106] August 4, the
matter was taken up by Congress: "Whereas, those counties
which are now represented in this Congress by a majority of

---

[101] The number of absences for each, in order: 1, 3, 5, 7, 8, 9.

[102] Absences: Lent 35, Strong 28, Lawrence 32, Williams 20, French 35,
Hicks 40.

[103] Absences: Marston 17, Franklin 36, Graham 20, Dayton 25, Thorne 29.
Swart 37; Watkins, Campbell, Seeley, and J. Woodhull were not present at all
during this period.

[104] Absences: Morris 7, L. Graham 8, J. Lawrence 7, Robinson 6, A. Yates 8,
Silvester 4, Livingston 11, Van Rensselaer 10, Glenn 12, N. Woodhull 12,
Hobart 11.

[105] *4 Am. Arch.*, **3:** 528.

[106] *Ibid.*, **2:** 1807.

the delegates . . . may be deprived of their weight of representation, by the absence of members upon the public service, Resolved, therefore, that all members who are absent by order of this House, or of the Continental Congress, shall be counted with those who actually appear, and when a majority shall appear upon such counting, then those members actually present shall give their vote for the said county, as if a real majority were personally present at this board."[107]   Both the resolutions of Albany County and of Congress are difficult to understand. Four members had frequently cast the vote of Albany County.[108] The assumption of the congress that a majority of the county delegation was necessary to make a quorum, does not accord with the facts.   There was no county, with more than two delegates, which had not frequently voted when less than half of its delegation was present.   If a majority of the delegates from a majority of the counties had been made the quorum requirement, Congress could hardly have lasted a month.   Perhaps the term "majority" in this resolution is equivalent to "quorum." However that may be, Congress was, during August and September, "frequently . . . unable to proceed to business for want of a sufficient number of members,"[109]—so frequently, indeed, that the quorum rule was sometimes ignored altogether, and on one occasion some important measures were carried when only six out of the fourteen counties were present.[110]

The problem of attendance and quorum might have been solved, doubtless, by a dissolution and new elections.   There were, however, two objections to such a procedure: to dissolve Congress before it had run its term would be an open confession of the very weakness which it was important to conceal, while a new election could hardly prove more satisfactory than the first one.   Ultimately a dissolution was inevitable, but for the present the difficulty was partly solved by a device of which even more

[107] *Ibid.*, 1816.
[108] July 1, only four were present; July 4, three cast the vote of the county; July 6, two cast the vote; July 5, 7, 8, only two present.   *Ibid.*, 1335–1346.
[109] *Ibid.*, 1278.
[110] October 24, there were two divisions with only six counties present; November 4, there was a division with seven counties present.   *Ibid.*, 3: 1303, 1323.

effective use was made in the second congress—the Committee of Safety. The first committe of safety was appointed July 8, after a session of six weeks and three days, when the attendance had fallen to an average of less than one-half of the membership. The committee, which was to sit for two weeks only, and to which nearly the whole power of Congress was intrusted, was composed of three members from New York with the privilege of two votes, and one member from each of the other counties with the privilege of one vote. The membership was apparently determined by each county delegation, but it is the membership that is significant. The three members for New York were P. V. B. Livingston, Lispenard, and MacDougall; the member for Albany was Gouverneur Morris of Westchester; for Dutchess, Jonathan Landon; for Ulster, Egbert Dumont; for Orange, David Pye; for Suffolk, Abram Brasher of New York; for Westchester, Gouverneur Morris; for Kings, Henry Williams; for Richmond, Richard Lawrence; for Queens, Alexander Mac Dougall of New York; for Tryon, P. V. B. Livingston of New York; for Cumberland, John Morin Scott of New York.[111] Eleven men thus made up the committee; five of the eleven were perhaps the most pronounced radicals of the New York delegation, and together they controlled six votes out of a total of fifteen, while Gouverneur Morris, a leading radical at this time, controlled two more, which made a majority. After reassembling July 26, Congress sat for five weeks and three days, and on September 2, with an attendance of forty-seven, a second committee of safety was appointed to sit for the month of September. In this committee New York had four votes, Albany three, and the other counties two each.[112] The concentration of votes was not so marked as in the previous committee, but six New York radicals controlled seven votes, and the additional votes necessary for a majority were in fact secured in the two instances where there was a division.[113]

Meanwhile, if the Provincial Congress did in fact represent the revolutionary party rather than the province as a whole, it was

---

[111] *Ibid.*, **2:** 1347.
[112] *Ibid.*, **3:** 580.
[113] *Ibid.*, 885, 911.

precisely for that reason necessary to proceed with great caution
in assuming the functions of a government. That it did proceed
with caution, but that it also became a government in no uncertain sense, a consideration of the measures which it carried
through will make abundantly clear.

To the important question of jurisdiction, which was taken
up at once, there were two sides: to what extent was Congress
prepared to enforce obedience to its own recommendations within
the province; to what extent was it prepared to submit to those
of the Continental Congress. Both questions were fairly raised
on the first day of the session by Isaac Low who moved: "that
implicit obedience ought to be paid to every recommendation of
the Continental Congress for the general regulation of the associated colonies, but this Congress is competent to and ought,
freely, to deliberate and determine on all matters relative to the
internal police of this colony." Debates arose, and it was resolved that the question "be not now put."[114] Two days later
it was moved "to give their entire and cordial accession to the
confederacy of the colonies," by formally approving of the proceedings of the first Continental Congress. The question was
again debated, and "deferred for further consideration."[115]

Whether the refusal to pass these resolutions marks the first
appearance of local jealousy which, under the lead of the radicals, was one day to develop into the doctrine of states rights,
is an interesting question. However that may be, a more satisfactory solution of the difficulty was found in the proposal to
continue the policy initiated by the city committee. On the
following day it was resolved that the members of Congress be
desired to sign the New York Association of April 29,[116] and
steps were taken to secure complete lists of signers and non-
signers throughout the province. Committees were to be appointed in all of the counties and districts, either by the inhabitants themselves or by their deputies in Congress, "to carry into
execution the resolutions of the Continental and Provincial Congress." The association was to be tendered to every inhabitant

[114] *Ibid.*, **2:** 1244.
[115] *Ibid.*, 1253.
[116] *Ibid.*, 1256.

in each district, and returned to Congress with the names of all non-signers, not later than July 15.[117] For the present, however, it was information that was wanted rather than the strict enforcement of obedience. The committees were instructed, accordingly, that "no coercive steps ought to be used to induce any person to sign the Association;" the example of the other colonies, and the necessity of "maintaining a perfect union in every part of the colony, it is presumed are sufficient reasons to induce the inhabitants of your county to comply with this requisition."[118] Without too hasty an assertion of its own authority or that of the Continental Congress, the way was thus open for whatever coercive measures future events might justify, or for countenancing any plan for conciliation that might prove practicable.

The question of conciliation was, indeed, closely related to the question of asserting governmental authority. Any complete and formal usurpation of power would necessarily discredit the claim that the colony desired a restoration of friendly relations with the mother country; and if there were some extreme radicals, like Isaac Sears, who cared nothing for conciliation, and some extreme conservatives, like Seabury and Wilkins, who had lost all confidence in extra-legal methods of obtaining it, there were many conservatives who would not abandon Congress so long as it made even an ostensible effort in that direction. Moderates and radicals alike, with few exceptions, were as yet too uncertain of their position to alienate unnecessarily any class, however small, which helped to bolster up their extra-legal organization. Therefore, while Congress was "acting with all the confidence and authority of a legal government,"[119] on the one hand, it did not neglect, on the other, to prepare a scheme for reconciliation. May 30, Benjamin Kissam, a conservative and ultimately a loyalist, moved that, "forasmuch as a reconciliation . . . on constitutional principles, is essential to the wellbeing of both countries, and will prevent the horrors of civil war, in

---

[117] *Ibid.*, 1256, 1257, 1261.
[118] *Ibid.*, 1261. *Broadsides*, **1.**
[119] Colden to Dartmouth, June 7, 1775. *New York Col. Doc.*, **8:** 579. *Letter-Book*, **2:** 419.

which this continent is now about to be involved," a committee
be appointed to prepare a plan to be presented to the Continental
Congress.[120] In a slightly amended form, the motion was considered on June 2,[121] the previous question, moved by Mac
Dougall, being lost by a vote of 17-8.[122] The resolution was
carried by the same vote, an additional clause was added, and
a committee of fourteen representing all shades of sentiment appointed to make a report.[123]

The plan, which was not reported for three weeks,[124] betrayed
a hasty and careless preparation. It was short, and in tone far
from conciliatory. The first article demanded the repeal of all
acts mentioned in the resolutions of the first Continental Congress, and of all subsequent acts in restraint of trade and the
fisheries. For this Gouverneur Morris proposed to substitute
"such acts of Parliament as the present Congress think fatal
to the liberties of America,"—a proposal which was voted
down.[125] The report further demanded that the colonial assemblies be limited to three years; that Parliament surrender absolutely the right of interfering "in the religious and ecclesiastical concerns of the colonies;" that the right of the colonies to
legislate for "all cases of internal police whatsoever, subject
only to the negative of their sovereign," be fully recognized;
that all duties raised by Parliamentary regulation of trade be
paid in to the colonial assemblies; that colonial assistance in the
defense of the empire be voted by the assemblies, or by a continental congress "deputed from the several assemblies" and
presided over by a president appointed by the crown. These
proposals were all adopted, except the last which was amended
to read "deputed by the several *colonies.*" The delegates at
Philadelphia, to whom the plan was forwarded, were not very

---

[120] *4 Am. Arch.,* **2:** 1265.
[121] The amendment withdrew the clause referring the plan to the Continental Congress. *Ibid.,* 1269, 1271.
[122] *Ibid.,* 1271.
[123] *Ibid.,* 1270.
[124] Report made June 22. *Ibid.,* 1311. Adopted by paragraphs. *Ibid.,* 1315-1318. Final Plan. *Ibid.,* 1320.
[125] *Ibid.,* 1315.

favorably impressed by this scheme of reconciliation, which was in fact never presented to the Continental Congress.[126]

Whether the adoption of a plan of conciliation, however unpropitious, strengthened Congress with the conservative classes cannot be determined. In any case, measures for the control of the colony were steadily elaborated. The New York Association had already been signed by ninety-nine of the original deputies, fourteen neglecting or refusing to sign,[127] and the district committees were preparing their lists to be returned in July. The official returns show in five districts of Orange County approximately 1,550 signers and 250 non-signers; in seven districts of Ulster County, approximately 1,770 signers and 80 non-signers, in seven or eight districts of Suffolk County, 2,060 signers and 200 non-signers; in six precincts of Dutchess County, 1,680 signers and 882 non-signers; in one district of Charlotte County, 110 signers; in three districts of Cumberland County, 123 signers and 10 non-signers; in Queens County, 17 signers and 209 non-signers.[128] June 7, Colden estimated the signers in New York County at 1,800.[129] August 5 the chairman of Rombout precinct, Dutchess County, requested more time to complete his list,[130] which he returned August 25, the delay being, he said, "on account of pursuing lenient measures."[131]

But refusing to sign the Association was one thing; refusing to obey Congress was quite another. It was desirable to know

[126] July 6, the delegates acknowledged the receipt of the plan. They informed the Congress that they had "unanimously agreed to be silent" on the religious liberty clause, so as not to introduce any thing "foreign to the present controversy." *Jour. of Prov. Cong.*, 1: 73.

[127] The list of signers is given in *Cal. Hist. MSS.*, 1: 85. *4 Am. Arch.*, 3: 581. Besides the 99 original deputies who signed, Isaac Sears, who replaced George Folliott, signed also, making 100. The deputies who did not sign were: Abr. Walton, Folliott, and Franklin, of New York; Chas. Clinton, of Ulster; Jas. Haven, of Suffolk; Rich. Stillwell, of Kings; David Watkins, George Smith, and Archibald Campbell, of Charlotte; Daniel Rapalje and Thomas Hicks, of Queens; Israel Seeley and Jesse Woodhull, of Orange; Jacob Baylie, of Gloucester.

[128] *Cal. Hist. MSS.*, 1: 5, 6, 10, 12–18, 24, 25, 27, 29–36, 44, 46–61; 63, 66–72, 74–83, 98, 99, 209. *4 Am. Arch.*, 3: 582–619. The numbers are given approximately; the lists in the Calendar and in the Archives differ somewhat, and there are some lists which are not definitely referred to any district.

[129] Colden, *Letter-Book*, 2: 424. *New York Col. Doc.*, 8: 579.

[130] *4 Am. Arch.*, 2: 1817.

[131] *Cal. Hist. MSS.*, 1: 86.

who were willing to abide by the recommendations of Congress, but those recommendations were to be observed by all alike. The harbor was carefully watched,[132] cargoes were disposed of by committees appointed for that purpose,[133] and in general the non-intercourse agreements were rigidly enforced.[134] But obedience was also exacted in matters not involved in the Continental Association. Shipping of supplies to Boston was prohibited under penalty of confiscation.[135] British army enlistments were punished by imprisonment in military camps.[136] A British ensign, living in New Jersey, and attempting to return to Boston, was sent back to the New Jersey committee, though without "unnecessary violence."[137] Persons "hostile to American liberty" were imprisoned for a time, and then released on "promises of amendment."[138] Some were declared public enemies for having misrepresented the conduct of the Continental Congress;[139] others were required to remain in certain districts without taking further part in the controversy.[140] "No one," wrote Cadwallader Colden, July 15, "dare now print, write or speak a word in favor of government."[141]

Meanwhile, under the direction of the Continental Congress, the province was put in a state of defense as rapidly as possible. Continental troops were raised,[142] the militia organized,[143]

[132] 4 Am. Arch., 2: 1574.

[133] Ibid., 965, 1046, 1645, 1815; 3: 16, 21, 66–67. Hist. MSS. Com., 14: Pt. 10, p. 350.

[134] "Non-importation strictly adhered to and non-exportation daily expected." Isaac Seagrove to Jno. Blackburn, July 2, 1775; Hist. MSS. Com., 14: Pt. 10, p. 324. Exportation was in fact supervised rather strictly even before the agreement became effective. 4 Am. Arch., 2: 934; 3: 445.

[135] Tryon to Dartmouth, August 9, 1775; New York Col. Doc., 3: 604.

[136] 4 Am. Arch., 2: 1297, 1298, 1299, 1301.

[137] Ibid., 1345.

[138] Ibid., 1793, 1800, 1806.

[139] Ibid., 3: 20, 21.

[140] Ibid., 2: 1815; 3: 15, 20, 21.

[141] Hist. MSS. Com., 14: Pt. 10. p. 330.

[142] 4 Am. Arch., 2: 1242, 1265, 1267–1270, 1275–1278, 1283–1286, 1333–1338; 3: 23–25, 238, 708, 1118. New York Col. Doc., 8: 589.

[143] 4 Am. Arch., 2: 1266; 3: 133, 139, 150, 213, 223, 235, 239, 262, 438, 459, 466, 543, 625, 627, 629, 639–641, 644, 653, 660, 681, 690, 695, 707–709, 726, 737, 750, 774, 778, 851, 936, 983, 988, 1150, 1181, 1206.

fortifications erected,[144] and ammunition and supplies secured.[145] The time had not yet arrived, however, for conscription. As late as August 22, the congress directed that every fourth man in the militia be appointed for minute duty, but only "of such persons as are willing to enter into this necessary service."[146] The most serious difficulty in this respect was naturally the raising of money. Resistance to English taxation did not imply a readiness to submit to congressional taxation: such a measure, we are told, "would give a disgust that might ruin all their schemes."[147] May 26, Congress began to work out a paper money scheme, which was afterwards merged in that of the Continental Congress.[148] Meanwhile, money was advanced from the treasury of the colony by Abram Lott on the personal security of the deputies,[149] by the Loan Office at Albany,[150] or by individuals.[151] But debts rapidly outran income, and in July the possibility of a tax was agitated. As "prudence or policy" dictated the "propriety of doing this in the manner least liable to popular disgust, or perhaps opposition," the congress suggested to the continental delegates that Holland tea, of which there were large quantities in the province, be sold under certain regulations, and bearing a "tax of one shilling per pound."[152] This

---

[144] *Ibid.*, **2:** 1265–1269, 1275–1286. *Broadsides,* **1.**

[145] *4 Am. Arch.*, **2:** 1046, 1242, 1265, 1285, 1292–1297, 1310. Ammunition was secured during 1774 and 1775 in large quantities from Holland, France, and England. *Cal. Home Office Pap.*, 1773–1775, Nos. 717, 732, 782, 793, 1074, 1093. *Hist. MSS. Com.*, **14:** Pt. 10, p. 366. *New York Col. Doc.*, **8:** 434, 509, 510, 528.

[146] *4 Am. Arch.*, **3:** 543.

[147] Colden to Dartmouth, June 7, 1775; *Letter-Book,* **2:** 419. This was recognized by Congress itself. *Cf. 4 Am. Arch.*, **2:** 1805.

[148] *4 Am. Arch.*, **2:** 1254, 1255, 1262. For continental issue, see Ford, *Journals,* **2:** 103, 105, 207, 221, 236. For later issues of Provincial Congress, see *4 Am. Arch.*, **3:** 565–567, 568.

[149] May 31, Clarkson, Lispenard, and MacDougall offered to be bound for sums advanced up to 1500 £. It was then resolved that all the deputies be bound personally, except Henry Williams who dissented. *4 Am. Arch.*, **2:** 1266.

[150] *Ibid.*, 1272.

[151] Clarkson gave a note for 200 £ on personal security of the deputies. *Ibid.*, 1271.

[152] Congress to the Continental Delegates, July 28, 1775; *Ibid.*, 1805. No direct reply to this letter has been found, but September 30, the tea scheme was mentioned in a letter on another matter. "You cannot be insensible of the delicacy of this subject, and how many difficulties we have to struggle with to accomplish your humane request." *Ibid.*, **3:** 750.

plan was abandoned, and August 30 a committee reported in favor of a tax of 15,000£. The report was not approved, however, and Congress issued 45,000£ in paper money instead.[153] A few days later the debt to the colonial treasury, incurred in May, was repudiated in so far as the money had been "applied for the public exigencies of this colony."[154]

While preparing for war in this fashion and endeavoring to suppress the enemies of America at home, Congress sought to maintain friendly relations with the agents of the English government, civil and military, who were stationed in the colony. After the proroguing of the assembly, Colden retired to his farm on Long Island,[155] and June 25, Governor ·Tryon returned from England.[156] Curiously enough, General Washington reached New York at the same time. Both men entered the city under escorts provided by the Provincial Congress,[157] and the same crowds which cheered Washington in the afternoon, huzzaed for Tryon in the evening.[158] Early in July the mayor and corporation proposed to wait upon the governor and deliver a formal address of welcome, but Congress resolved that it would be "altogether improper for the said Corporation, or any other body corporate or individual . . . to address His Excellency at this most critical juncture."[159]

But the chief source of irritation between the royal and revolutionary governments was the presence of the royal ship *Asia,* which had been stationed in the harbor since May 27,[160] and of the royal troops in the city. The troops were an eye-sore to the mob, and radicals like Sears and Willett were in favor of forcing the barracks and imprisoning those who would not desert. To avoid a conflict, it was proposed to remove the small

[153] *Ibid.,* **2:** 1817 ; **3:** 567, 568, 575-577.
[154] *Ibid.,* **3:** 578.
[155] *Cal. Home Office Pap.,* 1773-1775. No. 1057.
[156] Tryon to Dartmouth, July 4, 1775 ; *New York Col. Doc.,* **8:** 589.
[157] "That he have the residue of his Battalion ready to receive either the General or Governor Tryon, whichever shall first arrive, and to wait on both as well as circumstances will allow." *4 Am. Arch.,* **2:** 1318.
[158] Jones, *Hist. of New York,* **1:** 54.
[159] *New York Col. Doc.,* **8:** 594. The address was left with the governor, nevertheless, and he replied to it. *Ibid.,* 593, 594, 595.
[160] *Ibid.,* 581. *4 Am. Arch.,* **2:** 1257.

garrison to the ship *Asia,* and June 6 was set for the embarkation. The radical leaders, under the impression that the troops were to be taken to Boston, halted the procession as it marched down Broad street, and under the lead of Marinus Willett captured some carts containing equipment which, they insisted, the committee had not authorized to be taken from the barracks.[161] The committee itself, however, voted to restore the equipment.[162] Equally irritating to the radicals was the regular provisioning of the ship *Asia,* which the committee had authorized upon its arrival, and which had been continued by the Provincial Congress.[163] July 13 a boat belonging to Captain Vandeput was destroyed in the night.[164] It was ordered rebuilt by the congress, but was again destroyed, whereupon Congress ordered the persons involved to be punished as "enemies of their country."[165] The radicals succeeded in cutting out the phrase "enemies of their country," and the committee appointed to carry out the resolution reported that the guilty persons could not be found.[166] No carpenter dared undertake the task of rebuilding the barge, and it was finally constructed under the protection of a military guard furnished by the Provincial Congress.[167]

For about three months Congress carried out with no serious difficulty the cautious policy which has been described: exercising the functions of government in a tentative way; preparing for war without making war; securing obedience without inflicting harsh penalties. But from the close of August, a policy of moderation became increasingly difficult. It satisfied less than ever the extremists on both sides: conservatives were with-

---

[161] Willett's *Narrative,* 58–65. Colden to Dartmouth, June 7, 1775; *New York Col. Doc.,* 8: 582.

[162] *4 Am. Arch.,* 2: 1290.

[163] *Ibid.,* 1257. Admiral Graves wrote that there were many in the Congress who wished to keep the peace on account of their property, "through whose influence perhaps it is that, as yet, the King's ships have met with no difficulty in getting the provisions required." *Cal. Home Office Pap.,* 1773–1775, No. 1113. But he thought there was no telling how long it would last. *Ibid.,* No. 1057.

[164] Tryon to Dartmouth, August 7, 1775; *New York Col. Doc.,* 8: 597.

[165] Motion introduced by Low and Walton, both afterwards loyalists. *4 Am. Arch.,* 2: 1812, 1818.

[166] *Ibid.,* 3: 78, 79, 139, 535.

[167] *Ibid.,* 533.

drawing because of the failure of conciliation; radicals were urging more repressive measures. To understand the situation during the closing months of the first Provincial Congress, it will be necessary to consider briefly the progress of events outside of the colony.

Until the middle of the summer of 1775, those conservatives who still believed that conciliation was possible without unqualified submission, fixed their hopes upon two things: Lord North's resolution, and the assembly's petitions. It was late in February that North introduced his famous Resolution for Conciliation.[168] The unexpected move was regarded by the opposition as an effort to secure by *finesse* what could not be secured by a straightforward policy.[169] There was some justification for the charge. The government's best hope lay in breaking down the support which Massachusetts was receiving from the other colonies: if New York and some of the southern colonies could be detached from the continental union, the New England rebellion, it was thought, would collapse. The resolution of the first minister was in fact shortly followed by the acts restraining the trade of New England and of the southern colonies.[170] Neither act touched New York, and as the Resolution was held out to the colonies individually, it was expected that the favor thus shown to New York, combined with the well-known conservative temper of that colony, would once more justify the Roman maxim of *divide et impera*.[171] Unfortunately for such an expectation, the Resolution reached New York the day after the news

---

[168] The resolution proposed that when any colony made provision for its proportion of the "common defense," and for the colonial government, such colony would be exempt from further taxes except duties incidental to the regulation of trade, such duties to "be carried to the account of such province." *Parl. Hist.* 18: 320.

[169] Pownall, hitherto the staunchest friend of the colonies, now advocated the use of force. *Ibid.*, 322 ff. Fox thought the measure "founded on that wretched, low, shameful, abominable maxim . . . *divide et impera.*" *Ibid.*, 333. Burke "found the proposition altogether insidious in its nature." *Ibid.*, 335.

[170] *Ibid.*, 298, 411. *15 George III.*, chs. 10, 18.

[171] "I avow the using that principle," said Lord North, "which will thus divide the good from the bad, and give support to the friends of peace and good government." *Parl. Hist.*, 18: 334. *Cf.* London Letter, July 9, 1775; 4 *Am. Arch.*, 2: 1614.

from Lexington, when the city was already in the hands of the mob, whose control was shortly replaced by the more effective rule of the Provincial Congress.

The Provincial Congress ignored the resolution of Lord North, and formed a plan of conciliation of its own which, as we have seen, was referred to the Continental Congress. That the Continental Congress would reject the government's proposals was a foregone conclusion, for those proposals struck at the very union of which the Continental Congress was the chief expression. Before even considering the resolution, Congress very clearly defined its own position. Frankly accepting the Battle of Lexington as a declaration of war, it assumed more openly than the first congress had done the powers of a government. Massachusetts was recommended to form a state government, and to ignore the regulating act and the officers appointed to enforce it.[172] June 17, Washington was appointed "General and commander-in-chief of the army of the United Colonies," and invested with "full power and authority . . . . . . for the . . . welfare of the service."[173] June 30, rules for regulating the army and navy, were established;[174] and July 6, a declaration was put forth stating that the attempt of Great Britain to "effect by force of arms what by law or right they could never effect, renders it necessary for us also to change the ground of opposition, and to close with their last appeal from reason to arms."[175] After all this any measure looking towards conciliation could have at best but a conventional significance. The Petition to the king was felt to be entirely perfunctory,[176] and the reply to Lord North, which was delayed till July 31, was scarcely less so. The resolution was declared to be both "unseasonable and insidious," and the world would agree, it was thought, "that nothing but our own exertions may defeat the ministerial sentence of death or abject submission."[177]

---

[172] Ford, *Journals*, **2**: 83.
[173] *Ibid.*, 96.
[174] *Ibid.*, 111.
[175] *Ibid.*, 128.
[176] *Ibid.*, 158.
[177] *Ibid.*, 224.

If the hope of conciliation was failing in America, the reception of the assembly's restrained petitions by the English government was equally disappointing. Parliament refused to consider either the Memorial or the Remonstrance,[178] and Dartmouth informed Tryon that the government could not negotiate when "all America, Quebec, Nova Scotia, and the Floridas excepted, are in arms against Great Britain."[179] Equally remote from any prospect of conciliatory action on the part of England, was the rumor, which became current in August and September, that Congress had discussed independence, was preparing to confiscate the property of all those who had not taken an active part in resistance, to negotiate a treaty of alliance with France, and to open the ports of America to the commerce of Europe.[180] The issue was daily becoming more definite: more clearly than ever the conservatives found "themselves between Scyalla and Charybdis, that is, the dread of parliamentary taxation, and the tyranny of their present masters."[181] Many of them, convinced that conciliation was a delusion, were now going over to the position which Seabury and Wilkins and others had taken nearly a year before, the steady decline in attendance upon Congress from July to November being precisely a concrete expression of this fact. On the other hand, the very

---

[178] *Parl. Hist.*, **18:** 650, 688.

[179] July 5, 1775: *New York Col. Doc.*, **8:** 591.

[180] "It is said that a motion has been made at the Continental Congress for an Independency." New York Letter, July 5, 1775; *Hist. MSS. Com.*, **14:** Pt. 10, p. 326. "If no response is made to the last petition . . . Independency will be looked forward to and a European power asked for assistance if required." *Ibid.*, 331. Tryon wrote that it was said that within six months, in case Great Britain did not propose some scheme of reconciliation, independence would be declared, a European alliance secured, the ports opened to the world, and the loyalist's property confiscated. Tryon to Dartmouth, [Confidential], August 7, 1775; *New York Col. Doc.*, **8:** 603. The radicals were in fact urging these steps. "We ought to have had in our hands a month ago the whole legislation, executive and judicial of the whole continent, and have completely modeled a constitution; to have raised a naval power, and opened the ports wide; to have arrested every friend of government on the continent and held them as hostages." Intercepted Letter of John Adams, August, 1775; *Hist. MSS. Com.*, **9:** Pt. 3, p. 81. *Cf. ibid.*, 31, 82; **14:** Pt. 10, pp. 327, 364, 388, 399. Ford, *Journals*, **2:** 200.

[181] Tryon to Dartmouth, August 7, 1775; *New York Col. Doc.*, **8:** 604. Many who became loyalists still held to Congress in spite of all this. For a statement of their position, see John De Lancey to Oliver De Lancey, October 3, 1775; *Cal. Home Office Pap.*, 1773–1775, No. 1223.

events which were driving some conservatives into loyalism were forcing the moderates forward on the road to revolution. The Provincial Congress was bound to follow, however hesitatingly, in the steps of the Continental Congress, and whatever strengthened the loyalists increased the necessity of more repressive measures on the part of the revolutionists.

With conservatives withdrawing on the one hand, and radicals demanding an aggressive advance on the other, the Congress nevertheless maintained, as best it could, its old attitude of moderation, although making some concessions as the result of radical demands. An oath of secrecy was administered to the deputies.[182] Ships carrying provisions were forbidden to leave the port without a special permit.[183] In response to inquiries from county committees asking what should be done with persons "opposing the measures of Congress,"[184] a committee was appointed to report on that question. Its report, which was delivered September 1,[185] was substantially as follows: (1) Persons guilty of "attempting to furnish" the British army or navy with supplies contrary to the resolutions of Congress, or of giving information, or of advising expedients to be used against the colonies, were to be punished "at the discretion of the committee" of the district or county, not to exceed three months imprisonment; (2) persons guilty of "having furnished" provisions as above stated, were to be disarmed, to forfeit double the value of the provisions, and to be imprisoned at their own expense until three months after the payment of the forfeit; and for a second offense to be banished from the colony; (3) "although this Congress have a tender regard for freedom of speech, the rights of conscience, and personal liberty . . . yet, for the public safety," any person denying the authority of the Continental or Provincial Congress, or of any county or district committee, or dissuading any person from obeying their recommendations, shall be disarmed, and for a second offense confined at his own expense; where no county or district committee exists, the offense

[182] 4 *Am. Arch.*, **3:** 547.
[183] *Ibid.*, 559, 561.
[184] *Ibid.*, 527, 541, 566.
[185] *Ibid.*, 569, 573, 574.

may be tried in the next district or county, and enforced if necessary by the militia; in all such trials at least thirteen of the
county committee must be present, except Albany, where twenty-five, and New York, where the established quorum, was required; (4) all persons in arms against America, or enlisted for
that end, to be arrested and tried by the Provincial Congress;
the property of such persons to be seized, and "discreet" persons to be chosen to put a value upon it and report the same to
Congress; (5) in all trials under these resolutions the witnesses
were to take oath to speak truth, and judges to try the case on
the evidence without fear or favor.   These measures were not
drastic enough for the extreme radicals, and the second Committee of Safety voted to disarm all non-Associators by force
if necessary.[186]   But in October the resolution of the Committee
was disapproved by Congress by a vote of 11–4, when only six
counties were present.[187]   Its own rules had outlined a sufficient
policy; to be realized more effectively in the future,[188] it would
meanwhile justify the Congress to the friends of America
throughout the continent.

While the loyalists were becoming more and more troublesome, relations with the agents of the British government were
approaching a crisis. Boats belonging to Captain Vandeput were
destroyed,[189] and the mob, while engaged in removing twenty-
one pieces of ordnance from the Battery on the night of August
23, was fired upon by the British ships.[190]   Captain Vandeput
claimed that the firing was begun by the mob itself,[191] but a
committee of Congress reported that the "firing and attack
began from Captain Vandeput's boat."[192]   The affair was
thought to be serious, and on the morning of August 25 Tryon
came up to the city, assembled the Corporation, representatives

---

[186] *Ibid.,* 898, 912.
[187] *Ibid.,* 1303.
[188] For the execution of these rules, see *Ibid.,* 559, 879, 884, 916, 1305, 1321–
1323.
[189] *Ibid.,* 639. *Hist. MSS. Com.,* **14:** Pt. 10, p. 375. *New York Col. Doc.,* **8:**
632.
[190] *New York Col. Doc.,* **8:** 631. *Hist. MSS. Com.,* **14:** Pt. 10, p. 377. *4 Am.
Arch.,* **3:** 550.
[191] *4 Am. Arch.,* **3:** 550.
[192] *Ibid.,* 555.

of the city committee and of Congress, and restored semi-friendly relations by proposing that the stores should remain unmolested and provisions be furnished to the *Asia* by boats from the city instead of the royal barges.[193] In the afternoon, Congress accordingly "ordered that no more cannon or stores be removed from the Battery, until further orders from this Congress."[194]

At the same time it was found necessary to double the guard around the Governor's house. The position of the Governor, indeed, was fast becoming impossible. As early as August 22 he had been informed that the "Continental Congress has agreed to secure all the Crown officers and friends of government."[195] October 6, the Provincial Congress was in fact recommended to arrest every person in the colony "whose going at large may . . . endanger the . . . liberties of America."[196] That Tryon, who was constantly furnishing the English government with valuable information,[197] came under that category, there was no question. Tryon assured Mayor Hicks that, as his arrest might lead to a bombardment, he would embark on board the *Asia* if the people desired it.[198] Both the mayor and the city committee replied that the people wished him to remain in the city: they were "not apprehensive of the least danger to his person or property."[199] But the specific pledge of protection which Tryon demanded was not forthcoming, and on October 19 he removed to the *Halifax Packet*,[200] and subsequently to the ship *Duchess of Gordon*.[201]

Whatever danger Tryon may have been in at the hands of the mob, he was in no danger of arrest by the Provincial Congress. No recommendation from Philadelphia could be obeyed, the

---

[193] Colden to Dartmouth, September 5, 1775; *New York Col. Doc.*, 8: 632.

[194] *4 Am. Arch.*, 3: 558.

[195] *Hist. MSS. Com.*, 14: Pt. 10. p. 374.

[196] Ford, *Journals*, 3: 280. *4 Am. Arch.*, 3: 1280.

[197] *Cf. New York Col. Doc.*, 8: 604.

[198] *Ibid.*, 638. October 9, in spite of the orders of Congress, thirty or forty loads of stores were taken from the Battery. *Ibid.*

[199] *Ibid.*, 639, 640.

[200] *Ibid.*, 641. *4 Am. Arch.*, 3: 1054.

[201] *New York Col. Doc.*, 8: 643.

Congress substantially asserted, "that will bring on a cannon-
ading from the ships of war."[202]   The fear of bombardment was
in fact widespread, and the removal of Tryon seemed to confirm it.[203]   People began removing to the country, taking their
effects with them.[204]   Some of the delegates at Philadelphia,
we are told, "have moved their family and effects aback of
Esopus and even to 'Duane's Burrow.' "[205]   Deputies of Congress and members of the One Hundred did the same. The city
committee at this period frequently had no quorum;[206] was ordered to proceed without one,[207] and, to avoid the difficulty,
twenty new members were elected in September.[208]   The Provincial Congress was also frequently without a quorum, and it also
proceeded without one whenever necessary. On the occasion of
the firing upon the Battery, P. V. B. Livingston, President of
Congress, retired up the river.[209]   "It gives me great anxiety,"
he wrote, "that I cannot attend your deliberations at this crit-

---

[202] Letter of Congress in reply to a suggestion from the Continental delegates
to seize the king's stores. *4 Am. Arch.*, **3:** 1315.

[203] The fear was not unfounded. September 10, Graves wrote to Vandeput that
if supplies were absolutely refused after three days notice he was to fire upon
the house of Isaac Sears, "which I understand stands conspicuous, and beat it
down." In case of resistance, all vessels were to be sunk, and the homes of
rebels, so far as distinguishable, to be bombarded. *Cal. Home Office Pap.,*
1773–1775, No. 1245. *Cf. 4 Am. Arch.*, **3:** 902.

[204] *Cal. Home Office Pap.*, 1773–1775, Nos. 1223, 1291.

[205] "Most of the inhabitants moving their effects. and many . . . also
going with them, most part of which are our heroes led on by some of the
delegates from Philadelphia." John Cruger to Henry Cruger, November 1, 1775 ;
Cal. Home Office Pap., 1773–1775, No. 1291. Philip Livingston loaded a sloop
with every thing he had. Duane sent every thing to Duanesborough. Harris
Cruger to Henry Cruger, November 3, 1775 ; *Ibid.* "Mr. L——d. [Lispenard]
too . . . has taken the alarm, and begins to talk in a reasonable way,
but now they have raised the devil amongst them they do not know how to
lay him." Jacob Walton to Henry Cruger, November 1, 1775 ; *ibid. cf.* Ashfield to I. Wilkins, November 4, 1775 ; *ibid. cf.* New York letter, October 17,
1776 ; *Canadian Archives*, 1885, p. 206.

[206] In August and September, meetings of the committee fell to an average
of about one every five days, with barely a quorum there. *4 Am. Arch.*, **3:**
66, 78, 139, 235, 640, 652, 659, 702, 736.

[207] *Ibid.*, **2:** 1813.

[208] *Ibid.*, **3:** 702, 736, 940. The new members were : Peter Clopper. William
Hyer, Jeremiah Brower, Henry Roome, Richard Ten Eyck, Peter P. Van Zandt,
Anthony L. Bleecker, Garret Abeel, John Ramsey, Patrick Dennis. John Pell,
Samuel Johnson, Isaac Stoutenburgh, Leonard Lispenard, Jr., Abram W. De
Peyster, John Ray, Anthony Abrahams, Andrew Breasted, Richard Norwood,
Daniel Wickham. Pell became a loyalist. Sabine mentions a Samuel Johnson.

[209] *Cal. Home Office Pap.*, 1773–1775, No. 1291.

ical juncture. . . . With a continual slow fever, a reluctance to food, and a constant vigilance or want of sleep, I find myself reduced to the necessity of taking some measures to preserve life.''[210] He expressed his great desire to return to Congress as soon as he was able; but he did not return, except on one occasion, to this or the succeeding Congress, even when ordered to do so,[211] and ultimately a new election was held to fill his place.[212]

With an attendance constantly falling below quorum, hostilities threatening, and the inhabitants actively removing from the city, Congress of necessity was brought to the question of dissolution. October 18, the committee on dissolution brought in its report.[213] ''Whereas it is highly necessary . . . that the duration of the power of all persons intrusted with high authority should be limited to a short period,'' it was resolved that Congress should cease November 14, and that one week earlier elections should be held in the usual places for a new congress, the suffrage being limited to the electors of representatives in the assembly. To secure a properly distributed representation, it was directed that New York should choose twenty-one members, Albany twelve, Dutchess and Westchester nine each, Ulster, Suffolk, and Queens eight each, Orange six, Kings, Richmond, and Tryon four each, Cumberland three, Gloucester and Charlotte two each. A motion to use the ballot was defeated by a vote of 13–6;[214] but five days later it was resolved that, as the limitation of the franchise would deprive of a vote many who were ''interested for the fate of this country,'' all tenants ''possessed of lands or tenements . . . of the value of Eighty Pounds be permitted to vote in the said election.''[215] November 4, ten days before the appointed time, the first Provincial Congress adjourned indefinitely.[216]

---

[210] August 28, 1775 ; 4 *Am. Arch.*, 3: 559.

[211] *Ibid.*, 4: 390, 408.

[212] *Ibid.*, 5: 255.

[213] *Ibid.*, 3: 1294. It is stated here that the committee was appointed June 8, but I find no appointment under that date. In another place the order for the dissolution is given under date of October 10. *Ibid.*, 1005.

[214] *Ibid.*, 1295.

[215] *Ibid.*, 1305.

[216] *Ibid.*, 1751.

CHAPTER X

THE SECOND PROVINCIAL CONGRESS: LOYALIST REACTION

It was in the midst of the strong royalist recation, the beginnings of which have already been indicated, that the election of deputies to the second congress occurred. The result was very nearly disastrous to the revolutionists: Congress was barely able to hold together; it could better afford to offend the Continental Congress and the continental army than the governor or the commander of the royal ships in the harbor; for the execution of its decrees against the loyalists of Long Island it was under the necessity of seeking aid secretly from Connecticut and New Jersey; censorship of the press was enforced by mobs which the dominant party was in sympathy with but dared not recognize; it was impossible even to mention independence.

The causes of this reaction mainly centered in the declining hope of conciliation, the repressive measures of the first congress, and the steady drift of events toward independence. But these considerations were strengthened by the economic effects of the Continental Association. For a year now non-importation had been rigidly enforced; imports from England had all but ceased;[1] and the non-exportation agreement became effective in September. Business was at a standstill, and there were in the city hundreds of families without means of support.[2] It was inevitable that a self-constituted government which carried through a policy of economic decay and counseled starvation

---

[1] McPherson, *Annals of Commerce*, 3: 585. Imports dropped from 437 to 1 during this year.

[2] "Every office shut up almost but Sam Jones', who will work for 6d a day and live accordingly. All business stagnates." J. M. Scott to Richard Varick, November 15, 1775; *Mercantile Library Papers*, 84.

should lose prestige. The economic situation in the fall of 1775 and winter of 1776 thus forced the latent alternative into the foreground. Of two things, one was necessary: either to retreat or advance: to open the ports of America to the world and declare independence, or to submit and open the ports to England. The pressure of this alternative, which is clearly revealed in the debates in the Continental Congress,[3] was forcing many conservatives into loyalist opposition to Congress, as it was bringing others to realize the necessity of still more radical measures.

The loyalist reaction found concrete expression more particularly in two ways: in the election for the second Provincial Congress, and in the effort to revive the assembly and place the control of affairs in its hands.

The new elections were set for November 7. By November 14, the date on which the second congress was to have opened its first session, in only nine of the fourteen counties had there been any choice of deputies at all. These were Albany, Dutchess, Kings, New York, Orange, Suffolk, Tryon, Ulster, and Westchester. Except in New York and Albany, the election was by general meetings of freeholders, the representative character of which we can in most cases only surmise.[4] In most cases it is necessary to rely upon the bare statement contained in the official credentials. For Kings County no credentials even have been found, although two deputies attended.[5]   That these counties were unanimous for Congress is not to be supposed. We are told that there were many loyalists in Dutchess County: "Some of the convention and committee men . . . are false and treacherous; nothing can be concerted but it transpires to the tories."[6] One of the Tryon deputies resigned, and a second election was

---

[3] The subject of the trade of the colonies was debated frequently from October, 1775, till the opening of the ports in April, 1776. The situation was concisely stated by R. R. Livingston: "We are between Hawk and Buzzard; we puzzle ourselves between the commercial and warlike opposition." *Works of John Adams*, 2: 461. The close relation between the non-intercourse policy and independence will be brought out in a later chapter.

[4] *4 Am. Arch.*, 4: 384, note; 385½ note; 400.

[5] *Ibid.*, 3: 1753; 4: 383.

[6] *Ibid.*, 3: 458.

held November 25,[7] the new deputy appearing for the first time
February 12, 1776. Orange County was represented by one deputy elected by Goshen precinct alone.[8] Whether the suffrage
restrictions recommended by the first congress were observed in
any of these counties, except Albany and New York, it is impossible to determine.

October 30, the Albany committee directed that elections for
deputies be held in every district in the county, on November 7,
at the "usual places," and that each district at the same time
choose new members for the county committee which it was declared should be dissolved December 21.[9] Whether the general
committee nominated a ticket is not known, but there were rival
candidates at least in the city of Albany: R. R. Livingston appears to have been pitted against Francis Nicoll, James Barker
against Henry Oothoudt, and Peter Van Ness against J. J.
Bleecher.[10] The polls were returned November 10, and the following day the result was announced by the committee.[11] There
was apparently no contest for committeemen, save in the one
district of Kinderhook. This district, which was the home of
Peter Van Schaack and a loyalist strong-hold, was entitled to
four members on the general committee. November 7, the district committee accordingly opened the polls at the home of
Cornelius Vosburg.   Believing that the recommendations of
Congress respecting the suffrage applied to the election of committeemen as well as to that of deputies, seven persons were refused a vote as not being freeholders, whereupon Isaac Goes and
some others opened a second poll at Tobias Van Buren's house.
Both polls were returned to the general committee, which proposed to take two members from each list.[12] This proposal was
rejected by the district committee, which maintained that the
exclusion of seven voters did not in any way affect the result.[13]

[7] *Ibid.*, **4**: 251, 469 ; **5**: 251.
[8] *Ibid.*, **4**: 383.
[9] *Ibid.*, **3**: 1264. Minutes of the Albany Committee, **1**: 334, 339.
[10] *4 Am. Arch.*, **3**: 1413.
[11] Minutes of the Albany Committee, **1**: 336, 339.
[12] *Ibid.*, 346 ff. *4 Am. Arch.*, **4**: 210, 211.
[13] *Ibid.*, 211.

The new general committee, to which the matter was referred, proceeded to invalidate the Kinderhook election on the ground that it was not held at the "usual place," and that voters had been unjustly excluded.[14]   The new election, nevertheless, confirmed the position of the district committee, inasmuch as the old members were elected by a large majority.[15]   But the district committee had meanwhile protested against the new election, and had declared the district of Kinderhook as no longer represented on the general committee.[16]   Whether it was true, as Van Schaack asserts,[17] that still more vigorous measures were taken to secure a representation from Kinderhook, the incident was an indication of the fact that free elections could not long survive an appeal to the sword.

That the policy of conciliating loyalists and conservatives by giving them representation on the extra-legal committees and Congress could not be consistently pursued much longer, is even more strikingly illustrated by the New York election. The Committee of One Hundred appointed the election for November 7, and while it recommended that the suffrage be limited according to the congressional resolution, the old method of voting in wards was given up, the electors being requested to assemble at the city hall instead.[18]   According to custom the One Hundred nominated a ticket, which consisted of fourteen of the old deputies and seven new names.[19]   The seven old deputies who were omitted from this ticket included one loyalist who had taken no part in the first congress,[20] one loyalist who had been an obstructionist,[21] one radical grown timid,[22] and four others of no special

---

[14] Minutes of the Albany Committee, 1: 346, 347 ff.

[15] Ibid., 356. For a detailed account of the Kinderhook trouble by Peter Van Schaack. see Van Schaack, Life of Van Schaack, Appendix F. Also in Cal. Hist. MSS., 1: 609–615.

[16] 4 Am. Arch., 4: 579, 580.

[17] Van Schaack, Life of Van Schaack, Appendix F. Cal. Hist. MSS., 1: 611–615.

[18] 4 Am. Arch., 3: 1340. New York Mercury, November 6, 1775.

[19] 4 Am. Arch., 3: 1340.

[20] Richard Yates.

[21] John De Lancey.

[22] Leonard L Spenard.

significance. The seven new names[23] included four[24] who were
destined to take a more or less active part in the revolution.[25]
The ticket was, however, not satisfactory to the more radical element. An address was issued a day or two later, signed *Philelutheros,* which, while disclaiming any intention of undermining
the committee's authority, asserted that some members of the
old deputation had "vilely betrayed their trust," and ought not
to be returned. In place of the committee's ticket, a list was
therefore proposed of "such gentlemen as is believed would
answer the general expectations and wishes of the people; they
are men of known probity, and most of them have in a particular
manner distinguished themselves in the common cause."[26] This
ticket dropped four men from the committee's list, two of whom
became loyalists,[27] the other two being of loyalist sympathies.[28]
The election had meanwhile been postponed to November 10,
when the ticket of *Philelutheros* was elected "by a great majority."[29]

When the day arrived for the first meeting of the second Congress, there had been elected seventy-four deputies from nine
counties, of which thirty-five were new men. The thirty-nine
who were not reelected included seven or eight loyalists,[30] all of

---

[23] Comfort Sands, Isaac Ray, John Finlay, Benjamin Helme, G. H. Ludlow,
Theodorus Van Wyck, Anthony Rutgers.

[24] Sands, Ray, Finlay, Helme.

[25] *Ibid.*

[26] *Broadsides,* 1.

[27] Isaac Low, Abram Walton.

[28] John Marston. G. H. Ludlow. The four new men were Cornelius Clopper,
Th. Smith, John Morton. G. W. Ludlow.

[29] 4 *Am. Arch.,* 3: 1423, 4: 383, note. Only about 200 electors voted.
Cal. Home Office Pap., 1773–1775, No. 1291. Even as thus reconstructed, the
deputation was destined to be further changed. Seven members did not attend,
and Congress ordered their places to be filed by a new election, which was held
February 13. 1776. By this election P. V. B. Livingston. Benjamin Kissam,
John Morton. G. W. Ludlow, I. Sears, C. C'opper. Theodorus Van Wyck. were
replaced by Adrian Rutgers, A. P. Lott, Isaac Stoutenberg, Evert Bancker,
Thomas Randall. Samuel Prince, William Denning. 4 *Am. Arch.,* 5: 255. Thus,
as finally const'tuted. the New York deputation included twelve new delegates.
and nearly all of the loyalists on the old delegation had been dropped.

[30] Besides those dropped from the New York delegation John Foster was
dropped from the Suffolk delegation, and Philip Van Cortlandt from that of
Westchester.

those who had not signed the Association,[31] and most of those who had proved themselves luke-warm by non-attendance or otherwise.[32] Three of the old loyalists were returned,[33] and one of the new members was possibly a loyalist.[34] The radicals might well say that the deputies for the new congress were "changed for the better," as J. M. Scott in fact said of the New York deputies,[35] but in adding "all staunch Whigs now," he went somewhat beyond the mark. It was not the opinion of staunch Whigs elsewhere that the New York Congress carried vigorous Whig measures, even when the deputies could be assembled in sufficient numbers to carry any measures at all.

And this, from first to last, was one of the serious difficulties that confronted the second congress: to secure a quorum. While the first meeting was fixed for November 14, there is no record of any proceedings until November 22. On that day some deputies from New York, Westchester, Ulster and Dutchess, who had been present since the first day, dispatched a letter to Kings County urging the necessity of sending a delegation.[36] The following day deputies appeared from Kings and Suffolk,[37] but as there still wanted one county to make a quorum, a similar letter was sent to Orange County,[38] and on the next a third was sent to Richmond.[39] Another week passed and there was still no quorum. Finally, on December 1, the deputies then present took upon themselves to organize "for the sake of order, and for the purpose of reading several letters . . . and for tak-

---

[31] From New York, Abram Walton, George Folliott, Walter Franklin; from Ulster, Charles Clinton; from Suffolk, James Havens; from Kings, Richard Stillwell. Orange had not yet elected a full deputation; but later the new delegation did not include either Israel Seeley, or Jesse Woodhull.

[32] Such as Swart of Albany, John Marston of New York, Dumont of Ulster, Dayton of Westchester.

[33] Gilbert Livingston of Dutchess; Joseph Hallett of New York; Selah Strong of Suffolk.

[34] The Dutchess delegation included a Beverly Robinson, but whether he was of the New York family of Robinsons I am not certain.

[35] *Mercantile Library Papers*, 84. "Those of this city are all of the warm stamp." V. P. Ashfield to Isaac Wilkins, November 14, 1775; *Cal. Home Office Pap.*, 1773-1775, No. 1291.

[36] 4 *Am. Arch.*, 3: 1753.

[37] *Ibid.*, 1754.

[38] *Ibid.*

[39] *Ibid.*

ing . . . measures . . . for calling such other members
as are chosen and have not attended."[40]   There were present on
that day only twenty-three deputies out of the seventy-four that
had been chosen, which was twenty-six less than the full apportionment. Letters were at once sent to the counties of Orange,
Kings, Dutchess, Tryon, Charlotte, and Cumberland, urging the
extreme necessity of organizing a Congress: the anarchy of mob
rule or military government by the continental army was the
unpalatable alternative which would follow their failure to comply.[41]

Nevertheless, nearly another week elapsed before deputies
from the necessary eight counties appeared.   December 6, with
nine members from New York, five from Albany, three from
Dutchess, two from Ulster, three from Westchester, three from
Suffolk, one from Kings, and one from Goshen precinct, Orange
County, the second Provincial Congress was finally organized.[42]
With so small a margin, the problem of attendance was sure to be
inconveniently pressing.   The first session was not prolonged in
fact beyond sixteen days, and during that time the average attendance was twenty-seven, and twice a quorum was wanting.[43]   As
a partial inducement to attend, it was voted to pay the deputies in
future;[44] but to solve the difficulty more effectively, a committee
of safety was almost immediately appointed, consisting of twelve
members, with seven as a quorum.   The committee was empowered to sit until dissolved, or until the second Tuesday in
June, and to it practically the whole power of Congress was
surrendered, including that of calling an election for a new congress.[45]   The principle of representative government, which was

---

[40] *Ibid.*

[41] *Ibid.*, 1755.

[42] *Ibid.*, 4: 383.

[43] Based on lists in *ibid.*, 383–440.   The votes of Ulster, Kings, and Orange
counties were sometimes cast when only one delegate was present. *Ibid.*, 407,
409, 414.

[44] Five dollars per day. *Ibid.*, 414.

[45] *Ibid.*, 417.   The committee consisted of MacDougall, Scott, Jeremiah
Clarke, P. R. Livingston, Morris Graham, Abram Brasher, John Leffertse, Comfort Sands, Thomas Treadwell, John Finlay, Pierre Van Cortlandt, and Samuel
Brewster.   Five of the twelve were from New York.   If John Leffertse and
P. R. Livingston refused to act, their places were to be filled by Joseph Hallett
and Henry Oothoudt. *Ibid.*, 440.   The two latter in fact served in place of
the former. *Ibid.*, 1038, 1102.

claimed as the theoretical foundation of the revolutionary organization, was hardly to be recognized in this very practical device. Out of one hundred apportioned representatives of fourteen counties, seventy-four are chosen, in some cases by questionable methods, from nine counties; twenty-seven of these meet and choose twelve of their number to govern the province. It was, however, a condition rather than a theory which confronted the revolutionists; and for the maintenance of the revolutionary government they had now effectively provided, even if the Congress could never again be got together. After adjourning December 22,[46] the congress did in fact meet for a month in February and March, only to surrender its authority once more to a second committee, which sat until the organization of the third congress in May.[47]

Meanwhile the Committee of Safety was not itself free from the same difficulty. The members were urgently requested to attend promptly on the adjournment of Congress, which was fixed for the 22 of December, but no quorum was present until January 3, 1776.[48] One member was unwell and could not wear his shoes;[49] another was troubled with "scorbutic complaint" on his hands and legs;[50] another was detained by the illness of his wife.[51] During the entire six weeks of its session there was never more than a bare quorum in town, eight being the highest attendance on any day. Five times there was no quorum, and on four of these occasions business was transacted without the required seven members.[52] The second Committee of Safety was hampered by the same difficulty,[53] and the city committee, which had already been increased to one hundred and twenty members, and had reduced its quorum from thirty-three to twenty-seven, was compelled in February to fix the number at twenty-one,

---

[46] *Ibid.*, 440.
[47] *Ibid.*, 5: 386, 387.
[48] *Ibid.*, 4: 1017. A special letter had been sent to the members urging them to attend immediately after Congress adjourned, December 22. *Cal. Hist. MSS.*, 1: 203. *Cf.* 4 *Am. Arch.*, 4: 1037.
[49] Joseph Hallett to John McKesson, January 3, 1776; 4 *Am. Arch.*, 4: 561.
[50] John Finlay to the Committee, January 23, 1776; *Ibid.*, 817.
[51] P. R. Livingston to the Committee, January 17, 1776; *Ibid.*, 1054.
[52] Based on the lists in *Ibid.*, 1017 ff.
[53] *Cf. ibid.*, 5: 1432 ff.

and even this did not always suffice.[54] The reports of such conditions did not make pleasant reading abroad, and the dissatisfaction of the delegates at Philadelphia was reflected in a letter
from Jay to MacDougall.[55]

The difficulty of securing a quorum would remain, certainly,
as long as five counties neglected to send any deputies at all;
and very early in the session Congress· set about to remedy this
situation. While the congress was theoretically based on the
will of the people, the practical difficulty would disappear if
even a small minority in each of the five counties should formally
choose representatives. It was a delicate question, but the exigencies of war left the congress no choice; the Committee of
Safety could not go on indefinitely, and its powers had been unduly extended as it was; delegates must somehow be chosen, if
not voluntarily then under pressure. The threat of military
government had already been held out to the delinquent counties.
"On the one hand, should the reins of government be let loose,
and the mob direct matters at their pleasure, the horrors of our
situation may be more easily conceived than described. And, on
the other hand, should the Continental Congress find it necessary
. . . . for the want of a Congress, to put the colony under

---

[54] The difficulty of securing a quorum in the Committee was so great in January that on the 8th of that month a fine of 8 shillings was voted upon those
then present who failed to appear at any meeting until all unfinished business
was disposed of. *Ibid.*, 689. *Cf. ibid.*, 280. January 10, a broadside was
published by the Committee stating that, "Whereas the business of this Committee has been much impeded by reason of the absence of many members,"
the freemen and freeholders should be requested to assemble January 27 to reduce the quorum to twenty-one, or such other number as might seem desirable.
Committee Chamber, January 10, 1776: *Broadsides*, 1. *4 Am. Arch.*, 4: 692.
This announcement called forth a second broadside which recommended the appointment of a new committee of fifty members, with a quorum of fourteen, to
be named by the old committee. This recommendation was due to no dissatisfaction with the action of the old committee but to the fact that the few
"who have made it a point to attend . . . are now almost worn out."
Lucius to the Inhabitants of New York; *Broadsides*, 1. The old committee apparently acted on this suggestion. February 2, a meeting was called for February 8 to choose a new committee of fifty for six months, with the quorum
at 21 *New York Mercury*, February 5, 1776. I have no record at hand of the
election of the new committee, but it is clear that it was elected. *Cf.* Letter of
the Committee to the Provincial Congress, July 30, 1776; *Jour. Prov. Cong.*, 2:
289.

[55] *Cf.* letter of December 23, 1775; *Jay Papers*, 1: 40, and letter of March 23,
1776; 4 *Am. Arch.*, 5: 471.

military government, directed by a Major General and an army, and that at the sole expense of this colony, you may easily imagine what disagreeable consequences will ensue."[56] The response to this request was not all that could be wished, but it sufficed for the object in view. From two of the five counties deputies were, after some difficulty and delay, forthcoming; three remained unrepresented altogether.

The county of Orange, although nominally represented from December 6, requested Congress to fix another date for the election of a fresh delegation, "by reason of some misapprehension, and the situation of our county and inclemency of the weather."[57] December 9, some freeholders at Orange Town accordingly elected six deputies for the county, and after December 12, a quorum was generally present.[58] In Cumberland County there was a sharp factional dispute, which the committee of safety proposed should be harmonized by a characteristic device,[59] and after a short delay the county committee appointed two deputies for the county.[60] Richmond County, left to itself, would not have chosen any deputies. The county committee was duly called to meet after the dissolution of the first congress, but no quorum appeared and the election was dropped.[61] In response to the unofficial letter of December 2, advertisements were posted, and December 15 "a number of the said freeholders and inhabitants did appear; a regular poll was opened and continued till six o'clock; at the conclusion of which it appeared that a majority was for the present for sending no deputies."[62] In Queens County the question had already been presented in the same fashion. November 7, a poll was opened at Jamaica and votes taken for or against sending deputies; the result was 788-221 against sending any deputies.[63]

---

[56] 4 Am. Arch., 3: 1755.

[57] Ibid., 1763.

[58] Ibid., 4: 399.

[59] Recommends the election of a large and representative committee for the county. Ibid., 1031.

[60] Ibid., 426.

[61] Ibid., 3: 1755.

[62] Ibid, 4: 428. Clute. Staten Island, 170.

[63] 4 Am. Arch., 3: 1389. Onderdonck, Documents and Letters . . . of Queens County, 39.

It was meantime learned that the loyalists of Queens County were being supplied with arms from the royal ship *Asia,* which was in turn furnished with supplies from Long Island. A committee of the county, which was ordered to appear before Congress, ignored the summons, and on December 21, Congress proceeded to a consideration of the state of both Queens and Richmond. It was resolved that those who voted against sending deputies be "entirely put out of the protection of this Congress . . . . that all friendly and commercial intercourse between the said persons . . . and the other inhabitants of this colony, ought to be, and . . . as far as can be effected by the recommendations of this Congress, hereby is . . . totally interdicted."[64] The congress was altogether ceasing to be a party organization advocating a policy; it was rapidly becoming a government enforcing obedience. How that obedience was to be exacted was, however, a question that bristled with practical difficulties. To suppress the delinquents of Queens County by force of arms would bring on a bombardment of the city by the king's ships; supplies would be stopped, and the evacuation of the city which had been going on for two months would be greatly accelerated. "We have proceeded against them" the continental delegates were assured, "as far as prudent regard to the present circumstances of the capital of this colony . . . will permit." The impropriety of employing any of the inhabitants of the colony against the delinquents, "if others can be employed for the purpose," it was thought would be sufficiently obvious.[65] Against Queens County the Continental Congress ultimately employed "others," but Richmond County now submitted. January 19, the polls were again opened "without any opposition," and Adrian Bancker and Richard Lawrence were elected.[66] Queens County refused to rescind its resolution, and, together with Charlotte and Gloucester counties, remained unrepresented. Meanwhile seven of the New York deputies, who neglected to

---

[64] 4 *Am. Arch.,* 4: 372, 435.

[65] *Ibid.,* 435.

[66] *Ibid.,* 1069. *Cf. ibid.,* 5: 263, 283. Adrian Bancker was a delegate from New York County.

attend were replaced by a special election February 20, pursuant to the order of Congress.[67]

Both loyalists and conservatives had been disappointed with the action of the Continental Congress on Lord North's resolution, but neither had given up hope of accomplishing something by means of it. The conservatives still looked to the Provincial Congress to act upon it independently; the loyalists, failing to prevent the organization of the second congress, but encouraged by its weakness when organized, aimed to revive the assembly and place the direction of affairs in its hands. In December and January the revolutionists were mainly occupied in preventing the realization of these aims.

The opportunity of the conservatives was furnished by a letter of Governor Tryon to the people of the colony, in which he expressed his regret that there had as yet been no prospect of taking "the dispassionate and deliberate sense of its inhabitants, in a constitutional manner, upon the resolution of Parliament for composing the present ferments."[68] Acting upon this suggestion, Thomas Smith assembled a caucus of those members of Congress who were supposed to be favorable to such a project, and his brother, William Smith, opened to them a "plan toward a reconciliation under the form of instructions to the delegates . . . at Philadelphia."[69] These instructions I have not found, but on the 8 of December, Thomas Smith introduced into Congress resolutions that were intended, apparently, to pave the way for his brothers'plan.[70] These resolutions asserted "that this Congress conceive it highly necessary and expedient that his Majesty should know the sense of this colony on the Parliamentary Resolution of the 24 of February in such a way as his Excellency may conceive to be most constitutional."[71] William Smith thought these resolutions "incautiously framed."[72] There

[67] Ibid., 5: 255, 259.
[68] Ibid., 4: 173. The date of the letter was December 4, 1775. For the reply of "a Citizen," see ibid., 174.
[69] William Smith to Tryon. December 17, 1775; New York Col. Doc., 8: 653.
[70] 4 Am. Arch., 4: 394. New York Col. Doc., 8: 653.
[71] 4 Am. Arch., 4: 394, 395.
[72] New York Col. Doc., 8: 653.

was in them, certainly, too obvious a reference to the governor's letter; in any case they were inconsistent with the proposed plan inasmuch as instructions to the continental delegates would scarcely satisfy Tryon's idea of "the most constitutional" method of taking "the dispassionate and deliberate sense" of the colony. The "most constitutional" method could mean nothing less than a vote of the assembly, and William Smith says that his plan was opposed by those who "had private aims of gaining seats" in that body.[73] When Congress resumed consideration of Thomas Smith's resolutions on December 13, this opposition was strikingly manifest in the amendment offered by Hobart and Gilbert Livingston. The amendment omitted all reference to North's Resolution, but asserted that the colony had no desire for independence. Nor was it the "desire or design of its inhabitants to disuse, much less to oppose or obstruct the ordinary course of government or legislation: but that, on the contrary, they highly esteem, and will not willingly cede their right of being represented in General Assembly." The two concluding resolutions expressed the desire of the people that the assembly should be convened "not only that the ordinary business of the country may be dispatched, but also that their sense may be expressed, as well by their representatives in Assembly as in Congress, on the present unhappy controversy."[74] The amendment was carried by a vote of 17-2, and referred for consideration.

But the revolutionists had been at too much pains to get a Congress assembled to countenance measures which would either remove its very *raison d'etre* or detach the colony from the Continental Congress. Both attempts—the attempt to refer the resolution of Lord North to the assembly, and the attempt to get the Provincial Congress to act upon it independently—were accordingly summarily defeated. The amended resolutions were discussed in detail on the 14th, with the result of transforming them beyond recognition. As finally adopted the resolutions were in substance as follows: (1) That the people of the colony have not withdrawn their allegiance from the king; (2) that the "sup-

---

[73] *Ibid.*
[74] 4 *Am. Arch.*, 4: 406.

posed present turbulent state'' of the colony arises solely from the acts of Parliament ''devised for enslaving his Majesty's liege subjects;'' (3) that the inhabitants do not desire to obstruct the ordinary course of legislation, but that they ''highly esteem their right of being represented in General Assembly.''[75] The resolutions which recommended the calling of the assembly were omitted altogether, and two additional resolutions were added which expressed very clearly the attitude of the revolutionists on the whole question. The first was moved by J. M. Scott: ''Resolved, nevertheless, that . . . nothing of a salutary nature can be expected from the separate declaration of the sense of this colony on the Resolution of the House of Commons . . . and . . . it would be . . . highly inconsistent with the glorious plan of American union, should this colony express their separate sense on the above mentioned supposed conciliatory proposal.''[76] The second was introduced by MacDougall: it asserted that the colony was fully represented in the Continental Congress for dealing with all proposals for reconciliation, and that the Continental Congress had already expressed the sense of the colony on Lord North's Resolution.[77]

The loyalists, nevertheless, proceeded to convene a new assembly. December 17, William Smith suggested the idea to Tryon: ''The dissolution will enable men of temper to testify their disapprobation of the present violence, under a proper and safe cloak form a confederacy to correct and undermine the tyranny erected over the colony, turn the eyes of the multitude towards a power that is constitutional, and favor future overtures for a restoration of harmony.''[78] Acting on this hint, perhaps, and assured of loyalist support, Governor Tryon dissolved the assembly, January 2. and issued writs for a new election returnable February 14.[79] The Committee of Safety was much alarmed; and letters were dispatched to all the members of Congress and to such of the county committees ''as may be thought necessary.''

[75] *Ibid.*, 408.
[76] *Ibid.*, 411.
[77] *Ibid.*
[78] *New York Col. Doc.*. 8: 654.
[79] 4 *Am. Arch.*, 4: 542.   *New York Col. Doc.*, 8: 649.

The object of the new election, the deputies were assured, was "to take the sense of the good people . . . (in what the government calls "a constitutional way") on Lord North's motion;" but the late resolutions of Congress "we cannot suffer to be rescinded by any body of men in this colony." To prevent such a catastrophe, the congress was called to meet February 1, which it was hoped would "sufficiently awe a corrupt Assembly." Accordingly, the letter concludes, "we beseech, we obtest, we adjure you . . . that you meet punctually . . . on the first day of next month."[80]

The elections, which the deputies and county committees were directed to attend to,[81] were held towards the end of January. They aroused but little interest. In New York city a broadside appeared January 6 recommending that the delegates be definitely instructed.[82] January 17, some freeholders met at Vanderwater's and nominated P. Livingston, Jay, Alsop, and MacDougall, who were elected without opposition on the first of February.[83] Elections were held in every county in the province, but few details have been preserved.[84] February 14 thirty representatives appeared, of whom nearly one-half were members of the Provincial or Continental Congress.[85] The congress had itself assembled two days before,[86] and General Lee was already in the city making preparations for defense against a British invasion. The city was in a panic, and under the circumstances it was felt that nothing could be accomplished. The assembly was at once prorogued to March 14,[87] and then to April 17.[88] Tryon would have prorogued it once more, and he issued a sum-

[80] 4 Am. Arch., 4: 1028. Cf. Hamilton to Jay, December 31, 1775; Jay Papers, 1: 41.

[81] 4 Am. Arch., 4: 1020, 1028. Schoonmacher, Kingston, 178.

[82] Publicola to the Electors, January 6, 1776; Broadsides, 1. Hamilton was probably the author. Cf. Jay Papers, 1: 41.

[83] Loudon's Packet, February 8, 1776. New York Mercury, January 29, February 5. 1776.

[84] For Ulster County, see George Clinton MSS., 1: 79. For Kings and Suffolk, New York Mercury, January 29, 1776. For Westchester, 4 Am. Arch., 3: 1373.

[85] New York Mercury, February 19, 1776, 4 Am. Arch., 4: 1153.

[86] 4 Am. Arch., 5: 251.

[87] New York Mercury, February 19, 1776. 4 Am. Arch., 4: 1153.

[88] New York Mercury, March 18, 1776.

mons to the council to meet on board the *Duchess of Gordon,* but all intercourse with the royal ships had recently been interdicted and the New York Provincial Assembly was at an end.[89]

If the congress might now draw an easy breath so far as Lord North's Resolution was concerned, there were problems enough, bristling on every side of it, still to be solved. Anomolous situations are doubtless inevitable in a civil war: at least the situation in New York during the winter of 1776 was a curious one. In the midst of active warfare, with a continental army blockading British troops in Boston, active preparations for defense making in New York city, and new troops raising in every colony, the British men-of-war in the harbor were supplied from the city by direction of the Provincial Congress, while the city was itself supplied from New Jersey by boats that daily passed within hailing distance of the enemy's frigates.[90] The governor had long since retired to the *Duchess of Gordon* for safety; and although he had been ordered under arrest by the Continental Congress, the council passed back and forth periodically in the exercise of functions that were altogether usurped by the Provincial Congress.[91] A nominal inspection of the mails failed utterly, as everyone was aware, to prevent the transmission of the revolutionists' secret plans to the English government.[92] The truth was that Congress could not bring itself to pronounce the dread word "rebellion." It labored diligently therefore, succeeding, one must admit, wonderfully well, to carry the principle of accommodation to the verge of absurdity. To restrain and direct those who were pressing on eagerly towards independence, without alienating the moderate and conservative elements or precipitating an open attack from the ships of war in

---

[89] Tryon to Germaine, April 18, 1776; *New York Col. Doc.,* 8: 676.

[90] 4 *Am. Arch.,* 4: 1110; 5: 270, 276, 281, 287.

[91] *Ibid.,* 5: 363.

[92] William Smith furnished information to General Howe. See Letter of February 11, 1776; *Ibid.,* 4: 1000. Tryon, on the *Duchess of Gordon,* was well informed of what occurred in the city. *Cf.* letters, February to July, 1776; *New York Col. Doc.,* 8: 663–681. Brattle, a servant of James Duane, was employed by Tryon as a spy at Philadelphia, and copies of resolutions of the Continental Congress were forwarded to Tryon by way of New York. *4 Am. Arch.,* 5: 44. Duane, *Diary of Marshall,* 56. *Cf. Writings of Washington,* 4: 130, 215, note.

the harbor: this was the dilemma which confronted Congress. How it eased off the prick from either horn, as it were, may be indicated by exhibiting its treatment of loyalists, on the one hand, and its dealings with the continental army, on the other.

Outspoken opposition on the part of individuals was suppressed in much the same manner by the second congress as by the first, but rather more summarily: by imprisonment at the expense of the offender.[93] Although the first congress had directed that a fair trial should be given to accused loyalists, it frequently fell out that prisoners protested entire ignorance of the cause of their confinement,—close confinement usually, which, as one prisoner complains, "daily drives a nail into my coffin."[94] The influx of loyalists from other colonies led to the requirement that every stranger should present a certificate from some committee on pain of being treated as an enemy.[95] It was in those districts or counties where the loyalists were a majority that the problem was most serious, however, particularly in Queens and Richmond counties. The New York Congress had already put those who voted against sending deputies under boycott. The danger from the royal ships prevented the employment of force by that body, and it had already been suggested that the object might be accomplished by the Continental Congress.[96] Letters were at the same time written to the neighboring colonies stating that, in case the Continental Congress did not take up the matter, they were "at liberty to take such measures with the enemies of America in these counties as they shall judge necessary."[97] In fact the Continental Congress passed a resolution January 3, 1776, for disarming the tories of Long Island and for the imprisonment of twenty-seven of the

---

[93] This opposition took various forms, such as violating the Continental association, speaking disrespectfully of Congress, sending provisions on board the royal ships, enlisting men for service in the royal army, spiking cannon at King's Bridge, allowing prisoners to escape, disaffection in the militia, etc. *Cf. 4 Am. Arch.*, **3**: 1625–1627, 1629; **4**: 156, 185, 187, 203, 247, 280, 390, 393, 402–404, 415, 693, 818, 857, 923, 1043, 1050, 1070, 1072, 1076, 1103, 1105, 1120; **5**: 102, 344, 359, 390, 466, 548, 558, 788, 926, 927, 1428, 1445.

[94] *Ibid.*, **4**: 857. *Cf. ibid.*, 818, 923; **5**: 390, 548, 558, 788.

[95] *Ibid.*, **4**: 438; **5**: 250.

[96] *Ibid.*, **4**: 435.

[97] *Ibid.*

ring-leaders in Queens County.[98]   Colonel Heard accordingly overran Queens County, disarmed about six hundred inhabitants and carried off nineteen prisoners.[99]   In February the Congress of New Jersey ordered the colonel to secure Staten Island "from depredation,"[100] which he accomplished to the satisfaction of the New York Congress;[101] and about the same time Schuyler, by order of the Continental Congress, disarmed the tories of Tryon County.[102]

There was a touch of irony, perhaps, in the fact that the continental army itself, upon which had been shouldered the responsibility of suppressing the tories on Long Island, was to furnish the chief obstacle to the congressional policy of accommodation.   The army naturally had little sympathy with such a policy; it was in fact the resort of many irreconcilable radicals like Sears, Lamb, and Willett, who had been shouldered out of the revolutionary organization in New York by erstwhile conservatives like Jay and Duane.   A foretaste of the temper of the army had already been experienced in the preceding autumn. November 20, sixteen men under Isaac Sears, a disgruntled member of the first Provincial Congress,[103] left New Haven

---

[98] Ford, *Journals,* 4: 25.

[99] *Ibid.,* 47, 114. *New York Col. Doc.,* 8: 663. *4 Am. Arch.,* 4: 1119, 1181; 5: 273. For further information as to conditions in Queens County, *cf. Ibid.,* 4: 203, 372, 404–406, 434, 596, 858, 860, 1108, 1119; 5: 265, 273. *Cal. Hist. MSS.,* 1: 215. In March the Revolutionists succeeded in getting county and district committees appointed in the county. *4 Am. Arch.,* 5: 352.

[100] *4 Am. Arch.,* 5: 263. Richmond had already elected delegates to the Provincial Congress, and the Continental Congress directed that they might be received on condition that they and a majority of the inhabitants signed the Association. *Ibid.,* 264. The delegates did so, and assured the Congress that seven-eighths of the inhabitants had also signed. *Ibid.,* 284. The Congress stated that Colonel Heard was sent to Staten Island to prevent "depredation" by Clinton. *Ibid.* Clinton had, however, long since gone south.

[101] *Ibid.,* 276.

[102] Ford, *Journals,* 4: 109. *New York Col. Doc.,* 8: 663. *Cf. 4 Am. Arch.,* 3: 1963.

[103] Sears was one of those extreme radicals who had no sympathy with a cautious policy of any kind. He never was of any use on committees or in the Congress, his talent being for stirring up the mob. Like many others, he consequently found the army more congenial to his temper. Tryon called him a tool of the Continental Army, and reports him as saying that he worked independently of Congresses and committees. Tryon to Dartmouth, December 6, 1775: *New York Col. Doc.,* 8: 646. Charles Lee characterized Sears perfectly: "He is a creature of much spirit and public virtue and ought to have his back clapped." Lee to Washington, February 14, 1776; *4 Am. Arch.,* 4: 1145.

and marched into Westchester County, where they were joined
by about eighty men under Captain Richards.   Prominent
loyalists of Westchester County, among them Samuel Seabury,
were taken and sent under guard to Connecticut.   The rest of
the company then proceeded to New York.   Entering at high
noon to the accompaniment of cheers and a salute of two guns,
they marched to the home of James Rivington, wrecked his
presses, and scattered his type in the river.[104]   Whether the New
York Congress was privy to this expedition or not, it is certain
that no effort was made to prevent it.   The more radical members were doubtless well pleased with the result; the conservatives pleased that Congress was not responsible for it.[105]   The
responsibility was nevertheless thrust upon them: the event was
talked of outside the province, especially at Philadelphia, and
it was thought among the revolutionists to argue ill for the
reputation of the colony,—a reputation, Jay wrote to the Congress, which cannot be maintained "without some little spirit
being mingled with its prudence."[106]

Prudence was, however, the strongest instinct of the Congress;
and it is significant of the entire situation in New York that the
presence of the continental army itself did not suffice to give it
a bold front. Early in January Washington informed the Congress that he had sent General Lee to put New York in a state of
defense.[107]   The arrival of General Lee himself created something of a panic among the inhabitants, who feared that his object was to attack the fleet.[108]   The congress was assured that

---

[104] 4 Am. Arch., 3: 1707.   New York Col. Doc., 8: 646.   Sears had a personal
grudge against Rivington.   Rivington's Gazetteer, September 2, 1774.

[105] The Congress protested against the exploit in a letter to the Governor of
Connecticut.   4 Am. Arch., 4: 401.   It also requested the Continental Congress
to take measures to prevent such occurrences.   Ibid., 422, 423.   From Connecticut no answer was returned until June 13, 1776; and then the Governor very
effectively turned the edge of the protest by stating that the instigator of
the whole affair was a citizen of New York and a member of the New York
Congress.   Ibid., 6: 1398, 1399.

[106] Ibid., 4: 410.

[107] Ibid., 605.   The instructions to General Lee are in Writings of Washington,
3: 327.   Cf. ibid., 345, 364.

[108] Tryon to Dartmouth, February 8, 1776; New York Col. Doc., 8: 666. 4
Am. Arch., 4: 958.   Cf. letters quoted in Irving, Life of Washington, 2: 179.

such was not the case;[109] but the arrival of a committee of the Continental Congress to confer with the general,[110] so far from quieting the apprehension, served only to arouse the latent sentiment of opposition to external interference in the affairs of the colony. And this sentiment, which was one day to ripen into anti-federalism and states rights, was strongest among the very radicals who had formerly urged the necessity of continental union in resistance to British oppression. If New York was to become the seat of war, the Provincial Congress did not propose for that reason to surrender its authority either to civil or military agents of the Continental Congress. February 1, Scott and MacDougall were sent to confer with the continental committee.[111] The request for supplies was answered by a motion that the troops be stopped until a "further conference could be held." The motion was lost by one vote, Brasher, MacDougall, and Sands, voting the affirmative,[112] whereupon Scott moved that the troops be lodged in the Barracks "under the direction of this committee [of safety] or the Provincial Congress."[113] The motion was carried, but the continental committee replied that they could not agree that the troops should be under the entire direction of the Provincial Congress, "as that would be to exceed any powers lodged in them by the Continental Congress."[114] Colonel Waterbury also assured the Committee of Safety that he could not give up the control of the troops "without orders from the general."[115] If the divergent principles of nationalism and sectionalism had thus early made their appearance in the practical politics of New York, the exigencies of war for the present gave an immense advantage to the cause of union, and, after a second conference, the Committee of Safety declared itself satisfied, "as those troops are to be under the command of the

[109] 4 Am. Arch., 4: 605.

[110] Harrrison, Lynch, and Allen were appointed January 26, "and that General Lee be directed to follow the determination of the said committee." Ford, Journals, 4: 94.

[111] 4 Am. Arch., 4: 1096.

[112] Ibid.

[113] Ibid.

[114] Ibid., 1098.

[115] Ibid.

committee of the Continental Congress."[116] February 4, the very day that Clinton sailed into the harbor on his way to the South, General Lee arrived with a body-guard of riflemen, and a regiment of Connecticut men under Colonel Waterbury marched into the city. Two days later the little army was strengthened by four companies of Jersey troops under Lord Sterling.[117]

The question of defense was settled satisfactorily,[118] but the relation with the ships of war at once gave rise to difficulties. Having learned that Governor Tryon had induced some gunsmiths to desert the colony and establish themselves in England,[119] Lee "*pro tempore* interdicted all communication with the governor's ship."[120] A "committee of war" was at once appointed by the Provincial Congress, (which had meanwhile assembled), and although measures were taken to limit intercourse with the royal ships, it was resolved that such intercourse could not be cut off altogether.[121] The seizure of two supply boats from the Jerseys elicited a strong protest from General Lee,[122] but Congress replied that if intercourse were cut off, the city's supplies, which were secured from the Jerseys in the winter months, would be confiscated and sent to Boston.[123] Towards the end of February a servant of Tryon's, who customarily came on shore with linen to be washed, was locked up in the guard house,[124] port boats were fired on by the troops,[125] and once more Lee ordered all intercourse cut off.[126] Sears was reported to have damned the Congress; Waterbury asserted that the united colonies ought to crush New York.[127] New comm.ttees were ap-

---

[116] *Ibid.*, 1100.

[117] Tryon to Dartmouth, February 8, 1776; *New York Col. Doc.*, 8: 666.

[118] *4 Am. Arch.*, 4: 1106, 1107, 1109, 1112, 1116, 1121.

[119] The charge was quite true. *New York Col. Doc.*, 8: 647. But the Committee of Congress could not find that the Governor had any hand in it. *4 Am. Arch.*, 5: 274.

[120] *4 Am. Arch.*, 5: 272.

[121] *Ibid.*, 27C, 281.

[122] *Ibid.*, 283.

[123] *Ibid.*

[124] *Ibid.*, 326.

[125] *Ibid.*

[126] *Ibid.*, 332.

[127] *Ibid.*, 328.

pointed to inquire into all these matters,[128] and a resolution of protest was passed against an order to impose a test upon suspected loyalists.[129]   The choleric general was driven frantic by what seemed to him a gratuitous solicitude for the enemy's comfort,[130] and he replied that, having been sent to New York to prepare for defense, he could no longer permit intercourse with the enemy's ships nor suffer notorious loyalists at large within the colony.[131]

The withdrawal of Lee for the Canada expedition[132] postponed the breach for another month.   March 8, Lord Sterling, who succeeded to Lee's position, agreed to a plan for supplying the royal ships under more careful restrictions, and on the distinct understanding that the city's supplies should be unmolested.[133]   The mails were also continued, all letters being examined by a committee of Congress.[134]   Friction between the congress and the army consequently largely disappeared during the month of March; and meanwhile conditions were bringing Congress to take a less inflexible attitude: the defenses of the city were strengthened, and new troops were arriving;[135] the approach of Spring freed the city somewhat from dependence upon the Jerseys for supplies;[136] the royal ships, it was asserted, failed to observe the compact.[137]   Even these considerations would hardly have induced Congress to take the bold course; but when, about the middle of April, General Washington communicated one of those polite but scathing letters which he so well knew how to compose, the congressional policy of accommodation came to an abrupt end: if we are at peace, said the general, why are the ports blockaded, property destroyed, citizens made captive; if we are at war, "my imagination is not fertile enough

---

[128] *Ibid.*

[129] *Ibid.*, 75, 334, 342, 1392.   In the matter of the test, the Continental Congress supported the Provincial Congress.   Ford, *Journals*, 4: 195.

[130] *Cf.* characteristic letter to General Washington: 4 *Am. Arch.*, 4: 1539.

[131] *Ibid.*, **5: 344, 347.**

[132] *Ibid.*, 344.

[133] *Ibid.*, 348. 354, 355.   The plan was sent to Tryon.

[134] *Ibid.*, 1380.

[135] *Ibid.*, 4: 1121, 1122, 1123; 5: 381.

[136] *Ibid.*. **5:** 1451.

[137] *Ibid.*, 1424, 1451.

to suggest a reason in support of the intercourse.''[138]   On the following day Congress ordered all intercourse with the royal ships to cease absolutely;[139] the fleet dropped below the Narrows;[140] and some seamen who landed on Staten Island for water were fired upon by a squad of Lord Sterling's men.[141] The council, which had been summoned to meet on the *Duchess of Gordon* on the 17th of April to prorogue the assembly, was refused permission, and the assembly was thereby dissolved,—a strong evidence, wrote Tryon, of the slight attention paid ''even toward preserving the form of a legal and constitutional representation of the people.''[142]

The time for preserving useless forms had in fact passed, and the open breach with the royal ships may serve to mark, as well as any event, the point from which compromise and accommodation ceased to be the central policy of the Provincial Congress. The way was now open (which meant, with such conservative politicians as Jay and Duane, that all other ways were closed) for a more open recognition, on the part of Congress, of its revolutionary character, for more directly repressive measures against all irreconcilables, for open ports, and for independence. This change of attitude in America was accompained by a similar change on the part of the British Government.   November 20, 1775, Lord North brought in the bill repealing the restraining acts of the preceding session, laying new restraints on the trade of all the colonies, and authorizing the king to appoint commissioners.[143]   Former measures, said the minister, were ''civil corrections against civil crimes;'' the time had now come for the prosecution of war as against any foreign enemy.[144] The commissioners could hardly expect to succeed where North's Resolution had failed.   Burke's magnificent plea fell on deaf

---

[138] *Writings of Washington,* 4: 21. *4 Am. Arch.,* 5: 1451.

[139] *4 Am. Arch.,* 5: 1451. Th's was a mere form, as Washington had already ordered all intercourse to cease. *Ibid.,* 796.

[140] *New York Col. Doc.,* 8: 676.

[141] *Ibid.,* 675.

[142] *Ibid.,* 676. *Cf. 4 Am. Arch.,* 5: 1434.

[143] *Parl. Hist.,* 18: 992, 1065. *New York Col. Doc.,* 8: 648.

[144] *Parl. Hist.,* 18: 993.

ears; old arguments were discarded; a new note was sounded: in both England and America conciliation had failed.[145]

This change, so far as Congress was concerned, was slow enough; much slower than the fixing of any particular date may, perhaps, seem to indicate, and certainly much slower than the radicals within the colony could have wished. The Continental Congress had already, March 14, recommended the disarming of "all who have not associated, and refuse to associate, to defend by arms these united colonies."[146] After careful deliberation, the Provincial Congress passed this resolution on to the county and district committees, with the additional instruction to "use all possible prudence and moderation."[147] Long Island was still, in spite of the measures of February, the chief center of danger, and in March and April the recommendations of Congress were in part carried out in that region.[148] From the other counties the Committee of Safety had heard nothing by April 24, and a second circular letter was dispatched instructing the committees to execute fully the recommendations of the Continental Congress.[149] The non-intercourse policy had for some months been modified by resolutions looking towards open ports;[150] and the possibility of a congressional tax was broached.[151] The sentiment for independence had been steadily strengthened, especially since the publication of *Common Sense* in January,[152] and

---

[145] *Cf.* comment in *Annual Register,* 1776, p. 139–140, on the debates in March, 1776.

[146] Ford, *Journals,* 4: 205. *4 Am. Arch.,* 5: 1385.

[147] *4 Am. Arch.,* 5: 1409, 1410.

[148] March 14, a committee reported in favor of proceeding against Long Island tories. Mere disarming was, in their opinion, insufficient, as the tories could be supplied by the ships; it was therefore suggested that children be taken as hostages. *Ibid.,* 215. *Cf. ibid.,* 370, 405, 450, 766, 926.

[149] *Ibid.,* 1642.

[150] By authority of the Continental Congress, a limited exportation for securing the munitions of war had been going on. *Ibid.,* 4: 424, 1061, 1091; 5: 360.

[151] A tax had been broached in the first Provincial Congress. In December, 1775, Jay wrote to MacDougall: "It appears to be prudent that you should begin to impose light taxes, rather with a view to *precedent* than profit." *Jay Papers,* 1: 40. *Cf.* also Jay to MacDougall, April 27, 1776; *4 Am. Arch.,* 5: 1092. In March there was a proposal to permit Albany and Tryon counties to collect an old excise duty. *Ibid.,* 369. It was, however, voted down, as the levy of taxes would be "very inconvenient at this time." *Ibid.,* 373.

[152] *4 Am. Arch.,* 4: 1496; 5: 211, 758.

Congress practically sanctioned the forcible suppression of those who spoke against it—the destruction of Loudon's pamphlets being precisely a case in point.[153]

The second congress, nevertheless, most carefully refrained from mentioning the word independence. Even in calling an election for a new congress, the question was not in any way referred to the electors. This may have been because the recommendations for the election were made nearly a month before the final breach with the king's ships; at that time there was in any case so far from being any question of independence that the proposal to exclude non-associators from the suffrage was voted down by a vote of 23-2.[154] It was resolved, however, that as non-associators were to be permitted to vote, "the election should not be made by ballot."[155] No complete record of the provisions for this election has been preserved,[156] but indirectly it may be inferred that the suffrage was given to freemen, freeholders, and persons possessed of property valued at 40£.[157] The Committee of Safety sat till May 8, and the second congress, hastily summoned, from that day till May 14, which was the end of its term.

---

[153] An answer to *Common Sense* was handed to Loudon to be printed, and it was advertised in the newspapers. February 18, Loudon was ordered to attend the Mechanics Committee. Unable or unwilling to give the name of the author, he was threatened with the destruction of the pamphlets. The committee refused to refer the matter to the Committee of Safety, and the following evening the New York committee advised Loudon not to print the pamphlet, as his safety depended on it. He promised to comply, but the same evening Duychinck, chairman of the Mechanics Committee, Scott, Sears, Lamb, and others, entered Loudon's home and destroyed the pamphlets. March 20, Loudon presented his case on oath to the Committee of Safety; and April 13, a second memorial was presented,' but it does not appear that any reply or expression of opinion was made by the committee. Jones, *History of New York,* 1: 63-65. *4 Am. Arch.,* 5: 438, 439, 1389, 1441, 1442. The matter was presented once more to the third Congress May 30, but it was postponed indefinitely. *Ibid.,* 6: 1348, 1363, 1393.

[154] *4 Am. Arch.,* 5: 364, 365.

[155] *Ibid.,* 365.

[156] March 11, the rules were amended, and referred for further consideration "tomorrow." There is no record of further proceedings, however, in the *Journals* as printed by Force. *Cf.* Dawson, *Westchester County,* 160, 161.

[157] The election for the fourth Provincial Congress was directed to be held in the "manner and form prescribed for the election of the present Congress," *i. e.,* the third. *4 Am. Arch.,* 6: 1352. In accordance with these directions, the New York Committee called an election by the freemen, freeholders, and all other inhabitants "possessed of goods and chattels in their own right to the amount of 40 £." *Ibid.,* 744.

CHAPTER XI

INDEPENDENCE AND THE NEW STATE GOVERNMENT

When the elections for the third Congress came on in April, 1776, the radicals, under the lead of John Adams, were beginning to see their way clear to the declaration of independence.[1] For many months they had pushed forward to this object. But the contest had hitherto centered mainly in other measures upon which the main point depended: on the one hand, non-intercourse and the possibility of conciliation; on the other, open ports and the foreign alliance. At last, however, conciliation was becoming a vain hope,[2] and non-intercourse had proved a failure: April 6, the ports of America were opened to the world,[3] and independence was a foregone conclusion.

Throughout the colonies, and nowhere more than in New York, the practical consideration which worked most powerfully for

---

[1] *Works of John Adams,* **3:** 36, 45. Smyth, *Writings of Benjamin Franklin,* **6:** 446. *4 Am. Arch.,* **5:** 794. As early as February 13, 1776, an address drawn by Wilson, disavowing the desire for independence, was tabled by Congress. Ford, *Journals,* **4:** 134.

[2] Such hopes as still existed depended largely on the commissioners. But the feeling was strong that they would not come at all, or, coming, would not offer any terms that could be accepted. *Cf. 4 Am. Arch,.* **5:** 188, 757, 758, 993. *Hist. MSS. Com.,* **9:** Pt. 3, p. 83, 84. Franklin speaks of the "vain hope of conciliation." Franklin to Quincy, April 15, 1776; Smyth, *Writings of Benjamin Franklin,* **6:** 446. The commissioners had not been appointed, in fact, by the end of April. *Hist. MSS. Com.,* **9:** Pt. 3, p. 84. January 9, 1776, the New York Committee of Safety published the Petition of the Continental Congress to counteract the assertion that "Congress have made no approaches towards an accommodation with Great Britain." *4 Am. Arch.,* **4:** 606. April 4, 1776, a plan of conciliation was published at New York. *Ibid.,* **5:** 785.

[3] Ford, *Journals,* **4:** 257. The question was raised January 17, 1776, and during March was discussed at length. *Ibid.,* 62, 213, 229, 256. Adams says it was opposed because it was a step in the direction of independence. *Works of John Adams,* **3:** 29.

independence was the failure of the non-intercourse policy. The non-importation measure injured America more than it injured England. During the year 1775, English imports into the colonies fell from 2,687,000£ to 213,000£, or, excluding Georgia, to 100,000£[4] Exports had naturally increased very greatly,[5] but the non-exportation, which became effective in September, 1775, had already closed that source of trade as well. So drastic a self-denying ordinance could not long be enforced: it was confessed in Congress that it would put American virtue to "too severe a test."[6] "People will feel, and will say, that Congress oppresses them more than Parliament."[7] Besides, the measure was not accomplishing the thing for which it was intended. So far from bringing England to terms, the government promptly passed the acts restraining the trade of the New England and the southern colonies,[8] and when Congress recommended the exempted colonies not to take advantage of the exemption,[9] a new restraining act was passed affecting the trade of all the colonies alike.[10] A coercive policy against Great Britain which was promptly seconded by a law of Parliament, could scarcely be regarded as successful. Throughout the winter of 1776, therefore, pamphleteers in New York and elsewhere were advocating independence as the best remedy for ruined commerce.[11]

---

[4] McPherson, *Annals of Commerce*, 3: 564, 585.

[5] New York exports to England advanced from 80,008 £ to 187,018 £. *Ibid.* The total exports from the colonies to England advanced from 1,373,746 £ in 1774 to 1,920,950£ in 1775, dropping in the next year to 103,964£. *Ibid.*, 564, 585, 599.

[6] *Works of John Adams*, 2: 457.

[7] *Ibid.*, 453. For the opinion of Jay, *cf. ibid.*, 471.

[8] 15 *George III.*, ch. 10.

[9] Ford, *Journals*, 3: 314. The question of modifying the exportation policy was settled by a resolution not to export anything before March, 1776, without permission, except in accordance with the resolution for the importation of military supplies. *Ibid.*, 280, 314.

[10] 16 *George III.*, ch. 5. *New York Col. Doc.*, 8: 668.

[11] *4 Am. Arch.*, 4: 1496, 1522; 5: 96, 914, 211. The great influence of *Common Sense* was due to its timeliness rather than to its inherent merit. The economic distress in New York was such as to lead people to lend a ready ear to any proposal which looked towards a revival of prosperity. *Cf. 4 Am. Arch.*, 4: 270, 1479; 6: 627. *New York Col. Doc.*, 8: 666. *Mercantile Library Papers*, 84. *Letters of Papinian*, 62.

It is true that a clandestine trade, partly sanctioned by Congress for securing munitions of war, was being carried on;[12] and the extension of such trade did not necessarily involve independence. But there were other advantages to be gained by an open foreign alliance, the chief of which were money and troops. Money and troops the revolutionists were particularly in need of precisely because their extra-legal governments were not strongly enough grounded to raise money by taxation or troops by conscription. Such, at least, was strikingly the case in New York. Neither the first nor the second congress would consider the possibility of laying even "light taxes rather with a view to *precedent* than profit.'"[13] Paper money and vain laws for regulating prices must needs suffice.[14] Military service was likewise voluntary;[15] and local jealousy and secret disaffection deprived the militia of much of the value it might otherwise have had.[16] If, therefore, the foreign alliance would bring troops and money from abroad, independence and the establishment of new governments would, it was hoped, prepare the way for confiscation and conscription.[17]

---

[12] Ford, *Journals*, 4: 280, 314. Ammunition was secured during 1775 from France, Holland, and even England. *Cal. Home Office Pap.*, 1773-1775, Nos. 717, 732, 782, 793, 1074, 1093. *Hist. MSS. Com.*, 14: Pt. 10, p. 366. *New York Col. Doc.*, 8: 434, 509, 510, 528.

[13] Jay to MacDougall, December 23, 1775; *Jay Papers*, 1: 40. *Cf.* the reply to MacDougall's answer to this letter, April 22, 1776; 4 *Am. Arch.*, 5: 1092.

[14] 4 *Am. Arch.*, 3: 1625; 4: 355, 392, 397, 419, 422, 1025; 5: 324, 301, 362, 466. Ford, *Journals*, 3: 452. *New York Mercury*, March 11, 18, 1776. April 20, the Continental Congress ordered that the power of committees to regulate the price of goods should cease, save in the case of tea. Ford, *Journals*, 4: 340. The attempt to keep the price of tea at 6 *sh.* was evaded constantly in New York. A favorite device was to charge 6 *sh.* for the tea, and 2 *sh.* for the paper bags or the string. *Jour. of the Prov. Cong.*, 2: 144. 4 *Am. Arch.*, 6: 435, 568, 638, 725. It was found necessary to appoint a committee of Congress to investigate. *Ibid.*, 1346.

[15] 4 *Am. Arch.*, 4: 431, 1081; 5: 275, 278, 280.

[16] *Ibid.*, 4: 1474, 1480; 5: 137, 138, 291. 5 *Am. Arch.*, 1: 355.

[17] "But there is another matter, which I would not choose to make public, and that is you cannot command the militia throughout the county. Your government is not firmly enough established for the people to yield a willing obedience, and I think it dangerous at this critical time to put it to the test." Egbert Benson to the Representatives of Dutchess County, July 15, 1776; 5 *Am. Arch.*, 1: 355. Independence was urged for its effect on the finances. 4 *Am. Arch.*, 4: 470. There was strong pressure from the debtor class to abolish debts, especially where the creditors were loyalists. *New York Col. Doc.*, 8:

The elections for the third congress were thus held under very different circumstances than those which prevailed in November, 1775. While the question of independence was not specifically referred to the electors, it was well understood that the third congress would have to consider it. The loyalists, although far from being suppressed, had been driven, as it were, from the arena of politics into the arena of war: while more than ever a danger to the revolutionists as conspirators and armed foes, they had ceased largely to be a danger at the polls. Henceforth, accordingly, the question of political parties, strictly speaking, centers in the divisions which appear in the ranks of the revolutionists themselves. The striking feature of the elections in April, 1776, therefore, is the reappearance of earlier party distinctions: on the one hand, the conservatives, led by the continental delegates and the city committee; on the other, the radicals, intrenched in the Mechanics' committee, and backed by the moral influence of the army. Whether independence should be hastened or delayed, whether it should be declared through the continental delegates or by the people directly through their Provincial Congress, whether the new state government should be broadly democratic or reasonably "oligarchic,"—these were the issues which occupied the field when the failure of conciliation had once driven loyalists and revolutionists into hostile military camps; and in these issues may already be discerned the larger questions that created the federalist and republican parties of the early Republic.

It was in the city election that the reappearance of conservative and radical factional divisions is most clearly observable. The old Mechanics' committee, representing the more democratic views, was opposed to the appointment of the continental delegates by the Provincial Congress,[18] seeing in this procedure an indication of that "oligarchical" tendency which was so much

---

652. "No one thing made Independence indispensably necessary more than cutting off Traitors." Major Hawley to Elbridge Jerry, July 17, 1776; 5 *Am. Arch.*, **1**: 403. *Cf. Works of John Adams*, **2**: 420. *Letters of Papinian*, 62. *Jour. of Prov. Cong.*, **2**: 204.

[18] Committee of Mechanics to the Committee of Inspection, April 1, 1776. *New York Mercury*, April 8, 1776.

feared later in connection with the formation of a new government.[19] The conservatives were interested in keeping the direction of affairs in the hands of well-tried men like Jay, Duane,
and the Livingstons. They were, therefore, not only in favor
of having the Provincial Congress appoint the continental delegates, but, inasmuch as the third Provincial Congress would undoubtedly consider the important question of independence, they
wished to have these same men in that body also.[20] April 13,
three days before the election, the city committee accordingly
published a list of deputies, headed by the continental delegates, Jay, Livingston, Lewis, and Alsop, who were recommended as persons "worthy to serve in the ensuing Provincial
Congress." Besides these four men the committee's ticket contained only three men who were not members of the old congress.[21] The same day a broadside, published over the name of
Sentinel, presented a ticket similar to that of the city committee,
save that for Jay, Livingston, Alsop, Lewis, Broome, P. Van
Zandt, and Almer were substituted MacDougall, R. Ray, J. Ray,
A. P. Lott, Th. Marston, Adrian Rutgers, and Henry Remsen.
The electors were urged to "trust not men who are only remarkable for their noise and bustle; but seek for men of sound
judgment . . . who really know the science of political government."[22] April 16, the Mechanics' committee presented a
third ticket in which there were substituted for Jay, Livingston,
Alsop, Lewis, Sands, and Randall of the committee's list, the
names of R. Ray, A. P. Lott, Wm. Malcolm, Sears, Adrian
Rutgers, and Henry Remsen.[23] Finally, a fourth ticket, un-

---

[19] *Cf.* Mechanics in Union to the Provincial Congress, June 14, 1776; *4 Am.
Arch.,* 6: 895.

[20] This was quite possible as it had been ordered by the Provincial Congress
that only five of the delegates should remain at Philadelphia and that of these
three should be a quoroum. Ford, *Journals,* 1: 14. *Cf. 4 Am. Arch.,* 3: 1756.

[21] Committee Chamber, New York, April 13, 1776; *Broadsides,* 1. The Com-
mittee's ticket was as follows; those in italics were not members of the Second
Congress.   *John Jay, Philip Livingston, John Alsop, Francis Lewis,* J. Van
Zandt, *Comfort Sands,* Isaac Stoutenberg, William Denning, Jos. Hallett, Abr.
Brasher, J. Van Cortlandt, J. M. Scott, Jas. Beekman, Anthony Rutgers, Evert
Bancker, Th. Randall, I. Roosevelt, *J. Broome,* Samuel Prince, *P. P. Van Zandt,
Jas. Alner.*

[22] The Sentinel, April 13, 1776; *Broadsides,* 1.

[23] The Mechanics in Union, etc., April 16, 1776; *Broadsides,* 1.

signed and undated, presented a list identical with that of the committee, save that Alner was replaced by Duane.[24]   While the contest was not acrimonious, it is clear that the radicals wished to exclude the continental delegates from the Provincial Congress, and to elect in their stead less conservative men like Sears, Lott, and Wm. Malcolm.[25] The conservatives were successful in the main point; with the exception of Samuel Prince and J. Alner, who were defeated by Duane and Remsen,[26] the entire conservative ticket was elected.

In the other counties the elections were in most cases uncontested. They were very generally held in strict conformity to the regulations laid down by the second congres.[27] Before the end of April thirteen counties including New York had elected one hundred and one deputies; Gloucester alone was unrepresented. Much greater uniformity prevailed than hitherto. The elections were called ordinarily by the county committees, and were held in most cases in the districts. The polls were returned by the district committee to the county committee, which declared the result and fixed the quorum. So far as the records show, there were no contests in the counties of Albany,[28] Cumberland,[29] Dutchess,[30] Kings,[31] Orange,[32] Queens,[33] Richmond,[34]

---

[24] *Broadsides,* **1.** Duane was not put on the committee's ticket, probably because it was thought best to leave one of the city delegates at Philadelphia. This is borne out by the fact that, though elected to the Provincial Congress, he attended but once or twice.

[25] MacDougall was on the *Sentinel* ticket but not on the Mechanics' ticket. He apparently expected to be elected, and Jay expected that he would be. His failure was probably due to the fact that he held a military command. Jay to MacDougall. April 27, 1776; *Jay Papers,* **1:** 57. MacDougall had learned moderation since 1770 when he was the "Wilkes of America," and he was now more intimate with Jay and Duane than with Sears and Lamb.

[26] *4 Am. Arch.,* **6:** 1310.

[27] *Cf. ibid.,* **5:** 364, 365. Dawson, *Westchester County,* 160, 161.

[28] Minutes of the Albany Committee, **1:** 397, 405, 408. *4 Am. Arch.,* **6:** 1310.

[29] *4 Am. Arch.,* **6:** 1409. The delegates did not appear until June 17, so that Cumberland was practically unrepresented in the third Congress.

[30] *Ibid.,* 1310.

[31] *Ibid.,* 1311.

[32] *Ibid.*

[33] *Ibid.,* 1310, 1311. Thomas Hicks excused himself on account of ill-health, and Jno. Williams on the ground of ignorance of public business. *Ibid.,* 1352. I find a certain James Townsend attending, though there is no record of his election. He was a member of the fourth Congress. *Cf.* Onderdonck, *Docu-*

Suffolk,[35] Tryon,[36] or Westchester.[37]   The deputies were given full powers, save that Goshen precinct in Orange County withheld the right of choosing delegates to the Continental Congress, and the deputies of Ulster County were instructed to vote for George Clinton.[38]   The return made by the Charlotte committee was protested by William Duer on the ground of irregularity and corruption,[39] but the protest was apparently ignored.   Two sets of credentials were returned for the same deputies from Ulster.   It appears that the deputies were chosen April 16, and credentials were prepared reserving to the people the right of electing a continental delegate; a second election was accordingly held May 13, when it was decided to instruct the deputies to vote for George Clinton, and a second set of credentials was prepared to that effect.[40]   The promptness and unanimity which distinguished the elections for the third congress from those for the second does not mean that opposition had ceased; it means that the loyalists were withdrawing from the party contests, thus leaving the field to the revolutionists.

It is probable, though the evidence does not permit a positive statement on this point, that the elections in the rural counties registered a conservative victory.   Thirty-two of the deputies

<hr>

ments and Letters . . . of Queens County, 55.   The loyalists of Queens were sufficiently overawed by the treatment of March and April to enable the whigs to set up the committee system, at least nominally.   *Cf. New York Journal*, May 2, 1776.   Onderdonck, *Documents and Letters . . . of Queens County*, 56.

[34] *4 Am. Arch.*, 6: 1311.   Paul Micheau could not attend on account of illness. *Ibid.*, 1340.

[35] *Ibid.*, 1310.

[36] *Ibid.*, 1311.

[37] *Ibid.*, 1310.   *Cal. Hist. MSS.*, 1: 632.   Dawson, *Westchester County*, 161.

[38] *4 Am. Arch.*, 6: 1311, 1313.

[39] The contest in Charlotte was due apparently to rivalry for possession of the county committee; whether the division related in any way to the questions of independence and new government, it is impossible to determine. *Ibid.*, 1190, 1191.

[40] *Ibid.*, 898, 899, 1333, 1349.   The only conflict seemed to be whether the delegate to the Continental Congress should be chosen by the people or by the Provincial Congress.   J. Hardenburgh, late chairman of the committee, observed that "the conduct of the gentlemen present on that day deprived me of my birth right to elect a person to represent me in Continental Congress by ballot." *Ibid.*, 899.

to the last congress were dropped.[41] While three of these were loyalists,[42] there were four loyalists among the new members,[43] so that there were more loyalist members of the third than of the second congress.[44] It appears also that some prominent radicals of the second congress failed to be returned to the third—Mac-Dougall, A. P. Lott, R. Graham, being cases in point. Too much conservatism was no longer a danger in the revolutionist organization; it was a hasty and ill-considered radicalism that had to be guarded against. "The late election," wrote Duane,[45] "sufficiently proves that those who assumed power to give laws even to the convention and committees were unsupported by the people. There seems therefore no reason why our colony should be too precipitate in changing the present mode of government."

The difficulty of securing a quorum, which was so pronounced in the case of the second congress, was scarcely a problem for the third congress at all. After the 18th of May, there were few days on which a sufficient number of deputies did not appear, and it was not found necessary to appoint a committee of safety during the entire session.[46] During forty-three meetings of the congress in May and June, the average number of counties represented by one or more deputies was over ten. The county quorums were small, however, ranging from one to three, except in the case of New York where five were required. The attendance was accordingly small as regards numbers, the high-

---

[41] The list is as follows: *Albany*—P. Silvester, H. Oothoudt; *Cumberland*— Paul Spooner; *Dutchess*—P. Ten Broeck, B. Robinson, Cornelius Humphreys, Gilbert Livingston, J. Kaine, J. Everson, R. G. Livingston; *New York*—A. Rutgers, A. MacDougall, A. P. Lott, J. Finlay, B. Helme, T. Smith, S. Prince, J. Ray; *Orange*—A. H. Hay, T. Cuyper, Jer. Clarke; *Richmond*—A. Bancker, R. Lawrence; *Tryon*—Wm. Wills; *Ulster*—D. Wynkoop, And. DeWitt, And. Le Fefer, Th. Palmer; *Westchester*—S. Ward, Jos. Drake, R. Graham, J. Thomas.

[42] B. Robinson, G. Livingston. R. Lawrence.

[43] John Alsop, A. Cortelyou, Leffert Leffertse, Rutgert Van Brunt.

[44] There were at least eight altogether; besides the four new loyalist members, there were four old ones; Jer. Remsen, Jos. Hallett. Th. Hicks, Selah Strong.

[45] *Jay Papers,* 1: 61. *Cf.* Dawson, *Westchester County,* 162.

[46] May 14, there were 13 delegates from 8 counties. Most of the counties had no quorum. The members present took evidence relating to counterfeiting on Long Island. 4 *Am. Arch..* 6: 1299. 1306. 1309. Measures were taken, directly the Congress organized. to secure a full attendance. *Cf. ibid.,* 1322, 1323. 1324.

est being thirty-seven, the lowest ten, and the average twenty-eight.[47] The rules of voting were modified in such a way as to concentrate power in those counties which were most likely to be present. Hitherto the rule had given New York four votes, Albany three, and each of the other counties two. Henceforth the apportionment was: New York eight, Albany six, Dutchess five, Suffolk four, Ulster four, Westchester four, Queens four, Orange and Tryon three each, Kings, Richmond, Charlotte, and Cumberland two each, and Gloucester one.[48] By the former arrangement, seven counties was the least that could carry any measure; by the latter, New York and Albany, supported by any three of the counties of Dutchess, Suffolk, Ulster, Westchester, and Queens, made a majority. The relative influence of New York was increased from one-seventh to one-sixth of the total vote. An analysis of the attendance shows that the work of the congress was carried by a small part of the elected deputies. From Albany County, for example, seven of the twelve deputies never attended; the county was in fact represented by Cuyler, Glenn, J. Ten Broeck, Van Rensselaer, and Gansevort. Some of the absentees were in the army or at Philadelphia, as for example, Abr. Ten Broeck and R. R. Livingston. Three of the deputies from Dutchess never attended, two were present but three times, the county being virtually represented by P. Schenck, J. Livingston, M. Graham, and De Lavergne. Queens County was frequently without a quorum, and would have been so much oftener had it not been for Blackwell and Lawrence. The New York deputies all attended more or less, but the brunt of the work fell upon Bancker, Remsen, Stoutenberg, Hallett, Scott, Sands, P. P. Van Zandt, Randall, Broome, Jay, and P. Livington.[49]

The third congress was occupied with two main problems: (1) the suppression of loyalist opposition; (2) the closely allied matters of independence and the new government. If the latter was the more important, the former was the more pressing. The abandonment of the policy of accommodation, the

---

[47] Based on lists given in *ibid.*, 1299–1444.
[48] *Ibid.*, 1312.
[49] *Ibid.*, 1299–1444.

suppression of all intercourse with the royal ships, and the resort to the continental army in dealing with Queens County, drove the loyalists more and more into forcible resistance, while the prospective arrival of General Howe emboldened them rather more than the actual presence of Washington's army emboldened the revolutionists.   After April, 1776, therefore, the contest between loyalists and revolutionists ceased to center at the polls and in the press: for New York, civil war had begun in earnest.

It is true that tentative steps towards suppressing irreconcilables had already been taken.   As early as September, 1775, the Committee of Safety of the first congress had recommended the disarming of all non-associators.[50]   But in October, the recommendation was voted down by the congress itself,[51] although the Continental Congress had authorized such a measure.[52]   But in March, 1776, the resolution of the Continental Congress that all persons who refused to associate to ''defend by force of arms these United Colonies'' be disarmed,[53] was passed on to the county committees with instructions to proceed with all possible prudence.[54]   All possible prudence was used, apparently, for by the end of April the order had scarcely been attended to at all.[55]   In fact, neither the first nor the second congress made any serious effort to deal with loyalist opposition in a systematic or effective fashion.   The entire problem, consequently, confronted the third congress.

The rumors of plots and counter-plots, in the midst of which the new congress assembled,[56] left no room for delay.   A com-

[50] *Ibid.*, **3:** 898.

[51] *Ibid.*, 1303.

[52] Ford, *Journals,* **3:** 280.

[53] *Ibid.*, **4:** 205.

[54] 4 *Am. Arch.*, **5:** 1385.

[55] *Ibid.*, 1642. A difficulty arose in respect to this association. The militia law exempted members from service outside the province, and many refused this association for fear they would lose the advantage of the exemption. In June, a new assoc'ation was formed to obviate the difficulty. *Ibid.*, **6:** 1420.

[56] The old Congress, which had been hastily summoned by the committee of Safety to meet May 1, finally met May 8, and sat till May 14, being occupied with loyalist conspiracies. *Ibid.*, **5:** 1491 ff. The members of the new congress who were present from May 14 to May 18, were occupied with counterfeiting. *Ibid.*, **6:** 1299 ff. At the request of Washington, a "secret committee" was appointed as soon as a quorum appeared, May 18, to confer with the general relative to conspiracies. *Ibid.*, 1313. *Cf.* Jno. Varick to R. Varick, May 14, 1776; *Mercantile Library Papers,* 91.

mittee on ''intestine enemies,'' the record of whose appointment
I have not found, reported three days after the congress was
organized. The report was debated at length, and with some
slight modifications was adopted May 24.[57]   A second committee
was then appointed to ''frame a *law of this Congress* in pursuance of . . . that report.''[58]   The resolutions, which were
adopted June 5,[59] while elaborate enough, reflect the weakness of
a government which, claiming to be still seeking reconciliation,
was in no position to demand allegiance or punish treason.   The
action of Congress was carefully justified by referring to the
Continental recommendation of October 6, and the resolutions
were substantially as follows:,(1) Whereas certain disaffected
persons in the counties of Kings, Queens, New York, Richmond,
and Westchester, are corresponding with the enemy and preparing to join the army when it arrives, Resolved, (a) That the
following persons,[60] who would probably not appear if summoned, be arrested and brought before a committee to be appointed for that purpose; (b) That the following persons[61] be
summoned, or, failing to appear, arrested. (2) The above mentioned committee was directed to inquire whether the persons
brought before it, (a) afforded aid to the British fleet, (b) dis-
suaded any persons from associating for defense, (c) decried the
value of continental money, (d) retarded in any way the congressional measures for the safety of the colony.   (3) Such persons were, (a) if innocent to be discharged with certificates, (b)
if guilty to be confined, or dismissed on parole or other security
to their homes or to some prescribed district in a neighboring
colony.   (4) The committee was authorized to proceed against
suspected persons not named in the resolutions in the same manner, and the county and district committees were given equal
jurisdiction over suspected persons not known to the congress.

[57] *4 Am Arch.*, 6: 1324, 1327, 1331.   John Alsop, a mild loyalist, was chairman.
[58] *Ibid.*, 1335.
[59] The report is in *ibid.*, 5: 1331.   In the final form as a "law of this Congress," *ibid.*, 1365. •
[60] *Ibid.*, 6: 1366.   For Queens County 7, New York 3, Richmond 4.
[61] For Westchester County 25, Kings 2, Queens 3.

(5) Finally, the committee was directed to arrest certain persons,[62] either royal officials or notoriously disaffected, who were (a) to be discharged with certificates if innocent, (b) or, if guilty, to be paroled in neighboring colonies or, on refusal of the parole, confined. The decisions of the committee were to be based on the evidence of paid witnesses sworn to tell the truth.

The committee, which after some changes consisted of P. Livingston, J. Hallett, Jay, Treadwell, L. Graham, G. Morris, and Gansevort,[63] began proceedings June 12 at New York city.[64] It sat almost continuously, and was deluged with business. Forms of summonses and arrest were prepared, the execution of which was turned over to the continental army. The examinations were elaborate and thoroughgoing, the decisions, discriminating but moderate. The county and district committees were equally industrious.[65] "We grow weary," writes one chairman, "of being called together to deal with Tories. That has been our whole business ever since we have been formed into a committee."[66] Some loyalists were paroled;[67] many were exiled to Connecticut;[68] the jails were full.[69] But the slow-moving processes of judicial committees were altogether insufficient. The expected arrival of Howe, and the activity of Governor Tryon, encouraged the loyalists to renewed activity which steadily outran all efforts to suppress it.[70] More and more the revolutionists were

[62] *Ibid.*, 1368, 1369. For New York County, 23. The list included O. De Lancey, Wm. Smith, Peter Van Schaack, J. H. Cruger, Jas. Jauncey, Jno. Cruger, Jac. Walton, David Matthews, Th. Jones. Kings County 2, Richmond 2, Queens 26. The Queens' list included G. H. Ludlow, Geo. Folliott, Dan'l Kissam, John Townsend. Th. Hicks. Westchester 2.

[63] *Ibid.*, 1152. *Cf. ibid.*, 1370, 1400, 1405, 1406.

[64] *Ibid.*, 1152 ff. An excellent statement of the proceedings against the loyalists in New York prior to July, 1776, is to be found in Flick, *Loyalism in New York*, ch. 3.

[65] For action against the loyalists by the county organizations, *Cf.* Flick, *Loyalism in New York*, ch. 4.

[66] Salem, (Westchester) Committee, June 5, 1776; *Jour. of the Prov. Cong.*, **2:** 204. 4 *Am. Arch.*, **6:** 1385.

[67] 4 *Am. Arch.*, **6:** 1159, 1343, 1347. *Mercantile Library Papers*, 150.

[68] *4 Am. Arch.*, **6:** 1072, 1073. *5 Am Arch.*, **1:** 1415, 1417, 1419, 1441, 1445. *Cf. Letters of Papinian*, 16.

[69] *4 Am. Arch.*, **4:** 437; **5:** 1496; **6:** 794, 816, 1343, 1415, 1418. *Cal. Hist. MSS.*, **1:** 340. Minutes of the Albany Committee, **1:** 360, 364, 420, 433.

[70] *4 Am. Arch.*, **6:** 569-574, 1031, 1055, 1320—1321, 1343, 1344, 1347. *Writings of Washington*, **4:** 130, 131, 138.

forced to resort to summary processes.   June 12 a mob paraded
the streets of New York, searched everywhere for Tories, dragged
them from their hiding places, and for judicial procedure substituted the tar bucket and the rail.[71]   The congress mildly
protested,[72] on the one hand; on the other, it resorted more and
more freely to summary military methods.   Washington was directed to confiscate supplies on Long Island, and suppress loyalists in arms there.[73]   At the request of the county committee, a
militia of one hundred and fifty men was raised to overawe the
loyalists of Dutchess County.[74]   Five hundred troops were billeted
on tories in Queens County.[75]   A squad of twenty-five men was
sent to Ulster County "to get the rascals apprehended."[76]   The militia of Orange County could not be trusted.[77]   Late in June there
was detected at New York a serious conspiracy to capture Washington and carry the colony over to the enemy. The plot emanated
from Tryon, and involved David Matthews, the mayor of New
York, who was arrested, and Thomas Hickey, one of Washington's guards, who was hanged June 28.[78]

Meanwhile the question of independence and the establishment
of a new government was under consideration.[79]   May 10, the
Continental Congress had recommended those colonies where no
sufficient governments existed to adopt such forms as might be

---

[71] Jones, *Hist. of New York*, **1**: 100 ff.   "We had some grand Tory rides,"
writes Peter Elting, "in this city this week, and in particular yesterday, several of them were handled very roughly, being carried through the streets on
Rails, their clothes tore from their backs and their bodies pretty well mingled
with the dust.   .   .   .   There is hardly a tory face to be seen this morning." Peter Elting to Richard Varick, June 13, 1776; *Mercantile Library Papers*, 97.   *Cf. Mem. Hist. of New York*, **2**: 77.   *New York Hist. Soc. Coll.*, **6**:
288.   Moore, *Diary of the Am. Rev.*, 288.

[72] *4 Am. Arch.*, **6**: 1398, 1402.

[73] *Ibid.*, 842, 1118, 1405, 1427.

[74] *Ibid.*, 1415, 1418.

[75] *Ibid.*, 1054, 1055.

[76] *Ibid.*, 1111, 1112.

[77] *Ibid.*, 1442.

[78] *Writings of Washington*, **4**: 188.   Moore, *Diary of the Am. Rev.*, 255, 4
Am. Arch., **6**: 1054, 1101, 1117, 1119, 1148.

[79] The weakness of Congress on the executive and judicial sides is mentioned
as one reason for a new government. *4 Am. Arch.*, **6**: 1351. One author asserts
frankly that Congress and committees are not equal to the task of furnishing
protection. *Ibid.*, 825, 826.   *Cf. 5 Am. Arch.*, **1**: 403.   Moore, *Diary of the
Am. Rev.*, 253.

thought best;[80] May 15, there was added to the recommendation
the assertion, "as it is necessary that the exercise of every kind
of authority under the . . . crown should be totally suppressed."[81]   These resolutions could have but one sequel,—the
declaration of independence,—and the great question was at
last presented to the cautious revolutionists of New York. As
usual, three shades of opinion are discernible. Duane represented one extreme. "There seems no reason," he wrote May 18,
"why our colony should be too precipitate in changing the present mode of government." Let the people "be rather followed
than driven on an occasion of such moment. But, above all, let
us see the conduct of the middle colonies before we come. to a
decision; it cannot injure us to wait a few weeks; the advantages
will be great, for this trying question will clearly discover the
true principles and the extent of the union of the colonies."[82]
On the other hand, the Mechanics' committee, in an address to
the Provincial Congress, May 29, declared that it would give
their constituents the "highest satisfaction" should that body
think proper to instruct the continental delegates "to use their
utmost endeavors . . . to cause these united colonies to become independent of Great Britain."[83]   Between these two extremes stood John Jay, the most perfect embodiment of that
boldly cautious spirit that carried the revolution through in New
York: the very day that the Mechanics declared for independence, he was content to assert that a new government would
soon be necessary since the present one "will no longer work
anything but mischief."[84]

The recommendations of the Continental Congress were taken

---

[80] Ford. *Journals*, **4:** 342.

[81] *Ibid.*, 358. *4 Am. Arch.*, **6:** 466.

[82] *Jay Papers*, **1:** 61.

[83] *4 Am. Arch.*, **6:** 614.

[84] Jay to R. R. Livingston, May 29, 1776; *Jay Papers*, **1: 64. Livingston**
had written: "You have by this time sounded our people. I hope they are
satisfied of the necessity of assuming a new government." *Ibid.*, 60. *Cf.* Jay
to Duane, May 29, 1776; *ibid.*, 63. MacDougall was in favor of a new government, but not from reasons that one might have supposed. "I fear liberty is in
danger from the licentiousness of the people on the one hand, and the army
on the other." **Quoted in Pellew, *Life of Jay*, 58.**

up May 24.[85] The business was opened by Gouverneur Morris who delivered a long speech[86] urging the necessity of independence and maintaining that there was no reason for delaying the establishment of a new government since Congress was already a sovereign law-making body. In conclusion, he moved that the people be recommended to choose delegates, "to frame a government."[87] Morris undoubtedly represented the more radical views: immediate action by representatives directly chosen by the people for the special purpose. These views were more popular outside of Congress than they were in Congress. The Mechanics' committee and their supporters were very clearly jealous of the influence of men like Jay, Duane, and R. R. Livingston, who represented what they were pleased ·to call "oligarchic" tendencies. One writer condemned those who for "self-interest" were "for keeping as near the old form of government" as possible. Rich and designing men, he said, have recently been creeping in to the congress and committees; "they speak fair, they will join the country's cause so far as will be best, not to go too fast and run into danger . . . They will soon . . . subject you to British tyranny *or to a tyranny of oppression among themselves not much better.*"[88]

The aim of the more conservative leaders, if not exactly "oligarchical," was at least to keep the new government from embodying any rash democratic experiments,—to keep it, in fact, "as near the old form of government" as possible; and to effect this they proposed to keep the decision of the whole matter in the hands of Congress. The motion of Morris was therefore opposed by John Morin Scott, formerly an advocate of popular rights, on the ground that "this Congress has power to form a government." As an amendment, Mr. Sands moved that a committee be appointed to consider the resolution of the Continental Congress and make a report to the Provincial Congress. The

[85] *4 Am. Arch.*, **6:** 1332.

[86] *Ibid.* This is probably the speech of which extracts are published in Sparks, *Life of Morris*, **1:** 91 ff. To determine the date of the speech. *Cf. ibid.*, 107. and *4 Am. Arch.*, **6:** 793.

[87] *4 Am. Arch.*, **6:** 1332.

[88] *Ibid.*, 840, 895, 994.

amendment was carried by a large majority, and a committee, consisting of Scott, Haring, Remsen, Lewis, Jay, Cuyler, and Broome, was accordingly appointed.[89]

The committee's report which was adopted May 27, was the work of a mind much more shrewdly politic than that of either Scott or Morris. It was quite impossible to assert roundly that "this Congress has power to form a government;" ostensibly, at least, the authority to form a government must come from the people, the people being, of course, those who were prepared to renounce their allegiance to Great Britain. Yet it was not necessary to follow out the plan of Morris, which, apparently, contemplated a constitutional convention distinct from the congress; the congress itself might be authorized to establish the new government and declare independence whenever and in whatever manner seemed best. And this was in fact the essential feature of the committee's report, which, in substance, was as follows:[90]   (1) That the right of "framing, creating, or re-modelling civil government is . . . in the people;" (2) "That as the present form of government by Congress and committees . . . originated from, so it depends on, the free and uncontrolled choice of the inhabitants;" (3) That the present form of government, being instituted "while the old form of government still subsisted," is subject to many defects; (4) "That the old form of government is . . . dissolved" because of, (a) the "voluntary abdication" of Governor Tryon, (b) the "dissolution of the Assembly for want of due prorogation," (c) "open and unwarranted hostilities . . . by British fleets and armies;" (5) "Doubts having arisen whether this Congress are invested with sufficient authority to . . . institute such new form of internal government and police;" (6) Those doubts can be removed by the people only; (7) Therefore this congress ought to continue the full exercise of its authority; (8) While the people by plurality of voices authorize the present deputies, or others in their stead, to institute a new government. Certainly a truly British insistence upon legal justification for

---

[89] *Ibid.*, 1332.
[90] *Ibid.*, 1338.

innovation is strongly exhibited in this recommendation. It must have surprised Governor Tryon to learn that he had voluntarily abdicated, while he doubtless would have had another explanation for the dissolution of the assembly.

While the report had not minimized the importance of the congress as a legally established government, it was not yet worded with sufficient care. It was accordingly turned over to Jay and Remsen for final revision. The resolutions in their final form, which were adopted May 31, differ from the report mainly in respect to the final clause, which was made more elaborate and more ambiguous; more elaborate, inasmuch as the time and manner of the elections were more carefully defined; more ambiguous, inasmuch as the purpose of the elections was so worded as to make possible two opposite interpretations. "Either to authorize," so runs the central clause of this final ·resolution, "their present deputies, or others in the stead of their present deputies, or either of them, to take into consideration the necessity and propriety of instituting such new government as   . , by . . . the Continental Congress, is described and recommended; and if the majority of the counties, by their deputies in Provincial Congress, shall be of opinion that such new government ought to be . . . established, then to institute and establish such a government as they shall deem best .   .   . to continue in force until a future peace with Great Britain . . . ''[91] Did this mean that if a majority of the counties instructed their deputies for the new government, the congress must immediately, on its meeting in July, proceed to form such a government, or did it mean that the whole question was to be decided by the deputies voting according to the ordinary rules? While the first interpretation might be drawn, the last was undoubtedly the one intended; the new elections were intended to secure from the people a general authorization to the congress to proceed in the business when and in whatever manner seemed best. The resolutions were criticised—very gingerly, indeed, because opposition to Congress was easily identified with loyalism,—from

---

[91] *Broadsides*, 1. *4 Am. Arch.*, 6: 1351. *Cf. Jay Papers*, 1: 65.

both sides: the Mechanics' committee, in a long and wordy address, discanted on the danger of "oligarchy,"[92] while extreme conservatives complained of the measure "as declaring an independency."[93]

The question of independence had, in fact, not been mentioned in Congress;[94] and if the measures respecting the new government revealed the aristocratic leanings of the conservatives, their attitude towards independence certainly revealed a sufficient caution. Two days before the above resolutions were adopted, the Mechanics addressed a letter to Congress urging the propriety of instructing the continental delegates to "use their utmost endeavors to cause these united colonies to become independent of Great Britain."[95] Whether or not this letter was "as unwelcome as a snowstorm in summer,"[96] the reply of Congress was cool enough; it was also perfectly non-committal, and therefore perfectly expressive of the conservative position. "We consider the Mechanics in Union as a voluntary association . . . warmly attached to the cause of liberty. We flatter ourselves however, that neither the Association nor their committee will claim any authority whatever in the transactions of the present time. . . . This congress is, at all times, ready and willing to attend to every request of their constituents. . . . We are of opinion that the Continental Congress alone have that enlarged view of our political circumstances which will enable them to decide upon those measures which are necessary for the general welfare. . . . We are determined patiently to await and firmly to abide by whatever a majority of that august body shall think needful. We cannot, therefore, presume to instruct the delegates of this colony upon the momentous question to which your address refers, until we are informed that it is brought before the Continental Congress and the sense of this colony be required through this Congress."[97] The very next

---

[92] 4 Am. Arch., 6: 895.
[93] Cf. ibid., 825.
[94] Ibid., 633.
[95] Ibid., 614.
[96] Dawson, Westchester County, 183.
[97] 4 Am. Arch., 6: 1362, 1363. Cf. ibid., 725.

day a letter was received from Virginia, stating that the convention of that colony had, on the 15th of May, unanimously instructed her delegates to propose to the Continental Congress "to declare the United Colonies free and independent states."[98]

Virginia was, indeed, less patient than New York, and June 7, R. H. Lee introduced his famous resolutions.[99] In the debate which followed,[100] the New York delegates took little part. Jay and Duane were not present. Clinton spoke but little; "Floyd, Wisner, Lewis, and Alsop, though good men, never leave their chairs."[101] Far from feeling any inclination to speak, the delegates did not know, in fact, how to vote, some of them believing that their instructions bound them not to vote at all. June 8, an express was accordingly dispatched to the Provincial Congress for instructions.[102] Now that the "sense of this colony" was so soon required, the congress was apparently not ready. as it had intimated to the Mechanics' committee that it would be, to "instruct the delegates," nor altogether to "abide by whatever a majority of that august body shall think needful." Taking refuge in the convenient excuse of want of authority, the congress exhibited a determination to keep as close control of the question of independence as of the question of a new government. The Continental delegates were accordingly informed that they had no authority to vote on the question of independence, nor could the Provincial Congress give them such authority, and, furthermore, since measures were already under way to learn the sentiments of the electors with respect to the new government, it would be "inexpedient to require the sentiments of the people relative to . . . independence, lest it should create divisions, and have an unhappy influence on the other." Nevertheless, the delegates were assured, the earliest opportunity would be taken to secure proper instructions on the ques-

[98] Ibid., 1364.
[99] Ford, Journals, 5: 425.
[100] Ibid., 428, 433, 491, 504, 507.
[101] Rutledge to Jay. June 29, 1776; Jay Papers, 1: 67.
[102] 4 Am. Arch., 6: 1391.

tion of independence.[103]   Such a reply could have consoled the delegates but little, as it was obvious that the great question would come to a vote before any instructions could be secured from the electors, unless the opportunity of the present election was made use of for that purpose.

Such was the situation at the end of June.   Congressional measures for suppressing loyalist opposition were proving inefficient; and both the great questions of new government and independence waited the good pleasure of Congress for a solution, the good pleasure of Congress being altogether an unknown quantity.   Washington was dissatisfied with the deliberation and mildness of Congress in the former matter,[104] and John Adams was moved to a choleric outburst, mainly with respect to the latter.   "What is the reason that New York is still asleep or dead in politics and war?   Cannot the whole congregation of patriots and heroes belonging to the army, now in the province, inspire it with one generous sentiment?   Are the people destitute of reason or virtue? Or what is the cause?"[105]   The cause was simple: affairs in that province were directed by cautious and conservative politicians, who, in the face of an armed foe and surrounded by domestic enemies, were still determined to preserve the essential features of their ancient political system from what they conceived to be monarchical encroachments on the one hand, as well as from rash democratic experiments on the other.   And this achievement, if it could be effected, they were determined should be formally declared by the colony and not by the United Colonies.

How much weight the latter consideration had, it is impos-

---

[103] Ibid., 814. Cal. Hist. MSS., 1: 320. This letter is not quite consistent with the resolutions of which it was supposed to be an expression. As a result of the debate on the letter from the delegates, Jay introduced a resolution requesting the electors to invest their deputies with powers relative to independence at the coming elections. 4 Am. Arch., 6: 1395. The resolution was adopted, but then it was immediately "agreed" not to publish the resolution until after the elections. Ibid., 1396. What meaning the resolution could have if not published before the election, it is somewhat difficult to understand. I do not find that the resolution was ever published, except as a part of the Journals.

[104] Cf. Writings of Washington. 4: 130, 131. Ford, Journals, 5: 441. 4 Am. Arch., 6: 790, 1436.

[105] John Adams to Wm. Tudor, June 24, 1776; Works of John Adams, 9: 411.

sible to say.   Certainly there was no other sufficient reason at the close of June for refusing to authorize the delegates at Philadelphia to vote for independence.   The new elections had been held in nearly every county, Richmond and Kings excepted, and there appeared no opposition to the establishment of a new government, or to the declaration of independence.[106]   Both measures were in fact assured;[107] and the results of these elections might easily have been communicated to the delegates in time to have enabled them to vote with the other colonies.   But the third congress, having prepared the way, was not destined to take the final step.   May 31, two days after the British fleet sailed into the outer harbor,[108] an adjournment was voted, to meet at White Plains July 2.[109]   On that very day independence was voted at Philadelphia, and the New York delegates were writing again for instructions.[110]   The third congress never met again, however, and when the delegates received their answer, it was only to learn that the fourth congress had itself declared independence.[111]

With the election of deputies to the fourth congress in June,

---

[106] The credentials are in 5 *Am. Arch.*, **1:** 1385, 1386, 1387, 1392, 1393, 1402, 1411. 1457. 1506, 1524, 1525.   *Cf.* also, *Minutes of the Albany Committee*, **2:** 440. 445, 457.   *4 Am. Arch.*, **6:** 743, 996, 1014, 1056, 1352.   *5 Am. Arch.*, **3:** 268.   *Cal. Hist. MSS.*, **1:** 422.   Onderdonck, *Documents and Letters of . . . Queens County*, 73.   *Livingston Papers*, **1:** 187.   *George Clinton MSS.*, **1:** 95.   The elections appear to have become rather the formal confirmation of candidates selected by the leaders in Congress, than the free choice by the people.   May 29, Jay writes to R. R. Livingston "I shall inform the members of Dutchess of your willingness to serve, and advise them to elect you."   *Jay Papers*, **1:** 65.   June 11, he writes again : "I have settled matters with James Livingston, that if no other of the present members from Dutchess should resign he will in order to make room for you.   I have written to Benson on the subject."   Jay to R. R. Livingston. June 11, 1776 ; *Livingston Papers*, **1:** 187.

[107] 5 *Am. Arch.*, **1:** 14.

[108] *New York Col. Doc.*, **8:** 681.   *Writings of Washington*, **4:** 200.   *4 Am. Arch.*, **6:** 1123. 1196, 1234.

[109] *4 Am. Arch.*, **6:** 1443.

[110] *Ibid.*, 1212.

[111] The fourth Congress met July 9. and immediately "Resolved unanimously, that the reasons assigned by the Continental Congress for declaring the United Colonies free and independent states, are cogent and conclusive, and . . . we approve the same, and will, at the risk of our lives and fortunes, join with the other colonies in supporting it."   5 *Am. Arch.*, **1:** 1391.   The resolution was read in the Continental Congress, July 15, which was the first intimation the delegates had of it.   *Cf.* Alsop's letter of resignation.   *Ibid.*, 368.

and the declaration of independence by that body July 9, 1776,
the differentiation of parties into revolutionist and loyalist was
as complete as it ever became. The elections were held apparently without opposition, the suffrage qualifications being
the same as in the previous election.[112] About one-third of the
deputies were new men. None of them was a loyalist, and of
the eight loyalist members of the third congress, none was returned.[113] The declaration of independence destroyed all hope
of reconciliation. Most men had already given up that idea long
ago. Of those who held to it to the last, John Alsop was the
most distinguished. Since the formation of the Committee of
Fifty-One in May, 1774, he had been among the most active
members of the extra-legal organization, though not one of the
most influential. His attitude is clearly expressed in a letter
to the Provincial Congress, July 16, tendering his resignation
as a delegate in the Continental Congress. "As long as a door
was left open for a reconciliation with Great Britain, upon
honorable and just terms, I was ready and willing to render my
country all the service in my power, and for which purpose I
was . . . sent to this Congress; but as you have, I presume, by that Declaration, closed the door of reconciliation, I
must beg leave to resign my seat as a delegate."[114] So completely, for the individual, had the question ceased to be one of
rights, so obviously had it become one of allegiance, that no one
seemingly could longer miss the point.

But the differentiation of loyalist and revolutionist had not
yet been completed before the beginning of new party alignments are to be observed within the ranks of the revolutionists
themselves. Evidence of this has already been noted: the jealousy exhibited by the second congress of interference in the affairs of the colony by the army or by the continental committee;

---

[112] 4 Am. Arch., 6: 743. 996. 1352. 5 Am. Arch., 1: 1385–1387, 1392, 1393,
1402. 1411, 1457. 1506, 1524. 1525. Minutes of the Albany Committee, 2: 440,
445, 457. Cal. Hist. MSS.. 1: 422, 480. Jay Papers, 1: 65. Livingston MSS.,
1: 187. George Clinton MSS., 1: 95.

[113] Gilbert Livingston, who was a member of the second Congress. but not
of the third, was the one member of the fourth Congress, so far as I have
found. who can be classed as a loyalist.

[114] 5 Am. Arch., 1: 368.

the apparent determination of the conservative leaders in the third congress that the declaration of independence should be made by the colony rather than by the Continental Congress; the fear of "oligarchy" exhibited by the Mechanics' committee in respect to the formation of the new government; the corresponding fear, on the part of men like Jay, of a government too weak at the top and too broadly democratic at the bottom. Thus early in the revolution, unquestionably, are to be found the germs of those opposing tendencies which, after the war was over, were to separate staunch supporters of the revolution like Jay and Hamilton, from equally staunch supporters of the revolution like Clinton and MacDougall. These new alignments were merely the revival, in a slightly different form, of the fundamental party divisions which had existed from the time of the stamp act. The fear of British oppression was transformed into the fear of oppression by the national government, while the demand of the unfranchised classes for recognition in the extra-legal machinery of the early revolution' was to find its ultimate answer only in the achievements of Jefferson and Jackson.

Here the history of revolutionary parties properly ends. The fourth congress succeeded, after considerable delay, in forming a new government. The delay, which has been charged to the conservatives, scarcely needs any explanation other than that Congress was fully occupied with the military situation. It was indeed prudent, especially after the Battle of Long Island in August, "first to endeavor to secure a state to govern before . . . . a form to govern it by."[115] Five counties and parts of two others were speedily occupied by the British: once in possession of Westchester and Orange, wrote MacDougall, "they will get a majority of the state and make a surrender of our rights."[116] In order to preserve even a semblance of popularly sanctioned constitutional government, the congress paid the delegates of New York, Suffolk, and Queens counties to represent those counties, although the great majority of the inhab-

---

[115] *Ibid.*, 1541.
[116] *Ibid.*, 3: 1123.

itants of those counties had declared their loyalty to the British government. Even then a quorum could rarely be obtained, and the congress dwindled into a committee of safety which only the wildest imagination could conceive to represent the state. Under these circumstances, one wonders that there could have been established any constitution at all, rather than that it should have been delayed for a few months. Of the rivalry between conservative and radical, which the question of the new government gave rise to, we hear but little. Under the stress of military invasion and loyalist conspiracy, all internal dissentions were largely hushed up. Yet, although the conservatives were successful in securing a government measurably centralized and measurably aristocratic, we know that there was considerable pressure for a more democratic form. "Another turn of the winch," as Jay said, "would have cracked the cord."[117] This rivalry, however, belongs more properly to the history of the Federalist and Anti-Federalist parties under the confederation.

---

[117] Pellew, *Life of Jay*, 76.

BIBLIOGRAPHY

I. PRIMARY SOURCES

A. UNPRINTED

1. *Chalmers Papers.* Twenty-one folio volumes of manuscripts, collected by George Chalmers, are in the Lenox Library. Four of these volumes are entitled *Papers Relating to New York MSS.* 1608-1792. They contain more particularly some valuable letters from prominent men in New York to Monckton. The documents are arranged roughly in chronological order.

2. *George Clinton Papers.* The papers of George Clinton are contained in 47 large volumes in the State Library at Albany, New York. Volumes 1-16 contain material arranged chronologically covering the period from 1763-1783; volumes 17-23 cover the period 1783-1800; volumes 24-34 cover the period 1724-1844; volumes 35-47 contain private business papers. Volumes 1-23 are indexed and calendared; volumes 24-47 are calendared only. These papers are valuable more particularly for the military history of the Revolution, and for state politics during the time that Clinton was governor, but I have found them of some use for the earlier period.

3. *Colden Papers.* The Colden papers are in the library of the New York Historical Society, and the most important letters for this period have been printed in the publications of the Society (See below, No. 106), in Force, and in the *New York Colonial Documents.* Five volumes of transcripts made from these letters for George Bancroft are in the Lenox Library, and make part of the Bancroft collection. The transcripts are mostly letters, chronologically arranged, from 1732-1775.

4. *Johnson Papers.* The papers of Sir William Johnson are in 26 volumes in the State Library at Albany. Volumes 1-22 contain letters and papers arranged by dates mostly, and covering the period 1738-1774; volumes 23-25 contain papers falling within the period 1733-1775; volume 26 contains private business papers. The collection is carefully calendared and indexed. These papers throw much light on the party intrigues and methods of political management for the period 1748-1770.

5. *Lamb Papers.* The papers of John Lamb consist of a few letters and documents enclosed in envelopes. The first is marked 1765-6: it contains the correspondence of the Society of the *Sons of Liberty* in 1766, and also some papers relating to the events of the tea episode in 1773. A second packet marked 1774-5 contains a few letters for that period. A third packet is marked *Papers of the Society of Federal Republicans to advocate State Rights,* 1788-1789. *Lamb and Tillinghast Papers.* Many of these papers have been printed in Leake, *Life and Times of General John Lamb.* (See below, No. 167.) They are of most importance for the foundation of the Society of the *Sons of Liberty.*

6. *Livingston Papers.* Two volumes of the transcripts made for George Bancroft, and now in the Lenox Library. They contain some letters from R. R. Livingston, and other documents; useful for the period 1775–1799.

7. *Minutes of the Albany Committee. Minutes of the Proceedings of the Committee for the City and County of Albany, begun 24 January, 1775.* Two volumes covering the period 1775–1778. Through most of the first volume every page is numbered; towards the close of volume I the scribe was satisfied with numbering every other page; in most of volume II there is no pagination at all. These minutes are in the State Library at Albany.

8. *Minutes of the Committee of Fifty-One.* The records of this committee are in the New York Historical Society Library. As they are printed in full in Force, I have used them in that form. (*4 Am. Arch.,* 1.)

B. Printed

1. Newspapers and Periodicals

9. *New York Gazette,* 1725–1744. William Bradford. Conservative paper. Taken over by James Parker and continued as

10. *Weekly New York Post Boy,* 1744–1746. Title changed to

11. *Weekly New York Post Boy and New York Gazette revived in the Weekly Post Boy,* 1747. Title changed to

12. *New York Gazette revived in the Weekly Post Boy,* 1748–1752. In 1753 William Weyman becomes a partner and principal owner. Title changed to·

13. *New York Gazette, or, the Weekly Post Boy,* 1753–1759. Partnership dissolved and the paper continued by Samuel Parker under title of

14. *Parker's New York Gazette, or, the Weekly Post Boy,* 1760–1762. Taken over by John Holt, and published with the title of

15. *New York Gazette, or, The Weekly Post Boy,* 1762–1766. Resumed by Parker and published under same title till 1770. Taken over by Samuel Inslee and Anthony Carr, and published till 1772.

16. *Weyman's New York Gazette,* 1759–1767. William Weyman.

17. *New York Weekly Journal,* 1733–1751. Established by John Peter Zenger. Radical organ of the popular party.

18. *New York Journal,* 1766–1776. Established by Holt after he retired from the *New York Gazette.* Holt evidently considered the *Journal* as a continuation of the *Gazette,* for he began with number 1241, which was the number which the *Gazette* had reached. Suspended by the British occupation of New York. Resumed at Kingston, 1777. The most radical anti-British paper in the province.

19. *New York Mercury,* 1752–1768. Established by Hugh Gaine. February 1, 1768, title changed to

20. *New York Gazette and the Weekly Mercury.* 1768–1783. With the British occupation of New York, removed for a few weeks to Newark, New Jersey. Gaine soon made his peace with the British and returned to New York. Excellent for news; uncertain as to opinions.

21. *New York Evening Post.* Probably established in 1744 and discontinued about 1752. Henry De Forest. Very inferior.

22. *New York Pacquet,* July 11. 1763, Benjamin Mecom. Apparently a prospectus number. Nothing more is known of it. *Cf.,* however, Thomas, *Hist. of Printing,* 2: 115.

23. *The New York Packet and the American Advertiser*, 1776–1783. Samuel Loudon. During the British occupation of New York, printed at Fishkill. Continued after the war at New York.
24. *Rivington's New York Gazetteer; or the Connecticut, New Jersey, Hudson's River, and Quebec Weekly Advertiser.* 1773–1775. Established by James Rivington. The best news sheet in New York, strongly loyalist. November 23, 1775, the presses were destroyed by armed men from Connecticut under the lead of Isaac Sears. Returning from England Rivington began his paper under the original title in October, 1777; but after two weeks changed the title to
25. *Rivington's New York Loyal Gazette,* October, 1777—December, 1777. Title once more changed to
26. *The Royal Gazette,* 1777–1783. After the British Evacuation, Rivington attempted in vain to continue his paper under the title of
27. *Rivington's New York Gazette and Universal Advertiser.*
28. *The Remembrancer, or Impartial Repository of Public Events.* Established in London in 1775, and edited by John Almon and George Pownall. The publication was suggested by "The late interesting advices from America." Contains American news; strongly American in sympathy.
29. *The Annual Register, or a View of the History, Politics, and Literature for the year 1764.* London. Printed for J. Dodsley in Pall Mall, 1765. Published each year through this period. Contains, besides the excellent summary of Parliamentary proceedings, some news from America.

   Cf. *Bulletin of the New York Public Library,* 5: 27 ff. Thomas, *History of Printing,* 1: 291, 295, 298, 299, 300, 302, 303, 307, 312. *New York Gen. and Biog. Record,* January, 1899, p. 49. *New York Col. Doc.,* 8: 450, 508. Valentine, *Manual* (1868), 813.

2. BROADSIDES

30. *Broadsides, etc., Consisting of Addresses, Advertisements, Ballads, Handbills, Pasquinades, Proclamations, Patriotic songs, and other ephemeral Publications principally relating to America. 1700–1840. Chiefly collected by John Pintard for the New York Historical Society. Arranged under the direction of the Librarian.* 1847. 2 volumes.
31. *Lenox Broadsides.* The Lenox Library broadsides have been summarized and printed in the *Bulletin of the New York Public Library,* 3: 23–33. They cover the period 1762–1779. Part of a collection made by Gerard Bancker. The broadside *To the Freemen and Freeholders of the City and County of New York, March 4,* 1774 (p. 30), is incorrectly dated. The date should be March 4, 1775.

3. PAMPHLETS

32. *Address to the Freemen, Freeholders. and Inhabitants.* 1774.
33. *The Case of William Atwood, Esq. . . . Chief Justice of the Province of New York . . . with a true account of the government and people of that Province,* etc. London. Printed in the year MDCCIII.
34. Chandler, Thomas B. *A Friendly Address to All Reasonable Americans on the Subject of our Political Confusions: in which the Necessary Consequences of Violently Opposing the King's Troops and of a gen-*

eral Non-Importation are fairly stated. New York; Printed: London: Reprinted . . . 1774.

Ascribed also to Cooper. The original owner of the Lenox Library copy has written on the pamphlet: "By Dr. Chandler of New York." The style is not like that of Cooper's known pamphlets. Published between the middle of September and the middle of October, 1774. *Cf.* p. 44.

35. —— The same, abridged. New York. 1774.

36. —— *The strictures on the Friendly Address Examined and a refutation of its principles attempted. Address to the People of America.* Philadelphia. 1775.

37. *The Conduct of Cadwallader Colden. Relating to the Judges' Commissions—Appeals to the King—and the Stamp Duty.* New York, 1767.

38. Cooper, Myles. *The American Querist: or Some Questions Proposed Relative to the present Disputes between Great Britain and her American Colonies. By a North American.* The Tenth Edition. New York. Printed by James Rivington, 1774. Appeared after August 28 and before September 8.

39. —— *The Case and Claim of the American Loyalists Impartially Stated and Considered.* Printed by order of their Agents. London: . . . MDCCLXXXIII.

40. *Considerations upon the Rights of the Colonists to the privileges of British Subjects,* etc. New York. 1766.

41. Dickinson, John. *Letters from a Farmer in Pennsylvania to the Inhabitants of the British Colonies.* New York. 1768.

42. Galloway, Joseph. *Historical and Political Reflections on the Rise and Progress of the American Rebellion,* etc. By the author of Letters to a Nobleman on the Conduct of the American war. London . . . MDCCLXXX.

Written in great haste amidst a multitude of other engagements; published from the first draft "in a manner uncorrected." (preface)

43. —— *The Examination of Joseph Galloway, Esq. by a Committee of the House of Commons.* Edited by Thomas Balch. Philadelphia. 1855.

This Examination was conducted from five to fifteen years after the events upon which the questions were based, and the answers were given without reference to notes, nor had Galloway, we are led to suppose, refreshed his memory in anticipation of the examination.

44. —— *A Candid Examination of the Mutual Claims of Great Britain and the Colonies: with a plan of accommodation on Constitutional Principles.* New York. 1775.

45. Hamilton, Alexander. *Full Vindication of the Measures of Congress from the Calumnies of their Enemies; in Answer to a Letter under the signature of a Westchester Farmer.* New York. 1774.

46. —— *Full Vindication Supported; or the Farmer Refuted,* etc., *in Answer to a letter from A. W. Farmer entitled "A View of the Controversy between Great Britain and her Colonies,"* etc. New York. 1774.

47. *Importance of the Colonies of North America, and the interest of Great Britain with regard to them, considered. With remarks on the Stamp Duty.* New York. 1766.

Ascribed to Nicholas Ray by Thomas. *Cf. Hist. of Printing,* **2:** 584.

48. Inglis, Charles. *The True Interests of America Impartially Stated in certain Strictures on a Pamphlet entitled Common Sense. By An American.* Philadelphia. 1776.

49. —— *Plain Truth; addressed to the Inhabitants of America. Containing Remarks on a late Pamphlet entitled Common Sense,* etc. Written by *Candidus.* Second Edition. Philadelphia. London. Reprinted for J. Almon. 1776.

Ascribed by a contemporary to a "Mr. Duer." *Cf. Hist. MSS. Com.,* **15:** Pt. 6, p. 416.

50. —— *Letters of Papinian in which the Conduct, present State, and prospects of the American Congress are Examined.* . . . New York: Printed. London: Reprinted for J. Wilkie. 1779.

51. —— *The Claim and Answer with the Subsequent Proceedings in the Case of the Right Reverend Charles Inglis against the United States,* etc. Philadelphia. 1799.

52. *The other Side of the Question: or a defence of the Liberties of North America. In answer to a late "Friendly Address to all Reasonable Americans on the Subject of our Political Confusions."* By a *Citizen.* New York. 1774.

Ascribed to Philip Livingston by Thomas, *Hist. of Printing,* **2:** 647.

53. Paine, Thomas. *Common Sense Addressed to the Inhabitants of America on the following interesting subjects,* etc. London: Reprinted for J. Almon. 1776.

On Paine as the tool of Benjamin Franklin, *Cf. Hist. MSS. Com.,* **14:** Pt. 10, p. 439.

54. Seabury, Samuel. *Free Thoughts on the Proceedings of the Continental Congress Held at Philadelphia September 5, 1774:* etc., *in a Letter to the Farmers and other Inhabitants of North America in general, and of those of the Province of New York in Particular.* By a *Farmer.* Hear Me for I will Speak! Printed in the Year MDCCLXXIV. (Signed A. W. Farmer Nov 16, 1774.)

55. —— *The Congress Canvassed: or an Examination into the Conduct of the Delegates at their Grand Convention Held in Philadelphia Sept. 1, 1774. Addressed to the Merchants of New York.* By A. W. Farmer, etc. Printed in the year MDCCLXXIV. (Nov. 28, 1774).

56. —— *A View of the Controversy between Great Britain and her Colonies,* etc., *In a Letter to the Author of a Full Vindication,* etc. By A. W. Farmer, etc. New York. Printed by James Rivington. MDCCLXXIV.

57. —— *An Alarm to the Legislature of the Province of New York, occasioned by the present Political Disturbances in North America,* etc. By A. W. Farmer. New York. 1775.

I have not seen this pamphlet; but have used it through the quotations in Tyler, *American Revolution,* in which is an excellent summary of all of Seabury's pamphlets.

58. —— *What Think Ye of Congress Now? Or an Enquiry how far the Americans are bound to abide by and Execute the Decisions of the late Congress.* New York. Printed by James Rivington.

Ascribed to Chandler, Cooper, and Seabury. The style leads me to suppose that it was written by Seabury. There are some phrases almost identical with phrases in Seabury's other pamphlets; *e. g.,* the statement that not one-hundredth part of the inhabitants were concerned in the election of delegates to the first Continental Congress.

59. *A Serious Address to the Inhabitants of New York on the Boston Port Bill.* New York. 1774.

60. *Strictures on the Friendly Address to all Reasonable Americans.* New York. 1774.

Ascribed to Charles Lee by Thomas, *Hist. of Printing,* **2:** 646.

61. Willett, Marinus. *Colonel Marinus Willett's Narrative.* MS. in the possession of the Mercantile Library Association. Printed in *New York During the American Revolution.* See below, No. 88.

4. DOCUMENTS

62. Adams, John. *Notes on the Debates in the Continental Congress.* By John Adams. Printed in *Works of John Adams* and in Ford, *Journals.* See below, Nos. 81, 102.

63. *American Archives: Consisting of a Collection of Authentic Records, State Papers, Debates, and Letters and other Notices of Public Affairs,* etc. In six series. By Peter Force.
    The fourth series, consisting of six volumes, and three volumes of the fifth series, are all that were published. Covers the period from 1774–1776 inclusive.

64. *Aspinwall Papers.* In *Coll. Mass. Hist. Soc.* 4th Series, Vols. **9, 10.** Parts relating to New York, **9:** 441 ff; **10:** 489 ff. Of importance for the controversy over the Judiciary and the Stamp-Act.

65. Assembly Journals. *Journal of the Votes and Proceedings of the General Assembly begun April 9, 1691, and ended December 23, 1765.* New York, 1764–1766.

66. Brookhaven Records. *Records of the Town of Brookhaven, Suffolk County, New York.* By Authority of the Town. New York. 1880.

67. *The Burghers of New Amsterdam and the Freemen of New York.* 1675–1866. In *New York Hist. Soc. Coll.* 1885.

68. *Calendar of Historical Manuscripts relating to the War of the Revolution in the Office of the Secretary of State, Albany, New York.* Albany. Weed, Parsons, and Company, Printers. 1868.

69. (a) *Calendar of Home Office Papers of the Reign of George III. 1760–1765.* Edited by James Redington. London. 1878.
    (b) —— The same 1766–1769. London. 1879.
    (c) —— The same. Edited by Richard Arthur Roberts. London. 1881.
    (d) —— The same. 1773–1775. London. 1899.

70. Canadian Archives. *Report on the Canadian Archives.* By Douglas Brymer. 1886.

71. *A Census of the Electors and Inhabitants in the State of New York. Taken in the year 1790, in pursuance of a law of the said State.* In the New York Historical Society collection of Broadsides, Vol. I.

72. *The Charter of the City of Albany—1686, July 22.* Printed and sold by William Bradford, in New York. 1736.

73. *The Charter of the City of New York.* New York. 1735.

74. *The Colonial Laws of New York from the year 1664 to the Revolution.* Albany. James B. Lyon. State Printer. 1894.

75. Council Journals. *Journals of the Legislative Council of the Colony, 1691–1775.* Albany. 1861.

76. Dawson, Henry B., *Papers Concerning the Town and Village of Yonkers, Westchester County.* A Fragment. By Henry B. Dawson. Yonkers, New York. 1866.

77. *The Deane Papers, 1774–1790.* In *New York Hist. Soc. Coll.* 1886–1890.

78. Drake, Francis S., *Tea Leaves. Being a Collection of Letters and Documents relating to the shipment of Tea to the American Colonies in the year 1773 by the East India Company,* etc. By Francis S. Drake. Boston. A. O. Crane. 1884.

79. East Hampton Records. *Records of the Town of East Hampton, Long Island, Suffolk County, New York, 1639–1850.* Sag Harbor, 1887–1889.

80. Fernow, Berthold. *New York in the Revolution.* Prepared under the direction of the Board of Regents by Berthold Fernow. Albany. 1887.

81. Ford, Worthington C. *Journals of the Continental Congress, 1774-1789.* Edited from the original records in the Library of Congress, by Worthington Chauncey Ford. Washington. 1904.

82. Hastings, Hugh. *Ecclesiastical Records: State of New York.* Published by the State under the supervision of Hugh Hastings, State Historian. Albany. 1901-1905.

83. Historical Manuscripts Commission Reports.
   (a). *Fifth Report of the Royal Commission on Historical Manuscripts.* Part I. London. 1876. The Marquess of Lansdowne MSS. contain material on this period.
   (b). *Ninth Report,* etc. Part III. The Manuscripts of Mrs. Stopford Sackville. London. 1884.
   (c). *Tenth Report,* etc. Part I. London. 1885. (MSS. of C. F. Weston Underwood.)
   (d). *Tenth Report,* etc. Part VI. The Manuscripts of the Marquess of Abergavenny, Lord Braye, G. F. Luttrell, Esq. London. 1887.
   (e). *Eleventh Report,* etc. Part V. The Manuscripts of the Earl of Dartmouth. London. 1887.
   (f). *Fourteenth Report,* etc. Part X. The Manuscripts of the Earl of Dartmouth. Vol. II. American Papers. London. 1895.
   (g). *Fifteenth Report,* etc. Part VI. The Manuscripts of the Earl of Carlisle. Preserved at Castle Howard. London. 1897.
   (h). *Report on the Manuscripts of the Marquess of Lothian, Preserved at Blickling Hall, Norfolk.* London. 1905.

84. *Journals of the Proceedings of Congress held at Philadelphia, Sept. 5, 1774.* New York. 1774.

85. *Journal of the Provincial Congress, Provincial Convention, Committee of Safety, and Council of Safety of the State of New York.* 2 Vols. Albany. 1842.

86. Knight, Erastus C. *New York in the Revolution as Colony and State.* Supplement. Being a Compilation . . . of Documents and Records which were discovered by James A. Roberts. Albany, New York. 1901.

87. *Memorial of the Merchants of the City of New York to the Knights, Citizens, and Burgesses in Parliament Assembled, respecting the Stamp-Act, April 20, 1764.* New York. 1765.

88. Mercantile Library Papers. *New York City during the American Revolution, being a Collection of original papers from the Manuscripts in the possession of the Mercantile Library Association.* Privately Printed for the Association. 1861.
   Taken from the Tomlinson MSS. Edited with an introduction by H. B. Dawson. Contains, among other things, a letter of E. Carther, November 2, 1765, describing the Stamp Act riots, and the list of loyalist addressers to Admiral Howe and General Howe.

89. Munsell, Joel. *The Annals of Albany.* Albany. 1850-1859.

90. Niles, Hezekiah. *Principles and Acts of the Revolution in America.* New York. 1876.

91. O'Callaghan, E. B. *The Documentary History of the State of New York.* By E. B. O'Callaghan. Albany. 1850-1851.

92. —— *Documents relative to the Colonial History of the State of New York.* Procured . . . by John Romeyn Broadhead . . . and Edited by E. B. O'Callaghan. Albany. 1856-1858.

There are ten volumes and an index of this series. Three additional volumes, uniformly printed with the above, and numbered 12, 13, 14, edited by B. Fernow, Albany, 1877–1883, are usually included in the series. The outside title for the entire fourteen volumes is: *Documents Relating to the Colonial History of New York.*

93. Poll Lists. *A Copy of the Poll List of the Election for Representatives for the City and County of New York . . . in the year of our Lord MDCCLXI.* (New York. 1880).

94. —— Same for 1768.

95. *The Records of New Amsterdam from 1653 to 1674 Anno Domini.* Edited by Berthold Fernow. 7 Vols. New York. 1897.

96. *Report on the Difficulties existing between the Proprietors of certain Leasehold Estates and their Tenants.* Presented to the Assembly 1846. In Bigelow, *Writings of Samuel Tilden,* **1:** 186.

97. Roberts, James A. *New York in the Revolution as Colony and State,* etc. 2nd Edition. Albany. 1898.

98. Stamp-Act Congress. *Authentic Account of the Proceedings of the Congress held at New York in 1765 on the Subject of the American Stamp-Act.* Philadelphia. 1767.

99. *The Statutes at Large from Magna Carta to the end of the Eleventh Parliament, 1761.* By Danby Pickering. (After 1761, continued as Statutes at Large with various sub-titles).

100. Tucker, G. J. *Names of Persons for whom Marriage Licenses were issued by the Secretary of the Province of New York prevous to 1784.* Albany. 1860.

101. Valentine, David T. *Manual of the Corporation of the City of New York.* New York. 1857–1867.

5. BIOGRAPHIES, MEMOIRS, LETTERS

102. Adams, John. *The Works of John Adams . . . with a Life of the Author . . . by . . .* Charles Francis Adams. Boston, Little, Brown, & Co. 1865.

103. —— *Familiar Letters of John Adams and his Wife Abigail Adams during the Revolution, with a memoir of Mrs. Adams* by Charles Francis Adams. Boston. Houghton, Mifflin & Co. 1875.

104. Adams, Samuel. *The Writings of Samuel Adams.* Collected and edited by Harry Alonzo Cushing. New York. G. P. Putnam's Sons. 1904.

105. Chatham, William Pitt, Earl of. *Correspondence of William Pitt, Earl of Chatham.* Edited by the Executors of his son, John, Earl of Chatham, etc. London. John Murray. MDCCCXXXVIII.

106. Colden, Cadwallader. *Colden Letter Book.* In *New York Hist. Soc. Coll.* Fund Series, Vols. IX and X.

107. Donne, William B. *The Correspondence of King George the Third with Lord North from 1768 to 1783.* London. John Murray. 1867.

108. Duane, William. *Extracts from the Diary of Christopher Marshall, kept in Philadelphia and Lancaster During the American Revolution. 1774–1781.* Albany. Joel Munsell. 1877.

109. Franklin, Benjamin. *The Works of Benjamin Franklin . . . with notes and a Life of the Author.* By Jared Sparks. Boston. 1839.

110. —— *The Writings of Benjamin Franklin.* Collected and Edited with a Life and Introduction by Albert Henry Smyth. New York. 1906.

111. Grenville, George. *The Grenville Papers: being the Correspondence of Richard Grenville . . . and the Right Hon. George Grenville, Their Friends and Contemporaries.* Edited . . . By William James Smith. London. John Murray. 1852.

112. Hamilton, Alexander. *The Works of Alexander Hamilton.* Edited by J. C. Hamilton. New York. 1851.

113. Hutchinson, Thomas. *The Diary and Letters o; Thomas Hutchinson.* By Peter Orlando Hutchinson. Boston. Houghton, Mifflin & Co. 1884.

114. Jay, John. *The Correspondence and Public Papers of John Jay.* Edited by Henry P. Johnston. New York. G. P. Putnam's Sons. 1890.

115. Jefferson, Thomas. *The Writings of Thomas Jefferson.* Collected and Edited by Paul Leicester Ford. New York. G. P. Putnam's Sons. 1892.

116. Kent, James. *Memoirs and Letters of James Kent, LLD., late chancellor of the State of New York.* Boston. Little, Brown & Co. 1898.

117. Lee, Charles. *Letters and Papers of Major General Charles Lee.* In *New York Hist. Soc. Coll.* Fund Series. Vols. IV, V, VI.

118. Madison, James. *Letters and other Writings of James Madison.* Published by order of Congress. Philadelphia. J. B. Lippincott & Co. 1867.

119. Montressor, John. *The Montressor Journals.* Edited and annotated by G. D. Scull. In *New York Hist. Soc. Coll.* for 1881.

120. Moore, Frank. *Diary of the American Revolution.* From Newspapers and Original Documents. New York. Charles Scribner. 1860.

121. Morris, Gouverneur. *The Diary and Letters of Gouverneur Morris, etc.* Edited by Anne Cary Morris. New York. Scribners. 1888.

122. Morris, Lewis. *Letters of General Lewis Morris.* In *New York Hist. Soc. Coll.* Fund Series. Vol. VIII.

123. Robin, Isaac. *Letters of Isaac Robin Esq., Private Secretary to Hon. George Clarke, Secretary of the Province of New York. 1718–1730.* Albany. 1872.

124. Smith, Richard. *Diary of Richard Smith in the Continental Congress 1775–1776.* In *Am. Hist. Rev.,* 1: 289–310, 493–516.

125. Ward, Samuel. *Diary of Governor Samuel Ward, Delegate from Rhode Island in Continental Congress, 1774–1776.* In *Mag. Am. Hist.,* 1: 438, 503, 549.

126. Washington, George. *The Writings of George Washington.* Collected and Edited by Worthington Chauncey Ford. New York and London. 1889.

6. MISCELLANEOUS

127. Bartram, John. *Observations on the Inhabitants, Climate, Soil, Production,* etc., made by Mr. John Bartram, etc. London. 1751.

128. Denton, Daniel. *A Brief Description of New York formerly called New Netherlands,* etc. By Daniel Denton. London. 1760. Denton was a resident and a landowner in Queens County.

129. Grant, Anne McVicar. *Memoirs of an American Lady,* etc. By Mrs. Anne Grant. author of *Letters from the Mountains;* with a memoir of Mrs. Grant by James Grant Wilson. Albany. 1876.

130. Jones, Thomas. *History of New York during the Revolutionary War, and of the leading Events in the other Colonies at that Period.* By Thomas Jones. etc. Edited by Edward Floyd De Lancey. New York. 1879.

131. Kalm, Peter. *Description of New York in the year 1748.* By Professor Peter Kalm. In Valentine, *Manual* (1869), 837.
132. Miller, William. *A Description of New York . . . in the year 1695.* By the Reverend William Miller. In Gowan *Bib. Am.,* No. 3.
133. Smith William. *The History of the Late Province of New York from the discovery to the appointment of Governor Colden in 1762.* By the Hon. William Smith. New York. 1829. Printed as volumes IV, V, of the *New York Hist. Soc. Col.,* 1st Series.
134. Maps. For useful maps of New York: *Doc. Hist. New York,* **1.** *Mem. Hist. of New York,* **2:** 344, 455, 494; **3:** 53. Valentine, *History of New York,* 379. Valentine, *Manual* (1857). For check list of maps of New York in New York Public Library, see *Bulletin of the New York Public Library,* **5:** 60–73.

II. SECONDARY SOURCES

135. Almon, John. *Anecdotes of the Life of William Pitt,* etc. Dublin. 1792. Based on material "collected and preserved" by the author. Almon says that he kept a diary, and that the anecdotes were "all of them in their day very well known." (Preface V.) In the presentation copy of the *Anecdotes* sent to Lady Chatham, Almon wrote "From your Ladyship's noble brother, the late Lord Temple, I received the most interesting part of these anecdotes." (*Grenville Papers,* **3:** 366, note.) Almon was of strong Whig and American sympathies. (*Cf. Dict. Nat. Biog.*).
136. Anderson, Adam. *An Historical and Chronological Deduction of the Origin of Commerce,* etc. London. 1801.
137. Baird, Charles W. *History of Rye, Westchester County, New York, 1660–1870.* By Charles W. Baird. New York. 1871.
138. Bancroft, George. *History of the United States of America,* etc. New York. 1884.
139. Barber, John. *Historical Collections of the State of New York,* etc. New York. 1851.
140. Bayles, Richard M. *Historical and Descriptive Sketches of Suffolk County . . . with a historical outline of Long Island from its first settlement.* New York. 1874.
141. Beer, George Louis. *British Colonial Policy: 1754–1765.* In *Pol. Sc. Qu.,* **22:** 1–48.
142. Benton, N. S. *A History of Herkimer County.* Albany. 1856.
143. Bolton, Robert. *A History of the County of Westchester.* New York. 1848.
    An elaborate history of the county by towns, based on town records, newspapers and material in the New York Hist. Soc. Library. '
144. Campbell, William. *Annals of Tryon County; or the Border Warfare of New York during the Revolution.* New York. 1831.
    Based on papers of John Frey, chairman of the Tryon County committee, documents furnished by descendents and relatives of persons conspicuous at the time of the Revolution, documents in the office of the Secretary of State, and on traditions handed down.
145. Chalmers, George. *An Introduction to the History of the Revolt of the American Colonies.* Boston. 1845.
146. —— *Political Annals of the present United Colonies from their Settlement to the Peace of 1763.* Book I published in 1780; Book II published in *New York Hist. Soc. Coll.* (1868)
147. Clute, J. J. *Annals of Staten Island.* New York. 1877.
    Based on records and documents of churches, and on the "Memories of several old people."

148. Dawson, Henry B. Introduction to *New York During the American Revolution.* See above No. 88.
    Excellent description of localities during Stamp-Act period.
149. ―― *The Sons of Liberty in New York.* A Paper Read before the New York Historical Society, May 3, 1859. Privately printed, 1859.
150. ―― *The Park and its Vicinity, in the City of New York.* New York. 1867.
    Relates principal events occurring in or near the "Fields," now the City Hall Park. Quotes many documents at length.
151. ―― *Westchester County, New York, During the American Revolution.* Morrisania. 1886. Also printed as a part of Scharf, *Westchester County.* See below No. 184.
    A very careful study of the history of revolutionary parties in Westchester County, and of the early period in New York City. Dawson was a most careful investigator, but he shows strong pro-radical prejudice in his *Sons of Liberty,* and equally strong pro-conservative prejudice in his *Westchester County.* His style is exceedingly diffuse, and so involved as to be almost unintelligible at times. His works are especially valuable for the many documents incorporated in the text or in notes, some of which are not elsewhere printed.
152. De Lancey, Edward F. *Memoir of the Hon. James De Lancey, Lieutenant-Governor of the Province of New York.* In *Doc. Hist. of New York,* **4:** 1035.
153. ―― *Origin and History of Manors in New York and in the County of Westchester.* New York. 1886. Also in Scharf, *Westchester County.* See below No. 184.
154. De Peyster, Frederick. *The Early Political History of New York.* An address delivered before the New York Historical Society, etc. New York. 1865.
155. Dunlap, William. *History of the New Netherlands, Province of New York, and State of New York, to the Adoption of the Federal Constitution.* New York. 1839.
156. Flick, Alexander Clarence. *Loyalism in New York During the American Revolution.* New York. 1901.
    An excellent study, based on the *Transcript of the Manuscript Books and Papers of the Commission of Enquiry into the Losses and Services of the American Loyalists,* etc., in the Lenox Library, and on other manuscript material.
157. Ford, Paul Leicester. *The Association of the First Congress.* In *Pol. Sc. Qu.,* **6:** 613.
158. Frothingham, Richard. *The Rise of the Republic of the United States.* 4th Ed. Boston. 1886.
159. Hodge, Helen Henry. *The Repeal of the Stamp-Act.* In *Pol. Sc. Qu.,* **19:** 252.
160. Hunt, Agnes. *The Provincial Committees of Safety of the American Revolution.* Cleveland. 1904.
161. Hunt, Charles Haven. *Life of Edward Livingston.* New York. 1864.
162. Irving, Washington. *Life of George Washington.* New York. 1857.
163. Jameson, John Franklin. *Origin and Development of Municipal Government in New York.* In *Mag. of Am. Hist.,* **8:** 315, 598.
164. Keyes, Alice Maplesden. *Cadwallader Colden. A Representative Eighteenth Century Official.* New York. 1906.
165. Kip, W. Ingraham. *The Olden Time in New York,* etc. New York. 1872.
166. Lamb, Martha. *History of the City of New York.* New York. 1877.
    Based on extensive acquaintance with sources, both printed and unprinted. Many documents quoted in full. Valuable also for biographical sketches.

167. Leake, Isaac Q. *Memoir of the Life and Times of General John Lamb*
     . . . and his Correspondence with Distinguished Men of his
     Time. Albany. 1850.
     Based on Lamb Papers, (See above No. 5), Broadsides, (See above
     No. 30), and Newspapers. Valuable for some letters of Lamb not else-
     where printed. Nevertheless is very inaccurate, exhibits violent pre-
     judice, and is altogether without insight.
168. Lecky, William E. H. *A history of England in the Eighteenth Century.*
     New edition. New York. 1892.
169. Le Fevre, Ralph. *History of New Paltz, New York, and its old Families.*
     Albany. 1904.
170. Lossing, Benson J. *The Life and Times of Philip Schuyler.* New York.
     1872.
     Based on unprinted material in the possession of descendants of the
     Livingston and Schuyler families.
171. —— *The Pictorial Field Book of the Revolution.* New York. 1860.
172. McPherson, David. *Annals of Commerce, Manufactures, Fisheries, ana*
     Navigation, etc. London. 1805.
     Based to considerable extent on Anderson. See above No. 136.
173. Macaulay, James. *The Material, Statistical, and Civil History of the*
     State of New York. New York and Albany. 1829.
174. —— *The Magazine of American History.* New York. 1877–1894.
     Particularly valuable for New York. Contains some original docu-
     ments; and many articles and notes of antiquarian interest.
175. Onderdonck, Henry. *Queens County in Olden Times,* etc. Jamaica, New
     York. 1865.
     Based on local archives, newspapers, and state archives. A chrono-
     logical list of facts and events under exact dates, with references for
     each entry.
176. —— *Documents and Letters Intended to Illustrate the Revolutionary*
     Incidents of Queens County. New York. 1846.
     Based on the printed and manuscript journals of the Provincial Con-
     gresses, military papers of Richard Thorne and John Sands, Force's
     American Archives, the Newspapers, and "conversations with aged
     people of Queens County." (Preface.)
177. Ostrander, Stephen M. *A History of the City of Brooklyn and Kings*
     County. Edited by Alexander Black. Brooklyn. 1894.
178. Pasco, W. W. *Old New York. A Journal relating to the History and*
     Antiquities of New York City. New York. 1890.
179. Ricker, James. *The Annals of New Town in Queens County, New York.*
     New York. 1852.
     Based on printed and unprinted documents at Albany, Brooklyn, and
     New York. Valuable for genealogical sketches.
180. Roberts, Ellis H. *New York.* (American Commonwealth Series.) Bos-
     ton. 1887.
181. Ruttenber, E. M. *History of the County of Orange: With a History of*
     the Town and City of Newburg. Newburg. 1875.
     A careful work based on local records.
182. Ryerson, Egerton. *The Loyalists of America and their Times from 1620*
     to 1816. Toronto. 1880.
183. Sabine, Lorenzo. *Biographical Sketches of Loyalists of the American Rev-*
     olution, with an historical note. Boston. 1864.
184. Scharf, John Thomas. *History of Westchester County, New York,* etc.
     Philadelphia. 1886.
     Consists of a series of careful monographs. See above Nos. 151, 153

185. Schoonmaker, Marius. *The History of Kingston, New York.* New York. 1888.

A careful work, based on local records and private papers.

186. Schuyler, George W. *Colonial New York. Philip Schuyler and his Family.* New York. 1885.

An admirable genealogical study of the Schuyler family, and of other leading New York families. Historical introduction by the author.

187. Sedgwick, Theodore. *A Memoir of the Life of William Livingston.* New York. 1833.

Based on correspondence in the possession of the Livingston family. Prejudiced, and contains inaccuracies.

188. Smith, Philip H. *General History of Dutchess County from 1609 to 1876.* Published by the author. Pawling, New York. 1877. Of slight value.

189. Smith, Thomas E. V. *Political Parties and their Places of Meeting in New York City.* New York. 1893.

190. Sparks, Jared. *The Life of Gouverneur Morris, with selections from his Correspondence and Miscellaneous Papers.* Boston. 1832.

Based on manuscripts at Morrisania and the *State Archives.*

191. Stiles, Henry R. *A History of the City of Brooklyn,* etc. Albany. 1863.

A careful work, based on local records.

192. Stone, William L. *The Life and Times of Sir William Johnson, Bart.* Albany. 1865.

Based on the *Johnson Papers* at Albany. See above, No. 4.

193. Thomas, Isaac. *The History of Printing in America, with a Biography of Printers and an Account of Newspapers.* Printed as Volumes V, and VI, of *Transactions of the American Antiquarian Society.*

194. Talcott, S. V. *Genealogical Notes of New York and New England Families.* Albany. 1883.

195. Tuckerman, Bayard. *Life of General Philip Schuyler: 1733-1804.* New York. 1903.

Based on Schuyler's papers, on the Gates Papers, and on the Archives of the State Department at Washington.

196. Valentine, David T. *History of the City of New York.* New York. 1853.

197. Tyler, Moses Coit. *The Literary History of the American Revolution 1763-1783.* New York and London. 1897.

198. Van Schaack, Henry C. *The Life of Peter Van Schaack.* New York. 1842.

Based on the papers of Van Schaack in possession of the author, not accessible elsewhere. Remarkably fair account of the most distinguished and probably the ablest of the New York loyalists. Particularly valuable because Van Schaack was actively identified with the extra-legal movement until after the outbreak of hostilities.

199. Villard, Oswald Garrison. *The Early History of Wall Street: 1653-1789.* Half Moon Series. G. P. Putnam's Sons.

200. Weeden, William B. *Economic and Social History of New England: 1620-1789.* Boston. 1890.

201. Weise, Arthur James. *The History of the City of Albany.* Albany. 1884.

202. Wilson, James Grant. *The Memorial History of the City of New York, from its Earliest Settlement to the year 1892.* Edited by James Grant Wilson. New York. 1892-1893.

A cooperative history. Carefully done, but lacks bibliographical apparatus.

203. Winsor, Justin. *Narrative and Critical History of America.* Boston and New York. 1886-1889.

Principally useful for bibliography. *Cf.* **6:** 68-112, 172-230.

INDEX

Press, the, freedom of, suppressed by first Prov. Cong., 216; censorship of, 228.

Prices, effect of non-importation on, 159; attempt to regulate, 255.

Prince, Samuel, member of second Prov. Cong. 232; defeated in election for third Prov. Cong., 257, 258.

Princeton students, burn New York letter on the Association, 91.

Pro Patria, hand bill, 58.

Property, declines in value as result of Grenville's currency legislation, 71, 79; recovers after 1770, 96.

Provincial Congress. (See Congress.)
—— Convention. (See Convention.)

Provision bill. (See Mutiny Act.)

Public stores, seizure of, 193.

Pye, David, member of first Prov. Cong. and of Committee of Safety, 211.

Queens County, land grants in, 8; action of, on Association, 172; elects delegates to Provincial Convention, 189; but they are not allowed to vote, 190, 191; elects delegates to first Prov. Cong., 202, 208; signers and non-signers of the Association in, 215; refuses to elect delegates to second Prov. Cong., 237; strong loyalist sentiment in, 238; boycotted by second Prov. Cong., 238; measures taken to suppress loyalists of, 244, 245; elects delegates to third Prov. Cong., 258; measures of third Prov. Cong. to suppress loyalists of, 263, 265; declares loyalty to England, 275, 276.

Quorum, in Committee of One Hundreo, 198; in first Prov. Cong., 207, 209; rule for, ignored in first Prov. Cong., 210; difficulty of securing, in Committee of One Hundred, 226; and also in the second Prov. Cong., 232, 234; and in the Committee of Safety, 235; reduction of, in Committee of One Hundred, 235; of county delegations, 207, 258; presents no difficulty in third Prov. Cong., 260; difficulty of securing, in fourth Prov. Cong., 276.

Radicals. (See *Sons of Liberty*, Party.)

Ramsey, John, member of Committee of One Hundred, 226.

Randall, Thomas, charter member of Chamber of Commerce, 61; member

of Committee of Twenty-Five, 113; and of the Fifty-One, 114; resigns from the Fifty-One, 126, 127; member of Committee of Fifteen, 132; and of the Sixty, 168; and of the One Hundred, 197; delegate to the second Prov. Cong., 232; and to the third Prov. Cong., 257, 258.

Rapalje estate, 8.

——, Daniel, member of assembly, 177; and of first Prov. Cong., 207; but never attends, 209; refuses the Association, 215.

——, John, member of assembly, 177.

Ray, Isaac, member of second Prov. Cong., 232; and of Committee of One Hundred, 226; defeated in election for third Prov. Cong., 257, 258.

——, Nicholas, proposes to form a Liberty Club, 48.

——, Robert, member of Committee of One Hundred, 198; defeated in election for third Prov. Cong., 257, 258.

Reade, John, member of Committee of One Hundred, 198.

Regulation Act, for reorganizing East India Company, 97; for government of Massachusetts, 221.

Remonstrance to the Commons, voted by the assembly, 177; rejected by the Commons, 222.

Remsen, estate, 8.

——, Henry, member of Committee of Inspection, 75; and of the Twenty-Five, 113; and of the Fifty-One, 114; and of the Fifteen, 132; motion of, for electing delegates to first Cont. Cong., 134; acting chairman of the Fifty-One, 163; member of Committee of Sixty, 168; and of the One Hundred, 197; and of the third Prov Cong., 257, 258; helps to draw report on new government, 269.

Repeal of Stamp Act, 50; celebrations of, by *Sons of Liberty*, 85, 86.

Representative government, establishment of, in New York, 5; a class privilege only, 15.

Resignation, of the radicals from the Committee of Fifty-One, 126, 127; of John Alsop from the Cont. Cong., 274.

Restraining Act, directed against the New York Assembly, 56; never operative, 57; protest against, 64; on the